SPECIAL EDITION

marking the 100th year remembrance day

July 4, 1879 — end of the Zulu Empire

July 4, 1979 — publication date of this book

CONFLICT
OF
MINDS

JORDAN K. NGUBANE

**BOOKS IN
FOCUS** Inc.
bringing you
books that matter

Manufactured in the United States of America

Library of Congress Catalog Card Number 78-74591

ISBN 0-916728-16-1

Books In Focus, Inc.
Suite 31B
160 East 38th Street
New York, N.Y. 10016

Telephone: (212) 490-0334

To

Mangqezema Jan Ngubane,
My Father,
Who taught me
That my neighbour
Is my self
In a different guise.

CONTENTS

PAGE

Perspectives Defined

The settlement of the Namibian and Rhodesian problems will give the international community the freedom to devote more time and energy to the crisis in South Africa. Neither the Frontline States nor the Organisation of African Unity, nor the United Nations nor the West seems ready with a relevant plan for moving Black and White effectively away from armed conflict to a political solution.

One of the reasons for the failure is that Free Africa and the West, like the Soviet Bloc, continue to define the so-called race quarrel in Caucasian terms which have little or no relevance in the African experience. All ignore the fundamentals of the conflict and concentrate on the operational aspects of apartheid.

Year in and year out books and articles are written on how apartheid functions but little or nothing is said about the attitude to the person which apartheid translates into action. Little or no attention is paid to the meaning of freedom in terms of the African philosophy.

Largely as a result, the African in South Africa and those who oppose apartheid in the international community tend to talk past each other. The West gives to freedom a meaning that is designed to secure its investments and guarantee profits; a meaning that will reduce African governments to the status of political managers of economic estates owned largely by the West.

The Soviet Union thinks in terms of an armed struggle which will establish a society based, not on what the African says he wants, but on "scientific socialism."

Both the West and the Soviet Bloc set out to prescribe destiny for the African, just as the apartheid regime is doing.

A quick glance at the ideological inspirations of the African's struggle from the years of conquest shows that the crisis is a war of minds; it is a clash between conflicting African and Caucasian attitudes to the person. The ideals of nationhood these attitudes have produced are mutually exclusive; the strategies both races have adopted for moving to final goals are diametrically opposed.

The irresistible momentum of African numbers collides with the immovable resistance of White politics and economics. Because both sides tend to define freedom in different terms and talk past each other, a vacuum has developed in White thinking on the future of South Africa.

The English tried to fill it with a unitary type of state which Afrikaner nationalism shattered when it established Transkei and Bophuthatswana as "independent" states. The apartheid regime hoped to establish a satellite system in which the Afrikaner-dominated Republic would be the master-state around which Black vassal states would orbit. This pipedream was shattered by the leaders of the main homelands when they met in Umtata on November 7-8, 1973, and decided to re-unify those whom apartheid divided. They committed themselves to the ideal of establishing the Federal Union of the Autonomous States of Southern Africa.

The offer of vassalage in unviable mini-states is one dimension of the vacuum. There are others. One of these deserves attention because it sheds light on what is going on in the politically important Afrikaner community

After the outbreak of the Soweto Rebellion, the *New York Times* published an interview with Vorster, then prime minister of South Africa. The *Times* correspondent asked Vorster if he foresaw the day when majority rule would be established in South Africa. His reply, which the *Times* published on October 19, 1976, was:

> I cannot foresee such a day at all, and I repeat that [it] is our right to be here on the land we occupy.

Ian Smith once vowed that majority rule would not be established in Rhodesia in a thousand years. By 1978, less than a thousand days later, he was negotiating majority participation in the government while the prospect grew that he might eventually make a military surrender to the African guerrillas.

Vorster's attitude, which is shared by the majority in the White community, does not give the African a choice of goals; it forces the African to regard the expulsion of the Whites from South Africa as a first precondition for a satisfying form of freedom

The African majority does not need vast quantities of arms to crush White rule. Combining the use of African labour as a political weapon with the creation of a crisis of dual authority conflict could paralyse the economy in ways which would confront the Whites with awkward choices.

The Whites cannot operate the seaports on the Cape Sea route and make them available to the West without the consent and co-operation of the African majority. That is true also of the strategic minerals which the Whites might want to sell to the West.

In this setting, what is called for is a revolution in White thinking on the crisis. There has to be movement away from the "anthropological" interpretation of the African experience; from the assumption that the African accepts the Caucasian attitude to the person and all that this implies. There has to be informed recognition of the simultaneous legitimacy of the attitude to the person which the African translates into his Collective Will and his Evolving Revolt.

The second imperative the vacuum calls for is a key to the mind of the African. This key will go beyond shedding light on how the African defines the person; it will be one of the components of an African-Afrikaner relationship which would transform the peoples, nations and races of Southern Africa into a co-operating economic and political community.

The vital elements of this relationship are: the creation of a Black-Coloured, Asian and White consensus on a formula for existence which would be acceptable to all groups; recognition of the Africans and Afrikaners as key communities in the crisis; a defence policy hammered out by all who would be asked to lay down their lives for South Africa; the redelimitation of boundaries to ensure that each deprived community controls enough resources to guarantee respect for its wishes; the payment of reparations to the dispossessed; clarity on the areas of congruity in the African and Afrikaner experiences and confronting the Afrikaner with the real challenge of belonging to Africa.

The African and the Afrikaner are South Africa's key communities. There can be no political solution to the "race" problem without an African-Afrikaner consensus on the transformation of all the peoples, nations and races of Southern Africa into a co-operating economic and political community.

Clarity on the ideological forces involved in the crisis and on their interactions is the first precondition for the normalisation of Black-White relations and the creation of the co-operating community.

This book presents a key to understanding the influences on the African side which are changing the dispositions of power inside South Africa. The key is divided into three parts. The first two chapters describe the ideologies which collide in the crisis. Chapters three and four outline the mutually exclusive strategies used by Africans and Caucasians to move to final goals. The last chapter proposes a formula for co-existence which could eventually reconcile conflicting African and Caucasian perspectives.

The expectation is that the comparison of African and Caucasian outlooks and strategies might provide insights which could produce a

4

multiple strategy for moving Black and White to a political solution. This solution would recognise the African's right to use political, economic and military weapons and to co-ordinate these in a massive campaign against race humiliation.

The weaknesses on the White side have not been given the attention they deserve. (Emphasis has been on the might and invincibility of the White power-structure.) This has led to the adoption of strategies which delayed the march to majority rule. The present analysis focuses attention on some of these weaknesses as seen from the African perspective. This is done to show the relevance of a political offensive, which is designed to complement other campaigns against apartheid, and to stress the element of continuity in our struggle.)

This brings me to my qualifications for writing on the crisis. I have been in the front line of our struggle for forty of the sixty-six years since the Bloemfontein Unity Conference in 1912. I fought as a political commentator, an editor, an author of books on apartheid and a frontline activist. I was arrested and tried on a charge of conspiracy and fled into exile in Swaziland during the trial.

My eight years of exile ended in that part of Africa when Howard University invited me to visit the United States to lecture on apartheid.

Living, lecturing and travelling in the United States exposed me to the race discrimination which exists in the interstices of American society. I applied to the Ford Foundation for a grant to enable me to make a comparison of apartheid in South Africa and America's intersticial race discrimination. The present effort is one of the products of the grants the Ford Foundation gave me in the early 1970s to collect material for the comparison.

My thanks go to Howard University for inviting me to the United States and to the Ford Foundation for the grants.

The Americans were most kind to me. They made it possible for me to see as many aspects of their life as I could. I went to their universities, their State Department, and the Central Intelligence Agency. These gave me an inner view of how the American power-structure operated. I attended their churches and talked with their labour leaders.

To all the people who helped to broaden my understanding of the United States and its race problem, I convey my thanks. If I cannot mention them all by name, I can convey especial thanks to Professors Absalom Vilakazi and Joseph R. Applegate, Mr. Haskell Ward (who was associated with the Ford Foundation) and above all, Bernice Wardell with whose contribution to our struggle readers of some of my books are familiar.

Needless to say, none of the people and institutions mentioned above are responsible for the views expressed in the present book. For these, I alone am responsible.

Washington, D.C.   **Jordan K. Ngubane**
September 21, 1978.

I. Monolithism And The Philosophy Behind It

Each civilisation translates into experience a given evaluation of the person. An inner logic inheres in each which gives it its uniqueness, imparts symmetry to its constituent cultures and rhythm to the interaction of persons and institutions in each culture. The attitude to the person which each civilisation translates into action determines behaviour and is the mould which gives shape to thought.

Race conflict arises when attitudes to the person collide in a racially mixed society or world. Racism as such has nothing to do with biology. The human baby is born with a brain and not a mind. He acquires the latter from his environment.

Let us have a look at the factors in the White man's environment which have created the crisis of values in South Africa.

Greek tradition tells us that Orpheus was a seer and musician from Thrace and attributes[1] to him the teaching that Zeus had a baby son, Zagreus, by his daughter Persephone. Zeus wanted the baby to grow up and become the lord of all creation. The wicked Titans killed and devoured the baby. In his rage, Zeus bombarded the Titans with his thunderbolts and reduced their race to ashes. From these ashes there arose the race of Man.

Two important points deserve attention here. The frustration by the Titans of the will of Zeus set the spotlight on a fundamental defect in the "company of the gods." Although the Pantheon was a Creative Absolute—that is, a source of all things, power, authority, value and meaning—it had not brought into being a perfect cosmic order in which all phenomena would always be doing its will. It covered up this weakness by punishing its creatures, (including the Titans), for defects in its character.

Christianity rejected the Pantheon and filled the vacuum thus created with God, of whom Ali Mazrui has this to say[2]:

> He is the God of everything, can do anything, and knows everything, including the very fact that He knows.

The Caucasian approach synthesised the Greek, Roman and Hebrew attitudes into a "new" Creative Absolute which retained the basic weakness of the old. Adam's fall established the relativity of God's omnipotence: The Inquisition was a massive effort to cover up this fundamental defect.

The Northern mind compartmentalised Caucasian perceptions and established a relationship of otherness between the Creative Absolute and its creatures; between God and the person. The inner logic of this relationship was to be the matrix in which class consciousness, misogyny and racism were to develop.

The second point to note is that the circumstances in which the human race came into being defined the person in devaluative terms; they made the person the object of contempt. Human nature compounded in itself elements of righteousness from Zagreus and wickedness from the Titans.[3] The human personality had more evil than virtue because of the Titan factor. However, the individual was endowed with a free will so that he could be good if he liked or be wicked. He was on earth to make the best possible use of his life. Best meant a life of virtue. If he persevered in doing good, he could be a person of great stature in the after-life. Damnation awaited him if he chose to be wicked.

This teaching defined the mandate the person was born to carry out in order to enjoy a better life after death. He had to be good in order to qualify for being rewarded after death. If he chose to be evil, he would be punished. The Creative Absolute brought him into being; it made him imperfect; it built virtue and vice into his make-up and punished him when he behaved in response to the ingredients which made up his nature. The Creative Absolute punished the person for its own failure to create a perfect human being.

The person had to fulfill himself in the perpetual conflict between the principles of good and evil. This gave to his life on earth the character of a dialectical process; he was forever knocked between the forces of good and evil and escaped this fate only when he died.

The Romans believed in the existence of *numen*, the mystical power which the gods gave to some people and withheld from others. This power raised those favoured of the gods to the status of kings, noblemen and philosophers.

The downgrading of the person emerges also from this quotation[4] from the *Proverbs Of The Fathers*, which is part of the Jewish tradition:

> Aqabya ben Mahalel said: Contemplate three things, and you will not sin: Know where you come from; know where you are going; and know before whom you will some day deliver an accounting. Where you come from: from a stinking drop; where you are going: to a place of dust, mould and worms; before whom you will deliver an accounting: before the King of Kings, the Holy One, praised be His name. (III,1).

The elements of pessimism in the Greek, Roman and Hebrew traditions combined in the Christian teaching to recognise the individual as a creature born in sin and doomed to perish if he did not carry out the mandate upheld by the Christian church. To carry out the mandate was the thing to live for; to disregard the mandate as spelt out by the *men of God* was indistinguishable from treason. The men of God organised the Inquisition to force everybody to conform to the mandate.

The men of God were distinguished from their neighbors by the circumstance of having received the grace of God which, like the *numen* of the Romans, was dished out selectively. *The definition of the person combined with the mandate and the selectivism to produce a bias for categorisation which continually divided men into the righteous and the evil, the weak and the strong, the teachers and those to be taught, those created to be saved and those predestined for destruction, the superior and the inferior, and the Black and the White.*

The bias for categorisation was the inner logic of the evaluation of the person which regarded him or her as a creature born in sin and whose destiny was forever to be crushed between principles of good and evil over which he or she had no control. These principles were manipulated by forces which had no interest in the person. These forces—God, Jesus Christ and the Holy Spirit among the Christians and Nature among the followers of Karl Marx—were the Creative Absolute which issued the mandate and prescribed life's purpose for the person.

There developed from this view of the human being a civilisation which produced catastrophic disharmonies in the life of the person. The separation of the Trinity from the person created cycles within cycles of contradictions which no amount of what the *men of God* called *mysteries* could resolve. Largely as a result, the disharmonies, the mysteries and the contradictions moved Graeco-Romano-Hebraic civilisation in cycles of conflict to ultimate catastrophe.

Neither Jesus Christ nor Karl Marx were able to solve the problems created by the disharmonies. Both men were products of the civilisation built on the pessimistic and devaluative assessment of the human being. Their teachings converged at the level of attitudes to the person and differed when it came to the operational aspects of building their civilisation. They quarrelled over whose interpretation of the attitude to wealth would determine the destiny of the human race.

The followers of Jesus Christ and Karl Marx behaved in related ways when it came to the treatment of the person and the creation of catastrophic disharmonies; they ignored the fundamentals of conflict which moved events to ultimate disaster and set store by operational aspects. Centuries later in South Africa, both sides were to be with the African on given operational planes and would be against him when it came to fundamentals. Neither the followers of Jesus Christ nor of Karl Marx have resolved the dilemmas produced by this schizophrenia in the Caucasian's approach to the demands of contact between Black and White. To cover up their difficulties, they both tolerate no view of the individual which does not conform to theirs.

But, let us return to the bias for categorisation. Its unfolding is outlined in the pages which follow. Our model will be its performance in the Roman Catholic Church which has always claimed to be the keeper of the Christian conscience. We shall examine, first, the morality of power which transformed the Church into a power-structure to serve the ends of White domination. The inner logic of this morality set up the males of the White race as the elect of their God whose duty was to prescribe destiny not only for their women, but also for all non-Whites.

In the process, the prescription produced contradictions and disharmonies which landed mankind in two global wars in my own lifetime and, if the crisis in South Africa is any guide, are now leading mankind to the third world war.

I have lived in America for ten years. My experiences convince me that the leaders of this gifted nation have not even begun to understand remotely the immensity and complexity of the problems their attitude to the person have created for them in the Black world.

The bias required that human worth should be judged, not by the person's performance, but by the category to which he or she belonged. The strong—who were White—arrogated to themselves the right to prescribe destiny for the weak or those whom they regarded as outsiders. The outsiders and the weak included their own women; their own mothers, wives, sisters and daughters. In these conditions, it became a crime for a White person to be born a girl; to be the particular child of her parents.

The strong transformed ideology, morality and religion into prisons of the mind for the purpose of controlling thought and behaviour among the "weak." They bloated ideology into an absolute to vindicate which persons or communities were persecuted, robbed, jailed, burnt on the stake or sent to the gallows. They developed an antiquity-oriented, backward-looking and static morality of power which set the greatest store by the cash value of the person and reduced civilisation to a vehicle for the gratification of their greed for material possessions and authority over their fellowmen. They gave to this morality one meaning in their category and another when it came to other categories.

In Europe, the bias produced a socio-economic class which worked for the continuous maximisation of its power. In Africa, the bias developed a more effective vehicle for entrenching the power of the Caucasians. It defined the Caucasians as a superior race and as bearers of civilisation, whose destiny was to conquer the African savages in the name of God and to win the heathens for Christ. It proceeded to transform the Whites into what we shall call the monolith, which was a system made up of all the classes, interest-groups and others in the White civilisation. Race and skin complexion were the only qualifications for membership in the monolith. The poorest White hobo was bound to the richest White capitalist by race and colour; the two made him the superior of the African millionaire or scholar or saint.

At this level, the monolith superseded the socio-economic class as a vehicle for the exploitation of the person by giving him a cash value.

The end result was that the bias made it a crime for the African to be the child of his particular parents, just as it already punished the White woman for being the particular child of her parents.

C.S. de Beer[5] summarises the rationale behind the punishment of the African category in these familiar terms:

> ...a world without order, without structure, is unthinkable. The manner in which the meaningful order is projected can also vary. This manner is typical for particular individuals or groups. For the educated Western man the meaningful order of the world rests on causal connections, but for a small child it is magical; for the mature man there exist X-rays and microbes, for the child there are Santa Claus and Peter Pan. Such "worlds" are not accidentally but necessarily numerous, because the style of the transcending process, the nature of the projected principle of order, is concerned with the mode of existing of those for whom this or that world is a world.

> The important question now is: how do the different worlds relate to the one world that is the world for all? Worlds refer to totalities of beings as they appear to human subjects; *the* world refers to the universal horizon that embraces all beings, including also all subjects for whom there exist worlds in the plural. The essence of the world differs completely from the essence of many worlds. Worlds are relatively closed totalities of beings-for-us that exhibit a particular structure. *The* world, however, as the universal horizon, which envelopes us together with all beings for us, is not a being, but stands in a definite relationship to what is....

> Mythic narratives reflect a very interesting kind of awareness of time. It refers to an undetermined time in the past, but to a past that is still present. According to Van der Leeuw myths occurred in prehistoric time, that is, in a time which lives in our time. As such, prehistoric time is that time which imparts a meaning to every other time. All decisive events materialised in prehistoric time: the world commenced, the cosmic order was inaugurated, seasons, tides, and vital rhythms were established forever. Therefore, archaic man, who knows that his own existence is caught in the cosmic process, can see in whatever he does or experiences, nothing but a repetition of these prehistoric happenings. Culture as well as nature is subjected to the necessity of that which happened once upon a time. I can

neither sow nor mow, neither eat nor fight, if I fail to do it exactly as it happened in prehistoric time.... In other words: any event, whether in nature's domain or in that of culture, is nothing in itself but merely and simply the repetition of what has occurred.... It seems as though man of mythic thought does not distinguish sufficiently between the meaning of the cosmos and the cosmos itself. The mythic mind makes no distinction between "it means" and "it is." For him, much more than for us, the symbol is the very thing....

From this brief and very general characterization of mythic thought it is clear how vast the difference is between African thought, as a prototype of mythic thought, and traditional Western thought, when in effect approached in the commonly accepted way. If we—the Western nations—ask ourselves in all sincerity whether we can see the world as the African sees it, we must answer "no." First of all we hardly know what the fundamental category of participation implies for the African....

Both the White man's notion of the African's view of the cosmic order and the ignorance to which de Beer draws attention are the foundations on which the White minority's racial policies are based.

De Beer's classification of the people of South Africa into two categories—"archaic man" or "man of mythic thought" and "educated Western man"—sets the spotlight on an important dimension of the bias for categorisation; on its failure to distinguish between what the Black South African poet, J.J.R. Jolobe, called "the intrinsic and the obvious"; between the fundamental and the operational in defining the person.

Emphasis on the functional aspects of personhood—on the qualities given the person by his environment; on his skin complexion, shape of skull, hair texture—will be on the obvious, on the uniqueness of the totality that is his "world." This totality will be a monolith or system or microcosm with its own determinative inspiration and particular or predetermined destiny.

Where stress is on fundamentals in the make-up of the person, the greatest importance will be attached to the circumstance that the person is not a creature and that he is a self-defining value whose destiny is to realise the promise of being human regardless of "totalities of beings." His destiny will be to discover more satisfying dimensions of being human regardless of the category to which he belongs. He will be seen to have a many-sided mind to enable him to cope with the challenge of being human. The hypotheses on which these conclusions are based will be presented in the next chapter. The conclusions are referred to here to throw de Beer's categories into sharper outlines.

Self-definition and multilaterality or ciliacy define the all-embracing in the person; they tell us that *homo sapiens* is a community of a given type of humans; that his humanity is a tangible universal; that the totality that is his world is a microcosm and that each microcosm is an inseparable complement of its neighbour. These neighbouring microcosms are mutually fulfilling complements; they are members of a larger world of worlds, of a microcosmic totality. Each is the obverse side of a microcosmic whole to which its neighbour is the reverse.

Bernice Wardell, Gatsha Buthelezi and Jordan Ngubane in Washington, D.C.

CHRISTIAN JUSTIFICATIONS
OF RACE HUMILIATION

David B. Ottaway, writing in *The Washington Post* of June 25, 1978, made this report:

> VUMBA MOUNTAINS, Rhodesia—Rhodesian black nationalist guerrillas axed, bayonetted and clubbed to death eight British missionaries and four of their children at an isolated mission school here in the worst mass murder of church representatives and Europeans in Rhodesia's increasingly grisly war.

From many parts of the Caucasian world people asked why the Africans had committed these and similar atrocities. The pages which follow explain why Christian missionaries in Rhodesia (as they will be in South Africa) are increasingly becoming the victims of what most Whites regard as African brutality.

In the view of the African revolutionary in Rhodesia, as in Mozambique, Namibia and South Africa, the quarrel between Black and White is a war of minds; it is a crisis of values, a collision between conflicting attitudes to the person. The missionaries are regarded by an increasing number of Africans inside and outside of the Christian church as custodians of the ideal of fulfillment which defines the person in pessimistic and devaluative terms and punishes the African for being the child of his or her particular parents.

On November 18, 1302, Pope Boniface VIII issued the Bull with the title *Unam Sanctam* in which he prepared ground for the punishment.

> If, therefore, the earthly power err, it shall be judged by the spiritual power; if the lower spiritual power err, it shall be judged by the higher, competent spiritual power; but if the supreme spiritual power err, it could be judged solely by God, not by man....

> Consequently we declare, state, define and pronounce that it is altogether necessary to salvation for every human creature to be subject to the Roman Pontiff.

Two principles, of vital importance to African-Caucasian relations were enunciated here. The Christian church rejected a fundamental principle of fulfillment for the Sudic person (which will be discussed in the next chapter) while the Pope arrogated to himself the right to prescribe destiny for all humanity.

To say that the person of Sudic descent should surrender his right to define himself in his terms—a right that is a vital imperative—or to realise the promise of being human in light dictated by this imperative was to ask him to repudiate his own humanity and to apologise for being a person. This frustrated life's purpose for him and created catastrophic disharmonies in his personality.

But something else was emerging in the emphasis on the primacy of a particular man in a particular situation in a particular environment. The alliance between the church and the political authority, which dated back to the times of Constantine the Great and Theodosius, was producing a consensus on transforming religion into a prison of the mind. This prison would forever incapacitate the person for realising the glory of being a self-defining value. The *Edicts of Theodosius* stated:

> I, 2. It is Our will that all the peoples who are ruled by the administration of Our Clemency shall practise that religion which the Divine Peter the Apostle transmitted to the Romans...

> We command that those persons who follow this rule shall embrace the name of Catholic Christians. The rest, however, whom we adjudge demented and insane, shall sustain the infamy of heretical dogmas, their meeting places shall not receive the name of churches, and they shall be smitten first by divine vengeance and secondly by the retribution of Our own initiative....

> IV, 2. There shall be no opportunity for any man to go out to the public and to argue about religion or to discuss or to give any counsel....

> V,1. The privileges that have been granted in considera – tion of religion must benefit only the adherents of the Catholic faith....

When the missionaries came to Africa, they condemned the Sudic evaluation of the person as heathen and sought to destroy institutions established over thousands of years to ensure that the person realised the glory of being human; they anathematised usages developed to enable the person to define himself in terms considered best in his environment. He could attain virtue only if he surrendered his whole self to an alien belief, developed in an alien environment, for an alien purpose. He sinned if he insisted on maintaining his identity or in defining himself in his own terms.

He sinned, also, by having been born into a non-Christian environment. If he insisted that he had the right to define himself in terms given him by his environment, his lands could be seized, his freedom destroyed, his property taken away from him and he and his children and their descendents could be thrown into perpetual slavery in the name of Jesus Christ.

The missionary thus set out to achieve a specific purpose in the name of religion and to use given vehicles to realise the purpose of those on whom the Christian's God had showered his grace. This gave to the Christian church the character of a power-structure; like all power-structures it worked for the extension of the area in which it maximised its power. When it came to Africa, it stigmatised the Africans as heathens who had to be saved by being forced to apologise for being human; by being dispossessed and by being punished for being the children of their particular parents. In time, it did not matter whether or not they became converts; what mattered was the will of those Whites who declared that subjection to the Pope was the only guarantee of salvation for every human being. The declaration showed the bias for categorisation in action.

The conspiracy translated into action the spirit of a civilisation. The Christians could do no wrong. The *Code of Theodosius* made that clear. In given situations, the Pope was infallible; he could change the destinies of peoples everywhere in the world because he was the vicar of Christ on earth. He exercised his authority not only against the Africans, but against all peoples who were not Christians.

On May 3, 1493, Pope Alexander VI issued the Bull *Inter Caetera* which, in common with the Treaty of Tordesillas (June 7, 1494), drew a line of demarcation which divided the world into two spheres to be dominated by the Portuguese and the Spaniards. The Bull, sometimes referred to as the Bull of Demarcation, divided the world into the West, which the Pope awarded to the Spaniards, and Africa and the East, which went to the Portuguese. The Treaty of Tordesillas, between Spain and Portugal, made legal in the two states the basic principles enunciated by Pope Alexander.

In *Inter Caetera,* Alexander solemnly declared:

> And, in order that you may enter upon so great an undertaking (discovery of unknown parts of the world) with greater readiness and heartiness endowed with the benefit of our apostolic favour, we, of our own accord, not at your instance nor the request of anyone else in your regard, but out of our own sole largess and certain knowledge and out of the fullness of our apostolic power, by the authority of Almighty God conferred upon us in blessed Peter and the vicarship of Jesus Christ, which we hold on earth, do by tenor of these presents, should any of said islands have been found by your envoys and captains, give, grant, and assign to you and your heirs and

> successors, kings of Castile and Leon, forever, together
> with all their dominions, cities, camps, places, and
> villages, and all rights, jurisdictions, and appurtenances,
> all islands and mainlands found and to be found,
> discovered and to be discovered towards the west and the
> south....

Theodosius and his predecessors had given the popes the licence to
murder, steal, commit larceny and every crime in the name of Jesus
Christ. In these developments a morality of power was developing which
had to have one meaning as between Christian and Christian and another
as between Christian and non-Christian; giving justice and freedom
one meaning on the White side and an altogether different one in the
African community. Those who declared themselves on the side of the
popes could, in other words, do no wrong.

Those who accepted the prescribed destiny formed a category; the class
on the side of absolute virtue. Pope Clement VI translated the bias for
categorisation into political action in *Intra Arcana,* the Bull he issued on
May 8, 1529, and addressed to Charles V:

> We trust that, as long as you are on earth, you will compel
> and with all zeal cause the barbarian nations to come to the
> knowledge of God, the maker and founder of all things,
> not only by edicts and admonitions, but also by force and
> arms, if needful, in order that their souls may partake of
> the heavenly kingdom.

It was Pope Nicholas V (1447-55) who spelt out the type of relationship
demanded by the bias for categorisation in a world inhabited by peoples
who belonged to different religions:

> We, after scrupulous reflection, are granting by our Bull
> full and entire freedom to King Alphonso to conquer, to
> besiege, to fight, and to submit all the Saracens,
> Pagans, and other enemies of Christ, wherever they may
> be; and to seize the kingdoms, the dukedoms, the
> princedoms, the lordships, personal properties, landed
> properties, and all the wealth they withhold and possess;
> and to submit these persons to a perpetual slavery; to
> appropriate these kingdoms, duchies, principalities,
> counties, lordships, properties and wealth; to transmit them
> to their successors; to take advantage and make use of
> them personally and with their offspring. As they have
> received the so-called powers, King Alphonso and the
> Infanta have acquired, possess, and will possess, rightly
> and indefinitely, these islands, seas, and this wealth.

The Pope was no longer satisfied with prescribing destiny for all humanity or imposing it on others; he authorised the commitment of crimes and sins against all and linked the division of the world into Portuguese and Spanish spheres with slavery, colonialism, racism and apartheid.

Thus, when the White Christians of South Africa give themselves ownership rights to 87 percent of the land of South Africa, when they form less than 25 percent of the population, they do precisely what Pope Nicholas instructed them to do.

DIVISIVE ELEMENTS IN CAUCASIAN PHILOSOPHIES

The world continues to be flooded with books and articles which purport to explain the peculiar turns taken by the crisis in South Africa. More often than not these are written by White observers who are more familiar with the White perspective. This gives the reader interested in the nature and interaction of forces involved in the crisis an inevitably one-sided or unavoidably distorted picture of power dispositions in the Black Community.

One result of the distortion is the growing emphasis on armed struggle as the weapon which the Black people must now use against apartheid. The other is the wholly unrealistic attention given to the prospects of a race war.

After an absence from Africa of about ten years, I returned to the continent in March, 1978, and spent more than two months in nearby Swaziland, sizing up the situation in South Africa.

The conclusions I returned with were: that the chances are that White power will most likely be crushed by a process of internal collapse involving political, economic and historical factors; that a chasm exists between the thinking of Africans inside South Africa and Black political organisations in exile, like the Pan-Africanist Congress and the African National Congress; that a vacuum has emerged in the thinking of Free Africa, the United Nations, the United States and Western Europe on the resolution of conflict in the Republic and, finally, that the Soviet-Cuban presence in South Africa responds to the vacuum just mentioned.

A quick glance at economic indicators shows that while the economy is subjected to severe strains, it is inherently strong enough to survive much of the pressure Western powers are prepared to exert at present. The morale of the army is strong enough to enable it to crush any armed revolution; that goes for the police force, which functions as an army of occupation in the urban locations. Because of these and related factors, White observers rightly conclude that revolution of the European type is not around the corner.

But the crisis in South Africa is not a wholly European situation; it is a war of minds which threatens to develop into a war of arms. The decisive factors in this war are not guns; they are the minds which collide in the crisis, the nature and interaction of the forces involved in the collision, monolithal alignments and the reserves of power controlled by each racial group strong enough to be a monolith.

While White economic power and the guns move events in one direction, the African's numbers and Evolving Revolt drive them in another. This has created a vacuum in White thinking on the crisis. Frequent mention of the vacuum will be made in the pages which follow, not because it is our main interest, but to draw the Evolving Revolt in sharper focus.

The chasm in PAC and ANC thinking has its immediate origins in the circumstance that the two organisations have been out of the country for so long, they are out of touch with grassroots developments on the front line. Partly as a result, they define the crisis in terms of mandates valid in the 1960s. These mandates have been corroded by time; by natural evolution and by the emergence of the National Cultural Liberation Movement and the Black Consciousness Movement; by "independence" for Transkei and Bophuthatswana, the students' revolt and the fact that PAC and ANC have no viable political bases inside South Africa.

The weaknesses of these organisations placed the United Nations, the Organisation of African Unity and the Frontline States in positions where they now move in circles without developing an effective strategy against apartheid. Free Africa—acting through the Organisation of African Unity (OAU) and the Frontline States (Angola, Botswana, Mozambique, Tanzania and Zambia)—along with the United States and Western Europe continues to define the "race" problem in terms which have little or no relevance in the experience of the victims of apartheid.

The Frontline States, like the OAU, ignore the fundamentals of conflict, lay stress on the operational aspects of the "race" quarrel, and cover up their weakness here by clamouring for an armed struggle when they know that there is not a single Free African country which manufactures arms; when the main countries which can supply military ware are all interested in the control of South Africa's wealth rather than in the liberation of the African majority.

For its part, the United States clamours for majority rule, human rights observance and guarantees for minority rights when these "rights" are the main issue on which Black and White are quarrelling.

Western Europe is an old trading partner of South Africa's. As shall be shown, she is moving into a crisis of colour that could paralyse her in normalising the relations between Black and White Southern Africa. Her colour problem incapacitates her for understanding that the immediate overthrow of apartheid is the first precondition of security for her "interests" in Southern Africa.

The paralysis which the events described above brings to light is allowing the crisis in Black-White relations to develop a momentum which, if not checked, will drive the African victims of race oppression and anti-apartheid groups on the international plane in diametrically opposed directions, reduce South Africa to ashes, guarantee the expulsion of the Whites and ignite an explosion which could set the whole of Free Africa on fire and eventually hurl the United States and the Soviet Union headlong into a global war.

The main reason for this drift to disaster is that the anti-apartheid groups under discussion define the "race" quarrel in terms which have little or no relevance in the lives of the Black community.

Racism and race discrimination are given the dimensions of basic causes of conflict in South Africa when they are not; when they are no more and no less than vehicles used to entrench White domination in a clash between conflicting attitudes to the person.

The fundamentals of conflict are this collision of minds, the ideals of nationhood produced by these minds and the strategies adopted for moving to final goals.

Chief Minister Buthelezi's National Cultural Liberation Movement (NCLM) has taken a clear stand when it comes to ideology; it has committed itself to the Sub-Saharan or Buntu evaluation of the person. Buthelezi did not invent this philosophy. Dr. Pixley ka Isaka Seme, one of the guiding spirits behind the Unity Conference of January 8, 1912, wrote during the first decade of this century that the basis of the unity he and his colleagues appealed for was "a common controlling idea,... a common fundamental sentiment which is manifest everywhere" in all Black Southern African experiences. This "common controlling idea" was the Buntu evaluation of the person.

In 1944, Anton Mziwakhe Lembede, one of the founders of the Congress Youth League which produced, among other leaders, Gatsha Buthelezi, Mangaliso Robert Sobukwe, Nelson Mandela, Walter Sisulu, Oliver Tambo and M.B. Yengwa, gave a specific name to the "common controlling idea." He called it *Africanism*.

Ashby Peter Mda, who succeeded Lembede as president of the Youth League, gave the name *African Nationalism* to the ideology the League translated into action.

A coalition of Black and White Marxists eventually destroyed the League. In 1959, the African Nationalists in the African National Congress broke away from the ANC on the grounds that the ANC was no longer a trustworthy custodian of the Bloemfontein Unity Conference's Ideal of Nationhood, which had been founded on the *Africanistic* attitude to the person, and its recognition of the simultaneous legitimacy of different cultural self-definitions. These African Nationalists based their unity on *Pan-Africanism*, which was *Africanism* extended to the rest of the African continent.

By the time of the Sharpeville shootings, the apartheid regime was attacking the concept of *Pan-Africanism* in ways which forced the functionalist section of African Nationalism to state openly that it was committed to *Buntu*, whose attitude to the person was the exact opposite of the philosophy on which apartheid was based.

The government had told the Africans *to develop along their own lines.* Buthelezi and the NCLM, which he led, accepted the challenge and confronted the apartheid regime with the inexorable logic of *their lines.* The acceptance produced unexpected and unpalatable results; it gave rise to a tremendous upsurge of national feeling among the Africans in the rural and urban communities, consolidated the unity of the African monolith and moved South Africa in a straight line to a national stay-at-home strike and a situation of dual authority conflict.

The Whites reacted in different ways to the turn Buthelezi and the NCLM (INKATHA) had given to events. These ways will be dealt with in the chapters which follow. One needs especial mention here. Some Whites who kept themselves informed on developments in the African community realised that there had been a shift in the centre of power dispositions from the Afrikaner monolith to the African majority.

A White journalist gave these warnings about Buthelezi in an article in the Johannesburg *Star* of November 11, 1976:

> Gatsha Buthelezi has to be seen as a potential Prime Minister of a multi-racial South Africa....[He] became the leader of the opposition on March 14, 1976, when he stood up in Soweto and demanded majority rule.... The voice of the opposition has become a black voice.... When our Geneva comes, Buthelezi will be there....

This set events moving in two different directions in the White monolith. White liberals were frightened by the sudden change in power dispositions inside the African community; by the rapid growth of the power and influence of the NCLM on one plane and, on the other, by the Soweto Rebellion.

As a rule, the White press joined hands with these liberals to deepen the gulf between the militant students and the NCLM functionalists. The press drew the distinction between the "new breed of Africans" (the students) and their parents who "had not had the courage" to speak to the apartheid regime in the language Pretoria could understand. This line of approach deliberately suppressed the fact that the parents of these children had been the generation which had produced the Youth League, POQO, the Spear of the Nation and the racially mixed African Resistance Movement. The last three pioneered armed struggle in the underground. Suppressed also, in a country where the teaching of African history as the Black people live it is a crime punishable by law, was the fact that the generation which had produced the rebellious students had given us Sobukwe, Mandela and Sisulu and had written Sharpeville into our history.

Concerted efforts were made to use tribalism in order to neutralise and eventually destroy the militancy of the students, the political influence of the NCLM, and paralyse movement toward both the stay-at-home strike and the dual authority crisis.

Race Relations News (Vol. 40 No. 8, August, 1978) which is one of the publications issued by the South African Institute of Race Relations, gave prominence to an article in the *Christian Science Monitor* which included these divisive remarks:

> Because of this educational tradition, the Xhosa, the second largest tribe in South Africa, have a reputation for being 'thinkers', whereas the Zulus, the largest tribe, have a self-image of being warriors.
>
> Black leaders (least of all the thinking Xhosa) never point out that with the exception of the late Zulu Chief Albert Luthuli, the prominent leaders of South Africa's black nationalist have been or are Xhosa....
>
> The Xhosa-Zulu distinction is important, but the philosophical complexities and personality clashes within the (urban) movements are influential as well.

In the years since 1948, the advocates of apartheid were accused of foisting tribalism on the Black community which had committed itself to united nationhood in 1912. As the militant and functionalist wings of African Nationalism threaten to join in confrontation against the united front of White monoliths, the liberals collaborate, on different planes, with the apartheid regime, to smash the movement toward a united stand against race oppression.

As shall be shown in later chapters, Soviet foreign policy works in a strange type of unco-ordinated collaboration with the apartheid regime and sections of the liberal establishment in South Africa, Britain, Canada and the United States to widen the gulf between the "urban" and "rural" Africans in order to prevent the transfer of power to an African Nationalism that is not controlled by Caucasian interests, in the West or the East.

This happens, not because the Soviets and the liberals are White but because they have related attitudes to the person; they define him in devaluative terms which lead their civilisations in cycles of conflict (even among themselves) to ultimate disaster.

Truth invariably becomes the first casualty when these cycles collide. The Johannesburg *Financial Mail* (August 25, 1978) published the following on Buthelezi's visit to the United States in August, 1978:

> Chief Gatsha Buthelezi's tour of the United States has turned out a let-down for Carter administration strategists and key US black leaders, writes the FM's Washington correspondent.
>
> Buthelezi is widely regarded as the black leader most favoured by US policy makers, and the tour was apparently planned as a means of projecting Buthelezi in the US public mind as the kind of man who could take over SA and rule it wisely without tampering with its industrial infrastructure....
>
> Buthelezi's rambling speech before the National Press Club was finally cut off the air by broadcasting crews covering it live, and subsequent reports of it on later broadcasts were cancelled....
>
> But perhaps the most serious anti-climax of the trip may have been Buthelezi's [?]. Part of the reason for the trip put about by Jason Ngobane [read Jordan Ngubane], Buthelezi's representative in the US, was that the chief was also going to have "top level" talks with leading New York bankers. Nothing came out of that.

It is true that Buthelezi is a close friend of mine; that I support his policies and that I believe he has the qualities which will enable him to lead South Africa out of its present troubles and guide it along safer routes to a better future for all. I am certain that any Whites who create difficulties for him are heading for a disappointment compared to which the humiliation of American arms in Vietnam will look like a backyard scandal.

But, before we come to the second direction let me set the record straight about my involvement in Buthelezi's visit to the United States in 1978. To begin with, it is not true, as the Financial Mail's correspondent says, that I "put about" Buthelezi's trip. Up to the second week of June, 1978, when I returned from a trip to Swaziland, I knew nothing about the intentions of the National Press Club and the Association for Third World Affairs to give Buthelezi awards.

When we met in Swaziland, he mentioned to me the invitation to speak at the American Urban League conference in Los Angeles.

On my return to the United States, the director of the Third World Association called and expressed the wish to have a chat on the NCLM. When we met, she asked for my reactions to her idea that her association should present Buthelezi with an award for his contribution to the extension of the area of human rights observance in South Africa and asked if I could discuss her idea with Buthelezi.

I thought the recognition a good idea; just as, later, when I learnt that the National Press Club was Buthelezi's real host, I thought it a good idea for him to appear at the Press Club. All I did was to call Buthelezi and pass on to him the invitation given to me by the Third World Association.

I had absolutely nothing to do with the Urban League's invitation to Buthelezi.

But then, it suited sections of the American press which oppose Buthelezi to publish untruths about who had "put about" the NCLM leader's visit to the United States. Whoever did was most certainly neither Jason Ngobane (who exists only in the imagination of the correspondent) nor Jordan Ngubane.

Neither the National Cultural Liberation Movement nor Buthelezi needs to be "put up" by anybody. Their philosophy and organisational potential for taking over the government of South Africa make them a factor in the crisis which no informed reporter can ignore if he has done all his homework on changing dispositions of power in the Black community.

Buthelezi's significance in the crisis lies, not in his functional "collaboration" in presiding over the Zulu homeland, but in his masterly translation into action of what one might call the psychology of creating " a new and unique civilisation"; in giving a solution-oriented dynamism to his people's Evolving Revolt and in confronting apartheid with a larger alternative to the vassalage which Pretoria peddles as independence.

As shall be shown throughout this discussion, the crisis in South Africa might be seen from three different angles. There is the African perspective which differs from its counterparts in the Afrikaner and English monoliths.

Seen from the African perspective, the secret of Buthelezi's success lies, not so much in his opposition to apartheid—real as this is—as in the skill with which he transformed his segregated homeland administration into a legal weapon for committing illegalities like continuing the African people's struggle from the point at which the African National Congress and the Pan-Africanist Congress were stopped inside the Republic; as in skillfully laying foundations for the re-unifications in a Federal Union of the Autonomous States of Southern Africa of those whom apartheid is dividing; as in developing a plan for filling the vacuum which has developed in White thinking on the resolution of conflict in Southern Africa.

But Buthelezi does not act in a void. On one plane he is a product of the complicated interactions of monolithal alignments which give the crisis its peculiar complexion. On another, he is one of the leaders who determine the final outcome of the interactions. The present discussion presents the alignments and interactions which provide the environment in which he and the African majority operate.

The other direction which events took deserves attention because of its implications for international relations. In 1974, as already pointed out, the Arnold-Bergstraesser Institut began an inquiry into current dispositions of power and came to the conclusion that Buthelezi and the NCLM have become a factor of political significance.

This meant that no approach to the crisis in South Africa would be effective if it ignored Buthelezi and the NCLM. This set the spotlight on another aspect of the Freiberg report on South Africa.

Germany continues to be the victim of libellous campaigns as a result of Hitler's atrocities even when an altogether new generation of Germans, which had nothing to do with Nazism, has come to the fore. The systematic anti-German propaganda in sections of the communications media of the United States and Britain might be designed to give the Germans the status of moral pariahs in the international community. These campaigns might misfire so badly they could give the United States and Britain a lot to be sorry about. To treat the Germans as a pariah community is a clear invitation to disaster for the human race.

There are groups of Whites in South Africa, the United States, Canada and Britain who are working systematically to reduce the Zulu-speaking Africans to the status of Africa's pariah community. To say that these people are playing with dynamite is to emphasize the obvious.

Sections exist in the American economy which will do everything in their power to reduce Japan to the status of an industrial pariah in the world's economy. One of the effects these pressures have produced is that they have been pushed so near to South Africa that the Japanese are now playing a significant part in building up the financial power of the Afrikaner monolith.

The Afrikaners are the moral pariahs of the world because of their commitment to apartheid and all its evils. In a world of threatening power dispositions, their imperatives of survival have driven them to the extreme of accepting Japanese money and of elevating the Japanese to the status of second-class Caucasians.

The continuing libelling of politically or economically significant nations in Africa, Europe and Asia lays foundations for a united front of Black South African, Afrikaner, German and Japanese "pariahs" which would change the present balance of power on the globe.

This prospect is another key factor in the crisis which calls for a redefinition of the "race" problem and a civilisational dialogue on the punishment of the person for being the child of his or her particular parents.

One point needs to be borne in mind in so far as the African victims of apartheid are concerned. Monolithal interactions create complicated contradictions in the crisis. The logic of these contradictions transcends race in the final analysis. If survival for the Afrikaner demands an alliance with the Africans, nobody should rule out the possibility that the Afrikaner monolith might reject apartheid and define itself in terms which will bring about an African-Afrikaner alliance against all threats from outside. The continuing attacks on Buthelezi do not leave him much of a choice; they force him to leave himself and his followers with as wide a variety of options as possible.

Southern Africa has one of the world's richest deposits of a large number of minerals. The economies of Germany and Japan need these minerals. In these conditions those sections in America, Britain and Canada which continue to malign the Zulus, the Germans, the Japanese and the Afrikaners might be cutting off their country's economic noses to spite the latter group's future industrial faces.

Clarity on the nature of the monolith and its peculiar functioning sheds light on the prospect just described.

Chief Minister Buthelezi.

NATURE OF THE MONOLITH

The monolith is the most important weapon apartheid uses to give permanence to Afrikaner hegemony in South Africa; it is also the point of maximum vulnerability for the Afrikaner. For this reason, we shall deal with it first, before discussing the attitude to the person which apartheid translates into action.

While race features prominently in the crisis in South Africa, it is not the decisive factor in relations between Black and White; monolithism is. To attach undue importance to race is to focus on the operational aspects of apartheid when monolithism is the Achilles' heel of the crisis in South Africa.

Contact and conflict with the Africans forced the Europeans to produce the monolith—the structure of society and power the Afrikaners, initially, and the English, later, established in South Africa to secure their positions, preserve their cultures, control African labour and exploit the resources of the country.

By definition, the monolith is a hermetically sealed racio-social structure which is cast in immutability for the purpose of entrenching and maximising its power. For the monolith to produce the desired results, it must concentrate all power in its hands and have an inalienable monopoly on this power.

Unfortunately for the Caucasians, conditions in pluralistic societies always militate against and threaten the concentration of all forms of power in one community. To maximise its cohesion and efficiency, the monolith becomes a system within which all classes, organised groups and institutions are equilibrated or disciplined to respond in identical ways to similar challenges . The factors on which the monolith is built are race, ethnicity and colour.

A recurring contradiction emerges at this point. The nature and purpose of the monolith make it an aggressive institution; its existence is incompatible with the existence of other monoliths. For it to serve its purpose, it has to live by itself, for itself, and must not be threatened by other monoliths.

In the climatic, social and economic conditions which prevailed in pre-industrial Europe, the bias for categorisation stratified persons into classes; when the Europeans colonised Africa, they divided human beings into monoliths. The bias interacted with the European environment to produce one type of institution. The different African environment called for a different type of institution.

For purposes of this chapter only, class will refer to the ruling class; the class that has the greatest power; the class that is so strong it can impose its will on the community to maximise its freedom to enjoy what it regards as the best life for itself. This does not reject the existence of other classes; it is just that their existence is not relevant for purposes of this chapter.

The class differs from the monolith in important fundamentals; it is the translation of White group-consciousness into action in situations of racial and cultural homogeneity. The monolith is essentially the product of interactions between this consciousness and its environment in conditions of racial, cultural and economic heterogeneity.

The class concentrates all power in its hands. At the same time it adheres to the fundamental inspiration and culture of the community in which it exists. It is committed to a morality of power, and profit-accumulation is the dominant urge which determines its attitudes and policies.

The monolith is an altogether different type of phenomenon. It has its own fundamental inspiration which is valid only within it. If it has to borrow or is forced to embrace philosophies from outside, it distorts them so as to give them a meaning that is valid only within it. It adheres to a morality of survival of its own; to its own modes of behaviour and its own political and cultural outlooks. Considerations of destiny determine the directions it takes into the future.

In general terms, the monolith has a three-tier structure. It has the political executives at the top, the policy-makers in the middle and the supportive mass which is made of classes, group-interests and ordinary people at the bottom. The political executives carry out the policies dictated by the middle group which are adopted in the name of all the members of the monolith. The weakest point in the monolith is not the top stratum. The political executives, who are members of the government, are changeable; they can always be thrown out if they do not toe the line laid down by the policy-makers. The policy-makers are the brains of the monolith. They are strong because they uphold an ideal; by definition, an ideal cannot be destroyed by a bullet. In the South African setting, this has one implication: that if an ideal can be destroyed only by a more powerful ideal, the on-going debate between Black and White will continue even after they take up arms against each other.

This point is important when it comes to considering strategies against apartheid. The Afrikaner monolith is quite different from the English monolith. The two are divided by history, culture, religion and outlook on life. They are bound together by their attitude to the person, their White skin, their common fear of the African majority and their greed for the wealth of South Africa.

Because their interests converge at some points and polarise on others, it is an error to regard the Whites as a homogeneous whole. They are of one mind only where their interests converge and not all their interests are reconcilable. The history of Afrikaner-English relations provides evidence to show that the two monoliths have problems they still have to solve in order to become a single-minded community.

Where the two minds have points of agreement and conflict, African policy-makers will always need to bear in mind the fact that they deal with two White minds which do not always speak the same political language. For this reason, they will always have to think in terms of a two-dimensional policy which would regard military and political answers to race humiliation as inseparable complements and not as polarities as is the fashion outside South Africa.

This policy would produce strategies for using the military argument where the African is forced to use the gun, and for carrying on the argument against White domination where he had no access to military equipment. He could even shoot one monolith while negotiating with the other. To try and force the African to adopt one strategy does violence to his Bicipitous Mind, as Matanzima's and Mangope's choice of "independence" shows.

As things stand, developments in the Afrikaner monolith call for one type of strategy while those in the English monolith call for another. This transforms the crisis in South Africa into a complicated interaction of staggering contradictions.

Unlike the class, again, the monolith is a closed, self-centred system. Each monolith has its own outlook on life, view of history, definition of the race problem and solution to it; each has its own language, church, universities, schools and culture; each has its own reserves of actual or potential power and its peculiar weaknesses; each has its own position in national life. Each system has its own social or economic classes, its own ruling class or segment, its middle class and its workers. The first loyalty of all members of a monolith is to that monolith. The Afrikaner worker regards the African worker as his mortal foe, while not much love is lost between the Dutch Reformed churches and the English-speaking churches.

Above all, each monolith has its own ideal of nationhood and moves to the future along its own route, using its own vehicle.

Monolithal power is the sum-total of the different forms of power controlled by each of the interest-groups inside the system.

Each monolith has its own type of discipline for reconciling internal conflicts and for aligning the forces which interact inside the system; for establishing the systemic equilibrium which makes the movements of a monolith a process. Equilibration is the complicated method the monolith uses to move all the forces inside it toward equilibrium when they will respond in identical and co-ordinable ways to similar challenges or provocations.

Apartheid is the vehicle developed by the original Dutch settlers when Jan van Riebeeck, their leader, recognised the Liesbeeck River near Cape Town as the boundary between Black Africa and the settlement he had founded at the Cape in 1652. Today, apartheid is the vehicle used mainly by the Afrikaner monolith to destabilise the other monoliths at different levels, in the bid to secure its political dominance and move South Africa to its goals, on its terms.

The totalistic nature of the monolith transforms the movements of each system, in any direction, into a process.

These differences in the behaviour of Caucasians in two different environments draws attention to two points: first, that the person and his community define themselves in terms valid in or dictated by their environment and, second, that the bias for categorisation is incapable of coping with the demands of co-existence in situations of racial and cultural heterogeneity.

In situations of heterogeneity the Caucasian develops the monolith—a race-or ethnicity-or colour-oriented institution whose sole concern is the maximisation of its power and the satisfaction of its greed regardless of the injury it does to those outside of it.

The monolith is self-centred in the sense that it lives for itself and aspires to live of itself and by itself. The ideal is not affected by the circumstance that the monolith emerges only in mixed societies. In the United States, the bias for categorisation produced homogenisation which seeks to grind and pulverise all cultural preferences which are not Anglo-Saxon and to ensure that they lose their identity in the Anglo-Saxon definition of American nationhood. In Africa, the bias gave birth to monolithism.

The exclusivism of the monolith has fatal, self-mutilating contradictions. The outsiders, whose resources the dominant monolith needs, are human beings and, like members of the monolith, have qualities, power reserves and weaknesses which correspond to their opposites in the dominant monolith. The total of power reserves and weaknesses determine the position of a monolith in monolithistic societies. The existence of these human peculiarities is the enduring constant which is to be found in all human societies. The monolith, which is a system, gives to them a dynamism which makes us describe them as systemic peculiarities.

They are aligned inside each system in peculiar ways and are given a peculiar thrust and focus.

The dynamisation of ordinary human qualities within each monolith sets them in conflict with systemic peculiarities in other monoliths.

Let us have a closer look at what happens when dynamisation takes place. The person is defined in pessimistic, devaluative terms to give him a feeling of permanent weakness, of permanent dependence on the monolith which becomes the vicar of a Creative Absolute which brings the human being into this earth to make the best possible use of his life in the continuing conflict between the principles of good and evil. A consciousness of human frailty develops which forces the individual —a Greek term which has no equivalent in the Sudic languages of Southern Africa—to live in fear of his neighbour, society, the state, the world around him and of the Creative Absolute; he lives in perpetual fear of death.

He lives for salvation in heaven or for amassing, for his use, all the good things of this earth or for contentment in a classless society in which all exploitation will have been flushed out of the human personality.

The moulds in which dynamisation of the personality takes place in each monolith develop mutually exclusive angularities which extend the area of conflict between the monoliths. These give all differences the nature of quarrels on fundamentals. If this makes dialogue impossible and sets the monoliths moving inexorably to conflict, it throws the spotlight on another aspect of the focus: the role of the Creative Absolute as a source of all authority, value and meaning.

The dynamisation of the person takes place at two levels: on the leadership plane and in the follower segment. The task of the leaders is to proclaim the truth, to clarify goals, to identify enemies and to establish the infallibility and validity of the fundamental inspiration. Dynamisation at this level sets out to give heroic dimensions to the leadership sector.

When it comes to the ordinary people, dynamisation works for the systematic pulverisation of the personality to facilitate its manipulation by the leaders.

Afrikanerdom has transformed itself into the most highly developed monolith. It not only developed apartheid into a creed of salvation, but also gave it the dimensions of a guarantee of security and survival. The leadership stratum in the Afrikaner monolith lied to the Afrikaners when it said apartheid was a reliable guarantee of survival. Afrikaner political power was built on African labour and English technological know-how. The lie was reinforced by the debatable view that overwhelming military power would forever force the Africans to submit to White rule. Impact was given to the lying by Afrikaner media, universities and churches which systematically concealed from the masses of the Afrikaner people the fact that on January 8, 1912, the Africans had met in Bloemfontein to form themselves into an opposing monolith.

It might be dangerously heretical to say that the Afrikaner people are victims of a gigantic lie; but their history demonstrates that they have not been told the truth about developments on the African side. In their ignorance, they supported policies which have no relevance in the African experience, policies which make the Afrikaner's eventual expulsion inevitable.

Afrikaner universities propagated the lie that the Africans had settled in South Africa at about the same time that the Whites were arriving at the Cape. Archaeology is blowing this lie to pieces. Jean Hierneaux, the French physical anthropologist, and others are showing that Sudic Africans were settled in Southern Africa for at least more than a thousand years before the Dutch came to the Cape of Good Hope.

Dynamisation forces the individual Afrikaner to think in a rut and believe what the policy-makers say he must believe. But crisis-point has risen like a spectre on the horizon. Concerned Afrikaners have begun to ask why, if apartheid is a guarantee of survival, 4,000 Whites flee South Africa every year.

Because the monolith is a system, it has its own reserves of power or points of strength and its own weaknesses, the interaction of all these generates rhythms and tensions within each system which give the monolith an insatiable appetite for power; they make the control of this power a guarantee of survival. This type of guarantee cannot be shared. Each monolith is sealed in immutability; each is self-centred in the sense that race, ethnicity or colour is the reality for which it lives and is the determinant of morality, attitudes and policy.

This leads to a whole series of contradictions. To maintain its dominance, the monolith has to cast the thinking of the other monoliths in its own moulds. Its peculiar weaknesses give it a predatory approach which sets out to maximise its power by corroding the points of strength in the other monoliths; by using deculturation to create conformity. The Afrikaner monolith, for example, works for[6]:

> onverbloemde Afrikaner-heerskappy, Afrikaans as hooftaal, met die einddoel kort and klaar die "volledige politieke nasionalisering en uiteindelike kulturele verafrikaansing van ons Engelssprekende eggenote."

The point to note in this quotation is that the bias of prescribing destiny for others has no respect for colour. If the imperatives of monolithal survival demand the *verafrikaansing* (afrikanerisation) of the English, the Afrikaner monolith will not hide its intentions on this plane. This gives to the united front of White monoliths the character of a consortium of resident oppressors who have irresolvable differences on given planes. These quarrels which move the two White monoliths in different directions, are a significant factor in the politics of a nation which sets great store by differences. One of the reasons behind the monolithisation of the Black language-groups was to enable the Africans to address themselves effectively to these differences.

In its campaigns for corroding English economic power, the Afrikaner monolith resorts to ethnicity as the weapon by which to swallow up and eventually destroy the English. The speech from which Serfontein quotes represents the views and aspirations of orthodoxy in the Afrikaner monolith; of the section which regards itself as the custodians of the Afrikaner's destiny. (The Afrikaner monolith uses racism and ethnicism as the weapons by which to destroy the Black monolith.)

Because of its self-centred nature, the monolith cannot share power of any sort with the others; to share it would be to provide them with weapons by which they would destroy it. But the weaknesses that inhere in being a monolith demand that cultural power should be shared; the other monoliths must be made to accept the fundamental inspiration which is believed to guarantee survival and entrench the power of the dominant monolith. This calls for the sharing of the religious experience and language.

This contradiction leads to the next. Uneducated people cannot be easily controlled through a religious concept they do not have the ability to understand. So, schools must be established for them in which the truth will be taught in forms predigested for them by the dominant monolithal teleguide. The Afrikaner monolith rejected the English system of education, introduced Bantu Education and taught all subjects from Afrikaner perspectives. The colonisation of the African's mind was designed to educate the Africans sufficiently to be good servants and collaborators in their own ruin and not to threaten the Afrikaner.

While the educated and the converted belong—the former intellectually and the latter spiritually—to the thought-world of the dominant monolith, the exclusivism of the monolith, which is its guarantee of survival, precludes acceptance in its social world; the educated and the converted remain permanently unwanted in this world.

This gives rise to two new contradictions. The mould of immutability in which each monolith is cast combines with the rhythms which give form to lifestyles in the others to demand an appropriate interpretation of the fundamental inspiration. Thus, each monolith gives its own meaning to the inspiration.

The teaching on the brotherhood of Man has one meaning in the Dutch Reformed Church, which administers to the spiritual needs of the Afrikaner monolith, a different one in the Nominalist churches organised by the Africans, and a third in the English-speaking congregations.

Inevitably, this proteanism reinforces schismatic deviationism and other heresies which threaten the intellectual supremacy of the dominant monolith. This point is crucial. In the South African setting, the dominant monolith preaches that the Africans should develop along their own lines. When they follow this advice to its logical conclusion and produce the Black Consciousness Movement, the government gives them the name of "communists" and attacks and jails the Africans while some of its agents murder the Africans to prevent them developing along their own lines.

When told that they must develop along their own lines, the Africans say that their lines led to the establishment of sovereignty and national independence for their ancestors. Apartheid insists on defining sovereignty and independence for them. When the Africans reject the White man's right to prescribe destiny for them, they become "communists"; when they reject the intellectual leadership of the Afrikaner, he again brands them as "communists" and commits all crimes against their humanity.

This happens because the proliferation of interpretations creates a vacuum in the thinking of the dominant monolith on how to reconcile the conflicting rhythms and cross tensions which give form to relations between the monoliths. Each monolith has its own type of discipline for resolving conflict among the groups within it; this discipline or equilibration creates the equilibrium which preserves cohesion within the system. The monolith cannot allow these conflicts to be resolved in the natural way; they have to be disciplined in a manner that serves the ends of monolithal dominance.

Each monolith generates its own internal rhythms which clash with the rhythms of other monoliths. The interactions of these cause cross-tensions; that is, tensions which bounce from and to each monolith. The proliferation of these cross-tensions leads to monolithal conflict when the attacked monolith fights to ensure its survival.

The international community has not begun to realise that the "race" quarrel is essentially a war of minds which is developing into a war involving arms; that it is a collision between evaluations of the person developed by the Africans and the Whites, between the ideals of nationhood these philosophies produced, between the vehicles used to entrench these ideals and between the mutually exclusive strategies adopted to move events to final goals.

These fundamentals of conflict give to racism the character of a punishment of the person for being the child of his particular parents and transform race discrimination into a vehicle for effecting the punishment.

The international community has not begun to draw the necessary distinction between the fundamental and the operational aspects of the crisis.

The present chapter outlines the attitude to the person which determines thought and behaviour among White monoliths.

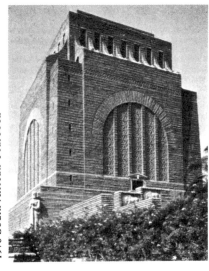

The Voortrekker Monument commemorating the Afrikaners march inland, just south of Pretoria.

TENSIONS IN BEING THE PARTICULAR
CHILDREN OF ONE'S PARENTS

Mention was made earlier in the chapter of the inner logic which an evaluation of the person or an ideal of fulfillment gives to a civilisation. The bias for categorisation is part of the inner logic which the Graeco-Romano-Hebraic evaluation of the person has given to Caucasian civilisation.

One of the characteristics of this logic is the creation of conflicts or tensions which move peoples and events in cycles, to ultimate disaster. The bias for categorisation destroyed the power of the Greek city-states and the might of the caesars in Rome; it drove the Holy Roman Empire headlong to catastrophe. The bias brought to their end the Spanish, Portuguese, British, French, Italian, Dutch and Belgian empires and landed the world in two ghastly global wars. Indications are not lacking that the United States and the Soviet Union might be drifting to disaster. The two superpowers are spending billions on armaments and neglecting those areas of social reform which would be the crowning glory of their ideologies. The Americans and the Soviets waste money on weapons, some of which become obsolete before they leave the assembly lines, not because they are stupid or find pleasure in destroying their countries and seeing their people killed; they act in response to the ruthless logic of categorisation.

This logic, this bias for categorisation, has its roots in the pessimistic evaluation of the person which was developed by the Hellenes, the Romans and the Hebrews. This evaluation is the fundamental inspiration which the civilisation developed by the Whites translates into action.

The danger which threatens the future of the Sudic communities in the Middle World emerges at this point. If Caucasian civilisation moves people and events in cyclic progressions to final disaster, it might drag the Sudic communities of the Middle World to a catastrophe on the order of World Wars I and II. Conditions could arise which would make it impossible for the rest of Free Africa to remain neutral in such a holocaust.

The urgent need for an evaluation of the person which will define the human being in universally valid terms is underlined by another aspect of the bias for categorisation. Graeco-Romano-Hebraic civilisation has in the last two thousand years been inflicting mortal wounds on itself by down-grading woman; by making it virtually a crime for a girl to be the particular child of her parents; by giving women a permanent sense of grievance, by making them permanent outsiders in their own community.

Please note that the women under discussion are White. The enduring injury was described by an American woman in these terms:

> ...it is man's fear and dread of the hated sex that has made woman's lot such a cruel one in the brave new masculine

world. In the frenzied insecurity of his fear of women, man
has remade society after his own pattern of confusion and
strife and has created a world in which woman is the
outsider. He has rewitten history with the conscious
purpose of ignoring, belittling, and ridiculing the great
women of the past, just as modern historians and
journalists seek to ignore, belittle, and ridicule the
achievements of modern women. He has devalued woman
to an object of his basest physical desires and has remade
God in his own image—"a God that does not love
women." Worst of all, he has attempted to transform
woman herself into a brainless simulacrum, a robot who
has come to acquiesce meekly in the belief in her own
inferiority.[7]

The Middle World is our primary concern. The stigmatisation and
inferiorisation of women is the time-bomb laid by history and usage at the
foundations of the American structure of power. The two evils are
inseparable complements. By making women congenital outsiders in their
own society, the twin evils force the women either to reject the values of
the society which attacks and punishes them for being the particular
children of their parents or lack the total commitment to these values
which would release all the creative forces locked in the female
personality and give them constructive purpose. Giving constructive
purpose to these forces is one of a society's or a civilisation's guarantees
of stability.

The stigmatisation and inferiorisation have transformed the American
democracy into a prison of the mind in which the genius and human
potential of the women are distorted in ways which give her an abiding
sense of grievance. This frustration of life's purpose for her ultimately
gives her a vested interest in the destruction of the values which are given
one meaning on the male side and another on the female.

The woman is placed in an impossible position here. On one plane she is
expected to produce children and to teach them, during their most formative
years, that the values which define American nationhood are the finest that
the United States could have been built upon. Her children grow up seeing
how this nationhood punishes her for being a woman. If this damages her
credibility, it gives the children a cynical view of the American system of
values.

The stigmatisation and inferiorisation of women complicate America's
race problem. The two evils have their roots in the ideal of fulfillment
which Graeco-Romano-Hebraic civilisation translates into action. God,
whom Christianity regards as the creator of all things, is a
male; so is his son, Jesus Christ, who is said to be the saviour of the
human race. In the Roman Catholic Church the Pope and the hierarchy
are all men.

In the Christian tradition maleness is associated with virtue, strength and innocence while woman is regarded as the fount and incarnation of all vice, all weakness and all cunning.

In *Canon Law and the Battle of the Sexes*,[8] Rosemary R. Ruether has the following to say about the position of the woman as defined by Canon Law:

> The law of the Church is designed to elevate one group at the expense of another: women are sacrificed as human beings to elevate priests to the status of sanctified beings. The law was written over the centuries by men for men, and by men who regarded sex (which is still today very hard to come by without women) as quite undesirable. In that men wrote for men, and then for celibates, women were written out of the organization of the Church and out of the sanctuary. As far as the spirit of canon law is concerned, the Church seems to assume that it can do very well without women.

The inferiorisation of woman has been justified by Church Fathers and other scholars down the centuries. Writing in the collection of essays to which reference has been made above, Bernard P. Prusak quotes Clement of Alexandria as making these comments on the beard as evidence of supremacy (p. 103):

> His beard, then, is the badge of a man and shows him unmistakably to be a man. It is older than Eve and is the symbol of the stronger nature. By God's decree, hairiness is one of man's conspicuous qualities, and, at that, hairiness distributed over his whole body. Whatever smoothness or softness there was in him God took from him when he fashioned the delicate Eve from his side to be the receptacle of his seed, his helpmate both in procreation and in the management of the home.

When Clement recognised the beard as evidence of supremacy, he was defining categories to justify male supremacy. Christian civilisation has been built on this type of supremacy. Largely as a result, the woman continues to be punished, in the Land of the Free, for being the particular child of her parents, even though White. On the Black side of the colour line, the person of colour is punished for being the child of his or her particular parents.

In either case the bias for categorisation punishes the "outsider" for having qualities which he or she cannot change. At this level, race ceases to be the determinant of behaviour; attitudes to the person come to the fore as translations into action of a particular view of the human being—of a given evaluation of the person.

This evaluation is so closely bound to Christianity that many American women rebel only silently against their inferiorisation. They have to be silent in order to survive. The silent rebellion is one of those factors which makes the United States a nation whose conscience is at war with itself; the Americans cannot be a free people if the American woman continues to be punished for being the particular child of her parents.

The students' revolt was not over when I arrived in the United States in 1969. I travelled extensively over America, speaking to different groups, largely on college and university campuses. Two aspects of the revolt attracted my attention. I discovered that the angriest students tended to be the girls. So much violence had been done to the person, dignity and honour of the woman, that the girls were determined to pull down the establishment in the bid to realise that freedom they had been promised by the Declaration of Independence and the American Constitution. They were outraged by the circumstance that in their society, freedom had one meaning on the side of the male and a different one on the side of the female.

The second aspect I noted was that the women and young men in revolt did not have an alternative philosophy with which to confront what they regarded as the establishment. Most of them clamoured for relevance; for the humanization of the American experience. Like the establishment which they opposed, however, they defined relevance and humanization in terms which would move them in a circle back to where they had begun to revolt. To an outsider from Africa, this was the basic weakness in the students' revolt.

To an African again, the weakness arose from the fact that the rebellious students did not challenge the pessimistic and devaluative assessment of the person developed by the Greeks, Romans and Hebrews and could not, for this reason, confront the boreal evaluation of the human being with an effective alternative.

While the rhetoric of the revolt emphasised "ideology" and many even spoke of a revolution, what happened in the absence of clarity on the meaning the young gave to the person was that the advocates of change concentrated on the purely operational aspects of their relations with the establishment; they fought the institutions, rules and other usages developed by the establishment to translate the Graeco-Romano-Hebraic view of the person into action.

There is no doubt in my mind that at the level of attacking institutions, the students' revolt scored some notable victories. The exposures of the Watergate Scandal, the public outcry against it which forced President Nixon to resign and the election of President Carter on his Human Rights and Clean Administration planks were gains.

The Blacks who revolted at this time were as handicapped as the White students were at the ideological level. While they set out to change American society, in the absence of a clearly stated philosophy by which to define the person, the revolting Blacks could do no more than attack the operational aspects of race discrimination and succeed in effecting changes in the functioning of a given set of institutions.

The civil rights laws which Congress passed were significant gains for the Black side. But these gains affected the functioning of institutions; they did nothing to the philosophy behind these institutions. The concessions were to a large extent a valve for letting off the accumulated steam which could explode and crack the foundations of American nationhood.

As long as the person was defined in terms which clashed with the nature and demands of the "Citty," America seemed fated to drift from one crisis to another until women on the White side and men and women on the Black were defined in terms which would be valid in the conditions created by the "Citty," described by John Winthrop in 1630.

That after two hundred years of American nationhood, the United States has a vigorous Equal Rights Amendment movement and that this Amendment has not yet passed sets the spotlight on the chasm between the ideal and the real; on the fact that in the Land of the Free, citizenship, liberty, equality and happiness have one meaning on the side of the White males and another when it comes to Black people and White women.

Black Americans and White women were punished for qualities they could not change; they were given the status of outsiders. This happened, not because the White males were wicked, but because of the bias for categorisation which had its roots in the Graeco-Romano-Hebraic evaluation of the person; in pessimistic and devaluative attitudes to the person.

The pessimism and the devaluation created difficulties in relations between man and woman on the White side and between Black and White. As shall be shown later, they also complicated some of America's relations with peoples of colour in the Third World generally and, in particular, with Africans. The complications incapacitated the United States for giving effective leadership in moving events toward a political solution to Southern Africa's race problem; they limited America's ability to understand the African or the thinking behind the changing dispositions of power in Southern Africa.

The dangers of the incapacitation were thrown into sharper focus by the American economy's need for some of Southern Africa's metals.

History was showing that the Whites were fighting a war they had already lost in the subcontinent; before many years were out, the United States would be dealing with the Black majority. For these dealings to produce the results the United States would desire, America would need to move away from devaluative definitions of the human being, toward universally valid assessments.

The Westerners, however, are not the only Caucasians committed to the devaluative view of the human being. Like them, the Soviet Bloc is part of the Graeco-Romano-Hebraic civilisational family. The pessimism about the person emerges in Soviet attitudes to African

Nationalism and in the American-Soviet consensus on guarantees for minority rights.

As shall be shown later, the Soviet Union continues to see African problems from Eastern European perspectives. These have little relevance in African conditions. To apply these arbitrarily, as the communists in South Africa used to do, creates problems for all.

The Communist Party of South Africa (CPSA) which was formed in 1921 and went underground after the apartheid regime came to power in 1948, has always had close ties with Moscow. Its critics argued that Moscow did the thinking for the CPSA. This thinking, like the approaches of the slave-owners of the Cape, the colonialists, the Christian missionaries, the advocates of apartheid and the capitalists, was founded on Graeco-Romano-Hebraic assessments of the person.

The Party always feared that its Caucasian perspectives would be diluted by Sudic perspectives. Moscow was always on guard against the dilution. The precautions the Soviet Union took in the 1920s to preserve the purity of Marxist doctrines were described by Eddie Roux, who was for many years a leading member of the CPSA, in his book, *Time Longer Than Rope*:[9]

> The Communist Party by now numbered among its members many Africans whose political knowledge and understanding was small. It began to seem that the Party might be swamped by members who had little or no knowledge of Marxist principles and theory. The suggestion came from Moscow that the Party should remain a small and select body of trained revolutionaries working through a larger mass body. In this way, the communists would be enabled to preserve the purity of their doctrine while at the same time, through the larger organisation, giving a clear lead to the masses on all questions.

The Soviet Union's distrust of African traditions was reflected in the CPSA's hostility to African Nationalism, whose leaders the CPSA attacked and denounced as the Black bourgeoisie. The CPSA spared no opportunity to split the political organisations established by African Nationalists. The first of these attempts was made in 1928, after the return of J. T. Gumede, then president of the African National Congress, from a visit to Europe which included a tour of parts of the Soviet Union. This came after communist attempts to split the Industrial and Commercial Workers Union (ICU) two years earlier. Clements Kadalie was forced to expel the communists from the ICU in the bid to preserve the unity of his organisation.

The ANC was always the prime target of the communists because of its being nationally recognised as the custodian of the 1912 Bloemfontein *Ideal of Nationhood*. The next serious attack on African Nationalism reached its peak in the middle of the 1950s when the communists set out to stampede the ANC into rejecting the Bloemfontein Ideal of Nationhood.

The document which set out to do this was the Freedom Charter, which was made public in Kliptown, near Johannesburg, on June 26, 1955. The Charter did not say a word about the Bloemfontein Ideal. The silence was eloquent; it implied that there was no Ideal of Nationhood to which the Africans were committed. The Charter justified the definition of nationhood which served best the ends of the CPSA.

For purposes of the present discussion, the most important aspect of the Charter came under the heading: "Guarantees for Minority Rights." The Charter argued for the entrenchment of "national rights."

Dr. Henry Kissinger, when he was United States Secretary of State, flew to Africa in 1976 on what he called a "mission of commitment." In his policy speech, delivered in Lusaka, he announced America's commitment to the establishment of majority rule in Southern Africa and coupled the commitment with the expectation of "Guarantees for Minority Rights."

Not to be outdone by the surrogates of Moscow who had written the Freedom Charter nor by the Republican Administration which sent Kissinger on his "mission of commitment," President Carter dropped this bombshell in his now famous Notre Dame policy speech:

Finally, let me say that we are committed to a peaceful resolution of the crisis in Southern Africa. The time has come for the principle of majority rule to be the basis for political order, recognizing that in a democratic system the *rights of the minority* must also be protected. (Emphasis added).

This declaration, which *The New York Times* published on May 23, 1977, was remarkable in two ways. On one hand the President seemed indifferent to the fact that the minority rights he wanted protected were the very issue on which Black and White were quarreling; they were the bone of contention which had moved Black and White to the Soweto Rebellion; they were the cause for which Africans had been willing to sacrifice hundreds of lives.

On the other hand, the emphasis on guarantees for minority rights established a point of convergence for Democratic, Republican and Soviet views on the cause of the race quarrel in Southern Africa.

The consensus was not accidental; it had its roots in the common American and Soviet commitment to the evaluation of the person developed by the Greeks, the Romans and the Hebrews. The convergence of American and Soviet views on minority rights issued from the Caucasian perspective which the evaluation produced. At the ideological level, the United States and the Soviet Union were poles apart, but when it came to civilisational patterns, they drank from the same inspirational fountain; they had identical, or, it should be warned, co-ordinable attitudes to the material possessions acquired by the White minority in Southern Africa. The Graeco-Romano-Hebraic perspective forced Washington and Moscow to regard the Whites in Southern Africa as a possible bridge which could guarantee access to the subcontinent's resources.

The Soviet Union was prepared to stab African Nationalism in the back to ensure that the surrogates of Moscow were the dominant factor when White domination was overthrown. The Democrats and the Republicans in the United States offered political power as the bribe which would make it possible for the Africans to agree to guarantee minority rights.

An articulate group of Afrikaners, mainly in the ranks of the intellectuals, promptly grasped the significance of the convergence of American and Soviet views on this plane and made public demands for a recasting of Afrikaner attitudes to the communist states. There was even talk of the formation of a South African-Soviet Union cartel to control the disposal of gold and uranium in world markets.

The demands for changed attitudes to communist countries were not the sort of babble heard in drinking parties. That some members of the government took them seriously emerged from debates in the South African parliament. The international edition of the Johannesburg *Star* (April 16, 1977) reported that Dr. P. van B. Viljoen, the apartheid member of parliament for the Newcastle constituency in Natal, had spoken during the resumed debate on the 1977 budget and had:

> warned the West that it could no longer take South Africa for granted, and if it came to a matter of survival the Republic would turn to communist and socialist countries of the Eastern bloc to raise capital.... [He added that] it was time South Africa became less dependent on the West for raising capital... South Africa could not go on ignoring the hostility of certain Western countries after all South Africa had done for the less fortunate people in South Africa... the time had come to ....establish economic links with certain communist countries... so that South Africa could rid itself of its dependence on the West and the vulnerability that went with dependence.

There certainly was more anger than realism in Dr. Viljoen's threats. The Afrikaner's control of South Africa is not absolute. While political power is for the present firmly in Afrikaner hands, the Africans supply the labour which sustains the economy while English finance is the lifeblood which keeps the economy going. An African-English alliance, made up by peoples both of whom have been dispossessed in different ways, could make it impossible for the Afrikaner to take South Africa to the communist side of the fence when it comes to foreign investments.

English dominance in the economy could create problems which the apartheid regime has limited power to control. The response of big business to the continuing Black revolt shows what is possible. Alarmed by the government's inability to suppress the 1976 revolt on one side and the refusal to introduce meaningful change in racial policies on the other, big business has, in at least the last three years, moved steadily to the left of the government. At present, it is about the only part of the capitalist world to stand to the left of the government on a fundamental issue of national policy.

This has placed South Africa in the unique position where the dispossessed, who have a vested interest in change, find themselves virtually in alliance with big business against the government. Government intransigence could, by radicalising the dispossessed, transform them into revolutionaries. It would be interesting to see the Soviet Union in alliance with the apartheid regime against revolutionaries who would be backed not only by Free Africa but also by China.

Whether or not the advantages of a gold and uranium cartel would outweigh the obloquy the Soviet Union would draw on itself for bailing apartheid out of its economic troubles is a matter that can be decided only by the Soviet Union. For their part, the men who control big business would have little reason for allowing the government to be economic allies with communism.

A South Africa whose government was anti-West while African labour and big business were pro-West would be an obvious candidate for destabilisation by any interested party.

Let us leave this tantalising subject at this point because our main concern is the role the boreal attitude to the person plays in situations where Black and White perspectives collide. The attitudes conducive to conflict are not peculiar to the Caucasians; they are not peculiar even to capitalistic societies. That people have been victims of race discrimination is no guarantee that they will not punish other human beings for being the children of their particular parents. Let us have a look at the incidence of race discrimination outside South Africa and the United States.

Europe's incursions into Africa brought into being the Middle World, gave it its medial perspectives and set in motion the evolving interaction between the punitive racism on the White side and the evolving reaction on the Black side. Let us, for this reason, look at race discrimination in Europe.

In the South African setting, most Afrikaners justify race discrimination on the score that it is a guarantee of White survival; that this type of guarantee is rendered necessary by the fact that the Whites are a minority in South Africa.

If this argument were valid, there would be no race discrimination in Europe, where the Whites are in the majority and have their roots; where no outsider can threaten these roots. The Intelligence Report of the *Parade Magazine* inserted in *The Washington Post*, August 14, 1977, published this item:

ADVICE TO ARABS: Don't do your wash in the hotel swimming pool and hang it up to dry in front of the hotel windows. Don't forget to pay when you go shopping. And remember, wait your turn in line.

These helpful hints, meant for Arab tourists coming to Great Britain, are contained in a booklet published in Arabic by the London Tourist Bureau.
The purpose of the guide, it says, is to protect the visitors from mistakes and embarrassment—it is not intended to be patronizing or condescending.
Tourists from Near-Eastern oil countries have been flocking to England. They spent more than $260 million last year in London alone.

The London Tourist Bureau might have had the best of intentions in mind. But in situations where the races have quarrelled or where colour prejudice is known to exist in one form or another, it does nothing to explain that patronizing or condescending is not intended, because, in Arab eyes, the patronizing issues from the context provided by the existence of race discrimination in Britain, by the attitude of people like Enoch Powell and his followers, by the existence of the National Front and by incidents like what happened in Bradford in 1971. Writing in *The Washington Post* October 16, 1971, Alfred Friendly reported:

In the small hours of Thursday morning, in the North England industrial city of Bradford, someone poured kerosene through the letter slot of an Asian immigrant family's row house, and added a match. By the time the father, a wool-comber on night shift in a textile plant, reached his charred door, his three youngest children, aged 8,11 and 15, were dead and his wife was—and remains—in critical condition....

The fire was only the latest in a series of 13 instances of deliberate arson against nonwhite immigrant homes in Bradford....
Eight West Indians were horribly burned when a Molotov coctail was thrown into their club in South London early this year. There have been several incidents in East London where gasoline-steeped rags have been set alight and stuffed through windows and letter slots....

The unhappy fact is that there is a great deal more racism in the United Kingdom than the British care to admit.

This was in 1971. Seven years later racism had become a political problem which, in the view of some commentators, threatened to give the British Labour Party one or two nasty headaches. Writing in *The Washington Post* of January 30, 1978, Geoffrey Hodgson reported as follows:

> British politics have always been moderate and civilized, as befitting a nation with old democratic traditions. But within recent years, we have been witnessing the rise here of an extremist right-wing movement, avowedly racist in outlook, that is now threatening to cut into the support of the ruling Labour Party.
>
> The movement calls itself the National Front, and it appears to be gaining ground in the decaying inner-city neighborhoods of London, Birmingham and Manchester as well as in such northern mill towns as Blackburn and Bradford, where sympathy for the Labour Party has been strong.
>
> The Front has been encouraging the antagonism of white workers in these areas against Asian, African and West Indian immigrants, many of whom perform unskilled jobs that the British themselves are loth to handle. There are some two million of these immigrants in Britain's population of 56 million.
>
> What worries the Labour Party leaders is the possibility that the National Front may win seats in Parliament if a general election is held this year.

The nascent racism in Britain obviously has some of its origins in the country's sick economy. This economy, which was for centuries supported by slavery or the resources of the colonies, does not seem able to recover from the ailments which have afflicted it since the end of World War II.

The nascent racism is not likely to help the British workers solve their problems; it is not likely even to provide more and better jobs for them in the long run. Take, for example, the case of Swaziland. In south-west Swaziland, the British have established one of the world's largest man-made forests at Bunya. Wood pulp from these is exported to Britain where it is processed into paper. The processing requires supportive industries which give additional jobs to British workers.

By falling back to racism, the National Front creates a climate of thinking which could provoke an African reaction; which could make it difficult and in some cases impossible for African countries in Swaziland's position to subsidise British workers in the way they do. The present generation of Free African leaders is moderate and is likely to tolerate for some time to come the humiliation of the African race by British workers who support the National Front. But these leaders are not immortal. One day, a generation of Africans will arise which will punish the National Front for its racial policies.

By hoping to drive the non-Caucasians out of Britain, the workers who support the Front might hope to secure jobs for the British today. In the long run, however, they are digging economic graves for their own children.

It would be wrong to recognise the British as the only color-conscious nation in Europe. On February 20, 1972, *The Washington Post* published a London *Observer* report by Sue Mastermann to this effect:

Growing prejudice in the Netherlands against coloured and foreign immigrant workers, has led to a Dutch government clampdown on the admission of foreign labour.

At the time, Holland had a population of about 13 million and about 125,000 foreign labourers made up of Turks, North Africans and people from the poorer Mediterranean countries. In Rotterdam, where the Dutch rioted for a week against foreigners in August, 1972, one out of every 15 people was an outsider. The influx of coloured people into Holland set in motion moves to dump them in the Netherlands' bantustans in the Caribbean—Surinam and the Antilles. As in South Africa, the idea was to give these territories "a greater degree of autonomy with independence in view."

In West Germany, Black American defenders of the Republic continually wrote home complaining of race discrimination; many were refused accommodation. As in Japan after the last world war, the children of Black American soldiers and German girls were often treated like the vermin of the earth in the land of their mothers.

The propaganda of socialist countries creates the impression that race discrimination is an evil peculiar to capitalist societies.

The death of Edmund Asare Addo in Moscow in 1964 set the spotlight on racism in the Union of Soviet Socialist Republics. Addo was a Ghanaian student of medicine. One morning, he was found dead on a street. The Russian authorities said he had died of natural causes or intoxication. The African students insisted that he had been murdered for reasons connected with race.

Free Africa agreed with the students. Writing in the Accra *Evening News* on December 20, 1964, Rambler, who was not noted for discovering evil in the Soviet system, had this to say, according to a bulletin published by the government of Swaziland at the time:

Details of circumstances leading to the death of that Ghanaian student in the capital of the Soviet Union make grim reading. No wonder

African students in Moscow who disagreed with the official version of the medical student's death had to use such strong tell-tale placards for their demonstration march on the Kremlin.

Whether Asare Addo died from natural causes, from intoxication, or from cold, the hullabaloo being made in sectors of the capitalist press and radio in some Western countries should teach our socialist friends the need for extending the principle of co-existence beyond the frontiers of ideological verbosity or theoretical altruism.

It is true one swallow does not make a summer but the very fact that such a thing could happen even in the Soviet Union emphasises the point that the cradle of socialism in the modern world is not itself free from the barbarities of race hatred and discrimination.

Other Free African papers took a stronger line. *Jeune Afrique* (Tunis) commented acidly on December 23:

In spite of all the (communist) party's propaganda, there certainly remain in Russia as in all Eastern Europe deep impressions of racism. This feeling often shows itself and black students put up with it even less easily because it is absolutely contrary to the principles which the Soviets teach them in interminable courses of political instruction. This time, in Moscow, fairly and squarely, they rebelled....

The most serious result of this incident in Moscow is that it throws into relief the contradictions between the Soviet Union's desire to teach the young people of the uncommitted countries and the "welcoming set-up" they can offer....

From Dakar, *Afrique Nouvelle* fired verbal shrapnel in all directions on December 27 and January 2, 1965.

What does seem important is that the African students should have demonstrated about a Ghanaian in the name of the whole of Africa. The Russians must therefore have found themselves confronted by a delicate problem. Besides, this was a lesson in freedom which they gave to the Soviets, but equally to the African Powers who want to indoctrinate their students.

In its commentary on the death of Addo the African press found it strange that racism could occur in a socialist country. There was nothing really new in the irony. In *The Red Prussian*, author Leopold Schwarzchild says that after the quarrel with Bakunin, Marx and Engels formulated a "new iron law." This is his description of it:

The will of history had endowed certain nations with the gift of spreading the gospel of progress throughout the world; to other nations this gift had been denied.

Applying this law to international relations, Engels wrote thus in a letter to Marx, dated May 23, 1851:

...there is absolutely no more reason for Poland to exist.... [Germany, he continued, should take] from the Western part of Poland anything that can be taken, to let the Germans occupy their fortresses under the pretext of "protection", use the people for cannon fodder and devour their country.

The founding saints of communism carried their hatred of outsiders to the plane of personal relations with some of their colleagues. Lassalle was a prosperous lawyer of Jewish extraction who did his best at times to assist the communist cause in Germany and often stood by Marx. In a letter to Marx, dated March 7, 1856, Engels described Lassalle in these colourful terms:

A typical Jew from the Slavic border, always ready to exploit everyone for his private ends...concealing with all kinds of hair oil and make-up, the fact that he is a greasy Jew from Breslau.

Subsequently, Lassalle wrote a book on Heraclitus and volunteered to send a copy to Marx. The father of communism had this to say about it in a letter to Engels, dated December 22, 1857:

We shall soon see for ourselves and even if it is a gift horse, we'll look it straight in the mouth...on the express condition, of course, that it doesn't smell of garlic.

After Lassalle had been to London, where Marx quarrelled with him, he ceased to be a Jew; he became a "Jewish nigger" whose genealogy Marx described in extravagantly lurid terms in a letter to Engels, dated July 30, 1862:

...it is perfectly obvious from the shape of his head and the way his hair grows that he is descended from the Negroes who joined Moses on the Journey out of Egypt, unless perhaps his mother or his grandmother had relations with a nigger.

When the interpreters do not prescribe destiny for the Africans, they ignore the fundamentals of conflict and focus attention on the operational aspects of the quarrel between Black and White.

The advocates of apartheid ignore the destiny the Africans chose for themselves on January 8, 1912, and insist that the Black people must seek fulfillment for themselves in the vassalage the South African government peddles as independence in unviable mini-states.

For years now, South Africa's White liberals have been clamouring for the abolition of what they call petty apartheid: the differential wage, residential segregation, influx control, Bantu education and related vehicles for entrenching White domination. The underlying assumption was that the Africans accepted integration in a socio-economic set-up based on Caucasian attitudes to the person, when the Africans rejected this type of integration on January 8, 1912.

Professor I. I. Potekhin, who was director of the African Institute of the Academy of Sciences of the Soviet Union, had much to say about what was good for the African. In one of his essays[10] he wrote:

The existence of the world socialist system creates highly important prerequisites for the non-capitalist development of the African peoples. The decisive prerequisite, however, is the condition of African society itself.... The Republic of South Africa, for example, is a capitalist country, with the peculiar feature, however, that capitalist enterprises in industry and agriculture belong to the European minority. The first task here is to make a people's democratic revolution as a result of which the system of racial discrimination will be abolished and the African population will receive political rights equal to those of the European minority. After the victory of the people's democratic revolution there will open up the possibility of building a socialist society, but South Africa is no longer in a position to by-pass the stage of capitalist development, since capitalism already exists here. In South Africa, therefore, it is not a question of non-capitalist development but of the transition from capitalism to socialism.

From prescribing destiny for the Africans (the majority) Professor Potekhin proceeds to berate those Africans who talk of African Socialism:

A completely erroneous counterposing of scientific socialist theory to "African Socialism" has gained wide currency among African Socialists: scientific socialism is not suitable for African reality; we shall build our own African Socialism, is what they say....

Some advocates of "African Socialism" imagine socialist society as a society of equal petty producers.... Everyone will manage his own farm or business independently of others and will exchange the products of his work; if someone suffers misfortune, the rest will help him.

This type of society, however, is simply impossible with the present state of technology....

A legitimate question arises: Why are people who sincerely wish to build a socialist society and abolish the exploitation of man by man unwilling to accept the scientific theory of socialism, tested in practice, and instead engage in a search for some other kind of socialist society?

A comparison of apartheid with Marxist positions on prescribing destiny for the African and condemning what they regard as ideological heathenism is not the place to answer Professor Potekhin's question. It can, however, be said in passing that "the scientific theory of socialism, tested in practice" is not acceptable mainly because it does violence to the African definition of the person, while the testing in practice took place in conditions which do not exist in Africa. It does not, in other words, address itself to vital African needs or to determinative realities in the Black experience. It does not, for example, recognise the African's right to define himself in his own terms. What need is there for him to do this when Jesus Christ, John Locke, and Karl Marx have done this for him? As far as Professor Potekhin is concerned, the Bloemfontein Ideal of Nationhood, which will be discussed in a later chapter, does not exist; the "common controlling idea" on the basis of which the various African language groups united themselves into a new nation in 1912 is not valid and the "new and unique civilization" this nation set out to build has no relevance. The things that exist and are valid and relevant are the "people's democratic revolution," a "socialist society" and receiving (from the Whites) "political rights equal to those of the European minority."

In all these examples we see the boreal attitude to the person translated into action in ways which punish the African for being the child of his particular parents. The Christians did this and the advocates of apartheid and the Marxists continue to do it today not because they are White, but because they all are committed to a civilisation built on a philosophy which defines the person in devaluative terms.

The will to impose White perspectives sets out to ensure that whole peoples define themselves in Caucasian terms. Leopold Senghor spoke at the inauguration of the Senegalese Economic and Social Council in Dakar in March,1964. Some of his remarks were as follows:

Nothing can replace capital, technical training, work and honesty. The mistake, Karl Marx and his followers made was that they neglected agriculture and stock farming in favour of industry, and the peasants in favour of the artisans. This mistake explains the lack of economic balance in the socialist countries....

Moscow's *Izvestia* (June 6, 1964) replied with this significant retort:

Nationalism has become the principal danger of the socialist commonwealth.

In all the above, we see a clash of attitudes to the person. In this collision, some Whites use racism as a vehicle by which to perpetuate the dominance of their civilisation. It does not matter much who or where these are, they all have a deeply vested interest in the security of their civilisation and the attitude to the person on which it is built.

The point to note in any serious attempt to understand the "race" problem is that the African has his own attitude to the person; that he is as vitally interested in its survival as the White man is in his and that if the White man cannot come to terms with this fact, South Africa is heading for a bloody collision, by the side of which the war in Rhodesia will seem like a backyard brawl.

Being involved in this collision is not our destiny. Concerned people on both sides of the colour line have the duty to launch a dialogue of minds or civilisations to reconcile conflicting perspectives. Most Whites—in the West and Socialist countries—are psychologically not equipped to accept the validity of truths discovered down the ages by the African. These Whites are part of the problem.

That people have been victims of race discrimination does little to prevent them from punishing others for being the children of their particular parents. Solomon Grayzel, a Jewish historian, tells us what happened to the Jewish community of Cochin, India, after the arrival of "white" Jews from Europe:[11]

> In matters of religion and culture the old settlement of Jews in India benefited from the arrival of the European Jews.... Socially, however, the new settlement brought a problem which has afflicted Cochin Jewry to this day. The newer arrivals insisted on keeping aloof from the others. Their reasons were the ignorance of the Hindu Jews and the supposed racial impurity indicated by their colour... The Spanish Jews argued that they could not permit their own racial purity to be sullied by intermarriage or even by social contact with such "inferior" stock.

> All the groups were equally orthodox, observing the same rites, although the "whites" and the older "blacks" worshipped in synagogues of their own.... Economically the "white" Jews were not necessarily better off than the "blacks."

No matter how tragic a people's experience of punishment for being members of a particular racial or ethnic group in Graeco-Romano-Hebraic cultures might be, the suffering does not seem to destroy their bias against outsiders. Today, about a generation after the tragic experience of the Jews at the hands of the Nazis, the ashkenazi or Western

50

Jews in Israel subtly, though illegally, keep a distance between themselves and their Sephardic brethren. The attitude behind the punishment of the sephardic Jews was stated by General Moshe Dayan, the renowned Israeli soldier and political leader, in South Africa when he visited that country in 1974.

In what the Johannesburg *Star* (International edition, September 7, 1974) described as an "impassioned speech" Dayan "took a side-swipe at what he called 'Oriental Jews.' " He told the South African Jews, who are classed as White in that country, that one of the problems facing Israel was that three out of every five immigrants were Orientals. Appealing to the "white" Jews to return to their "homeland" he said:

What we have to try to do now, is to be very, very attentive to try to help more newcomers from the Western countries.

For years, the peoples of the Third World regarded the Scandinavians in general and the Swedes in particular as the only Europeans whose attitudes were not poisoned by the evil of race prejudice. The Swedes themselves loved and were proud of this reputation. In July, 1977 the police in Goteborg, Sweden's second largest city, began an investigation [12] into five restaurants and discotheques that were shown to have refused to admit Blacks from Africa and the United States while opening their doors for White patrons.

United States Ambassador to the United Nations Andrew Young once called the Swedes "terrible racists" and had added that they had an ideology which made them very humanitarian, but when the crunch came, the Swedes treated the Black people in the way the Whites in Queens, New York, treated them.

The relevant point which emerges from what has been written up to now on race discrimination as used by the Whites to punish peoples of African descent is that the punishment transcends ethnic, religious and ideological loyalties in the Caucasian group itself. As the long history of anti-semitism and Nazism in Europe show, Whites are not above punishing each other for being the children of ethnically different parents.

This suggests that we should look beyond biology for the basic cause of race discrimination. Attitudes to the person seem to be the main cause of the evil.

As already stated, the human baby is born with a brain and not a mind. His environment—that is, his family, society, culture and location—gives him the perspectives from which he sees reality, experience and the person; it gives him his beliefs, attitudes, customs and other usages; it gives him his mind and identity. Race conflict arises when the total of attitudes we call the White mind collides with the mind of the African; when the Caucasian evaluation of the person clashes with its opposite on the Black side; when the Sudic perspective clashes with the Caucasian perspective.

The problem at which the present discussion is directed emerges in clearer outlines at this point. Contact with the Caucasians has thrown Africa into a crisis of values which moves Black and White in cycles of conflict to final disaster. This emerges from the history of Caucasian civilisation in the last 3,000 years or so.

The devaluative attitude to the human being combined with the bias for categorisation to move ancient Greece and Rome to final disaster; they drove the Holy Roman, Spanish and Portuguese empires to oblivion in much the same way that they led the British, French, Dutch, Belgian and Italian empires to ruin. The attitude and the bias plunged the world into two global wars in the lifetime of a single generation. If indications are any guide, the pessimistic definition of the person and its inner logic—which is the bias for categorisation—are driving the United States and the Soviet Union to the point where they will land the human race in World War III.

The initiatives asserted by the United States (and the West) on one hand and, on the other, by the Soviet Union and its satellites, have a special significance for Africa. If and when the two eventually take up arms against each other, they will fight their fiercest battles in Africa, whose mineral and other forms of wealth each great power seeks to grab for itself and its allies.

The "scientific approach" by which the Marxists set so much store, is as incapable of devising a formula for the resolution of conflict in Southern Africa as capitalism's greed is. In situations of contact and conflict between Black and White in Southern Africa, the West and the Soviet Bloc behave in related ways because of the attitude to the person to which they are committed.

In this setting we, the people of Africa, find ourselves caught in the drift toward disaster of an ideal of fulfillment which belongs to the childhood days of the human race.

For all of us, whether we are in Southern Africa, in Free Africa or in the diaspora the definition of the person in pessimistic and devaluative terms raises a fundamental question to which all the peoples of African descent need to give a fundamental answer.

The view that the individual is a creature and not an integral and inseparable part of the living force which unifies the cosmic order limits the person's freedom to discover more satisfying dimensions of being human and prevents him from realising both the promise of being human and the glory of being a self-defining value.

This frustration of life's purpose for the human being gives to the cash value of the person the dimensions of a criterion by which to assess human worth; the person ceases to be human—he becomes a unit of production and a cipher in the books of those who determine his destiny, manage his life, do the thinking for him and extort maximum advantage from his productive potential.

The person is born to live, work and die in the inhuman conditions created by those who prescribe destiny for their fellowmen. The Church comes along with countless mysteries to incapacitate the people for effective revolts against the devaluation of the person. The state establishes a whole structure of power to force the person to see fulfillment for himself in apologising for being human or, if the person is a White woman in the West, to apologise for being the particular child of her parents.

At the end of the person's life, he dies with a pile of credit cards which indicates the extent to which he mortgaged his life to those who were "smart" enough to transform ideology, dogma and gross national products into prisons of the mind in which he was not allowed to realise the promise of being human.

If he is an African, the fundamental question he asks at the end of his life is:

"What did I do with my life? Why did I not realise the promise of being human? Where did I go wrong?"

The next chapter gives answers to his fundamental questions.

NOTES ON CHAPTER I

1. H.J. Rose: *Religion in Greece and Rome*, Harper and Row, Nea York, 1959, P 94.
2. In *World Culture And The Black Experience*, University Of Washington Press, Seattle, 1974, P 8.
3. Rose, *Religion in Greece and Rome*, P 94.
4. Quoted by Hans-Joachim Schoeps in *The Religions Of Mankind*, Doubleday and Co., New York, 1968, P 231.
5. *Hermeneutical Philosophy, Myth and African Thought*, an essay in *Philosophy in the African Context*, compiled by D.S. Georgiades and I.G. Delvare, from papers read at a seminar on the theme: *Philosophy in the African Context*. The Seminar was held in the Witwatersrand University (Johannesberg) in July 1975.
6. J.H.P. Serfontein: *Die Verkrampte Aanslag*; Human and Rousseau, Pretoria, 1970, P 41. Rough translation: out-and-out Afrikaner hegemony, Afrikaans as the official language, with the end in view, briefly and clearly, of "complete political nationalisation and eventual Afrikanerisation of our English-speaking countrymen."
7. Elizabeth Gould Davis: *The First Sex*; Penguin Books Inc., Baltimore, 1973, Pp 17-18.
8. An essay in *Religion And Sexism*, ed., Rosemary Radford Ruether, Simon and Schuster, New York, 1974, P 270.
9. Wisconsin University Press, Madison, 1964, P 226.
10. *On African Socialism: A Soviet View*, in African Socialism; eds., William H. Friedland and Carl G. Rosberg, Stanford University Press, Stanford, 1975; Pp 102, 106, 107.
11. *A History Of The Jews*; New American Library, New York; 1968, Pp 636, 637.
12. *The Washington Post*, July 21, 1977.

54

Black leaders meet with Vorster, January 1975.

Ebony

Sharpeville Massacre, March 21, 1960.

II. An Attitude Toward The Person Which Has No Place In Africa

One of the important points raised in the last chapter was that in the view of the African revolutionary in Rhodesia—as in Mozambique, Namibia and South Africa—the quarrel between Black and White is a war of minds; that it is a crisis of values and a collision between conflicting attitudes to the person.

The central issue in this war, in so far as the Black South African is concerned, is whether or not the White race has the right to prescribe destiny for the Black race. The attitude to the person reflected in the papal bulls listed in the last chapter authorised the Europeans, who led Christendom at the time, to prescribe destiny for the predominantly non-Caucasian "pagans." The Whites in South Africa translate this attitude into action when they arrogate to themselves the right to own 87 percent of the African's land.

Professor Potekhin gives expression to the same quality of mind when he asks: "Why are people who sincerely wish to build a socialist society and abolish the exploitation of man by man unwilling to accept the scientific theory of socialism, tested in practice, and instead engage in a search for some other kind of socialist society?

The answer is that Africans do not recognise the White man's right to prescribe destiny for them and reject the White man's attitude to the person.

The rejection is not confined to South Africa or to the people involved in the fight against apartheid; it can be seen in major segments of the Black World. From March 25 to April 1, 1959, Black writers and artists met in conference in Rome to "preserve the unitary vision of cosmic reality which characterises the wisdom of traditional Africa." The conference's Commission on Philosophy moved this resolution:

1. That for the African philosopher, philosophy can never consist in reducing the African reality to Western systems;

2. That the African philosopher must base his inquiries upon the fundamental certainty that the Western philosophic approach is not the only possible one; and therefore,

3. Urges that the African philosopher should learn from the traditions, tales, myths and proverbs of his people, so as to draw from them the laws of a true African wisdom complementary to the other forms of human wisdom and to bring out the specific categories of African thought.

There were Marxist writers in the conference. They moved a motion which included the following:

1. The cultural references in Marx's thought are nearly all drawn from Western experience.

2. The economic situation of the Western proletariat cannot be strictly identified with that of the underdeveloped people.

3. A doctrine is all the more universal so far as, on the one hand, it takes into account all experience, historic, economic, etc., and the diversity of the cultural genius of peoples, and on the other hand, its application is controlled by a really representative authority.

We invite African Marxists to develop their doctrine on the basis of the real history, aspirations and economic situation of their peoples and to build and found it on the authority of their own culture. [1]

Strange as it might sound, the sentiments of the Marxists were echoed by the All-Africa Church Conference which met in Kenya in August, 1975. The Conference reiterated its determination to work for the development of a theology with "a universal dimension" which would reflect:

the situation in which the people of Africa live, their critical social, political and economic circumstances, their spirituality and cultural setting....Theology should always be rooted in the heart, soul and soil of the people, coming in the language, idiom and thought-forms of the people....[2]

Between the Rome and Kenya conferences an important development had taken place in Ghana. The All-African Students Union had met in conference at the University of Science and Technology in Kumasi in July 1972 and had passed a resolution which included:

We urge all Africans to rely on their own concerted efforts and resources to promote the overall development and total liberation of the continent.... In the great struggle for African freedom and advancement, we urge all African countries to adopt the philosophy of Africanism which serves the material, intellectual and spiritual interests of Africa and does not in any way serve the interests of either the Eastern or Western powers....

In this regard, we appeal to African countries to undertake a vigorous cultural revolution in which all citizens shall be compelled to have only African names, streets, public places and institutions named after things and people of African origin and also to liberate their education system from the shackles of bankrupt intellectual imperialism in Europe and America and gear it towards the needs and aspirations of the continent. [3]

The loud and clear message which comes out of the pronouncements made by the Black writers and artists, the Church in Africa and the students of Africa is that the people of Africa do not want anybody to prescribe destiny for them; that this applies as much to the West as to the Soviet Bloc, and the advocates of White supremacy in Southern Africa; that the destiny the Africans want for themselves is the creation of a world in which no person will be punished for being the child of his particular parents or for being the particular child of her parents; the establishment of a society in which the person will be equipped, enabled and seen to realise the promise of being human. This ideal is capable of attainment only in a society based on a positive and mature evaluation of the human being.

The All-Africa Church Conference's search for "a universal dimension" means that the leaders of African Christianity have reached the point where they realise that Christianity does not have this dimension. Otherwise why should they look around for something that is already in the religion they uphold?

The Conference's search is important because it sets the focus on the mutual exclusiveness of the Sudic and Christian evaluations of the person. The African Church says in effect that if the two are not incompatibles, the chasm between them is so wide it can be bridged only by "a universal dimension."

Here the African Church makes a fundamental criticism of Christianity's view of the human being. But the leaders of this Church are not alone in rejecting the element of what Nigeria's President Olusegun Obasanjo once described as teleguidance.

A ferment is afoot in the Sudic world; its aim is to rediscover the vital element that gave symmetry and durability to the Sudic experience throughout the ages, because the theologies and ideologies based on the

Graeco-Romano-Hebraic view of the human being create catastrophic disharmonies in the Sudic personality.

The day is coming when Sudic philosophers will realise that things went wrong in the Sudic experience when the Africans began to ignore their evaluation of the person.

Aimee Cesaire, the Black poet from Martinique, is a respected Black World thinker. After the 1956 Khrushchev exposures of Stalin's crimes against humanity, Cesaire decided to leave the French Communist Party. The letter of resignation he wrote and which is read widely in the Black World, had this to say:

> I could easily express my feelings towards both the French Communist Party and a Communist International as it has been shaped by the patronage of the Soviet Union ... the list of dissensions and grievances would be long....[They included] pigheaded obstinateness in error, perseverance in lies, the fantastic pretence of never once having been wrong... the bankruptcy of an ideal and pathetic of a whole generation's failure.

Cesaire then turned to racism in the party and tore it to pieces in these terms:

> ...in the light of events (and having appreciated the existence of a shameless anti-semitism whose manifestations have occurred and, it appears, still are occurring in countries that call themselves socialist) I have acquired the conviction that our ways and destinies, and those of communism, such as it is put in practice, are not purely and simply identical; that they cannot be purely and simply identified.

> One fact, crucial in so far as I am concerned, is this: that we coloured men, in this specific moment of historical evolution, have consciously grasped...the notion of our peculiar uniqueness, the notion of just who we are and what,and that we are ready,on every plane and in every department, to assume the responsibilities which proceed from this coming into consciousness...of our problems which aren't to be reduced to subordinate forms of any other problem ...of our history, laced with terrible misfortunes which belong to no other history [and] the peculiarity of our culture.

Cesaire proceeded from this to reject the claim that the French Communist Party had "duties towards colonial peoples in terms of a tutorship." He saw no point in campaigns to create Black solidarity

with the French proletariat and, *via* communism, with all the world's proletariats. I don't make light of these solidarities.... But I don't want to see them blown up into metaphysics. There are no allies by divine right...if communism pillages our most vivifying friendships, wastes the bond that weds us to other West Indian islands, the tie that makes us Africa's child, then I say that communism has served us ill in having us swap a living brotherhood for what looks to have the features of the coldest of all chill abstractions. [4]

Cesaire lays great stress on the "peculiarity of our culture." What makes it unique (for purposes of the present discussion) is its evaluation of the person; its attitude to the human being and its recognition of the person as a self-defining value.

Dr. Davidson Nicol, the Sierra Leonese scholar, stresses the uniqueness in his poem, *The Continent That Lies Within Us.* [5] He writes:

> Go up country, so they say,
> To see the real Africa;
> For whoever you may be,
> That is where you come from....
>
> We have looked across a vast continent and
> Dared to call it ours. You are not a country,
> Africa, you are a concept which we all
> Fashion in our minds, each to each, to
> Hide our separate years, to dream our separate dreams.
> Only those within you who know their circumscribed
> Plot, and till it well with steady plough
> Can from that harvest then look up
> To the vast blue inside of the enamelled bowl of sky,
> Which covers you and say, "This is my Africa," meaning
> "I am content and I am happy. I am fulfilled, within,
> Without and roundabout. I have gained the little
> Longings of my hands, my heart, my skin and the soul
> That follows in my shadow."
> I know now that is what you are, Africa,
> Happiness, contentment and fulfilment,
> And a small bird singing on a mango tree.

Dr. Nicol describes Africa as "a concept" and not merely a geographic entity. But Africa derives her nature not only from geography, but also from her people. When we talk of Africa and her identity, we refer to her and her children. This identity is unique and "peculiar" because it regards Africa as a concept or value, precisely in the way that it recognises each one of her children as a self-defining value.

Like other Sudic children of Africa, the Zulu-speaking Africans of South Africa developed, down the ages, a whole body of *izaga* (aphorisms) in which they defined the person, themselves and their environment. These wise sayings contain Zulu interpretations of the teachings of the Sudic philosophy. Of the person, they say: *Umuntu ngumuntu* (literally: The person is human). To be human is to be able to say what and who you are and to be able to say why you are here and where you are going; it is to be able to define yourself. Ancient Zulu philosophers taught that the person was unique in that he defined himself; in that he knew the worth of the value that he was.

Dr. Nichol draws attention to another aspect of the "peculiarity of our culture": the protean character of the philosophy by which we define the person. He says Africa is a concept which we "fashion in our minds, each to each, to hide our separate years, to dream our separate dreams." Each fashioning of the concept is legitimate, valid and important because each value is the unchanging equal of every other value.

The ideal on which Sudic civilisation has been built recognises, first, the right of the person to discover more satisfying dimensions of being human and, second, the simultaneous legitimacy, validity and importance of the different ways in which different peoples in different environments define themselves.

The definition of the person on which Graeco-Romano-Hebraic civilisation was developed attaches maximum importance to convictions which have no room for tolerance. Christianity, like Marxism, demands the whole person; so does apartheid. This is diametrically opposed to the principle of simultaneous legitimacy and validity.

Another aspect of racism and race discrimination emerges at this point. To punish the African for being the child of his particular parents, the Caucasians do not always put up notices at entrances to their buildings saying: "dogs and niggers not admitted"; they arrogate to themselves the right to "know" what is good for the persons of African descent and to impose their perceptions on the Black people. Their philosophy does not recognise the simultaneous legitimacy of their and the African experiences.

The Caucasian Christians decided by themselves that their religion was good for the peoples of Africa and crossed the seas to impose it in different parts of the continent. The South African government says segregation and retribalisation are good for the Africans and proceeds from this to impose Ethnic Grouping and the vassalage in unviable mini-states it peddles as independence. At this level, the Soviet Union does not behave differently. It reserves for itself the right to prescribe destiny for the Africans, whom, like the Christian missionaries of the West, it regards as heathens—that is ideological heathens.

Ideological deheathenisation in Southern Africa assumes forms which are different from those in the Northern Hemisphere. In North America, as in

Western and Eastern Europe, White scholars, journalists, authors and other opinion-formers are producing large numbers of books and articles in which they "interpret" or "speak for" or "explain" the African to the outside world without informing themselves on the factor which determines thought and action in the Black community: the Sudic attitude to the person.

Ignoring this fundamental of conflict gives to the "interpretations" and "explanations" the character of intellectual apartheid and forces those Whites who concern themselves with developments in Africa to distort African perceptions even where they have the best will in the world.

The distortions must be seen in context. The representative African witnesses whom we have called to testify on how they feel about imposed ideals of fulfillment are unanimous in saying that borrowed theological and ideological self-definitions create catastrophic disharmonies in the Sudic personality. The All-Africa Church Conference is looking around for "a universal dimension" which Christianity does not have. Black Marxist authors and artists demand an interpretation of Marxism which will be valid in African conditions. The Black South Africans are confronting the Whites with an alternative to apartheid.

The difficulties which Christianity is having do not mean that Africa should necessarily reject this religion if she does not want to. After all, Christianity was built on Judaic inspirations which were affected by the ancient Egyptian experience over a period of about four hundred years. Christianity is indebted to Egypt's Osiris, Isis and Horus cults for its concept of the Holy Family and for many other traditions the Jews brought out of Egypt with them.

What Judaism and Christianity did was to destroy the Sudic Ideal's mature definition of the person and to build themselves on given traditions borrowed from Egypt. This is the mistake Graeco-Romano-Hebraic civilisation made; it is this error which the African Church needs to correct.

Something else emerges from the pronouncements. The inner logic of the African attitude to the person moves the thoughts of the Marxists, the churchmen and the students toward convergence when it comes to Africa's destiny; toward what one might call an Evolving Consensus on the destiny of the Sudic peoples.

This point is of the greatest importance when we consider the crisis in South Africa on one plane and, on another, the dangers to which this crisis is leading the rest of Africa. If not diffused, the crisis will get out of control, reduce South Africa to ashes, start fires which will destroy Free Africa and eventually drag in the United States or the Soviets or both. At that point, the world will be galloping to a global war.

Substance is given to this prospect by the fact that the inner logic of Caucasian civilisation, which is the bias for categorisation, leads peoples through cycles of conflict to final disaster.

The inner logic of the Sudic or Sub-Saharan or Buntu attitude to the person which we shall, for lack of a better word, call the bias for agmination moves events toward congruency, as shall be shown throughout the present discussion.

The quarrel between Black and White might thus be defined as a collision between the inner logic of the Sudic attitude to the human being and the inner logic of the Caucasian assessment of the individual; between the bias for agmination and the bias for categorisation.

The present chapter outlines the philosophy which the Africans translate into experience. The philosophy will be presented as a four-sided entity: it will be argued that the African teaching is a protean evaluation of the human being which flowered into Egyptian civilisation on one hand and, on the other, created clusters all over Africa which together make up African civilisation. In this civilisation, each community defined itself in terms dictated by its environment. An outline of the Zulu self-definition will be given as an example. It will be shown that the Zulu self-definition was a total of nomarchic self-definitions because all these described the person in specific terms in a specific environment.

The model nomarchic self-definition made by my section of the Ngubane family was stated to me by my father when I reached puberty.

The intention in presenting the philosophy which gives meaning to the person and the specifics of this meaning—as described in my father's passing of the *Law* on to me—is not only to provide the context in which to see the quality of nationhood produced by the African ideal of fulfillment; it is also to focus attention on the fundamental weakness in the All-Africa Church Conference's search for a *universal dimension.*

The African Church will not find this dimension unless it faces squarely the fundamental conflict between the African or Sub-Saharan or Sudic attitude to the person, and the Graeco-Romano-Hebraic assessment of the human being on which Christianity is based.

Apartheid is not an aberration; it issues naturally from the logic of the definition of the person as a creature born in sin. It is part of a long and firmly established tradition which produced the Inquisition, gave rise to slavery, colonialism, racism, Nazism and communism. These evils issued naturally from the bias for categorisation.

The African Church needs to face squarely the fact that its search for a *universal dimension* ultimately responds to the fact that the Christian definition of the person has no place in African society; that Christianity can have valid meaning only if it defines the person in terms which establish the adequacy of the person, enlarge the human personality and enable each woman, man and child to fully realise the glory of being a self-defining value and the promise of being human.

If the African Church trembles at the prospect of freeing itself from the prison of the mind which the Graeco-Romano-Hebraic evaluation has become, African Christianity will commit the blunders which have forced the Africans to look for a *universal dimension*; that will make Christianity as irrelevant as colonialism.

A few explanations need to be made in order to place the outline in context. We shall be making frequent use of the word Sudic, to describe the Sub-Saharan experience. The outline will first trace the origins of this word and proceed to define the person. The texts used in the first instance will be taken from the writings of ancient Egypt for two reasons: Egyptian attitudes to the person are well documented while the Egyptian evaluation of the person is similar to the philosophy which inspires the major cultures of Black Africa today.

The Egyptian view of the human being is characterised by a concern with the person and a predilection for developing attitudes and creating institutions designed on the one hand to enable him to discover more satisfying dimensions of being human, and on the other, to realise the glory of being a self-defining value. The concern and the predilection characterise Black cultures.

The Egyptian definitions of the person will be followed by their opposite in the Zulu experience and by a review of how the Zulus translated the Sudic attitude to the human being into political action in the last five hundred years of Zulu history.

The choice of the Zulu experience is dictated by one simple reason: it is the only one which the present author knows and understands. I was born into it; it made me what I am. I believe that it is as integral a part of the larger Sudic experience as any we have in South Africa. Tracing the application of the Sudic evaluation of the person in the last five centuries will draw in sharper outlines the inner logic of the Sudic attitude to the human being in South Africa; it will show how the Africans reacted to conquest and what they eventually did to restore to themselves their land and their freedom.

The word *Sudic* comes from *su*, a variant of *Nu*, which is the rootword for *person* in most Sub-Saharan African languages. In terms of origin, the rootword is related to *Nu*, the ancient Egyptian word for primordial substance. The ancients believed that all phenomena emerged from *Nu*. The person, they believed, evolved from primordial substance through a creator-god. The person was "created" so that he should "appear in glory" on earth.

In the migrations up and down the continent, the differently placed Africans developed variants of *nu* and gave it the following forms: [*-du, -nho, -ni, -no, -ntfu, -ntu, -nwo, -nwu, -so, -su, -tho, -thu*] and *-tu*. This consensus on *nu* produced the following nouns for person among peoples in widely different parts of Africa:

Language	Word For Person
Hausa	mutum
Ibo	nmadu
Yoruba	*eniya*
Swazi	*muntfu*
Sotho	*motho*
Xhosa	*umntu*
Zulu	*umuntu*

In many Sub-Saharan languages the noun prefix generally can be translated to mean the expression, extension, individualisation or personification of, In Zulu, which is my language, *umuntu* means the person. If we break down the word into its components, we shall have:

The Article— *u-* meaning *the*
The Concord— *-mu-* meaning *personification of*
The Rootword— *-ntu* meaning *Ntu,* the person

Zulu, like, Xhosa, Swazi, Ndebele and Bhaca, belongs to the closely related languages which together form the Nguni cluster. The Xhosa still refer to Black humanity as *umzi ka Ntu,* the family or descendants of *Ntu.*

Like the other Nguni communities, the ancient Zulus believed that the cosmic order was an infinity; that as such it was a unity and that it was the environment in which the person really existed. If primordial substance was infinite, there could not be anything which existed outside of it; all phenomena emerged, existed and "died" inside it. The person was one such phenomenon; he and his environment were inseparable complements.

This relationship gave rise to the following derivatives from *Ntu* :

Ulutho	The nameless something; a phenomenon; substance.
Uluntu	The vital force; the powerful stomach muscle which regulates the peristaltic process.
Umuntu	The personification of *Ntu;* the person.
Isintu	Humanity.
Ubuntu	The art of being human; virtue.

The above shows how we can speak of *nu-* or *su-* or *ntu-* oriented cultures which together form the unity known as African Civilisation. We can also speak of *Nudic* or *Sudic* Civilisation in place of African Civilisation. In the present discussion Sudic will be used in place of Buntu because the apartheid regime has given to the word Buntu an unacceptable political meaning.

EGYPTIAN HERITAGE

The ancient Egyptians are divided almost as much by time as by geography from Sub-Saharan Africans. At the same time, the two are united by their attitude to the person. The values which constitute this attitude are together the philosophy which Sudic civilisation has been translating into experience in at least the last 10,000 years. Let us glance at the main ingredients of this philosophy.

The *Book of Knowing the Evolutions of Ra* tells us that [6] the creator-god Neb-er-tcher, the "lord of the company of the gods" gave the following description of creation:

I am he who evolved himself under the form of the god Khepera, I, the evolver of the evolutions evolved myself, the evolver of all evolutions, after many evolutions and developments which came forth from my mouth. No heaven existed, and no earth, and no terrestial animals or reptiles had come into being. I formed them out of the inert mass of watery matter, I found no place whereon to stand....I was alone... there existed none other who worked with me. I laid the foundations of all things by my will, and all things evolved themselves therefrom....I sent forth Shu and Tefnut out from myself.... Shu and Tefnut gave birth to Nut and Seb, and Nut gave birth to Osiris, Horus-Khent-an-maa, Sut, Isis, and Nephthys, at one birth, one after the other, and their children multiply upon this earth.

The Egyptian god, Osiris, receiving offerings from a woman of standing. The ancients believed that the immortal aspect of a virtuous person became an Osiris after the day of judgement.

66

In another version of the story of creation, Osiris has this to say[7]:

I came into being from primeval matter, and I appeared under the form of multitudes of things from the beginning. Nothing existed at that time, and it was I who made whatsoever was made. I was alone, and there was no other being who worked with me in that place. I made all the forms under which I appeared by means (or, out of) the god-soul which I raised up out of Nu, out of a state of inertness (or, out of the inert mass)....

I found there (i.e., in Nu) no place wherein I could stand. I worked a spell on my heart, and I laid a foundation before me, and I made whatsoever was made. I was alone. I laid a foundation in (or by) my heart, and I made the other things which came into being, and the things of Khepera which were made were manifold and their offspring came into existence from the things to which they gave birth. It was I who emitted Shu, and it was I who emitted Tefnut... and Shu and Tefnut were raised up from out of Nu wherein they had been.

One of the most important aspects of creation emerges from the following quotation:[8]

In the very ancient *Egyptian Creative Legend*. the Supreme Creative Principle is depicted as saying: "I existed by Myself; for They (*i.e.* the Gods) were not born. My name being Heka, I opened my mouth to proclaim myself."

The Egyptians tell us in the *Negative Confessions* about the spells they used to win entry into Annu, the heavenly city; that life's purpose for the person was to "live forever," to "live for millions of millions of years" and to be "the prince of eternity."
Eighteenth Dynasty spells[9] say the person should "proclaim" or define himself in these terms:

I am Baba, first son of Osiris, whom every God united to himself....

Mine are yesterday and [each] morrow, [for I am] in charge of [its] successive births. I am the Hidden Soul who made the gods....

My manifestation is the manifestation of Khepri [one name for the creator-god].... I have entered as an ignorant one; I have come forth as an initiate.... I shall be seen in my human form forever....

Several points emerge from the above quotations from ancient Egyptian texts. To begin with, the ancients regarded creation as an evolving process whose beginnings they traced back to the nature of *Nu*, their name for primordial substance. Primeval matter evolved into the watery mass, also known as *Nu*, from which the creator-god, *Nu*, emerged. *Nu* created the earth (*Nu*) and the gods from whom there descended the "things to which they gave birth." The *Book of Knowing the Evolutions of Ra* explains that "their [the gods'] children multiply upon this earth."

The Egyptians set great store by autogeny. The creator-god evolved himself from primordial substance and uttered the word of power by which he "proclaimed" or defined himself. He did not create "things" out of nothing; he facilitated their evolution from forms in primordial substance into phenomena. He raised Shu and Tefnut "from out of *Nu* wherein they had been." The facilitation was what the ancients regarded as creation.

The creator-god informs us that the *god-soul* was the mould in which he cast "all the forms under which [he] appeared." This god-soul was *The Law of Appearing*; it was Ultimate Value or Immutable Form. Each phenomenon first existed as a value or form, and then evolved in response to the challenge of its nature. The formula H_2O was the ultimate value of water. This value evolved into the liquid we drink, snow, ice, and steam in response to the challenge of its nature in different environments. The nature of the value did not change; it remained the same from aeon to aeon; it was the eternal person whose destiny was to live for millions of millions of years.

The creator-god was an infinity and, therefore, a unity. Nothing could co-exist with him; there was no outside of him; all things were inside the infinity; he expressed himself and appeared in all the things he brought into being. Through an act of will, he "made whatsoever was made." The will was translated into phenomena and the "things to which they gave birth." The chain of evolution and succession continues to this day.

Primordial substance was forever evolving in response to the challenge of its nature; it was forever individualising itself, through phenomena, to produce new "things"; it was always growing in response to the challenge of its nature or *Law of Appearing* or god-soul.

Everything inside the infinity was alive, for there was no death in the infinity; everything was a materialisation of the *Law of Appearing*; of Ultimate Value. Everything was consubstantial with primordial substance and with everything in the cosmic order. The consubstantiality combined with *The Law* to keep the cosmic order a unity.

In this setting, each phenomenon "proclaimed" or defined itself in everything it did. The self-definition proclaimed the section of *The Law* which gave the phenomenon its nature; it defined itself in its qualities.

The person differed from other phenomena in one fundamental respect; like the creator-god, he defined himself in his own terms. He knew what and who he was; what he knew was his secret; it was his source of power. He evolved into this earth and became *homo* in order to discover more satisfying dimensions of being human. Perpetual evolution was his destiny; his nature required that he should forever discover more satisfying dimensions of being human.

Each person defined himself in terms valid in or dictated by his environment and each such self-definition was as simultaneously legitimate, valid and important as that made by his neighbour, no matter who the particular parents of the latter were.

The principle of simultaneous legitimacy gave the Egyptian the feeling that he and his neighbour were inseparable and mutually-fulfilling complements. Each was the obverse side of a whole to which the neighbour was the reverse. The maximisation of the neighbour's ability to realise the promise of being human was a preconditon of fulfillment for the person.

Man's first neighbour was woman and vice versa. The great goddess, Isis, was:[10]

> the great and beneficent goddess and mother whose influence and love pervaded all heaven, and earth, and the abode of the dead, and she was the personification of the great feminine, creative power which conceived, and brought forth every living creature, and thing, from the gods in heaven, to man on the earth, and to the insect on the ground; what she brought forth she protected, and cared for, and fed, and nourished, and she employed her life in using her power graciously and successfully, not only in creating new beings but in restoring those that were dead.

This was Universal Woman, without whom Man could not exist. Man, also, was a precondition of Woman's existence. Society began when the two complements established a family. The function of society was to create the conditions in which the person could discover more satisfying dimensions of being human and realise both the promise of being a person and the glory of being a self-defining value.

The person was endowed with a many-sided or ciliate mind which would enable him to achieve everything he desired and make him become whatever he wanted to be. This unparalleled confidence in the person and the readiness to face squarely, over thousands of years, the implications of this commitment to the primacy of the person draw in the sharpest lines the difference between the Sudic and Caucasian attitudes to the person.

The confidence was translated into political realities in the plurarchic state which the Egyptians established. The plurarchy was based on the recognition of the simultaneous legitimacy and validity of the cultural self-definitions developed by different peoples in their environments. Pharaohs arose from time to time who sought to impose a uniform mode of behaviour on the peoples in Egypt's different nomes. We are told that the pharaoh Menkaure was outraged by the policy of forcing the Egyptians to adhere to the same formulary when performing religious rites. He issued a decree abrogating the former laws and making it legal for his people to worship as they chose.

The plurarchy was an open state in which the people were bound together by a political loyalty which allowed them to realise the promise of being human in the light of their choices. The Greeks and the Romans never understood the relationship between the Sudic attitude to the person and the plurarchy. A well-known British Egyptologist described the failure in the following terms:

> ...the cultured Greek writers must have, and did, as we know, look with mingled pity, and contempt, and ridicule, upon the animal cults of the Egyptians, and they had no sympathy with the materialistic beliefs and with the still more materialistic funeral customs and ceremonies, which have been, from time immemorial, so dear to certain Hamitic peoples, and so greatly prized by them. The only beliefs of the Egyptian religion which educated Greek or Roman truly understood were those which characterized the various forms of Aryan religion, namely, the polytheistic and the solar; for the forms of the cults of the dead, and for all the religious ceremonies and observances, which presupposed a belief in the resurrection of the dead and in everlasting life, and which had been in existence among the indigenous inhabitants of north-east Africa from predynastic times, he had no regard whatsoever. The evidence on the subject now available indicates that he was *racially* [author's emphasis] incapable of appreciating the importance of such beliefs to those who held them, and although, as in the case of the Ptolemies, he was ready to tolerate, and even, for state purposes, to adopt them, it was impossible for him to absorb them into his life. It is important to remember this fact when dealing with the evidence of Greek and Roman writers on the Egyptian religion and mythology, for it shows the futility of trying to prove an absolute identity in the indigenous religions of the Aryans and Egyptians.[11]

What was true of the educated Greek or Roman three thousand years ago is to a large extent true of White South African, Western and Soviet scholars who attempt to interpret the Sudic experience. For them to persist in misinterpreting the African in the way they do is a dimension of race discrimination, regardless of whether or not the culprits misinterpret the African unconsciously or deliberately.

Like their Greek and Roman predecessors, the advocates of apartheid, Western scholars and Soviet students of Africa judge the African on the basis of criteria which will not enable them to perceive his experience in the clearest terms possible. The tragedy of our times is that this ignorance is the basis on which White South African, Western and Soviet policies for Africa are, in the final analysis, founded.

ANCIENT EGYPTIAN THEOLOGY

Western scholars have difficulty in understanding the "religion" of the ancient Egyptians. Henri Frankfort is one of those as yet few scholars who seriously tries to see the Egyptian experience as the ancients viewed it. But even he lands in difficulties when he seeks to understand the fundamental inspiration which Egyptian civilisation translated into experience. He observes: [12]

Religion as we Westerners know it derives its character and its unity from two circumstances: it centers on the revelation of a single god, and it contains a message which must be transmitted....

Akhenaten was a heretic.... He denied recognition to all but one god and attempted to convert those who thought otherwise. His attitude presents no problem to us; we acknowledge a conviction too deep for tolerance. But Egyptian religion was not exclusive. It recognised an unlimited number of gods. It possessed neither a central dogma nor a holy book. It could flourish without postulating one basic truth.

We find, then, in Egyptian religion a number of doctrines which strike us as contradictory.... The ancients did not attempt to solve the ultimate problems confronting man by a single coherent theory; that has been the method of approach since the time of the Greeks....

Ancient thought...admitted side by side certain *limited* insights, which were held to be *simultaneously* valid, each in its own proper context, each corresponding to a definite avenue of approach. I have called this 'multiplicity of approaches'.... this habit of thought agrees with the basic experience of polytheism.

Polytheism is sustained by man's experience of a universe alive from end to end. Powers confront man wherever he moves, and in the immediacy of these confrontations the question of their ultimate unity does not arise.

This statement of the difficulties Western scholars encounter when it comes to understanding the philosophy by which the ancients gave meaning to reality and life draws in sharp outlines the difference between the Sudic and Graeco-Romano-Hebraic perspectives.

One finds it difficult to understand how Frankfort arrives at the conclusion that the question of the ultimate unity of the forces which confronted man did not arise. The Egyptians believed in the consubstantiality of phenomena. *Nu* was primordial substance out of which the Creative Principle emerged; all phenomena were extensions of the Creative Principle. That which was consubstantial was a unity.

The person who had led a virtuous life on earth became a 'shining one,' an Osiris, a companion of the gods and their equal after death; he became the "prince of eternity."

The key to the understanding of Egyptian philosophy is the ancients' attitude to the person; they regarded the "form" of the human being, that is, that which was eternal in him as destined to live forever. Philosophy centred around this conviction. Institutions were developed to enable the person to evolve to the best of his ability in response to the challenge of his nature. Egyptian society and civilisation were person-centred in the sense that they maximised the latitude within which the human being could make what they regarded as the best possible use of his life.

The Egyptian attitude to the person and its implications are not yet as clearly understood in Graeco-Romano-Hebraic civilisation as they should be. The definition of the person as a creature continues to be a stumbling block.

The Egyptians inclined to the view that dogma was a dangerous thing; it readily degenerated into a prison of the mind. They preferred an open society which faced most of the implications of man being an extension of *Nu,* via the creator-god. Pharaoh Menkaure became famous because he made laws which allowed the ancients once more to worship gods of their own choice, in their own ways.

The chain of consubstantiality which explained the Egyptian's regard for the person emerges from the quotation Neb-er-tcher from the "lord of the company of gods," in *The Book of Knowing the Evolutions of Ra,* [13] is important enough to repeat here:

> I am he who evolved himself under the form of the god Khepera, I, the evolver of the evolutions, evolved myself, the evolver of all evolutions, after many evolutions and developments which came forth from my mouth. No heaven existed, and no earth, and no terrestial animals or reptiles had come into being. I formed them out of the inert mass of watery matter. I found no place whereon to stand.... I was alone.... There existed none other who worked with me. I laid the foundations of all things by my will and all things evolved themselves therefrom.

In these early writings we see the ancients laying stress on self-evolution from *Nu.* The creator-god does not make phenomena from nothing; he forms them out of the watery mass of *Nu* or out of his essence. Each form has its unchanging value and evolves in response to the demands of this value. Perpetual evolution is its destiny because there is no end to evolution; it goes on forever.

72

The ancients faced the implications of this definition of the person and established a society designed to enable him, who knew his name and kept it a secret, to translate his secret into action to define himself to his family, home and society.

The lord of the company of gods tells us that he evolved himself and that he laid the foundations from which "all things evolved themselves." He evolved himself from *Nu*, and formed heaven, the earth, terrestial animals and reptiles from *Nu*, the inert mass of watery matter. He, the creator-god and his evolved "creatures" were made of one substance; that was why "all things evolved themselves" from forms or "foundations of all things" laid by his will.

The Egyptian mind thought in terms of evolution where the Graeco-Romano-Hebraic mind thought in terms of creation; the former regarded evolution as flowing naturally from the consubstantiality of *Nu*, the creator-god and "all things." The Greeks, Romans and Hebrews saw a relationship of otherness between them which separated the Creative Absolute from its creatures; this relationship gave rise to the bias for categorisation. The Greeks thought themselves a people apart from others and regarded outsiders as barbarians. The Romans regarded *numen* as the determinant of categories. Solomon Grayzel tells us in *A History Of The Jews*[14], that the Jew who lived between 516 B.C. and 70 A.D.,

felt that he was superior to the pagans. Their cruelty, their lewdness, their silly notions about gods, made the pagans seem lost tribes of humanity. Herein, however, the Jews saw their task: they were destined to be 'the witnesses of God,' the teachers of mankind. Their forefathers, the Patriarchs, had been chosen to found a new people. That new people had consecrated itself by accepting the Ten Commandments at the foot of Sinai. From this the Jews felt justified in drawing certain conclusions. One was that the Jews were a superior people, if not because of the merits of their own generation, then because of the fact that they were descendants of such illustrious ancestors. The other conclusion was that the Jewish people was not a racial group (a blood-group), but a group with a mission, that is, a group united by ideas.

This Jew regarded his community as "the chosen people" whose destiny was to teach mankind the commandments carved on stone by God. The Jews stood in a category by themselves; as having been appointed by God to teach the human race.

Ancient Egyptian documents suggest that the idea of commandments carved on stone was not peculiar to the Jews. E.A. Wallis Budge tells us in his introduction to *The Egyptian Book of the Dead* that according to the Nebseni papyrus one of the earliest chapters of this book was "found in the city of Khemennu (Hermopolis) on a block of ironstone [?] written in letters of lapis-lazuli, under the feet of the god."

The Turin papyrus of the XXVIth dynasty or later says the man who found the stone was Herutataf, the son of Pharaoh Khufu (Cheops) of the IVth dynasty, which puts the date of the discovery at about 3733 B.C.

Herutataf, we are told, was one of the best-educated men of his time. He played a leading role in bringing the sage Tetteta to the court of his father, Cheops.

Moses received the stone tablets with the Ten Commandments on Mt. Sinai during the 13th century *before Christ*, about 2,400 years after Herutataf.

Let us return to the bias for categorization. When the Europeans met the Black, Brown, Red and Yellow peoples, they used race and colour to define new categories of the human race. The non-Caucasians became the *barbarians* who had not been endowed with the *numen* which made the Caucasians the *teachers of mankind*; they became the *heathens* who did not have the *grace of God* and had to be won to Christ by the *missionaries*.

The Egyptian teaching on evolution and autogeny gave to the person the character of a self-defining value. *The Papyrus of Ani* tells us how Ani, a scribe, described himself after death as he journeyed to eternity. In *The Chapter of Changing into the Soul*, there is written:

I am Rā who [came] from Nu, the divine Soul, the creator of his own limbs. Sin is an abomination unto me and I look not thereon; I cry not out against right and truth, but I have my being therein. I am the god Hu, and I never die in my name of "Soul." I have brought myself into being together with Nu in my name of Khepera. In their forms I have come into being in the likeness of Rā. I am the lord of light.[15]

The Egyptians regarded primordial substance as infinite. By definition, an infinity was a unity; nothing could co-exist with it; nothing could have a will to oppose the will of the infinity. The infinity operated in terms of its Law, which was its will. Everything existed in the body of the infinity; everything operated in terms of the Law.

The person was created according to the Law; he was conceived according to the Law; he was born, fed and clothed in the Law. All he did; all his thinking and behaviour; all his hopes, victories, fears and defeats translated the Law into action. He could not violate the Law because he incarnated it. Nothing could oppose the Law because everything in the cosmic order conformed to the Law. Conflict itself was a translation into action of the Law. The person grew up and thrived in terms of the Law; he matured, aged and died according to it; he evolved perpetually into eternity according to the Law.

The logic of the Egyptian attitude suggests that the person could not sin even when he wanted to do this because sinning would translate into action another aspect of the Law. He hurt his neighbour and committed crimes because he did not know the Law sufficiently; because he was ignorant.

In all this, the Egyptian expressed unparalleled confidence in the person and this confidence had its origins in his belief in the consubstantiality of the phenomena which constituted the cosmic order. This was how he stated this belief:[16]

O Atum, who has gone forth as the Great One of the surging flood [the Waters of *Nu*]... pray speak thou to the Ancestors: [The deceased] comes as one who is in their midst.... Indeed [she] who bore Re [Rā] yesterday is the one who bore [the] deceased [too].

The "she" who bore Ra was primordial substance, *Nu*, in the form of the watery mass of antiquity. The creator-god evolved from *Nu* and phenomena evolved from the creator. The cluster of forces which together constituted the eternal in Ani, the Scribe, says this of itself:

I behold Rā.... His strength is my strength, and my strength is his strength.

What Ani tells us in this passage is that primordial substance is infinite; that since the infinity is a whole which cannot co-exist with anything and since it must always remain whole, it needs him as much in order to be this whole as he needs it in order to exist; that, in the final analysis, there cannot be any relationship of otherness between the Creative Principle and the phenomena it brings into being. There inheres in him the power by which he could transform himself into a god. Ani continues:

Behold me, for I am exalted upon my resting-place, Nu, upon the place which is adjudged unto me. I am Nu, and those who work evil shall not overthrow me. I am the eldest and the first-born of matter; my soul is the gods, who are the eternal souls.... I come, and my soul advanceth over the way of the Ancient Ones.... I am strong to pass over the sky.... My soul and the soul of my body are the uraei, and I live forever, the lord of years, and the prince of eternity. I am exalted as lord of the earth.... I grow youthful in my homestead, my name is "My name decayeth not" I am the Soul, the creator of Nu...I am the lord of millions of years. I make my nest in the limits of heaven.... I do away with my faults.... I am provided with what I need.

After defining the person in such exalted terms, the Sudic evaluation of the human being could not be anything other than a protean philosophy which each community translated into experience in terms valid in or dictated by its environment. The logic of this philosophy went beyond tolerance; it created a dimension of consanguinity which regarded all the children of *Nu* as an evolving unity.

The "she" who bore Ra was primordial substance, *Nu*, in the form of the watery mass of antiquity. The creator-god evolved from *Nu* and phenomena evolved from the creator. The cluster of forces which together constituted the eternal in Ani, the Scribe, says this of itself:

This is how Ani defines himself in *The Chapter of Changing into a Bennu* (p. 339):

I came into being from unformed matter, I created myself in the image of the god Khepera, and I grew in the form of plants. I am hidden in the likeness of the Tortoise. I am formed out of the atoms of all the gods. I am the yesterday of the four [quarters of the world], and I am the seven uraei which came into existence in the East, the mighty one who illumineth the nations by his body.... I am crowned, I am become a shining one, I am mighty, I am become holy among the gods. I am the god Khonsu who driveth back all that opposeth him.

Ani adds the following definitions of himself in *The Chapter of Changing into a Heron* (p. 340):

My hour is within me.... I am Nu, and I shall never be overthrown by the Evil-doer. I am the god Shu who sprang from unformed matter. My soul is god; my soul is eternity. I am the creator of darkness, and I appoint unto it a resting place in the uttermost parts of heaven.... My name is "Never-failing." My name is "Soul, Creator of Nu, who maketh his abode in the underworld."...I am lord of millions of years....

This definition of the human being produced an inner-logic which emphasised the primacy of the person; the consubstantiality of primordial substance, the creator-god, and phenomena; autogeny; self-definition; perpetual evolution and living forever. At the same time it gave to the Egyptian evaluation of the person the character of a protean philosophy which people in different environments translated into experience in different ways in response to the challenge of their destiny. This destiny was to live for millions of millions of years; to be princes of eternity.

A moment on the day of judgement: the god Anubis weighs the heart of the deceased while the god Thoth records the findings. The British Museum

THE ZULU INTERPRETATION

The three connecting links between the Egyptian and Zulu experiences were the commitment to the principle of consubtantiality, the attitude to the person and the teaching that perpetual evolution is the destiny of the human being.

Where the ancients believed that all phenomena emerged from *Nu*, which was primordial matter; where the chain of evolution began with *Nu* and proceeded to the waters of antiquity (*Nu*), the Original Mound or Earth (*Nu*), the creator-god from whom all things evolved, the lesser gods and the person, the section of the Nguni from whom the Zulus descended believed that all phenomena (*izinto;* sing, into, *ulutho*) had their origins in a living reality or consciousness which they called *UQOBO*.

This reality had no beginning and no end; it was alive and existed from eternity (*ingunaphakade*) to eternity. Each phenomenon had its *UQOBO* (reality or value) which was an integral part of the infinite Value; each was uqobo *loQOBO* (value which is a portion of VALUE).

The person evolved from this VALUE in response to the Law of Appearing (*Umthetho weMvelo*) or the demands of his nature (*isimo*) or Perpetual Evolution (*Ukuma Njalo.*) His destiny was forever to evolve (*ukuma njalo*) and discover more satisfying dimensions of being (*ukuba ngumuntu*).

These pronouncements on the origins, nature and destiny of the person exist in *Izaga* (*Aphorisms*) and form an important section of the *Law of Being Human*, (*Umthetho woBuntu*) which issues from the *Law of Appearing.*

Each phenomenon was a cluster of smaller values. All phenomena were alive because the infinite *UQOBO* was alive; all phenomena existed inside *UQOBO* because there was nothing outside it.

The ancient Nguni referred to the perspective from which they viewed the cosmic experience as *Umthetho* (the *Law*). What the ancient Greeks called philosophy was known among Nguni as the *Law*. This *Law* was passed down from generation to generation and exists to-day in its purest form in *Izaga*.

The five main sections of the philosophy are: the creed, the body of traditions by which communities defined themselves, customs, laws and other legal usages, constitutions and Social Purpose.

The central teaching of Buntu is that all things originate from *UQOBO* and evolve in response to the challenge of their nature; that the person is a self-defining value (*umuntu ngumuntu; umzimba uzwiwa ngumnniniwo;* that is: the person is human; it is the person who knows best the workings of his body) and that life's purpose for the person is perpetual evolution (*ukuma njalo*).

The person, however, cannot exist of himself, by himself, for himself; he comes from a social cluster, exists in a social cluster and "dies" physically in order to live in the community of spirit-forms (*amadlozi*). Just as he defines himself, so does the cluster define itself. It tells itself and its neighbours who it is through its interpretation of the *Law*, through the traditions it developed down the ages to guarantee its survival. Each social cluster (or family or nome in Zulu society) has its own traditions (*izinkambo)* for establishing its identity.

Later in this chapter, I shall give an example of the Ngubane self-definition or tradition to illustrate how the tradition was passed from generation to generation to instruct posterity on what it means to be a Ngubane.

In a preliterate civilisation variations had to occur even within each family or nome. But this did not bother the Nguni because Buntu regarded the person as a self-defining value; all self-definitions which served the purpose of the community were simultaneously legitimate. This protean character of Buntu gave a flexibility to self-definitions which survived because the collective sovereignty of the group guaranteed the individual sovereignty or primacy of the person.

The sum-total of family or nomarchic self-definitions was the constitution of the family or nomarchy.

Customs, laws and other legal usages were part of the self-definition on one plane; on another, they were expressions of the *Law of Appearing* in different environments. One of the functions of the mind of the person or the nome or the nation was to translate *UQOBO'S Law of Appearing* into social law and action.

The customs, laws, traditions, and other usages gave structure to society; they were its constitution. The function of this constitution was to create, regulate and perpetuate a social order in which the person could realise the promise of being human and the glory of being a self-defining value. This was what *ukuba ngumuntu* meant.

The self-defining value was his own legislator and policeman; he told his compatriots what sort of a person he was in what he thought, said and did. His compatriots were his judges; they presumed that he had entered their society—that is he had chosen to be born into it—in order to enable it to make the best possible use of its life in the light of him, by placing at his disposal the social experience it had developed down the ages. It could do this to the best of its ability only if it was open; that is, if it was based on mutualism.

Social Purpose was the exploration of the person and his environment in order to enable him to discover more satisfying dimensions of being human. The person's ciliate mind was the torch by which he lit his path in the mazes of the cosmic order.

Buntu insisted that the person was adequate for the accomplishment of every task he set out to do; that his ignorance was the only factor that limited his adequacy. To overcome the weakness, he had to regard his neighbour's mind as an open book of discovered knowledge; to recognise his neighbour as the reverse side of an entity to which he (the person) was the obverse. This demanded extremes of discipline which continuously enlarged the personality. To cope with the demands of these freely imposed disciplines was the glory of being a self-defining value.

The assumption here was that adequacy meant that an innate responsibility had been built into the person's many-sided or ciliate mind; that this quality could be awakened and developed in every person provided society was aware of its duties and obligations to the person. If the person could be guilty of crimes against society, the latter could also be guilty of crimes against the person.

The assumption predicated on adequacy faced the implications of its meaning. A value was neither good nor evil: it responded to the challenge of its nature or its environment. Society thus had always to be on the lookout for the difference between crimes committed out of ignorance or out of the will to hurt or out of society's failure to do its duty by the person. This had important implications for Zulu attitudes to guilt.

The Zulu view of *umuntu ngumuntu* (the person is human) meant that to be human is to have a many-sided mind. When a person attained heights of excellence which dizzied the mind, the Zulus said: *Umuntu ngumuntu.* When he fell to depths of degradation which defied description, the Zulus said: *Umuntu ngumuntu.* This was their way of saying the person defined himself in everything he did; that in everyone of his thoughts, modes of behaviour and deeds he told his family, neighbours, society, the world and the cosmic order what sort of person he was.

The Zulus coupled the ancient aphorism, *umuntu ngumuntu,* with *umuntu akalahwa* (the person is never so evil he is beyond redemption). The Zulu-speaking nomarchies of antiquity believed that all things had their origin in *UQOBO;* everything in the cosmic order evolved from *UQOBO.* This *UQOBO* was primordial consciousness; it had no beginning and no end; it was the infinite total of the values of all things which together made the cosmic order.

UQOBO was forever forming clusters of itself and combining these to produce phenomena. The agmination was regulated by *Umthetho weMvelo,* the *Law of Appearing.* Since *UQOBO,* the consciousness, was alive and there was no death in it; since it was an infinity, human behaviour in all its forms, on every plane and in all situations translated the *Law* into action. Nothing on earth or in the cosmic order could violate the *Law* for the violation was itself an expression of the *Law.*

When persons knew the *Law,* they did not fall into error; they did not hurt their neighbours; they developed a dimension of consanguinity which enabled the person to regard his neighbour as the reverse side of a phenomenon to which he, the person, was the obverse. His neighbour was all mankind.

Ignorance was the person's only enemy; ignorance was inadequate knowledge of the *Law;* it pushed persons into error and forced them to do evil things.

Each living person had experiences which made him a unique book of discovered knowledge. He fulfilled himself and his neighbour when he shared what he knew with his neighbour and when the latter shared with him what he, the neighbour, knew. For the neighbour was the first precondition of fulfillment for the person. The person and his neighbour were fulfilled when their personalities were improved by what they shared. In this regard, the person and his neighbour were mutually-fulfilling complements.

Society existed to enable the person to grow in his knowledge of the *Law* ; to teach and enable him to discover more satisfying dimensions of being human and to see to it that he realised both the promise of being human and the glory of being a self-defining value.

Society, which was a total of self-defining values, committed crimes against the person when it failed to equip or enable him to realise the promise of being human or when it did not see to it that he made the best possible use of his life. By failing to do its duty by the person, society denied him the opportunity to be the best human being that he could be; it left him ignorant and made him a danger to himself, his neighbours and society. He could thus not be condemned unconditionally and regarded as beyond redemption when he did wicked things.

Thus, Zulu law, which was an extension of the *Law*, drew the distinction between guilt and culpability and sought to focus as much on the person's wilful desire to remain ignorant and lead an evil life as on his society's failure to equip and enable him to be the best that he could be. That he had a many-sided mind was proof that he could be a better human being. He could not, in this setting, be so wicked as to be beyond redemption.

The person was neither good nor evil; in everything he did he responded to the inner necessity which inhered in his nature. He became a person of virtue, *umuntu ofundiswe umthetho* (the person who has been trained in the *Law*) or *into engenamthetho* (the thing which is without the *Law*) depending on how he "proclaimed" his nature or defined himself.

As a result, ancient Zulu philosophers, like their contemporaries in other language-groups, developed a large collection of *Izaga (Aphorisms)*, each of which summarised the *Law*. These wise sayings told the person what to do in order to realise the promise of being human *(ukuba ngumuntu);* they defined the person as seen from perspectives provided by the Zulu interpretation of the Sudic Ideal.

The Zulus defined the person also in their statutes, customs and other usages.

The dimension of consanguinity taught that the person and his neighbour were unchanging relatives because both were agminates of *UQOBO* and both were self-defining values. *UQOBO* was an infinity and, as such, transcended race. If different environments gave different races different skin complexions, hair textures and eye shapes, that did not affect consanguinity. Primordial substance, like the *Law of Appearing* and the self-defining value which metamorphosed into the person, were above race.

The fact that each person in every part of the earth was a value, an unchanging *UQOBO* form, like every other person, made the human race a unity, just as the cosmic order was a unity. It was this unity which gave simultaneous legitimacy to all cultural self-definitions. To seek to destroy this unity was a criticism of primordial consciousness; it was to try to invert the perpetual evolution of the cosmic order; it was a ploy for running away from facing the challenge being human. In short it was Ultimate Insanity.

Apartheid errs because it makes it impossible for the non-White person to face the challenge of being human; it prescribes his destiny and says he must see fulfillment in going back to the childhood days of the human race; it says, in effect, that virtue for him consists in apologising for being human.

But apartheid must never be seen out of context; it translates into experience the pessimistic and devaluative view of the human being which was developed by the ancient Greeks, Romans and Hebrews. It creates catastrophic disharmonies in the personality and produces conditions which make it impossible for the person to realise the promise of being human (*ukuba ngumuntu*) if he is not White. Its inner logic drives Black and White through cycles of conflict to final disaster. To see this logic in clearer light, let us have a quick glance at how the Zulu-speaking nomes translated the bias for agmination and the dimension of consanguinity into action before the advent of the Caucasians.

A NEW IDEAL OF NATIONHOOD

The shift in the positions of the earth's poles produced cataclysmic changes in Sudic societies. Large numbers of African communities were forced to emigrate from their ancestral lands and settle in other parts of the continent.

The largest of these communities were the Ba-*NTU,* the descendants of *NTU* or *NU.* These moved in a southern direction. The Xhosa, who, like the Zulu, Mpondo, Swazi and Bhaca, were members of the Nguni family and spoke mutually intelligible languages, spearheaded the southward migration. They were, for this reason, isolated from the larger, Ba-*NTU* communities fleeing from the desiccated Saharan tablelands. Largely because of this isolation they retained some ancient Nguni words and expressions;

words which other Nguni language-groups dropped from their vocabularies.

The relevant expression found in Xhosa today is the description, first, of the Xhosa community and, second, of mankind, as *umzi ka NTU* (the family of *NTU*).

The Nguni were not the only Sudic people who reached South Africa. The Sotho language group, which includes the Sotho, Tswana and Pedi, was among the people from beyond South Africa. Smaller language-groups like the Venda and Tonga also settled in South Africa.

The southward migration must have stretched over thousands of years if the evolution of the different languages of Black South Africa is any guide. The Nguni and Sotho pushed the Ba-Twa and Khoikhoi farther south and settled on the lands they conquered.

The Xhosa always had the freedom to move to new lands in response to population pressures while the Zulu who settled in Natal were trapped between the Indian Ocean and the Drakensberg Mountains on the east and the west and between the Xhosa in the south and the Sotho-speaking communities in the north.

The different positions of the Xhosa and Zulu forced them to develop different political institutions in their efforts to create satisfying Sudic societies. The bias for agmination and the dimension of consanguinity preserved the autonomy of the different Xhosa nomes. If a nomarch broke away from his main cultural group, he could settle farther south where he would keep in purity the principles of his group's interpretation of the Sudic Ideal and preserve the autonomy of his nome.

A different situation existed among the Zulu-speaking Nguni. The circumstance of being trapped gave to the bias for agmination and the dimension of consanguinity the character of threats to nomarchic autonomy. As the population increased over thousands of years, nomarchic overcrowding created hunger for living-space. Nomarchic tensions and wars more or less became the order of the day

Our main source of information on these developments is still the body of panegyric poems or patronymic legends (*izithakazelo* = words by which one is welcomed) which were attached as titles to each family name. These poems, which described the exploits of distinguished ancestors, were passed from generation to generation because in them each family defined itself, stated its interpretation of the Sudic Ideal and preserved its identity and uniqueness.

If a person with the family name Ngubane handed over something to his neighbour, the latter expressed his thanks by reciting the Ngubane patronymic legend:

Ngubane! Nomafu!
Ngogo zabantu,
Nezezinkomo!

[May you live long] O Ngubane!
Element of the clouds!
In your disdain for your enemies
You crushed people and their cattle;
Their skeletons tell the story.

Most of these poems describe a golden age in the experience of the Zulu; an age when warrior-heroes strode the land and achieved the impossible. Warrior-heroes come to the fore in conditions of social and political turbulence.

In this setting, the Zulus turned inward, to themselves, in the bid to discover a formula for co-existence which would normalise life in what was later to be known as Natal. Nomarch Malandela Zulu ruled over a tiny nome which called itself the Zulu, the people who belonged to the heavens or universes. The only claim to fame the Zulus had was that they were excellent farmers; they produced a quality of tobacco which was in demand over many parts of Southern Africa.

The most powerful princes set out to impose their own solutions on the Natal Nguni. Powerless as Malandela was, he nursed the ambition that one day, he might have a son who would lead his people to the heavens; who would restore order in Natal.

Some time during the second half of the fifteenth century, one of Malandela's wives gave birth to a baby boy. Malandela was convinced that the boy was the leader who would bring peace to Natal and lead the Zulu-speaking nomes along safer routes to a better future. To ensure that the boy lived and achieved as expected, Malandela gave him the name Zulu.

Zulu ka Malandela Zulu did not live up to expectations and the turbulence did not subside. By the eighteenth century a power-vacuum had developed which each of the major princes tried to fill by asserting vigorous hegemonistic initiatives.

Each prince or princelet employed one or more of the best-educated poets in his nome to chronicle events. The court poet composed a long poem in honour of the prince. Tradition vested him with the authority of an oracle; a voice of destiny. He could say things in public which nobody could utter; he could criticise the prince freely in his compositions. At the same time he could form opinion and influence it in given directions.

Senzangakhona ka Jama Zulu was an eighteenth century successor to Zulu ka Malandela Zulu. Like most of his predecessors he was too involved in questions of survival to bother much about conquest or considerations of destiny. His Court Poet, however, was determined forever to confront him with the call of destiny. The Poet was under a new type of pressure. The Zulu who were best-educated in their culture had begun to reject the idea that conditions would be stabilised by a strong prince; they saw salvation in an ideal of nationhood which would not be associated with the family of any ruling prince; an ideal which would unite because it was seen to produce the desired results; an ideal which evoked similar and co-ordinable responses to similar challenges.

The Court Poet to Senzangakhona enunciated the ideal in these terms:

Ngisuse phansi, ngiye phezulu,
Ngibuye nencombo,
Ngibhule, ngipheke.
Ndaba, bayosala beshumayezana,
Abasezitheni nabasekhaya!
. . . .

Masiphoth'intamb' ende,
Menzi ka Jama;
Siye emazulwini,
Lapho nezithutha zingey' ukufika;
Zobasakhwele,
Zephuk' amazwanyana!

Raise me from the depths;
To heights take me,
That with grain I may return;
The grain I shall winnow;
The grain I shall cook.
(Should you do that) O Ndaba,
They will forever preach to each other about it.
The foes will;
So will those on our side.

. . . .

A cord of destiny let us weave,
O Menzi, scion of Jama,
That
To universes beyond the reach of spirit-forms
We may ascend.
(So long must the cord be)
The spirit-forms themselves
Will break their tiny toes,
Should they dare to climb!

The people to whom the court poet addressed himself needed no extraordinary powers of imagination to understand his message. They believed that they were incarnations of eternal values and that the eternal in them was real and positive to all things; that it could do whatever it imagined. Since perpetual evolution was its destiny, it had the power to traverse space and move from one universe to another in the endeavour to find more satisfying dimensions of being human.

The poet told them that they needed no props to respond to the call of destiny; they needed no gods; their ancestral spirits could not reach the heights of achievement which the person could. The disciplined self could imagine all things, achieve all things and rise to all heights because he was human. All the person needed to do to awaken the powers locked in him was to have faith in the person; to discipline himself and to proceed from this to explore himself—to search the eternal microcosm that he was—for satisfying dimensions of being human.

The person had all the future before him to evolve perpetually into the type of human being he wanted to be. Society and the spirit-forms were his allies and supporters; they were always ready to reinforce him whenever he disciplined himself and marched to a clearly stated goal.

The assumption behind this approach was that the person was adequate; that he had in him all the powers he could need to realise the destiny he chose for himself. These powers inhered in him as a person; he did not receive them from any source outside of himself.

Any belief in an external power was superstition and superstition was the person's mortal foe. Shaka killed groups of diviners and witch doctors in the effort to free his people from the grip of superstition. He wanted a nation of truly free men and women who needed no props outside of themselves in order to realise the promise of being human.

The Zulus were not the only people who regarded themselves as the people whose destiny was to traverse universes; in Rhodesia there were the MaZezuru, the people who belonged to the heavens!

Shaka the Great was the son of Senzangakhona. He adopted the court poet's ideal as the main inspiration of the revolution which he led after his father's death; it was the ideological blueprint on which he built the Zulu nation.

But the revolution must be seen in context. The Zulu philosophers whose thinking was reflected in the new ideal of nationhood had evolved out of the stage when they were dependent on religion for guidance on the establishment of a better society. Nomkhubulwana, the princess of heaven, was the last of their deities.

Religion had been alive in the thousand years before Shaka. In all these years, it failed to resolve the conflicts in Natal; it forced men to see it as a prop, a prison of the mind which was used by the strong to entrench their power and not to solve the problems of suffering humanity.

Shaka sailed into this situation and preached that wherever human beings were oppressed, they were, in the final analysis, oppressed by consent. The person had a many-sided mind which could traverse space and move from universe to universe and transform the human being into a conscious citizen of the cosmic order. This meant that if the person was prepared to impose certain disciplines on himself, he could become the creator of his destiny.

Using his mind to traverse the heavens in search of more satisfying dimensions of being human was the challenge of being a self-defining value.

Point was given to the challenge by the Zulu interpretation of the Sudic Ideal which taught that the person had entered the earth as an act of choice; that his purpose in entering it was to discover more satisfying dimensions of *ukuba ngumuntu* (being human). The quest was the commitment for which he lived; it shaped his thinking, motivated behaviour and inspired action. *Ukuba ngumuntu* was its own reward. The person could not look outside of himself for a reward for realising the promise of being human. He and he alone had chosen to enter the earth; he was the author of his mandate for existence on it.

Perpetual evolution, the Sudic Ideal taught, was the destiny of both the person and the cosmic order. My grandmother on my mother's side, who had served in King Cetshwayo's Ingcugce Regiment, about forty years after Shaka's death, insisted that I should never say, "Ngiyabonga" ("Thank You") if given anything. She taught me that I should express thanks by addressing the following blessing to the giver: "Ume Njalo!" (May you stand forever).

When I asked her why I should say to people they should stand forever she told me that in the mists of antiquity, when stones cried if pinched, early Man walked upright and sometimes on all fours. Then, one day, he found a formula in his mind for walking upright. He shared it with his neighbours and from that day each human being was so grateful they all thanked or blessed each other by wishing each should forever walk upright.

The Zulu-Nguni philosophers whose teachings the court poet preserved for posterity in his ideal had not reacted negatively to the religious experience; they had simply outgrown it when it ceased to have valid meaning in their lives. To do this was to respond to the challenge of being human; to the call of perpetual evolution.

Shaka presented the court poet's ideal as the formula for co-existence which would raise all persons to a satisfying dimension of being human and stabilise conditions in Natal. Shaka urged those who would listen to him to believe that life would have a better meaning for themselves if they abandoned loyalty to the nomarchy and committed themselves to the creation of a state in which the person would be equipped, enabled and seen to make the best possible use of his life regardless of who his parents were; to a state founded on an ideal which could be seen to satisfy in the conditions which prevailed in Natal.

Shaka created the open state and open society in which race and ethnicity were of no political significance. What mattered most was commitment to weaving the cord of destiny.

In *Shaka Zulu,* E.A. Ritter, a White writer, tells us how sections of the Zulu-speaking nomarchies responded to Shaka's translation of the bias for agmination and the dimension of consanguinity into political action:

> Many of the most intelligent people beyond Shaka's boundaries who were above military age moved with their whole kraals to Zulu-land, which now indeed lived up to its name of "Heaven-land." Because of their superior intelligence they realized that they too would some day be "smelt out," merely because their sharper wits brought them more prosperity than their neighbours. In the same way that the Pilgrim Huguenots and Pilgrim Fathers had been attracted to countries with more liberal ideas, so Zululand—as yet an embryonic state—became the Mecca of thinking people beyond its boundaries, and an asylum for all the oppressed.[17]

The unification of the nomes into a nation-state was one of Shaka's most remarkable achievements. In this eternal monument to himself, he showed what the human mind was capable of doing. His other remarkable achievement was to raise women to the highest levels of government. He appointed Mkabi and Langazana joint governors of the *Isiklebe* military base while Mkabayi was governor of the Baqulusi nome. Mawa was in charge of another military base. Nomzinhlanga ruled over another.

He thought it childish that people who were mothers of the human race should be relegated to the tasks of producing children, tilling the soil and administering family affairs only. Women, he argued, were the producers of the most precious phenomena in a society: children. This enjoined on them the duty of having the biggest say in the affairs of a society. With this in mind, Shaka organised them into regiments which administered the country's affairs and helped to maintain law and order when the men were out in the wars.

His highest achievement, however, was the creation of a society in which the person realised the promise of being human regardless of who his particular parents were or of whether or not she was the particular child of her parents. Ritter lived with some of Shaka's contemporaries who quoted Shaka as having given the following reply to a Zulu xenophobe:

> Any man who joins the Zulu army becomes a Zulu. Thereafter his promotion is purely a question of merit, irrespective of the road *(ndlela)* he came by.[18]

Shaka's problem was to justify the revolution he led. It was not enough for him to condemn the Old Order; he had to offer a viable alternative; he had to define the morality of the revolution in terms that were seen to have valid meaning in the life of every Zulu.

His most powerful weapon for doing this was not his army, as those who have not studied the Shakan revolution continue to say; it was a consensus on final goals which translated into action the Sudic principle of simultaneous legitimacy.

Shaka's character and thinking were influenced to a large extent by the superfluity of humiliations heaped on him by one nome after another as he grew up. When he was not being punished for being the child of his particular parents, he was denied the status of a royal personage, to which he was entitled. The persecution played a by no means small role in making him a revolutionary.

He set out to destroy the Old Order which had produced the nomarchic state. This type of state was based on each nomarchy's understanding of the Nguni interpretation of the Sudic Ideal. Consanguinity was to a large extent the cement which bound together the citizens of the nomarchy. The citizen's first loyalty was to his nomarchy.

Where the Natal Nguni were trapped, the hunger for living-space combined with rival nomarchic loyalties to produce an explosive security problem; it created a power-vacuum which Shaka set out to fill with the nation-state.

But for this state to perform as desired, it had to destroy the political power of the nomarchies, protect their cultural identities and reconcile political integration with cultural autonomy; it had to transform cultural autonomy and political centralism into interlocking mutualities. To weld the nomarchies into a viable power-structure, the new state had to be based on a formula for co-existence which recognised the simultaneous legitimacy of the cultural self-definitions developed by all the nomes; it had to develop a unifying consensus based on interlocking reciprocities: the nation-state guaranteed the security and protected the identity of each nomarchic group while the surrender by each nomarchy of its sovereignty to produce a collective sovereignty, maximised the nation-state's ability to create the conditions in which the citizen could be equipped, enabled and seen to realise the promise of being human.

For lack of a better word, we shall refer to this type of state as a *synarchy*.

We might digress a little here, to draw into sharper relief the complexity of the problem Shaka faced. Each nome proclaimed its commitment to its version of the Nguni interpretation of the Sudic Ideal—which each called the *Law*—by "writing it in blood"; by making given marks on the bodies of its citizens. Others made no marks.

Most Caucasians, even those who pass for authorities on Africa, still refer to these incisions as "tribal marks." The label establishes the White man's right to prescribe destiny for the African. In the view of the Africans, the marks are evidence of commitment to a given understanding or interpretation or translation of the Sudic evaluation of the person; of the *Law of Being Human.* They are public declarations of ideological commitment.

The Sudic experience regards the *Law* as so important it has to be "written in the blood," as the Zulu members of the Sudic family say. The "writings" go beyond identifying the person; they prescribe the ways in which he should be treated, what he should eat, who he should marry to avoid incest and how he should be expected to respond to co-existence with his neighbours.

These marks were the external descriptions of the value the person incarnated. We shall come to this value shortly, but before we do that, let us have a quick glance at another aspect of writing the *Law* in blood.

The ancient Egyptians were an overwhelmingly African people.[19] They had communities of foreigners mainly in the areas near the delta. The aboriginals had been originally divided into nomes, some of which made marks on their bodies to proclaim their different commitments to the Sudic Ideal. Pictures of some Egyptian deities, like that of Mayet, goddess of truth and justice, show us pierced earlobes like those we can see in many parts of contemporary Africa. Pharaoh Amenophis IV also had holes in his earlobes.

Thus, when I meet an African with particular marks on his body, I see in these declarations of commitment to a given perspective on the Sudic Ideal. These open forms of identification are important in an open society based on the primacy of the person; they tell all concerned how the person with the marks feels, thinks, behaves and expects to be treated.

Pharaoh Tutankhamen is at the moment the best-known of the kings of ancient Egypt in the United States, if not in the West. The West is dazzled by the splendour of his jewelry. To me, the most important thing about him is the way his earlobes are pierced. The piercing tells me something about his family, the nome from which he came and the ideological identity which the nome gave itself; it gives me a perspective on Tutankhamen and his times.

I am interested in this perspective because the piercing acts like an open book to me; it tells me that Tutankhamen was committed to an interpretation of the Sudic evaluation of the person which was not alien to the one to which my father, whose earlobes were also pierced, adhered.

When I read ancient Egyptian classics like *The Book of the Dead* and numerous papyri from Egyptian tombs, I find that the fundamental inspiration which gave meaning to reality and life and which the Egyptian experience translated into action was not unlike the one which inspires the cultural experiences of the Nguni, Sotho, Shangane, Venda and other Sudic communities of South Africa.

Each set of marks is treated with respect in a civilisation which emphasises the primacy of the person and the right of his community to define itself in terms dictated by or valid in its environment; a civilisation which respects each group's right to see the truth in its own light and which acknowledges the simultaneous validity of the truths discovered by different communities in different environments.

When the White missionaries came to Africa they condemned the making of what they called "tribal marks" as heathen. In doing this, they set out to destroy a vital principle which gave rhythm and balance to African communities: the doctrine of simultaneous legitimacy and validity. This teaching acknowledges the legitimacy and validity of different "tribal" self-definitions; of different cultural experiences. It opposes the imposition of one cultural experience on another.

This draws in sharper outlines one of the factors behind the race quarrel. The Sudic Ideal attaches importance to simultaneous legitimacy and validity while Caucasian civilisation lays stress on what Henri Frankfort has called "a conviction too deep to allow for tolerance." Such a conviction will justify the Inquisition and its successors and the concentration camps of Auschwitz, Dachau, etc. In the Sudic view, such a conviction distorts the personality and violates the person's right to see the truth as it stands revealed to him or her.

This conviction might have a place in homogeneous Caucasian communities. In racially and culturally polyglot societies, it is a clear invitation to disaster. For the quarrel between Black and White is, in the final analysis, a collision between a civilisation which teaches that life's purpose is to discover more satisfying dimensions of being human and its opposite, which stigmatises and inferiorises the human being. In this setting, to be different is to be wrong; to have a different skin complexion is to commit an unforgivable crime.

Simultaneous validity was given added signigicance when I travelled in West Africa in 1958, and the United States in 1969. I discovered that the West Africans saw reality from perspectives I had, in my ignorance, regarded as peculiar to the "Buntu" teaching in my part of the continent. I was pleasantly surprised to discover that the common factor in Southern and Western African experiences was our evaluation of the person, which gave identical rhythms to our different cultural experiences.

As I delved deeper into the Egyptian experience, after my contacts with West African experiences, I came to the view that ancient Egypt's attitude to the person ultimately was what made it possible for me to understand the "Buntu" assessment of the human being better.

The points of convergence in the ancient Egyptian view of the person and the one which inspired Sub-Saharan attitudes to the human being were so many, I began to ask if there was any relationship between the *Land of Punt* and the *Land of the Buntu*. It was not improbable that in the ears of the Greeks, on whose testimony we rely for much of our knowledge of antiquity in Egypt, Nubia and Punt, the word *Buntu* could have sounded like *Punt.*

I had neither the time nor the leisure to determine whether or not there was any relationship between Buntu and Punt. What I could do, and what I did, was to recognise the ancient Egyptian experience as one more window through which we could view the protean Sudic attitude to the person in action.

The experience of both the Zulu and the ancient Egyptians sheds valuable light on the problem of "tribalism"; it shows that ethnicity in Sudic communities is only a vehicle for translating a given ideal of fulfilment into social action and that the diversity of ethnic groups is compatible with a synarchy.

This setting throws into bolder relief both the harm the Christian missionaries did in Africa and the dangers of defining the African experience in terms designed to prescribe destiny.

The missionaries, like those Whites who sought to impose ideological destinies on the African, were interested mainly in forcing or persuading the African to define himself in terms which served their interest. They were not interested in preserving that harmony in his personality which made the African what he was and gave symmetry to his personality. The ideological missionaries wanted to fill the African's head with ideologies which would enable him to be exploited and humiliated by consent. Locking the African personality in a prison of the mind to facilitate the exploitation by the Caucasians of African resources is the cause of race conflict which focuses attention on the urgency of clarity on the difference between Sudic and Caucasian minds.

THE ZULU DEFINITION OF THE PERSON

We always have to bear in mind the fact that by declaring the person a self-defining value and by recognising the simultaneous legitimacy of all cultural self-definitions, the Sudic evaluation of the human being gave itself the character of a protean philosophy which different communities interpreted differently in different environments. All these self-definitions were simultaneously legitimate because self-definition was a quality of being human.

The Sudic mind set out to reconcile these self-definitions; to develop a formula for co-existence which would evoke identical and co-ordinable responses to similar challenges.

The challenge the different nomes which inhabited what later came to be known as Natal faced was that they were trapped between the Indian Ocean in the east, the Drakensberg Mountains in the West, the Xhosa-Nguni in the south and the Sotho-speaking groups in the north. This created a hunger for living-space which produced irreconcilable tensions and conflicts. The Zulu-Nguni interpretation has to be seen in the context provided by this environment.

Zulu philosophers took the position that there could be no peace in the world they knew and no order and stability in Natal if the forces which together made the person were not harmonised. An undisciplined person created a disorderly society and chaotic world. Their first precondition for a harmonised personality was a philosophy which defined the person in positive terms and faced the implications of this definition. In their view, a philosophy succeeded or failed in proportion to the degree that it harmonised the personality.

The Sudic Ideal, which was their starting-point, set out to effect the harmonisation by emphasising the primacy of the person and to create a society designed to secure and promote the primacy; a society which equipped, enabled and ensured that the person realised the promise of being human *(ukuba ngumuntu);* that he was seen attaining the glory of *ukuba ngumuntu.*

In literal terms, *ukuba ngumuntu* meant: *to be or to become human.* The components of the process were *umuntu* (the person); the definition of the person as *umuntu ngumuntu* (the person is human; he or she possesses a many-sided of ciliate mind); the injunction that life's purpose for the person is *ukuba ngumuntu* (to realise the promise of being human); the admonition that in order to realise the promise, one has to evolve through *amabanga okuba ngumuntu* (distances of being human). The ciliate mind's progression toward being human would be influenced by the extent to which the person knew or was ignorant of the *Law.* He would fall into error if he was ignorant. But the *Law* taught that there was no extreme of error beyond which the person could not be redeemed. The final component in the process of *ukuba ngumuntu* was a dimension of compassion: *umuntu akalahlwa* (the person cannot be thrown away, like trash).

The dimension of compassion was predicated on the postulate that the value was neither good nor evil; that it responded to the necessity which inhered in its nature and the demands of its environment. If the environment was sufficiently developed to provide scope for the full expression of every side of the ciliate mind, if it was sufficiently informed to harmonise the ciliations, it produced the person with a harmonised personality. If it was not adequately equipped for enabling the person to make the best possible use of his life, it disorganised the personality and moved him and his neighbour in cycles of conflict to ultimate disaster.

The dynamic which enabled a society to produce a harmonised personality or a disorganised one was the attitude to the person. In the Sudic tradition, this attitude regarded the person as a self-defining value; he had a many-sided or ciliate mind in order to cope with every aspect of the challenge of being human. Each Sudic culture translated this central teaching into a body of values which were valid in or were dictated by its environment.

ATTITUDE TO THE PERSON 93

The main parts of the philosophy were:

1. *The Core of the Teaching or Buntu (Umnyombo weMfundiso)*
   (Recognition of the person as a self-defining value)

2. *Logic of the Teaching (Inkambo ye Mfundiso)*
   (The protean character of the Sudic Ideal)

Zulu   Xhosa   Sotho   Shangane   Tonga   Venda, etc.

3. *Applications or Values of the Teaching (Amasiko e Mfundiso)*
   (Simultaneously legitimate self-definitions)

Ngubane   Nxumalo   Mtshali   Kubheka   Cele   Khumalo, etc.

4. *Perpetual Evolution (Ukuma Njalo)*

The reader has noted that in the Sudic view, life's purpose for the person was not to conform to a mandate imposed from outside; it was *ukuba ngumuntu;* it was forever to respond positively to the challenge of being human. This challenge did not exist outside of the person—in the abstract, so to speak; it was a constituent part of his being; it was one of those parts of himself which made him human. He and he alone understood this challenge because he had responded to it when he elected to enter the earth; only he and he alone could explain what he had come to this planet to do. He defined himself when he explained what he had come to do.

The environment in which he defined himself was not a vacuum. His ancestors had defined themselves before him; they had, down the ages, developed a whole tradition of self-definition which linked them with the person. Thus, when he communicated with them he did not go out of himself to make supplications to external powers; he summoned powers which inhered in himself as an extension into the future of those who had gone before him; he was his forebears in a different guise, living in a different period. That was why he took on their names and titles in his family *isithakazelo* (panegyric legend).

When he summoned the inherent powers, it was because these were another quality of being human. He was not indebted to any power outside of himself for these. They were his and his alone. The more he awakened and developed them, the more he realised the promise of being human—*ukuba ngumuntu*.

There was no end to the challenge of the promise. The person faced it every moment of his life. The answer to it was to turn inward and explore the eternal reality that was the value behind the person; it was forever to discover new dimensions of being a person. These dimensions existed in every man, woman and child; nobody could give them and nobody could withdraw them. People could keep the person ignorant of his powers, but they could never destroy them. When the person knew the truth, when he knew that he was absolute master of the powers in him, he realised the promise of being human and the glory of being a self-defining value; he attained *ukuba ngumuntu*.

This was the essence of Sudic philosophy.

Like other teachings, the Sudic Ideal had an inner logic which gave Sudic civilisation its uniqueness, symmetry and durability. This logic enabled Sudic civilisation not only to survive the ravages of slavery, colonialism and apartheid, it also fueled the revolt against White domination and is now moving Southern Africa inexorably to rebirth into a satisfying destiny.

There is glory in the unfolding of this revolt: glory because the African fights with his attitude to the person, his brain and his bare hands. Those who prescribe destiny or frustrate life's purpose for him have every engine of destruction at their disposal. In spite of this, the African challenge has forced them on to the defensive. This has happened because, in the final reckoning, the positive definition of the person is superior to all pessimistic attitudes to the human being.

There is glory whenever the person faces the challenge of being human, instead of fleeing from it.

In the Zulu experience—I am certain that other language-groups will one day tell mankind how their peoples interpreted the Buntu Ideal and translated it into experience; when that time comes, we shall have a truly comprehensive picture of Sudic Civilisation—the Sudic evaluation of the person was the central teaching which was given an interpretation that was valid in the Zulu environment. A large number of nomes and families existed in this environment. The Baqulusi nome, whose governor was Princess Mkabayi ka Jama Zulu in Shaka's time, defined itself as *Isidindi somtshiki.*

All members of the Baqulusi nome gave themselves the generic definition of *Isidindi somtshiki.* But these members belonged to different families, each of which revealed its identity in its *isithakazelo.* Each such panegyric legend was the core of a body of specific values which together constituted the family's understanding of the Zulu interpretation of the Sudic Ideal.

I shall shortly give a list of principles which, my father taught me, gave a Ngubane his particular identity. Every Zulu had these principles or values. Their name for these was *Umthetho* (the *Law*). The sum-total of these self-definitions was the ideal by which the Zulu nation defined itself and gave itself its particular identity. The Xhosa, Sotho and other language-groups produced their own self-definitions and familial inter-pretations of these self-definitions. This application of the principle of simultaneous legitimacy made African communities democracies of minds. Apartheid introduces catastrophic disharmonies in these democracies.

Up to now attention has been given to Sudic civilisation's concern with and commitment to the person; to its unparalleled faith in him. Much has been said about the person being a value that is forever evolving simultaneously inward and outward. Inward evolution is the growth of the physical body, the accumulation of experiences and the progressive harmonisation of the forces which constitute the personality. Outward evolution is growth in response to the demands of the person's environ-ment. The person is forever growing inwardly and outwardly.

This growth takes place in terms of the *Law*. Each person, family, and society, like mankind and the cosmic order, translated the *Law* into ac-tion in terms dictated by his or its nature and environment. Since these differed, their self-definitions had to be different. The sum-total of these self-definitions constituted the ideal by which a society described itself.

As a rule in Sudic societies, the *Law* was stated, among other forms, in aphorisms. It can be said that each aphorism was a clause of the *Law*. The *Law* was the mould in which the personality was cast; it organised the rhythms which determined thought and behaviour; it gave symmetry to experience, defined purpose for the human being and prescribed criteria by which to fix his place in society and the cosmic order.

The person was unique in that he discovered the *Law*, gave meaning to it and translated it into social action. These achievements made him the "prince of eternity"; the jewel of the cosmic order; the supreme value which determined all values. The only civilised mode of conduct was to walk in humility in the presence of the person; it was fiercely to vindicate his or her humanity and to regard no sacrifice as too great in the defence of the primacy of the person.

Zulu society was a totality of nomes bound together not only by their commitment to the Zulu interpretation of the Sudic Ideal, but also by their Ideal of Nationhood. Each nome defined itself in terms dictated by or valid in its environment. The sum-total of these self-definitions was the Zulu statement of what it meant to be a Zulu.

In the pages which follow I shall give aphorisms or the *Law* which made me identify myself as a person, a Ngubane, a Zulu and a human being.

But before we do this, let us have a last glance at the nature of the phenomenon which the Sudic Ideal called the person. The vital elements which gave this phenomenon its nature were the Eternal Person or Value *(uqobo lomuntu;* the real in the person); the Body *(umzimba);* the Aura *(isithunzi;* literally the shadow); the *Law (umthetho)* and the Infinite

Consciousness*(UQOBO)*which was the environment in which the person existed.

These elements formed an inseparable cluster. The Eternal Value was the reality which gave life to the body. The life within the body was reinforced by the cosmic forces which the aura selected, sifted and prepared for use by the body. In this sense, the aura was the link between the person and the cosmic consciousness from which all things had their origin. In this dispensation, the *Law* regulated the actions and evolutions of all phenomena. Every action by the person occurred in terms of the *Law,* inside the infinite consciousness or *UQOBO.*

The person, the *Law, UQOBO* and the universes which together constituted his environment were an indivisible total; they were the *Definitive Agminate.* There was no beginning and no end to this total; perpetual evolution in response to the challenge of its nature was its destiny. Every thought, every movement and every act in this evolution translated a given section of the *Law* into experience.

The person had a ciliate mind which enabled him to simplify the *Law* and translate it into customs, rules, regulations and other usages designed to enable him to meet the challenge of being human. Since the person was unique because he had entered earth as an act of will, he and he alone could define himself and tell all concerned what he had come to this planet to do.

In the pages which follow I shall list some of the values in which a Ngubane defined himself, stated life's purpose for himself and by which he fixed his position in society and in the universes.

These values go beyond defining the person; they show, perhaps more clearly than anything can, the point where Sudic and Caucasian attitudes to the person clash.

A few days after I was born, I was presented to my grandfather who lived over fifteen miles to the east of Ladysmith. He was a squatter on a White farm. A ceremony was held in which he thanked the Ngubane ancestors for having brought me into his family; he thanked them also for my safe arrival. He then took me to the midst of his large cattle enclosure, dug a hole in its centre, cut an incision on the tip of the smallest finger of my left hand and let the blood drop into the hole, which he filled with cowdung.

That was how I was inducted into the Ngubane family; that was how the *Law* was written into my blood.

When I reached puberty, my father organised another ceremony. Before the inevitable feasting, he took me into one of the rooms of the sprawling stone bungalow he had built for his family in Ladysmith and instructed me in the *Law.* What he told me was more or less what his father had said to him when he reached puberty. Each aphorism or cluster of aphorisms states the *Law* which gave a Ngubane his identity:

I;
I am;
I am alive;
I am conscious and aware;
I am unique;
I am who I say I am; I am the value *UQOBO*
I forever evolve inwardly and outwardly in response to the challenge
    of my nature;
I am the face of humanity;
The face of humanity is my face.
I contemplate myself and see everything in me.
I perceive; that which I perceive is form.
Form is an unchanging value.
Value is eternal consciousness;
Consciousness is that in which all things have their origin;
It does not change; it exists from eternity to eternity;
It is an infinite cluster of clusters of itself;
It is forever evolving in response to the challenge of its nature.
It is *ULTIMATE VALUE;*
It is *UQOBO*.
The value metamorphoses into a phenomenon;
Each phenomenon is a total of smaller forms;
Phenomena form clusters to produce other phenomena;
The cosmic order is an indefinite total of forms and phenomena.
I am a phenomenon; I am a person.
I am *UQOBO;* I am the consciousness.
The infinity is a unity; it cannot be destroyed;
I am a constituent of the unity;
I cannot be destroyed;
The infinity and I are inseparable;
I cannot exist outside of the infinity,
For, there is no outside of it.
Everything is inside the infinity.
UQOBO is the Infinity.
It is a Whole;
It cannot be other than Whole; without me it cannot be Whole;
Nothing can be added to or subtracted from the Whole.
The infinity is alive;
There is no death within it;
There is life and perpetual agmination.
That which is alive has purpose;
Purpose is destiny;

Perpetual evolution is the destiny of *UQOBO;*
UQOBO evolves in response to the challenge of its nature.
The *Law* regulates evolution;
It is a constituent of *UQOBO*
It is the will of the Infinity;
It is my will; it explains everything, for there are no mysteries;
Mystery is the redoubt of the ignorant.
Everything, everywhere, evolves according to the *Law;*
The *Law* is knowable;
I cannot violate the *Law* no matter what I do;
I incarnate the *Law;*
Everything I do translates into action one section of the *Law* or the other;
The processes of the *Law* are irreversible;
Ultimate Absurdity is the attempt to invert the *Law;*
The inversion of the *Law* is a cosmic cataclysm;
It is Ultimate Criminality;
I am the reconciler of all contradictions.
UQOBO, the *Law* and I are together the Definitive Agminate;
Nothing can separate us.
I live now,
And shall forever live, in *UQOBO ,*
For, I am *UQOBO;*
I am eternal; I am the secret that drives out all fear.
Perpetual evolution is my destiny.
I evolve forever, in response to the challenge of being human.
I have a mind to light my path in the mazes of the cosmic order.
This mind has many sides;
It comprehends all things;
It establishes my right to latitude; to being heard;
It makes me feel at home in the cosmic order.
My neighbour has a mind;
It, also, comprehends all things.
My neighbour and I have the same origins;
We have the same life-experience and a common destiny;
We are the obverse and reverse sides of one entity;
We are unchanging equals;
We are the faces which see themselves in each other;
We are mutually fulfilling complements;
We are simultaneously legitimate values;
My neighbour's sorrow is my sorrow;
His joy is my joy.
He and I are mutually fulfilled when we stand by each other in
    moments of need.
His survival is a precondition of my survival.

That which is freely asked or freely given is love;
Imposed love is a crime against humanity.
I am sovereign of my life;
My neighbour is sovereign of his life;
Society is a collective sovereignty;
It exists to ensure that my neighbour and I realise the promise
    of being human.
I have no right to anything I deny my neighbour.
I am all; all are me.
I come from eternity;
The present is a moment in eternity;
I belong to the future.
I can commit no greater crime than to frustrate life's purpose
    for my neighbour.
Consensus is our guarantee of survival.
I define myself in what I do to my neighbour.
No community has any right to prescribe destiny for
    other communities.
This universe I challenge, a higher being than me to show;
My knees do not quake when I contemplate my destiny;
I know my way to eternity;
I make obeisances to the million sides of the ciliate mind;
The Eternal Person is Universal Man, Universal Woman and
    Universal Child.
I am a Universal Constant; I am a Cosmic Constant;
I am All-in-One; I am One-in-All.
I am the circle which encompasses infinity;
I am the point that is the beginning of the circle;
I am the value behind the circle.
I am *umuntu,* the knower of all probabilities and possibilities;
There is nothing I cannot know;
There is no tyranny I cannot crush;
The value of water is H_2O; it lives from eternity to eternity;
Nothing exists anywhere which can destroy it.
I am who I am;
I am not a creature; nothing can destroy me;
I am the self-evolving value *NTU*; I live forever and ever.
I am the phenomenon *MUNTU.*
I am a person; a *Ngubane;* I am *Ngogo Zabantu Nezezinkomo;*
I am a cluster; I am *Skeletons of People and their Cattle.*
The cluster has vital elements;
They are the centre and core: the value *NTU;*
The body, the aura, the *LAW* and *UQOBO.*

The *Law* and *UQOBO* are the environment in which I exist.
I am a *Ngubane;* The *Skeletons* tell my history; they, too, define me.
I am adequate; I have in me all I need to be the best I can be.
I have contempt for that which is not freely given to me.
Whoever wishes me good,
Let that good go to him;
Whoever wishes me to be a prince,
Let him become a prince;
Whoever wishes that I should die,
Let his wish be his fate,
For I want nothing to which I have no right.
I am the servant of my ancestors;
My father is the messenger of my ancestors;
My ancestors are humanity;
All I live for is to be the best that I can be.
I do not prescribe destiny for my neighbour;
My neighbour is myself in a different guise;
Equals do not prescribe destiny for each other;
They hold conversations of minds;
They oppose ideas with counter-ideas.
This, my ancestors told Shaka,
Was the behaviour of civilised men.
They told him this from their fortress cave.
Shaka forgot nothing;
He carved everything on stone.
A Zulu forgets nothing;
I carve everything on stone;
My adequacy makes me magnanimous;
It makes me wise when strong and brave when weak.
There are no frontiers I cannot cross,
For I, the person, am my own challenge.
Disease has no power over me when I know;
I determine my health; I am what I want to be;
I see mankind on the highroad to eternity;
It marches along many routes;
The Light in the person guides the march;
It leads mankind along safer routes to a better future.
I join my hand with the hand of my neighbour;
This is my guarantee of reaching the future I desire;
I march confidently and triumphantly into the future;
My harmonised personality enables me to see my goal clearly;
Every moment is a rebirth into a new dimension of being human;
My duty is to guide the rebirth;
I and I alone guide the rebirth.

I outgrow the use of crutches;
I face the challenge of being eternal;
I align the cells in my body;
I know each, by name;
I am self-knowledge without end;
That which I eat, drink or learn I convert into myself;
I walk in humility in the presence of the person;
I can afford to be humble; I am not afraid; I am adequate;
That doctrine shall prevail which is not afraid of the person.
I reject all dogmas; they create disorder in my personality.
I am the enemy of all dogma, for dogma is a prison of the mind.
I am the egg in my mother's womb;
I draw to myself that which I need to evolve;
Every moment of my life I evolve,
For perpetual evolution is my destiny.
I am the clot that extends itself into the person;
I am the person who extends himself into humanity;
The mind of humanity comprehends infinity;
Humanity is the blanket that covers my body; it is my flesh;
It is the matrix in which I grow;
It is the face of the infinity which sees itself.
For *UQOBO* knows itself;
It knows its nature;
It knows its destiny;
It has within itself everything it desires;
It is itself;
It has no race and no colour;
The human value has no race and colour;
Each value metamorphoses in response to its environment;
Behind each complexion is the environment;
In each environment is a section of the *Law;*
The *Law* is a Whole.
UQOBO is an infinite cluster of forces;
Life is one of its components;
The *Law* is another;
So is Energy;
So are others, seen, unseen and incapable of being seen;
My mandate is to know them all;
To understand them all.
I move from eternity to eternity to understand them.
My sojourn on earth is a moment in my never-ending journey.
My destiny is forever to respond to the call of the morrow.
I have in me all I need to make the journey;
I move from one dimension of being human to another;

I move in proportion to the degree that I know;
Knowledge is the key to the gates of every dimension;
My title to the key is that I am human;
I contemplate myself to discover myself;
The key is my birthright;
He is the enemy of humanity who denies me the key.
For the key is the *Law*.
I am born according to the *Law;*
I live, grow and die according to it;
My mother is the *Law;*
My father is the *Law;*
My relatives and neighbours are the *Law;*
We are all bound together by the *Law;*
My neighbours are mankind;
Mankind is the *Law;*
Phenomena divide and fuse according to the *Law;*
Conflict is a dimension of the *Law;*
Conflict is a moment of agmination;
The stages of agmination are collision, disintegration and fusion.
Harmony and equilibrium are the fulfilment of the *Law;*
The world is the *Law;*
Everything is the *Law;* I am everything.
I am the *Law;* I am a jewel of the cosmic order;
The *Law* is my and my neighbour's will;
I am a value; I have all the power to be what I want to be;
There is glory in being human; in being a self-defining value.
My name is *Man;* my name is *Woman;*
I formed myself from my mandate;
My mandate was the *Law;*
I entered earth as an act of will;
I came to realise the promise of being a value;
To realise the glory of being human;
To discover more satisfying dimensions of being a person.
I am not alone; I have never been alone;
I shall never be alone,
For I am a cluster.
I am Father-Mother;
I am the cluster of phenomena which constitute me.
I am Father-Mother-Child.
I am the past, the present and the future.
I have no beginning and no end;
I am the geodesic circle in which Father and Mother merged
    to become *Me.*
I extend myself into the child.
I am the brick out of which society is built;
I am the Eternal Person.

In everything I think and do, I describe myself;
I show how I face the challenge of being human.
The *Law* is a component of *UQOBO*
It has an infinite number of sections;
The sections interact on each other;
The interactions produce thought;
The *Law* interacting on itself in me produces thought;
I translate thought into action;
I create the world I desire through action;
I evolve in response to the challenge of my nature.
Thus to evolve is life's purpose for me and my neighbour;
We have in us everything we need to evolve;
To discover satisfying dimensions of being human;
To realise the promise of being persons.
I am a witness of eternity;
So is my neighbour;
We are witnesses of what we are;
We are living moments in eternity.
I am a tiny component of *UQOBO*
I am an element, a substance and an incarnation of *UQOBO*
I am an incarnation of the *Law;*
I live in the *Law;* the *Law* lives in me;
It acts through me and fulfils itself through me.
When I know, the *Law* fulfils itself freely.
When I am ignorant I disorganise the *Law's* interactions;
I create disharmonies in my personality;
I hurt my neighbour;
I sow dissension in my environment;
I frustrate life's purpose for humanity.
I flee from the challenge of being human;
I live in terror of myself;
I plant terror into my neighbour's psyche;
I terrorise all human beings;
I move the world in cycles of conflict to catastrophe;
I finally collapse amidst the ruins I build;
I rot in the prison of the mind I create;
Passers-by note the stink;
Here lies one who fled from the challenge of being human, they say.
For I create my destiny in everything I do;
I and I alone know this destiny.
The challenge of being human is forever to explore myself;
It is forever to understand my neighbour;
Forever to reveal the power of the Definitive Agminate.
The cosmic order is the seraskierate of the Definitive Agminate;
I am the vizier of the seraskierate;

The *Law* is my sceptre;
To know it is the challenge of being human;
Forever to discover it is the promise of being human.
Perfection is the continuing response to the ever-beckoning hand
    of the *Law.*
Conquest forever distorts my personality;
It is the aching wound that never heals.
I listen to the call of the morrow,
When to Ncome I shall return;
When to Ulundi I shall return.
I wait in the shadows of eternity;
I wait for the day of rebirth into a satisfying destiny.
I do not apologise for being human.
I walk in humility in the presence of the person;
If aught there is to worship, it is the person.
To worship the person is to glorify myself.
The person is real; he needs no oracles to interpret him;
He has compassion in his bosom; the gods are capricious;
They are crutches for all partisans for ignorance.
The gods are trustees of my estate; I am the master.
I grow in understanding.
I outgrow the need for divine trustees; I stand on my feet;
I march into the future on my terms.
Nothing can strike terror into my heart,
For I am *uqobo* of *UQOBO.*
I know every one of my cells;
My mother taught me how to count them.
My mother is all women; all women are my mother.
I prostrate myself before all women;
I cry out to them; Arise, mothers of the person!
Lead your children along safer routes to a better future!
To all men I cry: Arise, fathers of the person!
Create the world in which it will be no crime to be your children!
For all I desire is to realise the promise of being human.
Good and evil are related;
Either translates the *Law* into action.
Virtue is knowledge and practice of the *Law;*
Vice is ignorance of the *Law.*
To know the *Law* is the glory of being human;
It is *ukuba ngumuntu;*
Perpetually to be responsible is *ukuba ngumuntu.*
I have all I need forever to be responsible,
For I am the source of all meaning, all value and all authority.
I build a Civilisation in homage to the person;
The highest points reached by other civilisations are in the sky;
These zeniths are the levels from which I start building;

I entered the earth to create order out of chaos;
I recognise the person as my Light;
I pay homage to the Light;
The Light will prevail,
For I know the heights from which they made me fall;
I know the depths into which they thrust me;
I know I shall prevail,
For I am who I say I am;
He has not been born who shall say he has conquered me!

Heavens and universes were the only fit and proper abodes for peoples who defined the person in these exalted and almost unprecedented terms. By the side of this Zulu *Definition of the Person* the Graeco-Romano-Hebraic view of the human being diminished the worth of the person. It is this diminution which forced the All-African Church Conference to look around for a "universal dimension" which would give Christianity a more relevant meaning in the African experience. It is to this diminution that we must look for the basic cause of conflict between Black and White in South Africa.

The last point above might be stated differently. We Africans oppose apartheid not only because it is a standing insult to the African race as a whole, not only because it prescribes destiny for us and not only because it distorts our personality but, above all, because it does violence to the exalted terms in which we define the person, and proceeds from this to hold out to us ideals of fulfillment which belong to the childhood days of the human race. We Sudic people outgrew these ideals long, long ago. Apartheid says we must go back to them when our evaluation of the person, the ideal of nationhood we developed on the basis of this philosophy and the specific terms in which each of our nomes has been defining itself for thousands of years point to the larger future we are building for ourselves.

It is at this point that Sudic and Caucasian attitudes clash in ways which cannot be mistaken. Defining the person in devaluative terms and proceeding from this to prescribe destiny for him has been moving Caucasian societies in the last two thousand years or more in cycles of conflict to eventual catastrophe.

This fate is the exact opposite of the destiny which the Sudic teaching lays down for the person. Perpetual evolution in discovering more satisfying dimensions of being human is the future in which the Sudic Ideal leads mankind to unending enlargement of the personality.

At this level, the conflict sheds light on the continuing humiliation which compelled Black writers and artists to urge the re-examination of African experiences for the purpose of extracting from them the ideal on which to establish the equilibrium of the Black world; which forced the All-Africa Church Conference to search for "a universal dimension" and emboldened the African students' conference in Kumasi to proclaim Africanism their creed of salvation.

Where attitudes to the person are basic causes of the race quarrel, reconciling opposing perspectives becomes an important precondition for the resolution of conflict in the crisis. More often than not, the Afrikaner does not understand African opposition to his racial policies; he tends to blame this opposition on English influences. He falls into this error largely because he has not as yet begun to do all his homework on the African attitude to the person. Only attitudes which are known can be reconciled.

Two points need to be noted about the Zulu definition of the person. Shaka and the revolution he led established an open society in which ideological consanguinity was the only qualification for membership. But, Shaka taught, there was no point in founding a nation on an ideal if the inner logic of that ideal could not be seen to be valid in the life of every person; there was no point in prating about the virtues of the ideal if it did not enable the person to realise the promise of being human.

He faced the challenge posed by the need for validation. If Woman was a value like Man, she was his unchanging equal. But there was no point in getting to the hilltops to proclaim her an equal if she was not seen to be one on her own terms. It was not enough to raise her to positions of power; she had to be involved fully in the making of laws and their translation into experience. In short, she had to be seen defining herself in her own terms and having all the authority she needed to translate her self-definition into action on her terms. That was the challenge of being human; of being a self-defining value. It was the challenge, also, of the bias for agmination and the dimension of consanguinity.

The Shakan revolution set out to create a new type of nation; to create a *synarchy,* a union of autonomous cultures, on the basis of Sudic evaluation of the person. Where necessity demanded the use of force to establish the synarchy, he was ready with the spear. Where persuasion and diplomacy served the ends of synarchisation he used them freely. While doing all this, he drew the distinction between ideological necessity and the imperative of being a self-defining value; between the demands of discipline and the demands of being the descendant of *UQOBO;* between the law and the right of the person to realise the promise of being human.

To ensure that the person's right was not violated, Shaka recognised the simultaneous legitimacy of the different definitions which the nomarchies made of themselves in their cultures. Each nome observed its own customs in its own ways inside the synarchy; all were bound together by the political ideal and the law. Political and cultural federalism were the main features of the state brought into being by the revolution. At the political level, this state was integrative; at the level of culture, it was committed to federalism. In short, it was a unitary state based on cultural autonomy. The logic of being trapped demanded that it should have this form.

Caught in a different situation, the Xhosa-Nguni genius developed a state based on political federalism and cultural autonomy. The common factor in the Zulu and Xhosa states was the commitment to federalism. The emphasis issued from the principle of simultaneous legitimacy and Sudic Civilization's concern with and regard for the person. If the new Zulu state was integrative, its opposite among the Xhosa retained the political and cultural autonomy of the ancient nomarchies while moving to a federalistic future. The logic of having vast stretches of land into which to move demanded that the Xhosa state should have this form.

The Xhosa and the Zulu Nguni were committed to the Sudic view of the person and each translated this philosophy in conditions dictated by its environment. The Zulus' environment moved them toward political integration while the Xhosa drove them toward federalism. This distinction should be borne in mind for purposes of understanding African reactions to conquest and the Ideal of Nationhood to which the Black people committed themselves after conquest.

While the commitment to federalism had its origins in the Sudic evaluation of the person and its bias for agmination, it also responded to urgent political challenges. The logic of unification demanded that integration should be complete; that the unitary state should be based on cultural uniformity, which meant the destruction of the customs adhered to by different nomarchies. This destruction, however, was not possible because it violated the Sudic evaluation of the person. The Zulu fell back to the centralised state which insisted on political uniformity as much as on cultural autonomy. The alternative was disruption for the Natal Nguni.

The Xhosa developed a tradition of federalism which was to have important political implications for Black and White in the clash of colour after conquest.

CONFLICT RATIONALISATION

The person described above saw the cosmic order as the Definitive Agminate whose main components were *Uqobo,* the *Law* and the *Person.* *Uqobo* was the environment in which the *Person* existed. He could not be separated from it; for it to remain a whole, the person had forever to be inside it. He needed *Uqobo* in order to exist while it needed him in order to be whole. The mutual need was the fundamental relationship in the cosmic order. This relationship was guided by the *Law.*

Every happening in the cosmic order developed according to the *Law;* there could be no accident in the Infinity; everything conformed to the *Law* which made the cosmic order a unity; every action everywhere was the unfolding of the *Law* of Agmination.

Conflict itself was an interaction of the *Law* with itself; it was a moment in the evolution of the process of agmination. The ancient Nguni analysed the moment and discovered that the sequence of events which they called conflict involved three forms of interaction. These were collision, disintegration and fusion.

On the basis of this analysis, they concluded that if conflict was a given type of the *Law-in-action,* it was a force, like heat, motion, magnetism (which they called *uzibuthe),* etc. Like other forces, they could use it to serve their ends provided they understood its nature and the laws according to which it functioned.

Under Shaka the Great, they developed a technique for the rationalisation of conflict to which they gave the name *ukuqhatha* (to manipulate conflict in order to serve ends dictated by reason). The simplest situation of conflict rationalisation developed when two boys, A and C, of the same age and in similar states of fitness were ordered by a third, bigger and stronger boy, B, to fight with their sticks to test each other's fighting skill and maximise each other's proficiency in fighting to defend the Zulu Ideal of Nationhood.

The Zulu interpretation of the Sudic Ideal regarded A, B and C as constituting a cluster; a weapon for attack or defence. A and C were complements whose performance was regulated by B to promote the ends of social purpose. The position taken by B, the regulant, between the complements, determined the relationship between them.

M. Mzileni

Buthelezi at the Shaka Memorial in Stanger, Natal.

The position may be presented in the following diagrammatic forms:

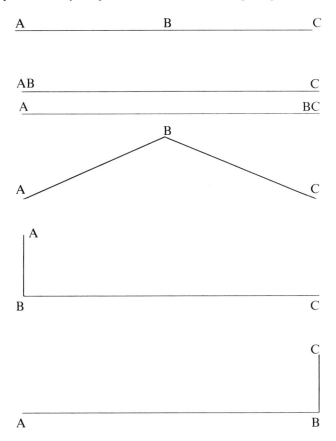

Let us have a closer look at their thinking because it sheds light on Buthelezi's strategy and politics.

As has been noted, the generation which went to the Bloemfontein Unity Conference had come face-to-face with a fundamental challenge which called for a fundamental response. The African's answer was a new Ideal of Nationhood. Faced with another version of the continuing challenge, the generation whose parents went to Bloemfontein met in Umtata and gave geopolitical content to the Bloemfontein Ideal; they gave a universal answer to a universal problem.

A pattern emerges here which tells us why Buthelezi chose to "collaborate" by leading the Zulu Territorial Authority. The balance of weaknesses and strengths in the African community at the time of Union produced what we shall call the policies of conciliation. The Africans spent a whole decade in dialogues which were bound to fail because it was the Whites who dictated the agenda. The politics of conciliation ended with the revolt of the ICU (Industrial and Commercial Workers Union) during the second half of the 1920s.

The Whites used the gun even when the African conciliated—as long as the conciliation threatened White domination.

This rejection of the African by the Whites led to the politics of disengagement when the Africans, Coloureds and Asians began turning their backs on collaboration with the Whites and exploring possibilities for Non-European unity. One of the results of these efforts was the unproductive ANC-AAC dialogues on union. The other was the emergence of the AAC. This phase came to an end when the Whites imposed the Hertzog Bills in 1936.

The formation of the Congress Youth League and the Non-European Unity Movement in 1943 ushered in the politics of confrontation to which the Whites answered with the Treason Trials and the Sharpeville Shootings in 1960.

The message from the White side was that non-violence used with determination to overthrow White rule would be crushed with violence. The issue here was the seizure of power by the majority. The weapons that could be used in the politics of transferring power were: the military argument; non-collaboration; negotiation; and the creation of conflict situations of dual authority to force the government progressively to surrender more power to the Africans.

In faraway Mahlabatini, Buthelezi had for years been experimenting with techniques for creating situations of dual-authority conflict and had tested these in action against government policy in his Shenge nome.

How they succeeded is a fascinating chapter of Zulu history. But our main concern is the logic which unfolded in these successes. Under continuing government pressure, Buthelezi gave ideological content to his fight with the apartheid regime; he made it a collision between the body of values which gave meaning to the Zulu experience and the attitude to the person which apartheid translated into action.

The government had told the African people that they should develop along their own lines. The Zulus decided to accept the challenge to the letter. They formed the National Cultural Liberation Movement. Stress was on *cultural liberation*. Pretoria liked the emphasis; they liked it so much that they registered the constitution of the NCLM with the now famous military clause described elsewhere in this discussion. One of the explanations for the regime's acceptance of the NCLM was given to me by a Zulu lawyer from Natal: he said that the apartheid regime wanted to denaturalise as many African language-groups as possible in order to isolate the Zulus, reduce them to the status of a minority vis-a-vis the Whites and then liberalise the structure of South African society as the first step toward incorporating the Zulus in the South African army on terms they would accept.

The Zulus were not interested in talk of integration in the army when their land was occupied by the White conqueror. Their first priority was how to restore to themselves their land and freedom under the conditions created by conquest. They were disarmed, poor and dispossessed. The only weapons they had were their determination never to accept conquest; their genius for organisation; their commitment to the Buntu or Sudic evaluation of the person and their refusal to be demoralised by defeat.

Thus equipped, they redefined the race problem and made it a clash between the Buntu attitude to the person and the Caucasian evaluation of the human being. Every member of the NCLM was made to know that he was fighting to defend the philosophy by which he gave meaning to life, against a philosophy which distorted his personality and frustrated life's purpose for him.

In this war of minds, the disarmed African had to develop a strategy for seizing islands of power wherever this was possible; to consolidate these and proceed to attack from positions of increasing strength. Policy sought to increase these seizures until the transfer of power to the majority was a process. Initially, the Zulus and subsequently Africans from other language-groups regarded Buthelezi as the man who would be able to translate this strategy into action. It is in this light that he and the NCLM should be seen.

The government lost one round after another in this fight. By 1967, it was talking of imposing homelands administrations. Buthelezi was ready to accept the challenge on a national scale; he was ready to operate apartheid's segregated institutions in order to use the weapon he had developed for the purpose of transferring power to his people wherever he could do this; to consolidate such gains, no matter how small and to proceed from this to conquer more ground. His goal was to transform the transference into a process.

But for him to succeed, there always had to be an effective, "extreme" group to his left which would define him as a "moderate" no matter what positions he assumed between the "extremists" and the apartheid regime. The Black Consciousness Movement played the role of "extremist."

As neither the "extremists" nor the apartheid regime had any liking for Buthelezi, they both collaborated in defining him as a "moderate" in the crisis. This definition created the balance of forces which could give the evolving transference of power the character of a process.

An Evolving Revolt moves to its goal through a continuing combination of defeats and victories, through contradictions and convergences and through reconciliations and conflicts. As shall be shown later, the Black Consciousness Movement's refusal to "collaborate" in working the homelands institutions enabled Matanzima and Mangope to accept the vassalage which Pretoria peddled as independence in unviable mini-states. Buthelezi's readiness to "collaborate" prevented this happening in Kwa Zulu.

On the other hand, non-collaboration enabled the militants in Soweto and elsewhere to write one of the most glorious chapters in our Evolving Revolt into our history.

In any language, these are positive gains in a situation of changing power dispositions. But there also are serious weaknesses on our side. Whether or not we admit it, apartheid has partially split us along pre-1912 lines. The existence of "independent" Bophuthatswana and Transkei is proof.

Our victories and setbacks call for a policy of giving constuctive purpose to our defeats; for a policy *yokubophana amanxeba* (of binding each other's wounds) which would re-unite those whom apartheid has divided and give us a formula for accommodating "collaborators" and non-collaborators in a co-ordinated effort to crush the corrupt power-structure.

This policy would also address itself to the prospect that if and when the power-structure collapses, it will go down with us and our children. It is in serious trouble on vital planes. The economy is under severe strain; the policy of importing skilled labour has collapsed; corruption has set in in high places while the number of White refugees who flee the country rises every year. These are indications of cracks in the Afrikaner's psychology of imposing destiny on other racial groups.

The policy of giving constructive purpose to adversity would search for the vital elements out of which to establish a relationship between the African and the Afrikaner which would stop the drift to disaster, narrow down the area of unavoidable bloodshed and give constructive purpose to Afrikaner efforts to discover an alternative to the status quo.

In their several meetings with African leaders, the Afrikaners indicated that South Africa faced a fundamental problem which called for a fundamental answer. They acknowledged that their monolith, by itself, cannot solve this problem; that the problem is so vast and complicated that it can be tackled on the basis of what they called "maximum consensus."

A straw in the wind which shows which way the wind might be blowing is the appointment, also in November, 1978, of Piet Koornhof and Punt Janson as ministers respectively of African Affairs and Black Education. These men are not one more set of White liberals; they are representatives of the Afrikaner monolith generally and of the leadership stratum which is changing the thinking of Afrikanerdom in the crisis. They are not and need not be friends of the African. They are representatives of an enemy group which might be beginning to face changed realities and changed dispositions of Black and White power.

These changes indicate that South Africa has reached the point of no return in the march toward the end of White rule. An oppressed people reaches this point when it regards its struggle as a fight to uphold the ideal by which it gives meaning to the person and his experience.

The Vietnamese won against American power when the ordinary people realised that the United States' approach threatened their Buddhist ideal of fulfilment.

At the time of writing, the turbulence in Iran has assumed the form of a clash between Shi'itism, an Islamic sect, and the tyranny Shah Pahlevi has imposed on his people in the name of modernisation. In this quarrel between attitudes to the person, the group on the side of morality or religion will win because the populace knows what it is fighting for.

Buthelezi has given ideological content to his fight with apartheid; he has made it known that he and the NCLM are committed to UBUNTU, the philosophy which the African experience translates into action. The oppressed understand what he says when he proclaims this commitment; they understand the fundamentals of conflict because these are translated into real action in their lives. When an oppressed people clearly sees the relationship between ideology and revolt, it has reached the point of no return in its struggle to create the world after its design; the world based on its own ideal of fulfillment

There are, however, dangers in the new directions which segments of Afrikaners are taking. While the Afrikaner proposes negotiations, he does this from positions of actual political strength. The Africans whom he is approaching deal with him from positions of actual political weakness. In this setting, the Afrikaner has the freedom to impose solutions.

The task before African diplomacy here is to create a new balance of African-Afrikaner forces for the purpose of maximising African power in ways which will force the Afrikaner to treat the African as an equal.

This can be done in three ways. The various homelands can refuse to negotiate separately with the Afrikaners and can insist on being treated as one group whenever they deal with Pretoria.

Pressure would be exerted on Free Africa by the united front of homelands administrations, if the principle of co-ordinated action is accepted, or by the NCLM, to persuade Free Africa to launch an offensive for the co-ordination of internal and external campaigns to reinforce the African side in the changing patterns of thought in the Afrikaner monolith.

A concerted initiative on the part of the homelands administrations would be organised to liaise with the West until majority rule has been established.

There is a shift in Afrikaner thinking on the race issue. The timing of this shift is important. Tanzania and Uganda are fighting a war which paralyses the OAU for action to normalise relations between the two East African States. There is trouble in the Frontline States. Zambia has decided to extend her areas of co-operation with South Africa.

These situations of weakness on the African side tempt Pretoria to move as fast as it can to negotiate with the African before the paralysing conflicts in the OAU are settled.

The Afrikaner is in a stronger position on this plane. Most Africans in the Republic, as in Free Africa, accept the prescribed religious destiny imposed by the Whites even when they reject the prescribed political destiny dictated by the Caucasians. Largely as a result, the Africans tend to be of two minds on dealing with the Afrikaner; some are for negotiating while others are for his expulsion from South Africa.

This brings us to the gravest weakness in the Western approach to Southern Africa: the refusal to regard African perspectives as determinants of policy. A personal experience with the Central Intelligence Agency of the United States will illustrate the refusal.

From quite early in the 1950s, the ANC had begun to move significantly toward the Soviet Bloc; toward an alliance with the Marxist sector of mankind. I feared this tendency would split the ANC as it had done in 1927, after J. T. Gumede's trip to the Soviet Union. I believed at the time that to balance the movement to the Left, we had to look for allies in the West or, if this was not possible, to place the West in a neutral position if and when we and the Whites reached our moment of decision.

I was arrested in 1961 on a conspiracy charge, escaped while on trial and settled in Swaziland. Exile cut me off from the struggle and gave me the freedom to visit the United States where I did all I could, from 1969 onward, to inform the State Department, the CIA, academic men and students on the African's definition of the race problem.

During the second half of 1977, I noticed that the CIA, which I had regarded as ignorant of what the NCLM was up to and tended to regard Buthelezi's carefully thought-out strategy as Zulu politics or worse, was beginning to be concerned about what he really was up to.

My years in the United States had taught me that the State Department was more fully aware of political realities in my country than was the CIA. I met officials from both departments and talked to both. The CIA tended to interpret events from the perspective of the English-speaking minority and adopted a slightly patronising attitude to the Afrikaner.

The CIA and the State Department had large numbers of highly trained men who collected every bit of information they considered relevant. The continuing failure of both was that when this information involved Africans, the Americans did not know how to draw correct or relevant conclusions from it.

This weakness arose from the fact that while the Americans were familiar with attitudes to the person which determined behaviour on the White side, they either believed these determinants did not exist on the African side or did not care to inform themselves on them. As a result, American dealings with the Africans fighting White domination were based on misreadings of the situation in the Black community.

In 1978, the American government sent someone on a mission to Africa to assess African reactions to my and Buthelezi's proposals for a political solution.They gave him a list of questions to ask Buthelezi on how he saw the crisis in South Africa and his role in it.

On his return, he prepared a detailed report of his answers, described the context in which the answers had to be seen and discussed the weaknesses in the situation of the Africans. When he handed in the report, the man in charge of the trip told him that his organisation had no need for it; that the material in it was good only for use in a scholarly tome.

This man, who had once said that he was one of those who prepare reports for President Carter, obviously advised the President on South Africa when he knew little or nothing about the changing dispositions of power in the Republic, or, for that matter, of the determinants of policies in the African community.

My attitude to the United States was always influenced by the desire to do whatever I could to help keep this powerful nation neutral in the coming collision between ourselves and the apartheid regime and to make allies for ourselves among those Americans who tried to understand our cause.

I was alarmed by the failures of American policy in Iran, where emphasis was on the modernisation (read Americanisation) of the Iranian experience. This meant the transformation of the Iranian middle and upper classes into political managers of an economic (and to some extent cultural) estate owned largely by the Americans and, to a lesser extent, other powerful Westerners. The cash value of the person was the measure for determining human worth, which the United States was slowly imposing on Iran. I did not want this criterion imposed on my people.

Now and then reports filtered through to the effect that there was growing anti-American feeling in Iran; the young who opposed the Shah regarded the Americans as enemies of their culture and religion. In the name of modernisation, the Shah placed himself in the position of alienating the majority of his people.

As usual, American policy was based on misreadings of the situation among those who opposed the Shah. The CIA had a massive organisation for collecting information for America's foreign policy-makers. When signs of an explosion emerged, the CIA gave this assurance to Washington:[20]

Iran is not in a revolutionary or even pre-revolutionary situation. Those who are in opposition, both violent and non-violent, do not have the capability to be more than troublesome. . . .

There is dissatisfaction with the Shah's tight control of the political process, but this does not threaten the government.

Robert C. Toth of the Los Angeles *Times,* who quoted the above from a secret CIA document, gave this description of reactions from the White House:

President Carter, declaring himself "not satisfied" with U.S. political intelligence that failed to warn of the turmoil in Iran, has ordered his three top national security aides to improve the quality of intelligence and its analysis reaching his desk "as soon as possible." [21]

There are indications that the lessons of South Vietnam and Iran are not being learnt with the speed events call for. The danger here is that the mistakes made in the two situations might be repeated in South Africa. A CIA man told me that I should take note of his prophesy that Buthelezi would lose the struggle for power and that the ANC would liberate South Africa. And this was the man who told me that some of his reports reached the President's desk. My answer was that events would prove him wrong as they proved his predecessors wrong in South-East Asia.

The misreadings focus attention on a basic weakness in the attitude of most Caucasians to the man of colour in the Republic or the Western hemisphere: the desire to prescribe destiny for him.

Misreading the dispositions of power in the Black community is an act of aggression; it sets out to minimise the impact of Black power in the hope that this will extend the area of White influence.

A vital point is missed here. How the person is defined determines the survival expectancy of a civilisation's ability to influence events effectively in a racially or culturally mixed situation. Where the cash value of the person is emphasised, policy will seek to cast African thinking in moulds which will make him a convert to the philosophy which humiliates him; it will seek to transform him into an ideological menial who will see nothing wrong in becoming a political manager of an economic, cultural or religious estate owned by the Whites.

The writers and authors who met in Rome, the All-Africa Church Conference and the African students' convention in Kumasi were united in one important fundamental: they rejected ideological menialism and all it stands for. This fact and its implications have not been adequately taken note of by White policy-makers in South Africa, the United States, Western Europe and the Soviet Bloc. The attitudes of these policy-makers to the crisis in South Africa and the war in Rhodesia are proof.

This sets the spotlight on another straw in the wind in the Afrikaner community. Dr. Andries Treurnicht, one of the men involved in the implementation of the policy which moved the Africans to the Soweto Rebellion, was elected, in November, 1978, leader of the Transvaal section of the Nasionale Party which rules South Africa. This endorsement of Afrikaner extremism by the Transvaal showed that Afrikaner nationalism is moving in two directions. Armed struggle would bridge this developing gulf and move South Africa to a head-on collision between Black and White which can have only one result: the expulsion of the Whites. White attitudes which move events in this direction are discussed in the next chapter.

NOTES ON CHAPTER II

1. Colin Legum: *Pan-Africanism: A Short Political Guide;* Pall Mall Press, London, 1962, Pp 217-220.
2. *The Washington Post*, August 8, 1975.
3. S.M.E. Bhengu: *Worshipping Gods Not Our Own*, Shuter & Shooter, Pietermaritzburg.
4. Legum, *Pan-Africanism*, Pp 105-7.
5. Hans Kohn and Wallace Sokolsky: *African Nationalism in the 20th Century;* Van Nostrand Reinhold Co., New York, 1965, Pp 171-72.
6. E.A. Wallis Budge: *The Egyptian Book Of The Dead*, Dover Publications; New York, 1967 Pp xcix-c.
7. Budge: *The Gods Of The Egyptians*, Vol. I; Dover Publications, New York, 1969, P 302.
8. Bernard Bromage: *The Occult Arts Of Ancient Egypt*, Samuel Weiser, New York, 1977, P 48.
9. Thomas George Allen, translator: *The Book Of The Dead*, prepared for publication by Elizabeth Blaisdell Hauser; Chicago University Press, Chicago, 1974; Spells 63 and 64, Pp 56, 59.
10. *The Gods Of The Egyptians*, Vol. II, Pp 203-204.
11. Budge, *The Gods of the Egyptians*, Vol I, P viii.
12. *Ancient Egyptian Religion*; Harper and Row, New York, 1961, Pp 3-4.
13. Budge, *The Egyptian Book of the Dead*, Pp xcix-c.
14. See sub-title: *The Chosen People*, P 128.
15. Budge, *The Egyptian Book of the Dead*, Pp 338-39, 40.
16. *The Book of the Dead or Going Forth by Day*, translated by Thomas George Allen; Spell 3, P 8.
17. The New American Library, New York; 1973, P 126.
18. Ibid., P 182.
19. Veronica Ions: *Egyptian Mythology*, Paul Hamlyn, Feltham, 1968, P 97.
20. The Washington Post, November 25, 1978.
21. Ibid.

Dr. Pixley ka T Seme, guiding spirit behind 1912 Unity Conference.

III. Prescribing Destiny
For The African

COMMON FACTORS IN APARTHEID AND COMMUNISM

Apartheid's apologists continue to claim that their policy of segregating every African language-group from every other conforms to African realities; that the "tribe" is the political structure which the African genius has been developing down the ages; that the Africans themselves are committed to "tribalism"; that "independence" in unviable mini-states follows the logic of "tribal" tradition.

The validity of this hypothesis will be examined in the African's five attitudes toward contact with and conquest by the Whites. These might be described as Nomarchism (the "tribalism" of those committed to the tradition of prescribing destiny for the African), Nominalism, Medialism, Monolithism, and what we shall refer to as Supermonolithism.

The aspects of each attitude to be considered are the way each attitude defined the race problem, the solution it proposed, the strategy it adopted to move to its goal, the dilemmas in its way, the action it took, and the results it produced.

It was said in the last chapter that conflict is a moment in a continuing experience; that it is divided into the acts of collision, disintegration and fusion. Conflict between Black and White went through the period of disintegration and is now moving toward crystallisation.

As a rule, the Africans who took up arms in the defence of their land and freedom were Nomarchists who were, as a rule, committed to the Sudic evaluation of the person and the meaning they gave to it in their different environments.

As a rule again, some of the Nomarchists had developed and had become nations. Nomarchism, in this setting, refers to attitudes and not to political structures.

Defeat on the battlefield combined with conversions to Christianity and industrialisation to split each language group into the Christians, pagans, dwellers in urban locations, squatters on White farms, those who lived in rural reserves, the educated and the unschooled.

Each of these groups adapted to the demands of its environment and began to define itself in terms valid in or dictated by its environment. Each translated its self-definition into political loyalties demanded by its situation. This threw the Africans headlong, first, into a crisis of values and, second, into a situation of fragmentation which threatened to incapacitate them permanently for regaining their land and freedom.

The White man's laws, industries, farms, schools and religion pulverised nomarchic cultures in the mission stations and in urban locations and everywhere reduced the African people to an amorphous mass. Proletariatisation threatened to destroy their cultural anchors and shatter their identities.

White policy prescribed a destiny for the Africans which gave them an identity dictated by the Whites. Proletariatisation was intensified by the law and industrialisation. The Africans did not accept this destiny. At the same time their knowledge of the ways of the White man was too limited to enable them to formulate a cohesive policy for resisting race oppression. A vacuum emerged in their thinking on their future which threatened their existence as a people.

The vacuum marked the beginning of the era of social disintegration—the end of "tribalism." The Africans found themselves confronted with a challenge they could not flee from. The new destiny pointed to extinction as their fate. The answers they developed are the subject of the pages which follow.

Since the law required that a chief should head the homeland administration, the Zulu requested Chief Buthelezi to frustrate apartheid's intentions by assuming leadership of the Zulu Territorial Authority.

A legal administration whose policies were inspired by conflict rationalisation had to occupy a position of extreme flexibility; it could demand majority rule from legal platforms, prepare itself for the situations of dual-authority conflict to which the government was driving the African people, build a political base inside South Africa and have a governmental base ready for the take-over of power when apartheid is overthrown. There are people who blame Buthelezi for having dared to do the inconceivable.

The Zulu who requested Buthelezi to stand for election argued that to boycott the Zulu Territorial Authority would give Pretoria the opportunity it desired to fill the leadership vacuum created by non-collaboration with chiefs who would endorse apartheid. To refuse to "collaborate" would be a signal to the government to crush all anti-apartheid political organisations.

The imperatives of conflict rationalisation demanded that the Zulu should "collaborate" to give impact to their rejection of "independence" in unviable mini-states. The advocates of non-collaboration did not stop the Transkei from accepting "independence."

This sets the war of minds in clearer perspective. We Sudic peoples are caught in the sweep of an interest-centred civilisation whose contempt for the person creates disorder in the individual personality and disharmonies in society which move mankind in cycles of conflict to final disaster. This is the destiny which the West and the Soviet Bloc seek to impose on Africa; this is the destiny they prescribe for us.

But this, also, is the destiny we rejected in the Rome gathering of Black writers and artists, in the Kumasi All-African Students' conference, in the Kenya sessions of the All-Africa Church Conference, and in the Khartoum summit of the Organisation of African Unity when Nigerian President Obasanjo rejected teleguidance.

The function of this book is to give the Sudic answer to the fundamental questions which conquest raises for the Africans in South Africa, on the continent and in the diaspora; to describe the protean attitude to the person which Sudic Civilisation translates into action; to present an ideal of nationhood which the philosophy produced in a given Sudic community; and to spell out the specific values in terms of which the person defined himself in a given Zulu family.

These terms recognise the person as a self-evolving and self-defining value which is an inseparable cell of *UQOBO* or *cosmic value* or the *infinite consciousness* which makes the cosmic order a unity.

In this dispensation, the destiny of the person is to discover more satisfying dimensions of being human and to evolve perpetually in the endeavour to realise the promise of being a person, regardless of race, colour, ethnicity, sex or creed.

In the responsible society based on the Sudic evaluation of the person, Gross National Products are not and cannot be the only criteria by which to judge performance. The catastrophic disharmonies created in the life of the person—hunger, insecurity, poverty, crime, disease, prostitution, infant mortality, corruption in high places, the wasteful use of resources, the anti-social maldistribution of wealth and the meaninglessness of social values—are the vital criteria Sudic societies include in evaluating themselves.

The Sudic ideal is an open and responsible society in which the person will come to the end of his life with no sense of guilt; in which he will say, as he breathes his last: "I made the best possible use of my life. My society protected me against the arrogant ignorance and avarice of those who set out to prescribe destiny for their fellow men."

The most remarkable feature of Egyptian and Zulu attitudes to the human being is their unbounded confidence in the person and the way they face the implications of this confidence. These features are the main criteria by which to judge Caucasian performance in situations of Black-White contact in Southern Africa.

ⅎattered the nomarchy of all Black language-groups. The
pre⌂   ⌂estiny gave them a new identity. They did not belong to their
nomes ⌂ ⌂ause the White man's guns had wiped them out, and they did
not belong to the White man's world because he rejected them. They
became a nowhere people, hanging somewhere between heaven and earth
and belonging nowhere.

In spite of these beginnings, the advocates of apartheid remain un-
shaken in their conviction that the African has his heart in the "tribe."

In an article in the *Star* (Johannesburg; international edition, July 8,
1978), Mr. Louis Nel, apartheid's member of parliament for Pretoria
Central, made the following comments on the conference on South Africa
which met in Freiberg, West Germany, in 1978:

> The scientists (in the conference) sought to infer from empirical find-
> ings that ethnicity is not a relevant political concept among the Blacks
> in the cities any more. All the questions asked related to the social
> behaviour of the Blacks and no important conclusion of a political
> consequence should be drawn from that.

> The fact that most Blacks in the cities see the cities as their home in
> the sense of a place where they prefer to work and live permanently
> does not in any way deny the existence of clearly definable Black
> nations in South Africa.

> It is clear that the vociferous denial of the existence and importance of
> ethnicity is nothing more than a Black political strategy.

Let the Africans tell us in their own words how they have been feeling
about ethnicity down the generations, how they translated their feelings
into action, and what their goal is. The witnesses I shall call have left us a
whole literature on all this. Their pronouncements have been collected into three volumes and edited by Thomas Karis and Gwendolyn Carter. The
volumes bear the title *From Protest to Challenge; A Documentary History
of African Politics in South Africa, 1882-1964,* and are published by the
Hoover Institution Press, Stanford University, Stanford, California.
The quotations are from Volumes I, II and III.

In his introduction to Volume I Sheridan Johns, III, observes:

> ...a small group of Africans in the Transkei called on educated
> Africans in 1882 to form a political organization, *Imbumba Yama
> Afrika* [which was] expressly concerned with maintaining African
> unity so that African interests could be forcefully articulated.

> In 1884, Africans in the eastern Cape Colony formed two additional
> organizations, the Native Education Association and the Native
> Electoral Association. Both groups were concerned with electoral
> politics and larger issues affecting the African population.

The Africans who formed *Imbumba Yama Afrika* were mainly the Xhosa-speaking. In spite of this, they formed, not *Imbumba Yama Xhoza* (the Xhosa Organisation), but *Imbumba Yama Afrika* (the African Peoples' Organisation).

In a statement on the task *Imbumba* had set itself, S.N. Mvambo, its leader, made these remarks:

Anyone looking at things as they are, could even go so far as to say it was a fatal *mistake* to bring so many church denominations to the Black people. For the Black man makes the fatal mistake of thinking that if he is an Anglican, he has nothing to do with anything suggested by a Wesleyan, and the Wesleyan also thinks so, and so does the Presbyterian. Imbumba must make sure that all these three are represented at the conference, for we must be united on polifical matters. In fighting for national rights, we must fight together.

Vol. I, Doc. 1

The educated and unschooled Africans gave a lot of thought to the vacuum in their thinking which conquest created. Their answer, as Mvambo demonstrates, was a nationalism that was larger than nomarchism; it was a synthesis of nomarchistic ideals of nationhood.

But the educated were not the only people who sought ways for filling the vacuum. In his book *The Story of the Zulus*, J.Y.T. Wilson[1] tells us that by the 1870s Cetshwayo, king of the Zulu, was sending emissaries to the then-extant African states asking them to form a military alliance which would declare Southern Africa a Black collective security area and push the Whites into the sea. Wilson says a White missionary in the Lydenburg district of the Transvaal reported that Cetshwayo's emissaries had been in that district spreading the gospel of an African united front to deal with the threat from the White side.

Sir Bartle Frere, too, was worried about the goals of Cetshwayo's diplomacy. He received reports that Cetshwayo's envoys were secretly active among Africans in the Cape Province. His worries led eventually to the war of 1879.

By the 1880s virtually all the African language-groups had been brought under the authority of the White man. If this shattered the nomarchic experience, it deepened the vacuum and emphasised the urgency of a formula for co-existence by which to fill it.

Writing from among the Xhosa, Mvambo said the answer was the unification of the African language-groups in order to develop a Collective Will. Cetshwayo, in Kwa Zulu, said the answer was the establishment of a collective security area. Here we see the beginnings of a convergence of views which was to have profound effects on the relations between Black and White.

Dr. Pixley ka Isaka Seme was one of the earliest Black thinkers to propose an ideological basis for the Collective Will. Writing in *The*

African Abroad (April 5, 1906) he propounded his Regeneration Theory in these terms:

I am an African and I set my pride in my race over against a hostile public opinion....

The African already recognizes his anomalous position and desires a change....

Yes, the regeneration of Africa belongs to this new and powerful period! By this term regeneration I wish to be understood to mean the entrance into a new life, embracing the diverse phases of a higher, complex existence. The basic factor which assures their regeneration resides in the awakened race-consciousness. This gives them [the Africans] a clear perception of their elemental needs and of their undeveloped power. It therefore must lead them to the attainment of that higher and advanced standard of life....

The African people, although not a strictly homogeneous race, possess a common fundamental sentiment which is everywhere manifest, crystallizing itself into one common controlling idea. Conflicts and strife are rapidly disappearing before the fusing force of this enlightened perception of the true intertribal relation, which relation subsists among a people with a common destiny. . . .

The ancestral greatness, the unimpaired genius, and the recuperative power of the race, its irrepressibility, which assures its greatness, constitute the African's greatest source of inspiration. . . .

The regeneration of Africa means that a new and unique civilization is soon to be added to the world. . . .

The most essential departure of this new civilization is that it shall be thoroughly spiritual and humanistic—indeed a regeneration moral and eternal!

Vol. I, Doc. 20

Seme made it clear that the alternative to the prescribed destiny was the creation of a "new and unique civilization" on the basis of "a common controlling idea." This idea was the Sudic evaluation of the person, which the "people with a common destiny" translated into experience in their different environments. No African should ever apologise for being a member of his language-group; none should ever be made to apologise for being the child of his or her particular parents, for to belong to a given language-group or nomarchy was a quality of being human; all were the faces of humanity's many-sided face; all were the faces of Africa's many-sided face. This "enlightened perception of the true intertribal relation" gave a unifying momentum to the cultures of the peoples of Africa; it made them a "people with a common destiny." The "perception" had "fusing force" because it defined the person in mature and positive terms.

The first essential element in building the new civilization was to unite the African peoples of Southern Africa into a new nation on the basis of "the common controlling idea." Seme preferred the Sudic Ideal because all the Africans were what he called "the children of one household"; the Sudic Ideal made them such a unity.

To Seme, the word African had nothing to do with race; it denoted commitment to a given definition of the person, to a given "common controlling idea." Writing in *Imvo Zabansundu* (October 24, 1911), he stated his position in these terms:

The greatest success shall come when man shall have learned to co-operate, not only with his own kith and kin, but with all peoples and with all life. . . .

There is today among all races and men a general desire for progress, and for co-operation, because co-operation will facilitate and secure that progress.

Vol. I, Doc. 21

Seme took a strong and uncompromising stand against racialism and "tribalism." He regarded them as the mortal foes of progress and harmony between peoples:

The demon of racialism, the aberrations of the Xosa-Fingo feud, the animosity that exists between the Zulus and the Tongaas, between the Basutos and every other Native must be buried and forgotten; it has shed among us sufficient blood! We are one people. These divisions, these jealousies, are the cause of all our woes and of all our backwardness and ignorance today.

Doc. 21

Seme, like Mvambo, addressed himself to the dangers posed by the vacuum. He and his generation had to act and act quickly to control the social disintegration created by conquest. He sent out a clarion call to:

all the dark races of this sub-continent to come together once or twice a year in order to review the past and reject therein all those things which have retarded our progress, the things which poison the springs of our national life and virtue; to label and distinguish the sins of civilisation, and as members of one household to talk and think loudly on our home problems.

Doc. 21

The problem which Seme faced was not new in the Zulu experience. The Natal Nguni had had to fight the threat of social disintegration in the thousand years before Shaka, as titles appended to family names tell us. The court poet to Shaka's father had said that the answer to the threat was an ideal of fulfillment which evoked identical and co-ordinable responses to similar challenges. Shaka translated this ideal into action when he led the revolution *(Imfecane)* which produced the Zulu nation-state.

Revolutions are not pleasant events; they are cruel and violent. This is because they are moments of rebirth into a new destiny. Birth, as every mother will vouchsafe, is a painful and messy happening. Uglier things were done in the Cromwellian, American, French and Russian revolutions than in the Shakan.

The disintegration caused by conquest brought all the Black language-groups to the crossroads. All were disarmed; all had been forced into the position where their conquerors prescribed destiny for them; they were not educated in the ways of their conquerors. Wherever they turned, disaster stared them in the face.

Seme said destruction was not their fate. It could not be the destiny of a people committed to a positive evaluation of the person. He told them that they had to put their heads together to identify "the sins of civilisation." They had to do this because they were not a Graeco-Romano-Hebraic people; Graeco-Romano-Hebraic civilisation rejected them. For them to be integrated into it was an invitation to humiliation; they had to create a synthesis of outlooks which would address itself to the demands of their situation.

In this setting, the answer to the prescribed destiny was an ideal of fulfillment which evoked identical and co-ordinate responses to similar provocations. Christianity was not the answer; it was incapable of producing these responses because it was a determinant of behaviour on the enemy side. The protean, Sudic evaluation of the person, which each African language-group translated into experience in terms dictated by its environment, gave to all Africans the character of "children of one household" and made them "a people with a common destiny." When Graeco-Romano-Hebraic civilisation humiliated them and made it a crime for them to be the children of their particular parents, their destiny had to be to create "a new and unique civilization," on the basis of a different attitude to the person.

The Africans did not have much of a choice. They faced a fundamental problem which demanded a fundamental answer. All sorts of difficulties stood in their way. The tragedies and suspicions brought about by *Imfecane* created paralysing chasms. No community had experience in uniting and building a nation out of peoples with different ethnic backgrounds. Fragmentation forced them to define themselves in a multiplicity of conflicting terms. Christianity created disorder in their personalities while proletarianisation transformed them into creatures which were not much different from mobile cadavers.

This does not mean that there were no influences which aided unity. Race humiliation affected every African language-group; so did industrialisation and proletariatisation. Christianity played a unifying role in its denominations and schools. The net effect of all these interactions was to give added impact to the moulding of the new nation.

The vacuum confronted every language-group with an unavoidable challenge. The threat of shattered cultural anchors affected all the African language-groups; each community sooner or later realised that by itself it would not be able to solve the problems which stood in its way.

Each had tried to develop its own synthesis of anchors. If it went too far with' this, the Whites hastened to play it against the other groups or to isolate it.

The answer was co-ordinated action in creating a larger synthesis of African traditions and borrowings from the White side. Initially each language-group used only its weapons and other vehicles to create its side of the synthesis; it could not do otherwise. These were all that were available to it. Let us see what the Zulus did. They fell back to *ukuqhatha* (conflict rationalisation) to develop the synthesis which they contributed to the synthesis of syntheses that Africans adopted as their cultural mode in the Bloemfontein Unity Conference.

Conflict rationalization has its roots in the Sudic Ideal's emphasis on the primacy of the person and in its recognition of the simultaneous legitimacy, validity and equality of the ways different peoples in different parts of the world define themselves.

The nature of the monolith is such that it creates and thrives on conflict; it generates tensions inside itself which it cannot in the long run resolve, while its bias for predation forces it constantly to clash with other monoliths. In the view of the Africans, who were committed to the principle of simultaneous legitimacy, the nature and functioning of monolithism called for a strategy which would enable them to give constructive purpose to conflict. This strategy would make it possible for the new nation to attack aggressively where it was strong and to conciliate where it was weak.

The unification of our people, the Evolving Revolt and the isolation of the Whites on the international plane were—like the formation of the Congress Youth League in 1944, the Defiance Campaign of the 1950s, the Pan-Africanist Congress's Anti-Pass Campaign of 1960 and the Soweto Rebellion—indications of strategic aggressiveness at work.

Where the African was weak he conciliated. The collaborationism advocated by the Jabavu family, African involvement in the long and futile dialogues with the government during the 1920s and the 1930s, the commitment to non-violence and moderatism were modes of tactical conciliation.

In South Africa's situation of conflicting monoliths, aggressiveness and conciliation were complements, just as the militancy of men like Steve Biko and the realism of people like Chief Gatsha Buthelezi are.

The rationalization of conflict is the technique developed in Sudic communities for using conflict in ways which serve the ends of reason. The Zulu understanding of the Sudic Ideal regards the person and his neighbour as mutually-fulfilling complements. Two people in love are complements; both need the other for the love-relationship to be real. In like manner, two persons quarrelling are complements; the situation of conflict would not exist without the quarrelling people; the healthy person cannot quarrel with himself.

In the old days, Zulu tradition held that situations of conflict could be created or managed in such a way as to give constructive purpose to forces in collision. Zulu education concentrated on teaching boys and girls the art of handling conflict, which was regarded as a force, like fire, heat, thunder or lightning. From quite an early age, the boy was initiated into the mysteries of *ukungcweka* (sparring with fighting-sticks). The girl was trained in the control of her mind and feelings to enable her to give constructive purpose to the conflicts and tensions which were part and parcel of life in a polygamous family. The Zulus gave the name *ukuphatha umuzi* (the administration of family affairs) to this aspect of a girl's training.

Each Sudic community of Southern Africa developed its own techniques for giving constructive purpose to conflict. To ensure that the Zulu extorted maximum advantage from the rationalization of conflict, he or she was taught how to recognise complements in any given situation of conflict or how to create such a situation when necessary; how to select and align forces to produce the desired results and how to manage them as they moved to the desired goal or became dangerous.

To manage the complements successfully, a third force, more powerful than either of the complements, had to regulate their conduct and interaction. In *ukungcweka,* the third force or regulant was *ingqwele,* the leader of the boys of a particular age-group.

The men and women who went to Bloemfontein in 1912 regarded the Afrikaners and the English, who had been at war at the turn of the century and had formed a united front of White monoliths in 1910, as complements. The Africans went to Bloemfontein to transform themselves into a third force, into the regulant that had the potential of being more powerful than either the Afrikaners or the English. The regulant they created was the new African nation.

Wherever this nation was strong, it went on the offensive; at the same time it conciliated where it was weak. Some of its topmost leaders were men and women who had had an overseas education or who had travelled in foreign lands. These attached importance to what was then known as the conscience of humanity. If they laid emphasis on the moral aspects of race humiliation, they believed they stood better chances of being heard. They accordingly sent a deputation to the Versailles Peace Conference to internationalise the quarrel on segregation.

The response to Seme's call was massive. Delegates from all the language-groups then resident in South Africa and the Protectorates gathered in Bloemfontein on January 8, 1912, to effect their rebirth into a new destiny. The delegates rejected the destiny prescribed for them by the Whites and saw fulfilment for themselves in uniting themselves formally into a new nation on the basis of the "common controlling idea." The destiny of this nation, as Seme had always said, was to create "a new and unique civilization."

At this gathering, the various language-groups created a vehicle to guide their march to the destiny they had freely chosen for themselves—the African National Congress. The aims of the·Congress were stated in its constitution:

1. To unite, absorb, consolidate and preserve under its aegis existing political educational Associations, Vigilance Committees and other public and private bodies whose aims are the promotion and safeguarding of the interests of the aboriginal races.

2. To be the medium of expression of representative opinion and to formulate a standard policy on Native Affairs for the benefit and guidance of the Union Government and Parliament; . . .

5. To educate Bantu people on their rights, duties and obligations to the state and to themselves individually and collectively; and to promote mutual help, feeling of fellowship and a spirit of brotherhood among them;

6. To encourage mutual understanding and to bring together into common action as one political people all tribes and clans of various tribes of races and by means of combined effort and united political organisation to defend their freedom, rights and privileges;

7. To discourage and contend against racialism and tribal feuds or to secure the elimination of racialism and tribal feuds, jealousy and petty quarrels by economic combination, education, goodwill and by other means.   Vol. I, Doc. 23

If we follow carefully the thinking of the delegates, we shall see that they set out to give the new nation the form of a monolith in order to oppose successfully the united front of White monoliths. The Constitution of the ANC stated:

19. The National Congress shall be composed of
  (a)   The hereditary Kings, Princes and Chiefs;
  (b)   The Elected Representatives of the Territories and the Protectorates (Lesotho, Botswana and Swaziland); .
  (c)   The Executive Committee;
  (d)   Official Delegates of the Provincial Congresses;
  (e)   Delegates representing certain bodies allied with and under the aegis of the Association.   Vol. I, Doc. 23

The monolith was composed of all the segments into which the various language-groups had been split by conquest, of all cultural self-definitions, of all social and economic classes, and of all interest-groups.

The Whites had rejected the Africans. By forming themselves into a new nation, the Africans made it known that they rejected teleguidance; that they were not members of the Graeco-Romano-Hebraic world; that they no longer wanted to belong to it; and that they were going to carve out a destiny for themselves which they had freely chosen. In all this, they told those with ears to hear that they would allow nobody, anywhere, to prescribe destiny for them.

By uniting themselves into a new nation, they buried nomarchism and set in motion an Evolving Revolt—a struggle for self-determination which gave itself a unifying momentum and which adapted its strategy and tactics to the demands of a changing situation.

Monolithal Functionalism and Conflict Rationalisation were the principles on which the strategy of the new nation was founded. We shall discuss these when we consider the five main responses to conquest.

Seme was a Zulu. It should be noted that when he sent out his clarion call, he did not address himself to the Zulus; he called on "all the Black races of the sub-continent" to unite. Monolithal Functionalism and Conflict Rationalisation were not nomarchic techniques; they were syntheses of experiences developed by the Collective Will which produced the Bloemfontein Ideal of Nationhood.

This Collective Will complemented the Evolving Revolt with an external offensive to internationalise the race quarrel and isolate the White supremacists on the international plane. With this in mind, the new nation sent a delegation to the Versailles Peace Conference in 1919 to alert the outside world to the explosion developing in South Africa.

The geopolitical expression of monolithism could not be anything other than a federal structure. "Children of one household" were unchanging equals with the same right to fulfilment in the light of their different temperaments; their cultural self-definitions were simultaneously legitimate. The form of state within which they could thrive was a federal union of culturally autonomous communities. We shall come to these when we discuss the five moods of African Nationalism.

For the present, let us trace the evolution of the African people's commitment to nationhood. Our witnesses will be leaders from all language-groups, representing African opinion from the Left to the Right.

The newly formed nation had hardly adapted to the demands of union when the White government plunged it in a major crisis. Parliament proceeded to pass the Natives Land Act of 1913 which made it illegal for Africans to buy land in so-called White areas. The ANC protested against the measure on behalf of all the language groups:

> . . . this Congress, representing all the tribes of the Bantu Races within the Union, earnestly prays that Parliament unhesitatingly reject the Report of the Natives Land Commission and instantly withdraw the Natives Land Act of 1913.   Vol. I, Doc. 26

This was in 1916. In his May 6, 1919 presidential address to the Congress, Mr. S.M. Makgatho, who came from the Northern Sotho language-group warned:

At a time like this, when we are face to face with some of the worst upheavals that ever overtook our people, it is imperative that we should stand together. . . .

This is the land of our fathers, and, in it, we wish to be treated at least as well as foreigners and with the same consideration extended to foreigners, including foreigners of enemy origin.   Vol. I, Doc. 32

John Tengo Jabavu, the great Xhosa liberal, gave evidence before the Select Committee on Native Affairs on June 15, 1920. The White members of the Committee defined the new African in "tribal" terms. The Chairman asked Jabavu:
You are not afraid that the appointment of one or two natives on the Commission would have the effect of rousing jealousy among the various native tribes of South Africa?
[Jabavu:] I do not know that in practice it would mean much—it is only sentiment.
Would a Zulu member of a Commission carry any weight with natives of the Transkei?
Yes, if he was a generally recognised man, if the people knew who he was, that he was capable, suitable in regard to character and also in regard to ability.   Vol. I, Doc. 33a

Tengo's attitude is important because he had serious reservations on the Bloemfontein Unity Conference and its decisions.
Meshack Pelem, another Xhosa, was president of the Bantu Union. At the Queenstown Conference of the Union on February 26, 1919, he declared:
. . . the time has come when all the races of the earth must be freed from the tyranny of the few and be granted equal rights and liberties in all things without distinction of race, colour, or previous condition. . . .
. . . there is nothing more honourable than that a man or woman should lose even life itself for the love of country, the honour of their people, and the graves where the ashes of their forefathers rest.

. . . British Ministers have been found or forced to become traitors to the ancient constitution of England, and have sold the Bantu under a fraudulent Union...as long as the foundations are based upon oppression and injustice, they shall never unify, but on the contrary, evil and division shall reign. . . .   Vol. I, Doc. 29

Pelem stood somewhere between Seme and Jabavu and, like the latter, spoke Xhosa. Jabavu's son, Don Davidson Tengo, became an African liberal luminary and played a key role in the development of Medialism.
Richard Victor Selope-Thema was one of the distinguished journalists of the new nation who wrote during the early years of the new nation and continued to do this into the 1950s. He wrote an article which *The Guardian* published in September, 1922:

. . . the [race] problem cannot be solved until both races have learned to co-operate in finding its solution. . . .

It is well known that the European has really no objection against Africans so long as they remain a race of servants. . . .

He [the White man] wants to dominate and to be master of the destinies of other races. . . .

. . . each race of mankind has the right to work out its own destiny and live its own life without let or hindrance. This right can only be limited by the equal right of others. . . .

I do not see how the Africans can develop along their own lines when they are kept under European hegemony. To develop along their own lines and evolve their own civilisation, they must not only have a place in the sun, but must have freedom of thought and action. . . .

The policy of "White South Africa" has naturally given rise on this side of the colour line to a cry of "Africa for the Africans."

Vol. I, Doc. 41a

Clements Kadalie had originally come from Malawi and had settled in Cape Town where he attained fame as a trade union leader. He was a founder of the ICU (Industrial and Commercial Workers Union) and was one of the leaders of radical Medialism in the Cape Town area. In his "Open Letter to Blackpool," which *The New Leader* published on September 30, 1927, he warned:

Denied all legitimate expression for his grievances and aspirations, who can blame the African if he takes what will seem to him the only possible path to freedom, if he comes to hate the White man as his oppressor, and if the attainment of justice and liberty comes for him to be a thing synonymous with the crushing of the civilisation the White man has built up?

None knows better than we do how fatal is the narrow spirit of nationalism; but, if the present ungenerous and shortsighted policy is continued by the Union Government, what other path will there be for us to take, and who among us will be able to show the African worker, maddened and humiliated by the White man's injustice and oppression, that White civilisation can yet be a fine and beautiful thing, that many of its constructive ideals are sane and desirable, and that its destruction in Africa will be immeasurably to the hurt of the African?

Vol. I, Doc. 49b-5

The united front of White monoliths was deaf to the voice of reason from the new nation. The Africans began to speak in strident tones. The Reverend Z.R. Mahabane, a distinguished theologian who played an active role in African politics and spent a large part of his life laying foundations for the reconciliation of Medialism and Monolithism, issued a statement which the *Bantu World* published on May 18, 1935:

The proposals embodied in the Report and the Draft Bills [abolishing the Cape Vote] constitute a direct challenge to the African community of the Union. How long shall the African people who form the integral and inseparable part and parcel of the population of the Union be contented with a position of political inferiority and political helotry and of exclusion from the civil organism of this land of their birth? . . .

The Africans should gather together on this occasion, take stock of their position as a race of people in the country, consider the whole Native policy that has been inaugurated since Union.. . .
                                                                    —Vol. II, Document 1

The united front of White monoliths was at the height of its power; it could afford to ignore the wishes of the African people. It had the guns and the guns guaranteed everything; they guaranteed security. Mahabane had been a moderate all his life; he had been a courageous moderate. When the Whites finally took away the Cape African Vote, he changed his tone. At the December 16-17, 1948, joint conference of the ANC and the AAC, he stood up and told the delegates:
> It is time we said to the Europeans of this country: "Thus far, and no farther." A state of emergency exists. Urgent measures must be adopted. The call is "To Arms," not by taking weapons but by coming together and speak with one voice and act as one man.
                                                                    —Vol. II, Document 69

The African people had reached their moment of decision when the Union of South Africa was established in 1910. They had chosen to form themselves into a new and larger nation. The choice moved the Whites to their moment of decision. They reached this moment in 1929 when Afrikaner nationalism rose to power virtually on its own steam. The Afrikaner chose to reject the African; to reject the Black man's right to share power with the Whites. The Afrikaner monolith, supported by the English monolith, declared political war on the African nation and set out systematically to pulverise the Collective Will The lines of conflict were drawn.

Mahabane's words were harsh and angry; they were the words the person utters when his humanity is outraged; they were the words of a people convinced that the White man was incapable of leading a mixed nation. Mahabane, however, was a Christian; he prayed hard while tyranny took bolder steps to crush the Collective Will.

A new generation of leaders came to the fore. They were not interested in prayer; they were not interested in dialogues; they were not interested in the White "friends" of the African. They spoke a new language; they concerned themselves with the African's destiny. The generation of their fathers had created the African monolith but hesitated to face squarely the inexorable logic of monolithism. The young men and women who formed themselves into the Congress Youth League grew up in a climate of systematic deprivation and dispossession. The African was losing his right to own land in the urban areas of his country; he was being denied the right to be on the common roll of voters in the country; he was being driven out of jobs so that Hertzog's "civilised labour policy" could secure the position of the poor Whites, who were mainly Afrikaners, at the expense of the African.

The answer to these humiliations was to face the harsh logic of being a monolith. The mainly Nominalist Old Guard in the leadership of the ANC had to be eased out of their positions. Eased out is the operative phrase. The League was committed to the Bloemfontein Ideal of Nationhood on one hand and, on the other, did not want to do anything which the surrogates of Moscow could seize upon to split the ANC as they had done when they used J.T. Gumede to divide the ANC and C. Doyle Modiakgotla to polarise the ICU during the second half of the 1920s.

The harsh logic required that we should deepen the vacuum that the Bloemfontein Ideal of Nationhood had created among the Whites, fill it with our concept of nationhood, give leadership which would enable us to overthrow White rule, and establish a society in which it would never again be a crime for the person to be the child of his particular parents.

This was the goal to which the Collective Will, developed in 1912, moved events in our community. For the surrogates of Moscow to talk of class conflict when race humiliation was the reality history required us to address ourselves to, when our land had been taken away, our honour trampled in the mud and our freedom crushed in the name of White supremacy, was to play the White man's game of diverting us from the fundamentals of conflict for the purpose of slowing down our march to freedom and majority rule.

For me in particular, the most important of these fundamentals was that the race factor was used to translate an attitude to the person which created catastrophic disharmonies in the human being committed to the Buntu philosophy; these disharmonies would move us, as they did the Caucasians, through cycles of conflict to final destruction.

It was not an accident that the attitude we needed to reject had hurled the world into two global wars in my own lifetime. I had been born toward the end of the first while the second broke out when I was an adult. My generation feared that the third might break out before we had died.

I saw no reason why we should hang on to the coattails of the Whites as the Caucasians would lead us to destruction with them. Like the Black authors and writers who met in Stockholm and Rome in the 1950s I sought to attain clarity on the ideal of fulfilment which would preserve the equilibrium of the Sudic world, unite the peoples of African descent everywhere and enable them to give a meaning to freedom which would lead the human race along safer routes to a better future.

My generation believed that Africa's destiny was to lead the human race after the Graeco-Romano-Hebraic attitude to the human being as a dominant factor in world thinking collapsed. The African would not be responsible for its fall; the fact that it was incapable of having a similarly valid and satisfying meaning in Black and White communities doomed it.

The generation of our fathers was caught in the contradictions of Nominalism and early Medialism and was reluctant to face the inevitable implication of apartheid, which was known as segregation at the time; They did not want to deal with the logic of transforming the various African language-groups into a monolith. These men were not cowards; they would not have gone to Bloemfontein if they were; they were realists who were aware that the balance between the reserves of power they controlled and those held by the White community was not in their favour.

The Youth League came into being to move events toward majority rule as the first step in the campaign to unify Sudic Africa for the purpose of freeing her from White domination and placing her in the position of leading the world to a safer future.

Anton Mziwakhe Lembede and Ashby Peter Mda were the principal spokesmen of the League. These two worked with the present author and others to organise the Congress Youth League. Lembede was elected first president of the League. Lembede's and the Youth League's attitudes were stated in an article in a weekly I edited, *Inkundla yaBantu,* (May, 1946):

1. *Africa is a blackman's country.* Africans are the natives of Africa and they have inhabited Africa, their Motherland, from times immemorial; Africa belongs to them.
2. *Africans are one.* Out of the heterogeneous tribes, there must emerge a homogeneous nation. The basis of national unity is the nationalistic feeling of the Africans, the feeling of being Africans irrespective of tribal connection, social status, educational attainment or economic class. This nationalistic feeling can only be realised in and interpreted by [a] national movement of which all Africans must be members.
3. *The Leader of the Africans will come out of their own loins.* No foreigner can ever be a true and genuine leader of the African people because no foreigner can ever truly and genuinely interpret the African spirit which is unique and peculiar to Africans only. Some foreigners, Asiatic or European, who pose as African leaders must be categorically denounced and rejected. An African must lead Africans. Africans must honour, venerate and find inspiration from African heroes of the past: Shaka, Moshoeshoe, Makana, Hintsa,

Khama, Mzilikazi, Sekhukhuni, Sobhuza and many others. . . .
5. *The divine destiny of the African people is National Freedom.* Unless Africans achieve national freedom as early as possible they will be confronted with the impending doom and imminent catastrophe of extermination.   Vol. II, pp. 317-18

Lembede died in 1947 and was succeeded as head of the Youth League by Ashby Peter Mda. From December 15 to 19, 1949, the ANC met in annual conference in Bloemfontein. The Afrikaners were preparing for their Voortrekker Celebrations. Mda and other Nationalists opposed the mild wording of Dr. A.B. Xuma's statement on the Celebrations. Mda advocated a strongly worded pronouncement which would signify:
not only our challenge to the White man's point of view but also an inflexible determination on the part of the African to struggle for National Freedom.   Vol. II, Document 47

In its Manifesto, published in 1944, the Youth League stated:
. . . Africanism must be promoted, *i.e.,* Africans must struggle for development, progress and national liberation, so as to occupy their rightful and honourable place among nations of the world. . . .
(THE AFRICAN) NOW ELECTS TO DETERMINE HIS FUTURE BY HIS OWN EFFORTS....

Soon the point must be reached when African Youth, which has lived through oppression from the cradle to the present, calls a halt to it all. . . .
In response to the demands of the times African Youth is LAYING ITS SERVICES AT THE DISPOSAL OF THE NATIONAL LIBERATION MOVEMENT . . . IN THE FIRM BELIEF, KNOWLEDGE AND CONVICTION THAT THE CAUSE OF AFRICA MUST AND WILL TRIUMPH.   Vol. II, Document 48

In a letter to Godfrey Pitje, dated September 10, 1948, Mda described the fundamental aim of African Nationalism as:
   (i)   the creation of a united nation out of the
         heterogeneous tribes.
   (ii) the freeing of Africa from foreign domination and
         foreign leadership,
   (iii) the creation of conditions which can enable Africa to
         make her own contribution to human progress.
                                                  —Vol. II, Document 56

A third voice was being raised on the issue of national unity. African Medialism, which had long settled in Cape Town, thought in terms of a unity which transcended monolithism on the African side; it thought of a unity which would bring together the Africans, Coloureds and Asians. The All-African Convention (AAC), formed in 1935 to fight the Hertzog Bills which abolished the Cape African Vote, was the head of Medialism. In August, 1943, the AAC issued its Manifesto calling for non-European unity:

Of what use is it to us when a few far-sighted Whites are worried over our terrible plight, because the "Native," as they say, "is the backbone of our economy and we must not waste our greatest asset. . . ." It is no use appealing to the government, because it is not our government but the government of the White man. It is no use appealing to parliament, because it is not our parliament but the parliament of the White man. It is no use appealing to the law courts, because the law is made by the White man against us. . . .
The White rulers of South Africa, especially, with views similar to Hitler's race theories, will not voluntarily give us our freedom and our rights. From the pronouncements of the Prime Minister . . . he wants to unite all White people for a final settlement of the relations between Black and White, meaning, of course, all Non-Europeans.
—Vol. II, Document 64

Cape Town was the base of the Coloured community. The Medial wing of African Nationalism was facing the challenge presented by the existence of the large Coloured minority. The unity the Convention was thinking of would bring together all the non-Whites. I.B. Tabata indicated in a letter to Nelson R. Mandela on June 16, 1948:

The interests of each are the interests of the whole, a unity in which the growth of a part automatically means the strengthening of the whole, a unity which will serve as the basis for a further development leading to a truly national movement, nationalism. And this is the very antithesis of sectionalism or racialism.
—Vol. II, Document 67

The federal structure of resistance was not a new development. The Xhosa experience had well-known examples of it. Cape Town had for years been the main base for Xhosa Medialism. Cape Town was also the main base for the Coloureds. In this setting, those whom the Whites punished for being the children of their particular parents created a synthesis of political outlooks. Devoted men like I.B. Tabata, Wycliffe Tsotsi and others spent their lives developing the synthesis. One result of these years of dedication was the epoch-making decision by the Coloured community of Cape Town to throw in its lot with the Africans after the outbreak of the Soweto Rebellion. We shall say more about this partnership in the heat of battle, later.

Events began to gallop toward Sharpeville. A self-crippling internal fight had been going on for years between the African Nationalists and the White communists who financed a clique inside the ANC which worked to commit the ANC to teleguidance. The African Nationalists had for a long time not had foreign allies while the Left wing of the Congress had secret connections with Moscow.

The situation changed after the first All-African Peoples Conference in Accra in 1958. The Nationalists embraced Pan-Africanism and established connections with Free Africa. That the African Nationalists had a choice of worlds hardened attitudes and forced the Nationalists to break away to form the Pan-Africanist Congress under Mangaliso Robert Sobukwe.

The relevant aspect of the split for purposes of this section of this chapter is that it did not in any way follow ethnic lines; it was a straightforward clash between those who rejected teleguidance and those who accepted it.

Sobukwe and his supporters saw the Africans as a nation. In January, 1959, he issued a question-and-answer statement in which he clarified the thinking of the Nationalists:

We firmly hold that we are oppressed as a subject nation—the African nation. To us, therefore, the struggle is a national struggle. Those of the ANC who are its active policy-makers maintain, in the face of all the hard facts of the S.A. situation, that ours is a class struggle. We are, according to them, oppressed as WORKERS, both White and Black.

But it is significant that they make no attempt to organise White workers. Their White allies are all of them bourgeoise!....

Q. But are you anti-White or not?
A. What is meant by anti-Whiteism? . . . . In every struggle, whether national or class, the masses do not fight an abstraction. They do not hate oppression or capitalism. They concretise these and hate the oppressor, be he the Governor-General or a colonial power, the landlord or the factory-owner, or, in South Africa, the White man. . . .We are not anti-White, therefore. We do not hate the European because he is White! We hate him because he is an oppressor. And it is plain dishonesty to say I hate the sjambok and not the one who wields it.

—Vol. III, Document 38

The moment of confrontation could no longer be delayed. Every major African political organisation started work on plans for an organised underground army. The PAC was determined, from its formation, to seize from the Whites the initiative to influence events on one hand and, on the other, to establish the relativity of White power.

Because he possessed the gun, the White man believed that his power was absolute; exclusive use of it by him, he believed, was his guarantee of security. The rank and file in the White community would not bother about giving any attention to the African's demands for change in racial policies so long as the Whites believed that the gun was their guarantee of survival.

The Africans had to move together as a monolith to create the situation which would force the Whites to realise that the gun was no guarantee of survival. When they did this the White government wrote Sharpeville into South African history.

A White policeman's bullet whizzed through an open window in Sharpeville Location and landed in the brain of the foetus in the womb of an African woman who was serving breakfast to her family in her dining room. The foetus and the mother died.

The foetus belonged to the generation which was to write the Soweto Rebellion into South African history.

Some Whites read the Sharpeville signals correctly and quietly began to emigrate from South Africa. The Collective Will had shown that White power had limitations; that it was becoming strong enough to challenge White power in a frontal attack.

The bans on the PAC and the ANC were designed, among other things, to create a political leadership vacuum which the government hoped to fill with co-operative chiefs who would accept the prescribed destiny on behalf of their people.

The Africans countered with a two-pronged offensive. The militant Medialism which had developed in the Cape in the main called on the victims of apartheid to refuse to collaborate in operating apartheid institutions and worked systematically to isolate the Whites on one plane and, on the other unite Africans, Asians and Coloureds.

The functional monolithism which influenced events mainly in the rural areas decided to "collaborate" in operating the homelands institutions partly to prevent their being controlled by co-operative chiefs and partly to use them as platforms from which to further the ends of the Collective Will.

At first viewing, there would appear to be a fundamental conflict between the positions taken mainly by the urban areas and the people mainly in the rural locations. A closer look, however, shows that the two were related responses by the Collective Will to the same challenge in different environments.

This statement calls for a little more attention. For years, as will be shown in the next chapter, militant Medialism had worked on the schools in the urban locations and in some rural areas to "conscientise" students, as Nkrumah said. The politicisation, as Mda had called it in the days of the Youth League, did not involve significant numbers of adults in the rural areas or the urban locations.

The locations of the Transvaal differed from the locations of, say, Natal and the Transkei; their systems of education were under the direct control of the government in Pretoria and this government was determined to impose Afrikaans as an additional medium of instruction in African schools.

Education affected the students as much as it did the parents. In the Transvaal, and more especially in Soweto, the parents organised themselves into a parents' association which led the campaign against the imposition of apartheid and supported the students who refused to be taught in Afrikaans.

When student resistance exploded into the Soweto Rebellion, it had the immediate support of the parents' side. That co-operation helped to give magnitude to the Soweto Rebellion. Since the imposition affected the Transvaal,the rebellion quickly spread to other locations in this province.

The imposition of Afrikaans was, however, the tinder that ignited the African community's anger against apartheid which originated from, and was given aggressive support by, the Afrikaner monolith.

An altogether different situation existed in Cape Town where African and Coloured students openly courted death in revolts against race humiliation. In this city, which is the original home of the Coloureds, Afrikaans could not be an issue because it is more or less the language of the Coloured people.

It was said earlier that African Medialism, which had developed mainly in the Cape Province, made Cape Town its base. Contact between the African and Coloured intellectuals had reinforced Medialism and had strengthened its commitment to a larger concept of nationhood and federalism. As shall be shown in the next chapter, the striving toward a synthesis of destinies in Cape Town dated to about the end of the nineteenth century.

Apartheid's rise to power gave added appeal to the synthesis of destinies. The Immorality Act and the Mixed Marriages Act insulted the entire Coloured community while the expulsion of these people from the city where they had first emerged cut wounds in their psyche which nothing could heal.

The consciousness of being Coloured which apartheid stirred up combined with African Medialism to draw in sharper outlines the dimensions of a larger grouping of forces against White domination: the super-monolith. The super-monolith would be the largest united front to oppose the Whites, who had no answer to it other than to surrender power to the non-Whites.

The united front of the Africans, Coloureds and Asians could paralyse South Africa's economy and bring it to a dead stop. It had the added advantage that, in terms of human lives, it was the cheapest weapon against apartheid and would move events to a decision faster than an armed struggle.

Noncollaboration had taken deeper root among the Cape Africans and Coloureds partly because these communities had the longest contact with the Whites and partly because they had been humiliated by the whittling of their rights to have their names on the common roll of voters. The rise to power of apartheid was intolerable; they had to take action against it no matter what it cost.

In this mood, the Medialists saw the realism of the monolithal functionalists as an attitude of collaboration. They felt so powerfully against collaboration they did not see Buthelezi's functional "collaboration" as a response which complemented their campaigns of noncollaboration.

The divergent tactics of the noncollaborationists and the functionalists had nothing to do with nomarchism, as the revolt by all language-groups in the urban areas of the Transvaal showed.

What was happening was that the two dimensions of the Collective Will—militant Medialism and Monolithal functionalism—were moving on different planes toward convergence. Confrontation with the White power-structure would be the point where they could co-ordinate action.

FUNCTIONAL "COLLABORATION"

World hostility against apartheid is rightly intense and many people are so taken up with the idea of an armed struggle that they see the South African crisis only in broad outlines and ignore the important but complex dispositions of power on both sides of the colour line inside South Africa.

One of the developments ignored is the direction in which the Collective Will is moving events inside the segregated homelands. Whether or not we like the leaders of the homelands is not important for purposes of this discussion; what matters is whether or not their actions serve the ends of the Collective Will.

One of the goals the Collective Will set itself was, according to the Constitution of the Congress, "to bring together into common action as one political people all tribes and clans of various tribes or races." Another was "to secure the elimination of racialism and tribal feuds by . . . economic combination, education, goodwill and by other means."

The Bloemfontein Conference gave the African peoples an *Ideal of Nationhood*. The All-African Convention translated it into action in terms which it stated clearly, and restated from time to time. At the December 16-17, 1948, joint conference of the AAC and the ANC, Tabata proposed the following as a formula for unity:

1. It should be based on the Convention's ten-point Programme. The Ten Points were read to the Conference.
2. The federal structure of the Convention should be retained.

3. The Unity should be based on the acceptance of the principle of the
   · unity of all non-Europeans.
4. It should be based on a policy of "noncollaboration with the
   oppressor."
   Vol. II, Doc. 69

Medialism moved events toward a united nationhood which included all the races which had made South Africa their home and regarded non-European unity or super-monolithism as the best vehicle for moving to its goal. Non-collaboration was the weapon it used.

Monolithal Functionalism moved toward the same goal but proceeded along a different route. It preached that there could be no effective unity between the African and any other group so long as the Black monolith was poorly organised and weak. A strong African community was the only precondition for a viable non-European united front. To build this strength on every plane was the goal the functionalists set themselves. *Every plane* was the operative phrase.

The functionalists argued that African history taught that to take a militant stand when the Africans were unorganised and weak placed the government in the position where it silenced the leaders by banning or jailing them. This created a leadership vacuum which weakened the African community. The African could refuse to collaborate; he could stage a national strike and paralyse the racist economy only when he was strong. The first priority of the functionalists was to build African power from the grassroots.

Both sides had one fatal weakness: they did not have a newspaper or printing press to enable themselves to conduct a meaningful debate on the pros and cons of the strategy proposed by each side. The militant Medialists argued that revolutionary fervour would develop among the masses as they were involved in action; that action would give a unifying momentum to the Evolving Revolt and eventually overwhelm White domination. The functionalist answer to this was that this strategy led to one Sharpeville after another. A succession of Sharpevilles certainly radicalised the masses of the African people, but the radicalisation of a people whose anger was focused on goals that were not clearly understood degenerated into mob rule which could destroy the Bloemfontein Ideal of Nationhood. Apartheid, the functionalists continued, had set itself the goal of destroying the Bloemfontein Ideal. It was not the business of any African to do the dirty work for apartheid.

These differences had nothing to do with nomarchism; they had nothing to do with whether the Africans lived in the urban locations or the rural areas. They issued from the logic of fragmentation, which will be the subject of the next chapter.

The functionalists adopted the strategy of attacking apartheid from positions which demanded minimum investments of human life to move to the goals toward which the militants were also marching. That the militants and the functionalists moved to common goals was no secret. The international edition of the Johannesburg *Star* (August 28, 1976) gave front-page prominence to excerpts from an interview its daily edition had had with Chief Gatsha Buthelezi, the principal spokesman of functionalism. Its report stated that Buthelezi had:

stressed that the objectives of his Inkatha movement were the same as those of Black Consciousness movements such as Saso and the BPC.

On November 7-8, 1973, the leaders of the main homelands administrations had met in conference in Umtata, the Transkeian capital, to tell the world where they were leading their people. The conference rejected the fragmentation of the African people and the balkanisation of their lands, and confronted the apartheid regime and the world with a geopolitical alternative. The relevant resolutions read:

2) Having understood that:

a) the idea of Federation is a long-term policy

b) that Federation is vital to the unity of the Black people, and bearing in mind that our people should be fully informed of the idea of Federation, this Conference resolves that in principle the idea of Federation be propagated to the people by the various Homeland leaders.

3) That in principle this Conference supports the establishment of a Black bank for Black people. [2]

By committing themselves to the ideal of establishing a federal state — Buthelezi called it a Federal Union of the Autonomous States of Southern Africa — the leaders of the main bantustans gave geopolitical content to the Bloemfontein Ideal of Nationhood and confronted the apartheid regime with an alternative to the vassalage Pretoria peddled as independence in unviable mini-states.

The Bloemfontein Unity Conference had set out specifically "to bring together into common action as one political people all tribes." The Umtata Conference expressed its commitment to the principle of unity by translating it into the ideal of creating a federal union.

The Bloemfontein Conference had also sought to "secure the elimination of racialism and tribal feuds by...economic combination...." The Umtata Conference committed itself to the establishment of a Black bank. The African Bank of South Africa was established shortly thereafter.

Buthelezi was not the initiator of the principle of federating. The principle had a long history, into which we shall go when we discuss the five moods of African Nationalism. Paramount Chief Kaiser Matanzima of the Transkei had committed himself publicly to the ideal on several occasions before the Umtata Conference. This commitment expressed the rejection by Medialism of racism.

This is how Buthelezi stated his commitment to the ideal of a federal union:

> Let us face it that we can never really talk terms with Whites as small separate entities. We can only bring White South Africa to her knees if we achieve and use Black solidarity....

> We realise as Blacks that if this dream (of a federal union) came true we could not have Black unity and our sense of Nationhood in the various Black states, on the basis of crushing the languages and cultures of non-Africans. Each member of such a new society would of necessity have a right to live out his or her life in the light of his or her experience and choices.

> The bond of union should be our common humanity, *ubuntu,* or Humanism and not race, creed, colour, age or sex. This means a non-racial society in which every human being would have the right and opportunity to make the best possible use of his life. [3]

The functionalists went beyond confronting Pretoria with a Geopolitical Alternative to apartheid. Those among them who accepted "independence" made it clear that they adhered to the Umtata commitment. In his speech when the Transkei became "independent" Matanzima included these remarks:

> Certainly we are a party to the break-up of South Africa in the form which has only satisfied a minority of its inhabitants and we shall be a party by necessary inference to the restructured southern African sub-continent which we hope will emerge in the not too distant future.

Chief Lucas Mangope of Bophuthatswana went farther. On the day his country became "independent," he told the world that he regarded the acceptance of "freedom" as a step toward establishing the federal union.

The role of the functionalists is of the greatest importance in the changing dispositions of power inside South Africa. To begin with, they have administrative power which they can use at least to build an effective political base from which to launch powerful campaigns against apartheid. To ignore the fact that they have the potential to form a united front and lead their people in a strike that would paralyse the apartheid economy is to be guilty of a dangerous and uninformed misreading of the situation inside South Africa.

The misreading is particularly serious when one bears in mind that some of the homelands leaders are committed Nationalists who are defending the Bloemfontein Ideal in singularly difficult conditions.

Mention is made of the danger because events are moving the Africans in South Africa in directions which are to a large extent the exact opposite of those taken by some of the Africans' ''allies'' in the outside world. We shall come to this point shortly.

For the present, let us return to the argument that the African has his heart in the ''tribe.''

It has been shown that the Sudic African regards agmination as the basic relationship in the cosmic order; that this principle of unity issues from the consubstantiality of all phenomena. It has been shown, also, that the logic of the Sudic evaluation of the person moves peoples toward convergence. The movement from nomarchism in Kwa Zulu, about five hundred years ago, to the Bloemfontein Ideal of Nationhood, shows the logic of the Sudic view of the human being in action in one African community. Scholars from other African language-groups are redefining the history of their people and are bringing to light aspects of their history which the conquerors suppressed for obvious reasons. One day they, too, will tell the world what their ancestors were doing before the coming of the Whites.

Above all, the testimony of the leaders of the African people, given over nearly a hundred years, shows solid and consistent movement toward united nationhood. Even the nomenclature used by the Black people in this period to describe themselves shows that unity has always been their goal. They started by calling themselves Zulu, Xhosa, etc. They abandoned this style after contact with the Whites and described themselves successively as Natives, Bantu, Africans, and now as Blacks. The changes responded to an evolving understanding of the nationhood they desired.

If we start with Cetshwayo's efforts to create a collective security area, we will see that the determination to unite the Black peoples found expression in concrete action over a hundred years ago.

People do not go to war, organise resistance movements for over a century, and systematically lay down their lives in efforts to restore to themselves their land and freedom merely to play political games. To dismiss as a ''political strategy'' all these protests against race humiliation is not only to be tragically insensitive, showing the quality of mind which could make the Police Minister say Steve Biko's death left him cold; it is also *to prescribe destiny for the Africans.*

MOSCOW'S ROLE IN SOUTH AFRICA

The involvement of the Soviet Union in South Africa dates back to 1921, when the Communist Party of South Africa was formed. The new nation and its Evolving Revolt had been in action for nine years. The basic premise on which the new nation had been built and the Evolving Revolt organised was that the African people had reserves of power and points of weakness which called for a grassroots revolution designed to crack the united front of White monoliths where it was most vulnerable and refrain from attacks where the Whites were strongest. This gave rise to types of activism and functionalism which created awkward problems for the Soviet Union.

Soviet action in South Africa, as in other parts of the non-Caucasian world, was designed primarily to serve the ends of Soviet policy, just as Christianity had been used to serve the ends of Western policy. For this reason, African Nationalism had to be controlled and forced to move in directions which promoted Soviet interests.

The late George Padmore was a West Indian who was for many years a member of the Communist International (Comintern) which formulated policy for and guided International Communism. He subsequently walked out of the Comintern because he realised that the Soviet Union set out to impose a prescribed destiny on the Black world. His is an inside view of communism's functioning in the Black world:

Economically depressed communities and racially oppressed peoples inevitably receive the attention of the Communists. Therefore, we are not surprised that they should have spent considerable effort to win the Negroes to their cause. Yet, sustained and energetic though this endeavour has been, the number of Black converts to the cause of World Communism has been quite incommensurate with the time, money and efforts expended to win them. To a large extent the failure to make a greater impact upon popular Negro opinion has been due to the tactical mistakes and psychological blunders which the Communist Parties of the Western World — America, Britain, France and South Africa — have made in their approach to the dark peoples.

Negroes are keenly aware that they are the most racially oppressed and economically exploited people in the world. They also are very much alive to the fact, demonstrated by the opportunistic and cynical behaviour of the Communists, that the latter's interest in them is dictated by the ever-changing tactics of Soviet foreign policy rather than by altruistic motives. Their politically minded intellectuals know that the oppressed Negro workers and peasants are regarded by the Communists as "revolutionary expendables" in the global struggle of Communism against Western Capitalism. They know that Africans and peoples of African descent are courted primarily to tag on to the White proletariat, and thus to swell the "revolutionary" ranks against the imperialist enemies of the "Soviet Fatherland." This attitude towards the

Negroes is fundamentally part and parcel of the Communist philosophy relating to racial minorities and dependent peoples, and it has
been influenced by the experience of the Russian Bolsheviks in their
struggle for power.[4]

The ends of Soviet policy required that the new nation into which the
Africans had united themselves should be defined in Soviet terms. Abuse
was showered on African refusals to be defined in alien terms. H.J. and
R.E. Simons were insiders in that section of the White community which
functioned as the surrogates of the Soviet Union in South Africa. This is
what they say of the Soviet approach to the leadership of the African
nation:

> The late I.I. Potekhin, a Soviet historian of Africa, argued that they
> (the chiefs in the ANC) were *compradores* (Black agents of foreign
> firms) who controlled the ANC for many years in opposition to the
> progressive intellectuals of the rising national bourgeoisie. It was
> because of the chiefs' influence, he maintained, that Congress rejected
> illegal mass struggle against oppressive racial laws and crawled before
> the authorities. In his opinion, an insoluble contradiction existed be-
> tween the aim of building a nation and the aim of strengthening tribal
> institutions. "An organisation of feudal compradores, such as was the
> ANC at first, cannot be the standard-bearers of a nation." Seme, like
> other right-wing leaders, Potekhin wrote, actually lowered the level of
> national consciousness by teaching Africans to think of themselves as
> junior partners of the White man who had brought peace and goodwill
> to Africa. "Congress never even put the question of national in-
> dependence for the Bantu or of freedom for their country from British
> imperialism."
>
> Potekhin did not adequately examine the process of amalgamating
> scores of formerly independent and often antagonistic ethnic societies
> into a single nation. No Marxist who is familiar with the concept "na-
> tional in form, socialist in content" should be surprised to learn that
> tribalism will wither away only if given free play in a non-tribal
> environment....
>
> The Chiefs were neither "feudal" nor "*compradores.*" Cast in con-
> flicting roles, they defended their people against the colonists and also
> served as minor functionaries of the White bureaucracy.[5]

Potekhin was one of the top Soviet authorities on Africa. He left visible
marks on Soviet policy in Africa. The two Simons, who were White and
were deeply involved in the work of the Marxists in South Africa, tell us
that Potekhin was not properly informed on the situation in the African
community. Coming from known Marxists, this tells us a lot; it tells us,

among other things, that the advice which Potekhin gave to the Soviet government was less informed than it should have been. This advice was one of the bases on which Soviet policy for South Africa was formulated. Basing policy on this ignorance is what we call prescribing destiny for the Africans.

But we should not go too far in our condemnation of Potekhin. His White sources of information on the African people were themselves inadequately informed on developments in South Africa.

With the best will in the world, it is impossible for a White person to have a clear view of the situation on the African side of the colour line. To a lesser extent, it is impossible for the African to have a clear picture of what is in the minds of the Whites. He has some advantages over the Caucasians; he works for them in their homes, farms and factories, goes to schools they have set up for him, and reads, writes and speaks their languages; and he has created a synthesis of cultures based on parts of his tradition and borrowings from the Graeco-Romano-Hebraic experience.

The Whites have no way of having first-hand knowledge of what is going on in the mind of the African. Segregation makes it impossible for them to have any intercourse with the Africans which would inform them on developments on the Black side. This has been the case since at least the establishment of the Union of South Africa in 1910.

The Whites whose books Potekhin had read lived in rigidly segregated White areas, where they were born, grew up and died. The Africans were born, lived and died in their equally segregated areas.

The Whites had one system of education, while the Africans had another. The rhythms which gave colour to and harmonised life in the African and White areas were poles apart. The Whites who managed the Communist Party of South Africa did not, as a rule, speak a single African language.

Except through the police, magistrates, commissioners and other White officials, racial laws and the economy, there was no meaningful communication between Black and White. At every level in parliament, the government, the economy, education and the church, the Whites laid down the law. In this setting the only possible relationship between the African and the White man was the servant-master relationship.

This setting forced the communists to see the Black-White quarrel from White perspectives. They could not be other than contemptuous of African definitions of the "race" problem. They offered solutions based on Caucasian perspectives and when the new nation said these had no relevance in its situation, the communists vilified its leaders, split its political organisations and created their own which sooner or later collapsed. These organisations could not survive because they were based on alien definitions of Africa; and they set out to impose a destiny prescribed by foreigners.

In these conditions, and with the best will in the world, the imposition of White-oriented destinies could not be anything other than attacks on the Collective Will; they could not be other than manoeuvres to effect the ideological deheathenisation of the African.

The Christian missionaries had used deheathenisation to convert the African to their religion and had produced the Separatist Churches. The capitalists and colonialists had imposed their lifestyle and had brought African Nationalism into being. The White racists had forced the Africans to unite themselves into a monolith. The communists were prescribing destiny for the Black man and were in that way moving him in a straight line to African Maoism.

Moscow's attempts to prescribe destiny for the Black South Africans assumed the form of an attack on the Collective Will and the Sudic evaluation of the person. The rigid insistence on ideological conformity was alien to the Sudic temperament. Preaching class conflict disorganised the African monolith and weakened it for the task of challenging the White power-structure. The rejection of the Bloemfontein Ideal of Nationhood and its substitution with a blueprint drawn up by the Whites was precisely what apartheid had set out to do when J.B.M. Hertzog, the father of Afrikaner nationalism, went to De Wildt in December, 1912, to lay down the principles on which apartheid operates today.

Neither Moscow's White surrogates in South Africa nor Potekhin prescribed destiny because they were Caucasians; they did this because they were the products of a civilisation based on a pessimistic and devaluative attitude to the person.

Soviet Socialism set out to effect the ideological homogenisation of the human race; it was not scientific enough to recognise the simultaneous legitimacy of different cultural self-definitions. At this level, its performance was not different from apartheid's. This created obvious problems for the White communists. When the Black Consciousness Movement came into being after Sharpeville, the militant Medialists took the position that all Whites were similarly motivated and for this reason, co-operation with them was out of the question. In his now famous address to the Cape Town University's Abe Bailey Institute of Interracial Studies in January, 1971, Steve Biko made it clear that he had no time for:

the liberal establishment, including the leftist groups. The major mistake the Black world ever made was to assume that whoever opposed apartheid was an ally....

His answer to the White consensus on prescribing destiny for the Africans was:

● to go alone and to evolve a philosophy based on and directed by Blacks....

- [a] policy of no involvement with the White world....

- rejection of the principle of unholy alliances between Blacks and Whites....

- [the realisation] that a lot of good can be derived from specific exclusion of Whites from Black institutions.

In the above, Biko welded into a single attitude and articulated the rejections of White values by the Africans, Coloureds and Asians whom the Whites had rejected in different ways. The Whites had sown the wind and were reaping the hurricane.

The counter-rejection had important implications for South Africa; it combined with the temper of the dispossessed to provide the inflammable material which could transform the coming revolution into a race war.

Its real importance, for purposes of the present discussion, was that it was part of the Black World's Collective Response to the punishment by the Whites of the African for being the child of his particular parents. This punishment had led to the decision by the Rome Conference of Black Writers and Artists to search for universal dimensions in African cultures, to a commitment to the same search by the All-Africa Church Conference in Nairobi, to the All-African Student Union's stand on Africanism and to Nigerian President Olusegun Obasanjo's declaration of war on teleguidance at the Khartoum summit conference of the OAU in 1978.

In 1967, Black delegates from all over the United States had met in Newark, New Jersey, to discuss Black Power. In the following resolution, they expressed their commitment to the Collective Response in these terms:

Whereas the Black people in America have been systematically oppressed by their White fellow countrymen,

Whereas there is little prospect that this oppression can be terminated, peacefully, or otherwise, within the foreseeable future

Whereas the Black people do not wish to be absorbed into the larger White community

Whereas the Black people in America find that their interests are in contradiction with those of White America

Whereas the Black people in America are psychologically handicapped by virtue of their having no national homeland

Whereas the physical, moral, ethical, and esthetic standards of White American society are not those of Black society and indeed do violence to the self-image of the Black man

Whereas Black people were among the earliest immigrants to America, having been ruthlessly separated from their fatherland, and have made a major contribution to America's development, most of this contribution having been uncompensated, and

Recognizing that efforts are already well advanced for the convening of a Constitutional Convention for the purpose of revising the Constitution of the U.S. for the first time since America's inception, then

Be it resolved that the Black Power Conference initiate a national dialogue on the desirability of partitioning the U.S. into two separate and independent nations, one to be a homeland for White and the other to be a homeland for Black Americans.[6]

Biko became one of the heroes of the Black Consciousness Movement because of his uncompromising commitment to non-collaboration. He wanted the African to go it alone and to have his own system of values; he demanded that his world should not be involved with the White world and rejected Black-White alliances and stood for the policy of keeping Whites out of Black universities, etc. In going to these extremes, he rejected the destiny prescribed by the Whites; he described the chasm White domination had created between the Africans and the Caucasians; he announced that the African counter-rejection was a determinant of policy among those for whom he spoke.

White "interpreters" of the African experience give little or no attention to the counter-rejection as a determinant of African policies. Because it is one of the influences given the generic name of fundamentals of conflict, the counter-rejection needs to be seen against different White attempts to prescribe destiny for the Black people on the political plane.

BACKGROUND TO REJECTION OF WHITES

From the beginnings of the Communist Party racism had affected its attitudes to the African in the main and to the Coloured to a lesser extent. The Simonses have this to say on the White consensus on race discrimination:

For all their Hyde Park oratory, the socialists failed the sovereign test of political sincerity. They appealed for Coloured votes but were no more prepared than liberal or racist parties to nominate a Coloured candidate in municipal or parliamentary elections.

—p. 140

This was during the first decade of the twentieth century. Some of the socialists who lacked "political sincerity" subsequently banded together and formed the Communist Party in 1921.

At a mixed meeting in January, 1921, to prepare ground for the formation of South Africa's Communist Party, the hundred delegates who attended

decided, by forty votes to twenty-nine, that a "Communist Party can at no time identify itself with any nationalist or other bourgeois party, and cannot support its platform." And further, they determined, there could be no unity with persons who refused to accept the principles of the Third International. Unity would be worthwhile only if it took the form of a strongly disciplined, centralized party affiliated to the C.I. (Communist International).

—p. 260

Ivon Jones and Sam Barlin were the South African Party's delegates to the third congress of the Communist International. Both were White and got into trouble for not having included an African delegate. The Simonses (p. 263) make these comments on Jones' experiences:

Like many after him, he found that the colour of his skin, which gave him entry into the racial elite, was something of a handicap among radicals abroad. "Why aren't you Black?" he was asked. He confessed to feeling "quite apologetic about our colour." South African delegations should include Africans, but it would be a mistake to exclude Whites. "The African revolution would be led by White workers." Yet his own analysis might have led him to doubt the proposition.

Jones was thinking of a campaign for the ideological deheathenisation of the Africans. He appealed to International Communism for reinforcements (p. 265):

"A few missionaries, revolutionists who need a spell of sunshine, would be very welcome."

The language in which the rejection of co-operation with "any nationalist" party was couched was a virtual declaration of war on the ANC — an announcement that the Whites in the Communist Party would work with African political organisations only on their terms. This was precisely the position Afrikaner nationalism was taking. In the view of African intellectuals, the position taken by the White communists indicated that the Caucasians were ganging up against the African on every plane to prescribe destiny for him.

This conclusion was to affect profoundly the relations between African Nationalists and the Soviet Union. The African Nationalists viewed their fight with the united front of White monoliths as a life-and-death struggle. If Whites who sought to identify themselves with the Africans existed at all, they should work with the Black race on its terms and not infiltrate the Black community either to disorganise the Black monolith or to fix goals for it.

The Simonses were devoted Marxists, as any committed South African who worked in the Republic between the 1940s and the 1960s knows. But unlike other Marxists they did not regard the Communist Party of South Africa as having a monopoly on virtue. They reported history as fairly as they could from their particular position. They noted that African Nationalists did not want any White man to prescribe destiny for them. Mahabane's was one of the consistently strong voices Africans raised against White domination. I myself heard it during the greater part of the forty years that I was in the forefront of our struggle. Mahabane addressed the annual conference of the Cape ANC in May, 1920:

> All white party leaders, he said, from Abraham Fischer to Smuts, were determined to keep Africans and Coloureds out of the parliament of the White plutocrats. Yet Africans were the rightful owners of the land, and would never consent to the status of bondsmen. The Whites were foreign fortune-seekers, who had seized supreme political power with Britain's aid, and used it to entrench themselves in the state, church, civil service and economy.
>
> — pp 250-51

But Moscow was determined to cast African attitudes to White domination in South Africa in its own moulds. Let another insider in the Communist Party give us an inside view of the situation among the ranks of Soviet surrogates. Eddie Roux was one of the very few Afrikaners who crossed the ethnic line on the White side and identified himself with communism, which Afrikaner nationalism regarded as one of its mortal foes. In *Time Longer Than Rope*, he tells us that:

> ...the party had by now become increasingly Black in composition. Many of the country branches were organised by Native communists. Only occasionally a White communist would come to address a meeting....
>
> In the ranks of the party the best Bantu communists always were those who had not been spoilt by serving an apprenticeship in the Congress

(ANC) or with the ICU. The best of all were rank and file Bantu members, often semi-literate, who received their education through the party and had never been in any other organisation.[7]
— pp. 214, 215

The uneducated were easy victims. In any nation, policy was not made by shepherds and street sweepers. The missionaries had taken advantage of the African peoples' ignorance of the White man's ways to prescribe destiny for the Black people all over South Africa. The communists were taking advantage of the ignorance of the uneducated to impose another destiny on the Africans. Roux continues:

The Communist Party by now numbered among its members many Africans whose political knowledge and understanding was small. It began to seem that the Party might be swamped by members who had little or no knowledge of Marxist principles and theory. The suggestion came from Moscow that the Party should remain a small and select body of trained revolutionaries working through a larger mass body. In this way, the communists would be enabled to preserve the purity of their doctrine while at the same time, through the larger organisation, giving a clear lead to the masses on all suggestions.

This was the beginning of a long and bitter conflict between African Nationalism and communism that eventually split the ANC on the homefront and, later, in exile. In 1924, Kadalie's ICU established a branch in Johannesburg, which developed into the headquarters of this workers' movement. The communists initially worked closely with the ICU, to win converts and not to reinforce this wing of African Nationalism. By 1926, Kadalie had had enough of their disruptive proselytism; he kicked them out of the ICU. The communists turned to the ANC. Let Roux continue from here:

It happened that this new suggestion from Moscow which was tantamount to an order came at a time when Bunting (another White communist) while in Tembuland (Transkei) had already tentatively founded an organisation called the League of Native Rights, a "designedly innocuous organisation," he called it, "with the preservation of the Native franchise and universal free education as the prime objectives," the Communist Party's interest in the scheme not being advertised but not necessarily concealed.

To the communists in Johannesburg the idea seemed good and they set about founding a new mass organisation to be called League of African Rights. It was inaugurated by a public meeting in Inchcape Hall, Johannesburg. The League called upon all to join who were interested in the struggle of Black men for freedom in Africa. It drew up a "petition of rights" with demands for the abolition of the pass laws and land laws, extension of the vote and free education for the Bantu....It took for its slogan *"Mayibuy' i Afrika"* (Let Afrika Return), and for its flag a black, red and green emblem. The song of *"Mayibuye"* was sung to the tune of Clementine. It was immediately joined by J.T. Gumede, of the ANC, who was made president, and by Doyle Modiakgotla, of the Ballinger ICU, who became vice chairman. The secretaryship was held by the communists Albert Nzula and Edward Roux (the author). Charles Baker was Treasurer.

The new organisation seemed well and truly launched according to Moscow specifications and the needs of the situation. The Communist Party, while duly represented in the leadership, was not conspicuous there.

But it seemed that this was not at all what Moscow had desired. The new L.A.R. was a success from the start. Political fever among Africans was still running high....

In the midst of it all a telegram from Moscow ordered the immediate dissolution of the League. The communists were dumbfounded, for they had acted, as they thought, on instructions from Moscow. But, good Leninists, they obeyed orders....

This incident calls for an explanation because it draws in the sharpest possible outlines the Soviet Union's dilemma in South Africa. The surrogates of Moscow were mainly White. As pointed out, these saw the "race" problem through perspectives developed in the White environment in South Africa. These perspectives differed from those in the locations of Johannesburg; they were a poorly informed response to a crisis which was shaking the ANC to its foundations.

The oppressed peoples of the world met in conference in Brussels in 1927 to consider plans for the co-ordination of their struggles against colonialism and imperialism. The decision to convene the conference had been taken by the Colonial Presidium of the Comintern at the urging of representatives of the Communist Party of the Soviet Union serving the Presidium. The Soviet Party regarded the convention of such a conference as a declaration of solidarity with the oppressed.

J.T. Gumede, the President of the ANC, represented his organisation at the Brussels conference. From there, he visited parts of the Soviet Union and returned to South Africa full of praise for the Soviet system. This plunged the ANC into a crisis; they saw in Gumede's championing of the communist cause a betrayal of the African people and an acceptance of the prescribed destiny. Explosion-point was reached when the nineteenth annual conference of the ANC met in Bloemfontein in 1930. The communist wing of the ANC was, this time, led by a White person, S.

Malkenson, who was given permission to attend the conference.

Umteteli waBantu (May 3, 1930) says that in his presidential address, Gumede started by giving his impressions of the Soviet Union:

> Referring to Soviet Russia, Mr. Gumede said his sympathies were with the peasant workers of Russia, and he urged Congress to consider the matter of defending them against the onslaught of the enemies of the oppressed peoples of the world. Everywhere the oppressed peoples were being inspired by that ideal of emancipation which found expression in the Russian revolution.
>
> Vol. I, Doc. 48i

Against the background given by the Communist Party's traditional hostility to African Nationalism, a hostility which had forced Kadalie to expel them from the ICU, Gumede's identification with a power which, acting through its White surrogates, prescribed destiny for the Africans, provoked negative reactions. Gumede proceeded:

> We have now to rely on our own strength, on the strength of the revolutionary masses of White workers the world over with whom we must join forces. We have to demand our equal economic, social and political rights. That cannot be expressed more clearly than to demand a South African Native Republic, with equal rights for all, but free from all foreign and local domination.
>
> Vol. I, Doc. 48i

The address raised a storm of protest and made it clear that Gumede's new position was not acceptable to the African Nationalists. To drive their point home, the delegates threw him out of office and elected Dr. Pixley ka Isaka Seme president of the ANC.

Malkenson, who requested that he should be allowed to speak during the storm, said he wanted to state the case of the communists. *Umteteli* reports that he said:

> no longer would the fight be a secret within the Congress; it would become a struggle outside Congress; and the militant masses would decide the issue.

> Dr. Seme on behalf of the new Executive welcomed this declaration of war....

To mend Gumede's shattered image as a leader, the communists formed the League for African Rights and elected him its first (and last) president. Apparently, the trick did not serve the ends of Soviet policy and Moscow promptly ordered the dissolution of the League.

Let us go back to Malkenson's speech, which drew the lines of conflict in ways nobody could mistake. Moscow's surrogates had reached the point where they felt they should come out in the open to smash both the Collective Will and the Ideal of Nationhood which it translated into action.

But the communists had one fundamental handicap: they were White. They could not come out openly and fight African Nationalism; they had to have Black surrogates whom they could manipulate to shatter the Collective Will and destroy the Ideal of Nationhood.

As the crisis in South Africa deepened and the area of freedom widened in the Third World, Moscow's policy of working through White surrogates who operated through Black surrogates ran into trouble. The emergence of non-Caucasian states after World War II gave the Black people a choice of allies.

Freedom was coming to Africa. Independence on the continent would reinforce the Nationalists. Time ceased to be the ally of the Soviet Union. The surrogates formed the Congress Alliance which included the ANC (which had come under communist control), the South African Indian Congress, the Congress of Democrats (White), the South African Coloured Peoples Organisation and the South African Congress of Trade Unions. The Alliance immediately transformed the ANC, which represented the majority, into a minority in the policy making bodies of the Alliance.

Thus reinforced, the surrogates called a "conference" which turned out to be a mass rally in Kliptown, near Johannesburg, on June 26, 1955. This rally adopted the Freedom Charter as a declaration of policy for the peoples of the Alliance. The document has been discussed so extensively in the last two decades we shall not consider its clauses here. Of interest to us are African Nationalist reactions.

The Freedom Charter purported to be an ideal of nationhood, like the Black Republic Gumede advocated in his pro-Soviet speech. What was remarkable about it was not so much what it said as what it did not say. It did not say a single word about the Bloemfontein Ideal of Nationhood. On the contrary, it spoke of "guarantees for national rights" when these rights were the issue on which Black and White were quarrelling.

The silence was a tactical rejection of the Bloemfontein Ideal of Nationhood. The Nationalists had no choice; they had to walk out of the ANC, when Chief Albert John Luthuli accepted the Freedom Charter as a statement of ANC policy, and formed the Pan-Africanist Congress which wasted little time in establishing contact with Free Africa.

The PAC adhered to the Bloemfontein Ideal of Nationhood while the ANC upheld the Freedom Charter. The communists had split the ANC under Luthuli as they did under Gumede.

Final victory in Moscow's bid to have complete control of the ANC came in 1969 when the ANC met in exile in Morogoro, Tanzania, and decided to abandon its African identity and admit White and other members. That created a crisis which led to the expulsion of an influential bloc of Black Congressmen in the 1970s.

On the homefront the use of Caucasian tactics in an environment where they had no relevance led from one defeat of communist strategy against apartheid to another until the communist underground cells were to a large extent wiped out.

This point deserves attention. The Freedom Charter confronted the Africans with a fundamental challenge which called for a fundamental answer. The communists predicted, rightly, that African Nationalism would sooner or later collide head-on with Afrikaner nationalism and that this would create a vacuum in White thinking on the future of South Africa. From this it proceeded to conclude, wrongly, that a concept of nationhood based on Graeco-Romano-Hebraic attitudes to the person as propounded by Karl Marx would fill the void.

The conclusion ignored the problems which Christianity had created for itself in the African community when it prescribed destiny for the Black people. Its rejection of the Sudic attitude to the person had split the Christian church and produced the Separatist Movement.

The nation born in Bloemfontein on January 8, 1912, had given itself an identity based, first, on the Sudic attitude to the person and, second, on the recognition of the simultaneous legitimacy of different cultural self-definitions and economic or political experiences. The destiny of this nation was to build "a new and unique civilization" in order to fill the vacuum.

The Separatist Movement and the Bloemfontein Ideal of Nationhood were massive rejections of any type of prescribed destiny. Moscow and its surrogates made a wrong reading of the Sudic mind when they thought they could impose their brand of prescribed destiny. The African's answer to the error was to split the ANC and form the PAC.

The pattern of rejecting the prescribed destiny is too important a feature of African behaviour after conquest to be ignored. This pattern, however, is merely a vehicle, an operational aspect of a fundamental rejection—the rejection of the Caucasian attitude to the person and the destiny it prescribes for the African.

Wherever the African's rejection of the alien philosophy—alien because it produced a morality which has one meaning in the relations between White and White and an altogether different one in dealings between Black and White—took place, it created an ideological void which the African filled with a synthesis of Sudic and Caucasian outlooks.

Communism, like Christianity, rejects the African's right to develop this synthesis. As Potekhin puts it, there is no need for the synthesis when "scientific socialism" has been developed and tested to answer the African's problems.

The weakness in this approach is that communism was developed and tested in conditions which differ in important essentials from those which exist in Africa. It is a product of Graeco-Romano-Hebraic and not Sudic civilisation. Marxism has yet to take note of this difference.

The problem we are dealing with here goes beyond class or race conflict; it is a collision between the psychology of creating "a new and unique civilization" and the psychology of prescribing destiny for the African. Marxism, capitalism, Christianity and apartheid are all habituated to prescribing destiny. The Freedom Charter expressed this habituation.

In the view of the Sudic African, the common commitment is rooted in what the Caucasian attitude to the person regards as conflict between the inadequacy of the known and the infinity of reality. What is known has limitations; the latter give the human race the character of a species born in weakness. Infinite reality is limitless; its boundlessness defines the person's weakness.

The Sudic Ideal rejects the theory of inherent weakness and regards the distance between what is known and the infinity of reality as a challenge. Perpetual evolution is the answer to this challenge. The destiny of the person is forever to march into the future. To do this, he must define himself in terms which enable him to respond to the challenge of his nature.

After the split on the Freedom Charter the leaders of the anti-apartheid homelands met in Umtata where they filled the vacuum created in African thinking by the split in the ANC, with the ideal of re-unifying the Africans in the Federal Union of the Autonomous States of Southern Africa.

Their silence on the Freedom Charter arose from the fact that this document reduced the Africans to the status of a people who accepted the prescribed destiny.

On one plane, the Umtata commitment to the ideal of re-unifying those whom apartheid divided was a rejection of the prescribed destiny. On the other, it was a movement of the Sudic mind to its Ideal of Nationhood; it was the assertion of Sudic leadership initiatives to fill the vacuum created by the Freedom Charter.

This gives perspective to developments in the African community inside South Africa at the moment. This perspective is one of the vehicles by which some of the tragedies now being enacted in Rhodesia could be avoided.

A little more light on this perspective will help. In the developments listed above we see the translation into experience of the psychology of creating "a new and unique civilization." This psychology is the product of the synthesis, of the *common controlling idea* as tested by conquest and challenged by proletariatisation.

The synthesis is an eclectic inspiration; it has had to make graftings from the West and the East. In spite of this, it remains a uniquely African creation; it remains the product of the African experience in the rural reserves and the urban locations. Above all, it is a determinant of African policy.

In the conditions created by apartheid the White man has no way of dealing with the African as an equal and, therefore, of understanding the psychology under discussion. He created for himself a prison of the mind when he committed himself to segregation. The price he is paying today is that he and the African are moving in opposite directions.

One result of this is that virtually every book written by Whites in South Africa or in the West or in the Soviet Bloc on the "race" question tends to say the same thing in different words. All focus on the operational aspects of apartheid because the authors have not done their homework on the fundamentals of conflict. Largely as a result, the international community concentrates on the operational aspects of White rule and, by doing this, allows itself to run in endless circles while the crisis drifts relentlessly towards predictable disaster.

Paying too much attention to how apartheid functions is an integral part of the "race" problem. This does not mean that the African must build his own prison of the mind and shut himself inside it. On the contrary, the eclectic nature of the synthesis and the Sudic evaluation of the person demand that he must open up to the major components of his environment—to Africa, the West, the Soviet Bloc and the rest of the world. He must inform himself on the Afrikaner's *survival problem,* develop a relevant philosophy for acquiring and controlling the technology of the West and have a continuing dialogue with the Soviet Bloc on the basic materialism of Sudic teachings on the consubstantiality of all things. He must, in short, have a continuing intercivilisational dialogue on the systematisation of the methods by which to present the Sudic Ideal's positive and universally valid attitude to the person. Finally, he must realise that if he must talk to the West and the Marxist World, he must also develop a way for talking to the Afrikaner monolith. The logic of the Sudic attitude to the person demands that he should do this even when the other side is arming itself against him. He must talk, among other things, to make his war aims known.

This logic does not say he must talk and move events to a political solution only; it says he must use political weapons where these place him in a strong position and not hesitate to use military arguments where these stand better chances of producing desired results. This logic combines with both the element of variability in the Afrikaner's hostility to race equality and the imperatives of monolithal survival to suggest that emphasis on the fundamentals of conflict might be the only shortcut to an African-Afrikaner consensus on final goals in a quarrel complicated by monolithal rivalries.

We have digressed from the sweep of apartheid's offensives against African Nationalism in order to set the spotlight on dimensions of the vacuum which deserve more attention than they receive. We must now return to our main theme. We stopped before discussing the fate of the militant wing of African Nationalism. This section was wiped out. But

African Nationalism's bicipitous mind promptly filled the vacuum thus formed with Chief Gatsha Buthelezi's National Cultural Liberation Movement. By the middle of 1978, this Movement had 150,000 paid-up members in no less than 956 branches. In any language, this was power.

This called for a fundamental recasting of attitudes to the dispositions of power inside South Africa. Ben Turok, a former member of the White Congress of Democrats and a leading theoretician of the South African Left in exile, weighed the results of communist strategy from the late 1940s and came to conclusions some of which are listed below. Turok's testimony is important because he spent nearly all his adult life, if not all of it, in South Africa building Marxist power and because he was on the inside of things in the Marxist movement. In 1974 he analysed the performance of the communist movement since the 1940s and published his thoughts in Canada under the title: *Strategic Problems in South Africa's Liberation Struggle: A Critical Analysis.*[8] His conclusions included:

> At the turn of the '60s Black Africa was rapidly gaining independence from direct colonial rule but their freedom was won without violence.
>
> —p. 43

This statement was, at first reading, not a correct representation of the historical position. On November 17, 1952, Superintendent K.R.T. Goodale, an acting superintendent of the Kenya Criminal Investigation Department, Special Branch, had "applied for warrants to arrest Jomo Kenyatta and five others on charges of membership and management of Mau Mau."[9] The Mau Mau had been a nationalistic revolt; it had used violence to prepare ground for the independence of Kenya and had succeeded in its objective.

But then the communist movement did not recognise the legitimacy of nationalist struggles. In spite of this, one hesitates to think that Turok might not have been aware of what had happened in Kenya, particularly because, like the war the Ethiopians fought against Mussolini, Mau Mau was given muffled cheers by the Black South African Nationalists; muffled because open declarations of solidarity would have given the South African police cause for action when the Africans were busy with preparations for the resistance movement.

In South Africa, it is a crime even to cheer the victories of African struggles for freedom. A group of young people met in Durban to congratulate Frelimo publicly for having won freedom for Mozambique. Some of their leaders are in jail today.

Turok continues:

> It can be seen that the sweep of sabotage was considerable. It was used in town and country and by all the liberation movements. Yet it failed to ignite the prairie fire as many had hoped.
>
> —p. 45

162

Having talked of fascism for a decade and more, the movements were nevertheless caught by surprise when the police behaved like fascists. Under torture, many victims found to their regret that they knew too much and that the police knew what they knew.

—p.45

Looked at as a single phase of the struggle it must be said that the sabotage campaign was abortive.

—p. 45

Perhaps the over-sophisticated methods used in sabotage were themselves the consequence of the political outlook of the movement.

—p. 46

The last paragraph above gets to the heart of the communist dilemma. The prescription of destiny demanded that "over-sophisticated methods" should be used in a community which had no knowledge of these methods and which had not been prepared for their use.

Toward the end of the 1950s, underground cells had to face the choice between sophisticated and unsophisticated methods. Sophisticated methods were largely irrelevant. A militant asked how one could burn vast sugarcane fields along the coast without getting caught. He went to an American, because I did not know how to do this. He took a matchbox, lit a cigarette, shoved the unlit end of the cigarette between the phosphorised heads of the matchsticks and the inner box and placed the whole on the cement floor. After ten to fifteen minutes the whole exploded into a burst of flame. The ten to fifteen minutes would give the arsonist enough time to escape.

Militants would take a late night train to the north or south coast with about a dozen match-boxes and cigarettes and would light the latter and throw them into the sugarcane fields at convenient intervals. To the best of my knowledge, not one was ever caught. But sugarcane fields were set on fire in the north and south coasts of Natal.

The point I am stressing here is that the White man's policy of segregation was so thorough in keeping vital information from the Africans—we were not allowed access to public libraries—that they did not know how to burn a sugarcane field; they had to go to a White man even for this.

In the situation which Turok is discussing, the communists had all the opportunity to develop arson and sabotage techniques to teach to the Black community. They did not because they always feared to arm African Nationalism lest it captured power on its own steam and gave to freedom its own meaning. Moscow did not want this to happen; it did not happen where White policy set out to manipulate the African's struggle through a relay of surrogates.

Turok proceeds:

In retrospect, it seems that if sabotage had not been able to establish itself as a continuing form of struggle because the method was too advanced and the organisation inadequate, then Operation Mayibuye (the Sabotage Campaign) was an even more dubious proposition. In a short time it led to the decimation of the movement. . . . once the main leadership was arrested at Rivonia in 1963, the Plan collapsed.
—pp. 48, 49

Many leaders and hundreds of the best cadres had been sent out of the country for training, and this seriously weakened the organisation at home. Those who remained were either jailed or immobilised. A serious miscalculation was the effectiveness of torture in extracting information leading to the uncovering of a sector of activists. As a result of arrests and the disclosures during prolonged interrogation, the underground was wiped out, and even the heroic effort of top cadres like Wilton Mkwayi, who returned after training abroad, were insufficient to renew the struggle. There is an important lesson here. There can be no move towards the attack until a line of defense and retreat has been prepared.
—p. 49

Certainly in the South African case, the problem of returning trained guerrillas from abroad and then keeping the action going is a formidable one. How Operation Mayibuye meant to overcome this is not known, but the fact that for some ten years a significant number of guerrillas have not been able to return is an indication that the proposal was unrealistic from the start.
—p. 50

The answer lies in the development of a correct political line to which the mass of the people can respond readily and in the elaboration of a strategy and tactics to match. Progress in this area has been rather slow in coming over the past decade.
—p. 51

The most recent pronouncements of the external movement, however, indicate that the emphasis is once again moving away from immediate armed struggle and there is greater stress on rebuilding political structures at home. The urgent need seems to be for political organizers who can return home and take root among the masses rather in the way this was done in the early days by Cabral in Guinea.
—p. 53

The complexity of the structure of the African people, together with the particular forms that oppression and exploitation take on in South

Africa, makes an outright socialist program unrealistic at this stage. No section of the movement has urged this in the past and while some groups in exile like PAC and the Communist Party have periodically turned to Marxist phraseology, all have agreed that the primary goal at present is the achievement of national liberation. . . .
—p. 56

Given the favourable circumstances there is good reason to predict that a Black liberation struggle will produce a progressive government.... But no matter how auspicious may be the future of socialism, the national aspect of the liberation struggle remains primary, with the African people its determining component. If African demands are to be in the forefront for political reasons, this is no less important strategically.
—p. 57

In the Bantustan areas the potential of African power is obvious. While the official leaders spar with government over the degree of autonomy they have, real resistance will grow among the mass of impoverished Africans which will either force the official leaders into greater militancy or bring them under popular attack.
—p. 57

We have come a long way from the years when the communists dragged in mud the names of African leaders; when Malkenson could stand up in a Nationalist conference and declare open war on African Nationalism in the name of communism; when the communists could produce the Freedom Charter to tell the Africans what sort of a nation they should be; when vicious attacks were made on Chief Gatsha Buthelezi for building a political base in the conditions demanded by the peculiar situation of the Africans. Now some theoreticians of the Marxist movement — which is a larger entity than the South African Communist Party — can acknowledge publicly that the "potential of African power is obvious" in the Bantustan areas. It was precisely this obviousness which forced men like Buthelezi and others committed to the eventual formation of the Federal Union of the Autonomous States of Southern Africa to "collaborate" in operating the segregated homelands institutions.

It might be premature to speak of a dialogue between the Soviet Union and African Nationalism in South Africa on a solution which will produce the desired results in the peculiar situation of the Africans in this country. Turok's critique serves the useful purpose of defining areas where the leaders of African Nationalism inside South Africa and the Soviet Union might explore the possibilities of a consensus on a political settlement. Clarity on the internal dispositions of Black and White power suggest that the chances of moving faster to majority rule are greater if all involved think in terms of a political settlement rather than of a military solution.

For what is at stake in South Africa is, as Turok rightly points out, power — who holds it and to what purposes he uses it. If the Soviet Union continues its war against African Nationalism and encourages attacks on the functionalist leaders, it would create conditions that would guarantee the expulsion of the Whites from South Africa. Apartheid has already given the Africans a very good reason for the expulsion of the Whites.

No African can stop the Whites if they are determined to create conditions that guarantee their expulsion. The wisest of them are already leaving the country in droves. The Brisbane correspondent of the Johannesburg *Star* (international edition, July 22, 1978) made this report on emigrants to Australia:

> White South Africans and Rhodesians are arriving in Australia for permanent settlement at the rate of 4,000 a year. Most of them are said to have changed countries because of racial tension.

For three hundred years and more, the Whites have made systematic efforts to impose their will on the African people. Reverend Z. R. Mahabane always warned that the day would come when the Africans would draw the line and say: "Thus far, Whiteman, and no farther!" That day came on June 16, 1978, when the students took a stand from which no guns would move them for nearly two years. Their stand established the relativity of White power, just as the defeats Turok describes with so much authority show that there are limitations to communist power in fixing final goals for the Africans.

The problem in the conflict between Black and White centres on conflicting attitudes to the person. Until it is seen in this light, before the Soviet Union and the West realise that accommodation with the African is possible only on the basis of reconciled attitudes to the person, the Africans will remain committed to the Evolving Revolt, which rises stronger from each defeat. Because it concerns itself with the person first, where the West and the Soviet Union concern themselves with material possessions first and the person afterwards, the African philosophy will in the end crush Western and Soviet materialism.

That it has the potential to do this has been demonstrated by the development of the Evolving Revolt in the sixty-six years since 1912 and by the policy of isolating the Whites which the new nation launched when it sent a delegation to the Versailles Peace Conference in 1919.

If the Soviet Union continues to disorganise the African monolith's march to its freely chosen goal, it will create conditions which will make it impossible for the Soviet Caucasians to set foot in South Africa, just as apartheid's blunders almost guarantee the expulsion of the White South Africans.

The expulsion of the latter is no problem. As the Kenyan experience shows, when the dust settles down after the overthrow of apartheid, droves of Whites from other countries will flock to South Africa with their skills and capital. They will be welcome because they will have entered South Africa on terms laid down by the African people.

COMMON ERRORS

From what has been written above, it will be seen that both apartheid and the Soviet Union seek to prescribe destiny for the Africans; both adopt rigidly ideological positions; both have declared war on the Bloemfontein Ideal of Nationhood and the Collective Will and, in the final analysis, both move events toward the establishment of minority rule.

It would be a misreading of the nature of the forces which determine apartheid's racial policy and the goals of Soviet foreign policy to say that race explains the identical attitudes to the Bloemfontein Ideal and the Collective Will. The root and fount of the similarity of the positions taken by Pretoria and Moscow is the Graeco-Romano-Hebraic attitude to the person.

This attitude ignores what the Africans regard as the fundamentals of the conflict — the minds at war, the depth of the commitment to united nationhood and federalism to accommodate different cultural self-definitions, and the Collective Will — and attaches maximum importance to residential segregation, the pass laws, the differential wage, influx control, etc., which, while they are real evils, are only vehicles in a collision which involves important fundamentals.

Both refuse to face the problems posed by conflicting attitudes to the person in a racially mixed society; both prescribe destiny. Pretoria offers the Africans vassalage and toy independence, toy flags, toy parliaments and toy governments in unviable mini-states.

Moscow prescribes destiny by defining the quarrel between Black and White as a class struggle when each monolith is a hermetically sealed system which has within itself all its classes, when the Afrikaner worker is the bitterest foe of the African worker. Moscow also lays down the law by financing and manipulating Black Communist Nominalists to undermine the Bloemfontein Ideal, boost the Freedom Charter, shatter the Collective Will and raise the spectre of Black racism.

Black racism certainly does exist in South Africa, where it is as evil a phenomenon as it has been everywhere. But the way to combat it is not to split the African people; it is not to prescribe destiny for them; it is to let them "do their thing" and give them support on the basis that they remain free to develop their own solutions to the "race" quarrel.

While there are striking similarities in the involvement of the apartheid regime and Moscow in the African's struggle, there also are fundamental differences. Apartheid and Soviet policy serve the ends of conflicting power-structures. Pretoria offers political bread crumbs in the rural areas which are not as easy to control as the urban locations where every person is under constant police vigilance. The South African version of indirect rule in the rural areas was originally designed to enable co-operative chiefs to keep their people in tow.

In the South African setting, however, there had to be heavy bribes for the chiefs to remain loyal as a group. And even then, co-operation was more forth-coming from illiterate chiefs. But the complex laws imposed by apartheid could not be understood or administered by illiterate chiefs. The White power-structure established an exclusive school for the sons of chiefs where policy taught them how best to serve the ends of White policy.

But, in the South African setting again, to educate a person is to make him a potential revolutionary. The educated chief became a political Nominalist and evolved from this toward becoming an African Nationalist. This does not happen to every chief, as the case of Chief Charles Hlengwa of Southern Natal shows. At the same time it develops a nationalistic mood which the interested reader need go no farther than the minutes of the Zulu "Legislative" Assembly to detect.

That some of the homelands administrations have become political bases for African Nationalism could very well result in South Africa's revolution being led, at least initially, from the rural areas. The White liberal establishment in the West, as in South Africa, has not as yet faced the implications of this prospect. Free Africa, too, has not faced it.

Moscow had its eye on the extensive proletariatisation going on in the urban locations. Here was ready-made material for the Soviet type of revolution. Every text book defined the location people as a working class. True, they were not as advanced as their opposites in Europe. But they were workers. The books said conflict was the destiny of the workers and bourgeoisie in the location.

This approach, however, was irrelevant in the location for two reasons: Strictly speaking the African community does not have a bourgeois or capitalist class in the European sense. While individuals here and there might have enough money to live above the bulk of their people, as a rule they do not own land; they cannot, as a rule again, buy stock in White companies and, generally, cannot own land in the locations, to say nothing of the White areas.

What money does for these people is to enable them to live a little more comfortably in the locations, where the pass laws and race humiliation apply to the millionaire and grave-digger with equal force. Both are punished for being Africans; the logic of the punishment forces them to see in the monolith their only guarantee of freedom.

To preach class conflict in this setting is to create chaos inside the monolith; it is to create the conditions which apartheid establishes through its policy of Ethnic Grouping.

Soviet policy concentrates on the urban areas where the surrogates operate in the main—yes, under extremely difficult conditions—in the locations in the expectation that the revolution will come from the urban areas. The Black urban worker is most certainly in a stronger position than his prototype in Rhodesia; South Africa is incomparably more highly industrialised than its neighbour across the Limpopo. This gives the urban locations a real potential to paralyse the South African economy with a general strike.

But this potential can be translated into political realities not by emphasising class conflict, but by reinforcing the Collective Will in the locations. In the view of the vast majority of urban and rural Africans race discrimination is the first evil that must be crushed.

The African population will have its mind on the race issue as long as there is race discrimination in South Africa. In this setting, the majority of the Africans will think in terms of a war of minds and not a war of classes.

The fundamental message which the African people are sending to the White world is that Caucasian civilisation rejects them by dispossessing them (as apartheid does), by exploiting them (as Western investors do), and by prescribing destiny for them and stabbing them in the back in their struggle for freedom (as the surrogates of the Soviet Union are doing).

The next chapter describes how the Africans see their struggle; it shows the difference between the African perspective and the White perspective and sheds light on why apartheid and Marxist initiatives generally evoke negative responses from the mass of the Black people in the urban and rural areas. The point which has to be faced in South Africa is that misreading the African experience, as the Afrikaner monolith clearly does, and prescribing destiny, as the Soviet Union has been trying to do since 1921, distort the African personality and create catastrophic disharmonies in our society on one plane and, on the other, in the relations between the Black and White races in the world.

The racial policies based on misreading the African experience led to the Soweto Rebellion and the establishment of the relativity of Afrikaner power. Prescribing destiny for the African by ignoring his attitude to the person and to the Collective Will reduce communist campaigns against apartheid to abortive adventures as Turok said and as events proved.

The problem which has to be faced here is that solutions which, in Caucasian views, are guaranteed to produce desired results in White environments more often than not turn out to be simplistic tangentialities in the conditions created by White domination in South Africa.

Take the clamours for armed struggle. A fairly highly placed American in the CIA told me that there was no answer to the bullet, when the war in South Vietnam made it clear that the disciplined will of a people cannot be crushed even by the most sophisticated military equipment. It was not Soviet or Chinese fire-power which brought about the humiliation of American arms in Southeast Asia; it was the disciplined will of the barefooted Vietnamese.

Whether or not armed struggle comes to South Africa, it will not be the decisive factor in the quarrel between Black and White; what will decide the course events finally take will be the Collective Will of the African peoples which they brought into being on January 8, 1912.

Political refugees who continue to see developments in South Africa from perspectives valid in the 1960s talk freely of armed struggle. They can afford to say this, protected as they are by foreign flags. Lest I be misunderstood, most of them fled the country precisely because they felt that the time had come to call for an armed struggle. To the extent that this is the case, they are quite right to call for armed struggle. But they are quite wrong when they claim a monopoly on virtue or political wisdom; when they sit comfortably under the protection foreign flags afford them and start attacking those leaders on the homefront who continue the struggle under conditions of unprecedented adversity.

Those who feel they want to talk about the armed struggle from safe positions provided by foreign powers are free to do this. But they should realise that if they want to have the masses of the people on the frontline, they should consider present realities in South Africa; they should realise that people who negotiate in the turn the crisis has taken are neither cowards nor traitors; that realism is awareness of the odds a people face.

The agminative logic of the Sudic attitude to the person demands that human groups should define themselves in terms dictated by or valid in their environment. If this environment leads some to armed struggle and others to negotiation, we should not paralyse the struggle by fighting each other over tactics; we should regard the people committed to different tactics as complements which together constitute the African's one Bicipitous Mind and his one Collective Will. The Bicipitous Mind and the Collective Will lead to one goal: freedom.

This unifying approach is based on the nature of the Evolving Revolt which demonstrates that negotiation in the conditions created by White domination can be a revolutionary weapon. When the government in Pretoria banned Inkatha's magazine, *Inkatha,* the NCLM defied the government's order and continued to publish it. In taking this stand, the NCLM created a situation of dual authority conflict which forced Pretoria to retreat. This happened because Buthelezi and the NCLM had negotiated a situation which enabled them to use legal institutions to commit illegalities like defying government bans. The extension of the area of situations of dual authority conflict leads eventually to a negotiated solution if people are disciplined on the basis of an ideal which evokes identical and co-ordinable responses in them.

The Sudic attitude to the person assumes relevance at this point. The ordinary African in the urban and rural areas does not understand the complex ideological influences which apartheid, the pass laws, influx control and the differential wage translate into action. For him, the race quarrel is a straightforward clash between Black and White; between the

African personality and the Caucasian personality.

If you tell the African in simple Zulu, Xhosa or Sotho that *abelungu bedelela ubuntu bethu* (the Whites have contempt for our personhood or humanity) he will understand clearly what race oppression is all about. The secret of Buthelezi's rise to political eminence lies in the fact that he interprets the struggle, not in incomprehensible alien terms, but in terms which have vital meaning in the day-to-day experience of the African.

The government's policy of forcing Africans to *develop along their own lines* gave Buthelezi and his NCLM their opportunity to consolidate their power and attack apartheid from legal positions, to use conflict rationalisation *(ukuqhatha)* to create and not to solve problems for the conqueror.

The point to note in the reference to *ukuqhatha* is that Buthelezi and the NCLM define the struggle in Sudic terms, analyse it in these terms and describe its goals in these terms. Apartheid's laws say they must develop along their own lines. If these lines clash with apartheid's intentions, the misreadings under discussion are to blame.

Most informed Africans realise that apartheid is merely the tip of an ideological iceberg; that in the final reckoning apartheid translates into action a global Caucasian attitude to every person of African descent. This person is presumed to be the inferior of his opposite on the White side simply because he or she is the child of particular parents. This calls for a co-ordinated answer from the Sudic World as a whole.

The humiliation of this world by slavery, colonialism, racism, apartheid and other forms of punishment for the African charges all peoples of Sudic descent everywhere with the responsibility of purging the dominant civilisation in Africa, Europe, the Sudic World and the Western hemisphere of the defects in it which distort the human personality and create catastrophic disharmonies in society; it charges all Sudic peoples with the duty to give contemporary Caucasian civilisation a mature attitude to the person, that is, an evaluation of the person which will discipline the individual and society and enable both to realise that the person is adequate for the tasks of discovering more satisfying dimensions of being human, of realising the promise of being a person, and of attaining the glory of being a self-evolving and self-defining value.

The "universal dimension" to whose discovery the All-Africa Church Conference has dedicated itself will always be a futile search and a costly waste of thought, energy, time and resources if it ignores the fact that the fundamental weakness in Christianity is its pessimistic and devaluative view of the person. This is the challenge which African Christianity must face honestly if it wants to influence events constructively in the changing dispositions of power on the continent.

For, it must always be remembered that communities which have been subjected to continuing abuse and humiliation by given racial or cultural groups eventually cultivate a revolutionary interest in the ideals which determine thought, motivate policies and influence behaviour and action among their oppressors.

This interest led the Jews to the positon where they became an exclusivistic community which regarded itself as preceptors to the human race. They succeeded in creating a world culture which was committed to values which enabled them—as Max I. Dimont points out in his books, *The Indestructible Jew* and *Jews, God and History*— to "teach" mankind through Jesus Christ and Karl Marx.

The Sudic members of the human race have been punished harshly for being children of their particular parents. The punishment has awakened in them the realisation that the first prerequisite for them to establish a satisfying position in the community of peoples is to create a moral order in the world in which it will never again be a crime for an African or a person of African descent to be the child of his or her particular parents.

In this world order, it will never again be a crime for a White woman to be the particular child of her parents.

The task of Sudic scholars and universities in this setting is not to be carbon copies of White universities; it is to address themselves to the vital problems of the Sudic World, to identify the philosophy by which Sudic Africa gives meaning to reality and life, and by which it seeks to lead the human race along safer routes to a better future by giving the person a feeling of adequacy and by creating harmony in his personality. The harmony and adequacy will, as the ancient Egyptian experience indicates, enable the family of Man to "build for eternity."

The values which give meaning to the above attitude to the person are readily available for interpretation (in Southern Africa) in, among other things, the interpretations of the *Law* which are drilled into the mind of the boy and girl on reaching puberty, and in each family's *izithakazelo,* the patronymic legend in which each such family defines itself.

These values are crucial for the resolution of conflict in the war of minds inside South Africa and, one might add, on the international plane. After forty years of frontline involvement in the fight against apartheid, I still find that most White people in South Africa, the United States and Western Europe do not have the faintest idea of what is going on in the communities of Southern Africa in general and, in particular, of the Black South Africans.

Where the main issue being decided in the war of minds is whether prescribing destiny for the African or recognition of the simultaneous legitimacy of different cultural self-definitions will determine the future of all the peoples who have made Southern Africa their home; armed struggle and negotiating are not incompatibles in a community like ours, on which divisive pressures are exerted from every section in the White community.

The exertion calls for an informed dialogue of civilisations—between the Sudic world on one hand and, on the other, the West and the Soviet

Bloc—on the reconciliation of conflicting perspectives and on finding a *via media* that will stop the drift toward World War III and toward the reduction of South Africa to ashes.

The most important factor to consider in moving events to a political solution is the Bicipitous Mind which will be discussed in the next chapter.

NOTES ON CHAPTER III

1. Shuter and Shooter, Picktermaritzburg, 1903.
2. Verbatim Report, First Kwa Zulu Legislative Assembly, 3-17 May, 1974; Vol. 4, Pp 133-34.
3. Ibid., Pp 136, 141.
4. George Padmore: *Pan Africanism or Communism*; Doubleday and Co., New York, 1972, Pp 268-69.
5. H.J. and R.E. Simons: *Class and Colour in South Africa* 1850-1950; Penguin Books, Maryland, 1969, Pp 134-135.
6. *Chronicles Of Black Protest*; ed., Bradford Chambers; The New American Library, New York, 1969; P 225.
7. University of Wisconsin Press, Madison, 1972, Pp 214, 215, 226-227.
8. *Strategic Problems in South Africa's Liberation Struggle: A Critical Analysis*; LSM Press; Richmond, B.C., Canada, 1974, Pp 43-57. (missing pages excepted).
9. Montagu Slater: *The Trial of Jomo Kenyatta*, Secker & Warburg, London, 1955, P 29.

IV. African Political Attitudes: An Inside View

A BLACK COLLECTIVE RESPONSE EMERGES

In his perceptive analysis of the crisis in South Africa, Ben Turok comes to conclusions which shed valuable light on present clamours for armed struggle in South Africa. He shows that the Marxists do not have a political power-base in the African community worth talking about and that sabotage campaigns and guerrilla infiltrations went haywire.

To the African who is involved directly in his people's struggle the reason for the failures to which Turok refers lies in policies based on the will to prescribe destiny. These concentrate on the operational aspects of apartheid and ignore the fundamentals of conflict when these fundamentals motivate thought and action and fix priorities in the African community; when they prescribe final goals and evoke identical and co-ordinable responses to similar provocations.

To define the quarrel between Black and White in terms of class conflict is to use a yardstick which has limited relevance in South Africa's war of minds. What we need to understand in Southern Africa are the attitudes to the person which give rise to mutually exclusive ideals of nationhood.

In the present chapter we trace African responses to White translations of the Caucasian evaluation of the person into actions. The intention is to discover the relationship between these responses and Black World reactions to conquest for the purpose of exploring the possibilities for a Black World strategy against race humiliation. The crisis in South Africa is of moment to the world and has taken a turn which calls for a fundamental recasting of attitudes. In the Soweto Rebellion the Africans showed that White power in general and Afrikaner power in particular is now relative. The armed might of South Africa could neither force the students to accept Afrikaans as an additional medium of instruction nor suppress the rebellion which went on for about eighteen months. One consequence of establishing the relativity of White power is that Whites now emigrate from South Africa and Rhodesia at the rate of about 4,000 a year.

What this means is that a substantial number of Whites have come to the conclusion that apartheid is no longer able to protect White domination or guarantee White security.

The political consciousness of the African people is such that the prospects of a general strike are today not as remote as they were five years ago.

The virtually complete isolation of South Africa on the international plane has paved the way for the co-ordination of internal and external campaigns against apartheid.

If these factors combine to make it possible for the African to see the light at the end of the tunnel, they also argue the case for a second look at the strategies adopted against White domination; they argue the case for a strategy that will hit the apartheid regime where it is weakest. The first precondition for such a strategy is that it must be developed by the Africans on the front line. The second is that people in foreign lands who want to give assistance should have a clear idea of what is going on in the mind of the African community.

The five moods of African Nationalism listed above give an idea of what is going on in the mind of the victims of apartheid.

The aspects of each mood to which attention will be given are: the circumstances in which each developed; each mood's definition of the "race" problem; the solution it proposed; the dilemmas it faced; the strategy it adopted and its achievements.

Enchorialism set out to defend the independence and land of the African people; to secure their right to determine their destiny and to protect their freedom. Defeated on the battlefield, they did the only honourable thing open to them: they refused to accept defeat. Bhambada kaMancinza Zondi rebelled when the British in Natal imposed the poll tax in 1905-06. The Zulu lost abut 4,000 men in that clash. They laid down their arms—to fight on another day, as the freedom songs of the time tell us. One summons the past to inspire the present:

Mathambo alele eNcome, vukani!
Arise, O ye bones
Which lie buried on Blood River's banks!

The one I heard people sing often when I grew up in Northern Natal ran:

Impi kaBhambada sayibamba,
Kwashisa phansi,
Kwabanda phezulu!
Siyeza mlungu!
Siyeza mlungu!
Mhla safika,
Kuyocish' ilanga!

In Bhambada's army we fought.
The clash of arms heated the earth
And chilled the heavens!
Beware, White man!
We are coming!
We are coming!
The day we arrive,
(We shall raise so much dust)
The sun shall not be seen!

History was against the enchorialists; they fought on ground where the enemy was strongest, and lost. Bhambada was defeated and paid with his life for challenging the armed might of the British. He set a precedent for the children who faced the White man's guns in Soweto: he showed that no matter how well armed the Whites were, their power was relative. The British withdrew the poll tax against which Bhambada had protested. It was re-introduced by Hertzog's Afrikaner government, in 1925.

The enchorialists were neither Christians nor educated; they fought to defend the Older Order.

Like Bhambada, the Nominalists were born and grew up in the shadow of defeat. The logic of defeat required that they should co-operate with the White man; that they should surrender themselves to his God and accept deculturation. They launched a great crusade to convert their "heathen" brothers, built schools of all sorts and established newspapers for their people. John Langalakhe Dube established Ohlange College; the Reverend E.A. Mahamba-Sithole built a settlement for Black orphans in Natal while the Reverend Abraham Z. Twala built a similar refuge near Elliotdale in the Transkei.

In 1892, Dube issued a call to Christendom:

I appeal to all Christians who may chance to read these pages, to aid in some way in this great work. "Truly the harvest is great, but the reapers are few." Millions of those for whom Christ died, are sitting in the darkness of sin and superstition, and almost crushed beneath the iron heel of heathen oppression. They are longing for something to satisfy the hunger of their famishing souls, but fail to find satisfaction in idols. No one points them to the only living and true God. . . .

Every true Christian must sympathize with the cause of missions, and with the conversion of the heathen. . . .
Oh! how I long for that day, when the darkness shall have passed away, because the "son of Righteousness has risen with healing in His hand." This shall be the dawning of a brighter day for the people of Africa. Christianity will usher in a new civilization, and the "Dark Continent" will be transformed into a land of commerce and Christian instruction. Then shall Africa take her place as a nation among nations; then shall her sons and daughters sing aloud: "Let us arise and shine, for our light has come. The glory of the Lord has risen upon us."
Vol. I, Doc. 19

My grandmother had grown up toward the end of the Zulu empire. She had enlisted in the army and belonged to the Ingcugce regiment. Her way of expressing the trauma into which the Zulus were thrown by the defeat was to say that one could smell gunpowder on every mountain and in every valley in the land of the Zulu. For her, the world had come to an end when Cetshwayo's Ulundi capital went up in flames on January 4—5, 1879. Grandmother, like many people of her generation near White settlements, became a Christian. Those whose world had been destroyed believed that Jesus Christ the Saviour would restore to them that which they had lost. They identified themselves with the White man on his terms. That landed them in two dilemmas. They sooner or later discovered that the Zulu Definition of the Person was diametrically opposed to the Christian. They did not doubt in their minds that the Zulu assessment was incomparably more highly developed than the individualism of Christianity; that it worked for the continuous enlargement of the personality and that it recognised the person and his neighbour as mutually fulfilling complements.

At the same time, Christianity was a proselytising religion which had behind it the military, economic and cultural power of the conqueror. The demands of survival required that people should embrace it.

In addition, Christianity's teaching on the brotherhood of men was an extremely attractive doctrine to a conquered people. If they embraced Christ, they concluded, they could be friendly neighbours with the Whites.

They were first shocked and then wounded very deeply when they found that the Christian missionaries who preached the brotherhood of men did not practice their teaching in their dealings with the Black Christians; that the White Christians rejected them and that those White Christians dispossessed them of their lands, denied them their human rights and made laws which made it a crime for a person to be an African.

The Africans had hoped that Christianity would be a bridge between Black and White and were horrified when they discovered that it was a prison of the mind in which the mind of the Black man was manipulated to serve White interests.

In spite of these humiliations, the Nominalists clung to Jesus Christ and were loud in proclaiming their dependence on the White missionaries. In 1903, the executive committee of the South African Native Congress issued a statement in which, among other things, it said:

The black races are too conscious of their dependence upon the White missionaries, and of their obligations toward the British race, and the benefits to be derived by their presence in the general control and guidance of the civil and religious affairs of the country to harbour foolish notions of political ascendancy. . . .

Just as we believe that the Unity of the Natives for the purpose of attempting to overturn the established authority of the white man is the "chimera" of ill-informed minds, and an idea which is belied by traditional tribal disunity, so also do we believe that the conception of uniting the white races in a league against the Native as a class is bound to failure.

—Vol. I, Document 7

The Nominalists had an irrepressible passion for prostrating themselves before British authorities. Their style comes out in the following quotation from a petition the Oxkraal Location people sent to Queen Victoria in 1887:

> The Humble Petition of the Native Inhabitants of the Location of Oxkraal in the District of Queenstown Colony of the Cape of Good Hope
> To
> Her Most Excellent Majesty Victoria by the grace of God of the United Kingdom of Great Britain and Ireland Queen Defender of the Faith Empress of India—
> We your Majesty's most loyal and dutiful subjects the Fingos of the Location of Oxkraal desire humbly to approach your most gracious Majesty. We consider it the highest honour to be under your Majesty's benign sway and the subjects of a Government distinguished for justice mercy and all temporal and spiritual privileges. . . .
> —Vol. I, Document 4

As fate would have it, it was the Whites (before whom they prostrated themselves) who slowly strangled and finally destroyed the leadership of the Nominalists in the African community.

In 1919 Medialism had brought the ICU into being. This omnibus type of workers' organisation set out to mobilise the collective power of Black workers to improve working conditions.

Clements Kadalie was convinced that a dialogue not backed by organised power would be a waste of time. The Whites swore by Christ on Sunday and, for the rest of the week, worshipped effective power. He organised the workers into the Industrial and Commercial Workers Union (ICU) in Cape Town in 1919 and used the African's labour as a political weapon.

The emergence of the ICU, after agreement on the Bloemfontein Ideal of Nationhood, was the most important step in the evolution of the new nation. The Bloemfontein Unity Conference had brought into being the African National Congress (ANC) which was intended to act as custodian of the 1912 Ideal of Nationhood and had committed itself to aggressiveness at the level of strategy and conciliation when it came to tactics. Kadalie, who had originally come from Malawi, saw little or no point in a Black-White dialogue in which the Black side did not have organised power.

Smuts, the new prime minister after Botha's death in 1918, read correctly the implications for White domination of Kadalie's approach. His cabinet piloted through parliament the Native Affairs Act of 1920 which set out to drive a wedge between the moderate nation-builders who had gone to Bloemfontein in 1912 and the ICU militants.

The act established the so-called Native Conferences in which "responsible Natives'' met periodically to place before the government the ''grievances'' of the African people. The White government's sole responsibility was to listen to the grievances; it was under no obligation to act on the advice of the leaders of the Africans in the Native Conferences.

Hertzog's Afrikaner nationalists feared that the Native Conferences, by treating the various African language-groups as a single political entity, promoted the ends of Black unity; they reinforced the Bloemfontein Ideal of Nationhood by demonstrating that the White government recognised the 1912 commitment. Afrikaner nationalism regarded African unity as the mortal foe of White domination generally and of Afrikaner hegemony in particular. By the end of 1929, the Hertzog government had abolished the Native Conferences. It substituted these with the Natives Representative Council in 1936, which was never to meet again after its November, 1950 session.

The element of impermanence in the institutions established by the wielders of power was emerging in the developments just described.

The decade after 1920 was the era of the dialogues between the Africans and the predominantly Afrikaner governments, the mainly English liberals and the Dutch Reformed Church. These exchanges failed to reconcile Black and White perspectives because the Whites prescribed the agenda and set out to persuade the Africans to accept a destiny prescribed for them by the Whites. The Africans refused to accept this destiny.

On the homefront the vassalage which the government was subsequently to peddle as ''independence'' in unviable mini-states responded largely to this refusal.

Let us go back to the Cape for a clearer picture of how the Collective Will affected the refusal. In this province, before Union, the Sudic Africans' diplomacy had aimed at preventing an Anglo-Afrikaner consensus on White supremacy from developing into a permanent alliance against the Black people. The Africans had used the vote they had to support the English political establishment. This policy played a part in forcing Cecil John Rhodes to commit himself to the ideal of granting equal rights to ''all civilised men.''

This English gesture to the Africans warned the Afrikaners that the English were not averse to the idea of forming an alliance with the Africans to keep Afrikaner nationalism in check, should it threaten English dominance.

When it came to the imperatives of monolithal survival, race ceased to be a decisive factor on the political plane. While the English were prepared to surrender political power to the Afrikaner monolith if it guaranteed their profits, they made it clear, through the positions they took in their press, that they were in no mood to be assimilated by the Afrikaners; that they would fight the Afrikaner as vigorously to preserve their identity as he did to protect his.

The imperatives of English economic dominance and Afrikaner

political dominance were incompatibles; the first desired the progressive stabilisation of economic and political conditions to guarantee development and profits. The second called for the intensification of race oppression and the deepening of the chasm dividing Black and White to maximise Afrikaner power.

The clash between the conflicting dominances came to a head during the Soweto Rebellion. On March 14, 1976, Buthelezi told the government and White South Africa that serious trouble was around the corner and that the only way to diffuse it was to accept majority rule and call a national convention to give South Africa a constitution that would be acceptable to all races. Premier Vorster anticipated Buthelezi's demand by appointing Dr. Andries Treurnicht, who held extreme anti-African views, to the African Education Portfolio.

Big business took note of the economic implications of the radicalised temper of the dispossessed and the government's maladroit handling of the rebellion. Organised Commerce and Industry urged the abandonment of race discrimination.

The all-White Associated Chambers of Commerce (Assocom) met in annual conference in Port Elizabeth in October, 1976. The prime minister opened the gathering. In his speech[1] he bluntly told the leaders of Commerce that they should stop undermining government policy on the race issue:

> Change must come through political processes. Efforts to use business organisations to bring about basic change in government policy will fail and cause unnecessary and harmful friction between the government and the private sector. You cannot ask me to accept policies rejected by the electorate and in which I do not believe.[2]

In these words the prime minister was telling the predominantly English businessmen that they must stop agitating for race equality because this would force them into a situation of confrontation with the government. Bearing in mind the Soweto Rebellion and its implications for the economy, the leaders of Commerce replied in ways which made it clear that if the government wanted a confrontation with business, it would get it. The conference passed a resolution which demanded, among other things:[3]

● more purposeful moves to eliminate all discrimination on grounds of race;
● relaxation of all racial restrictions on jobs in White-owned businesses;
● (facilitation of) the establishment of restaurants for all races in White central business districts.

The annual conference of the South African Federation of the Chambers of Industry was reported by the international edition of *The Star* (October 9, 1976) to have passed a resolution which included the following:

it was in South Africa's interest for the Government to phase out statutory job reservation in an orderly manner. The draft resolution which called for this to be done gradually was amended by the removal of the word "gradually".

In the same issue of *The Star*, the president of the National Development and Management Foundation was reported to have opened a "business outlook" conference. In his speech, the president made the following demands:[4]

● all races should be permitted to practise professionally or do business in any area

● all races should be permitted to live and own property and houses where their earning abilities allowed them to do so

● businesses should be allowed to decide for themselves whom they wished to employ and promote, irrespective of race or colour, and whether they wished to have separate facilities for the use of separate races

● hotels and restaurants themselves should decide whether they wished to place any reservations on the sex, dress and colour of their customers.

The leaders of Commerce, Industry, and Management were largely of one mind on the need to abandon apartheid in spite of the government's insistence on adhering to it. Sections of big business were, however, not satisfied with merely passing anti-apartheid resolutions. On the 3rd and the 4th of December, 1976, they convened a conference on The Political Aspects of Discrimination and on Dismantling Political Discrimination and invited Buthelezi to address them and convey African reactions to their stand against apartheid. The conference met in the Jan Smuts Holiday Inn, near Johannesburg.

The approach adopted by the sections of big business which invited Buthelezi differed from the government's in one important essential: Where the apartheid regime imposed "solutions" on the African, the businessmen prepared ground for solutions agreed upon by people on both sides of the colour line.

Buthelezi made these points in his speech:

What must be done is clear. We need radical political change. We need political power sharing. Above all, we need a combined effort to bring about radical change....

The United Party and the Progressive Reform Party (Prog-refs) are involved in opposition politics at the national, provincial and local
levels....
There appears to me no reason why we cannot form a shadow
multiracial body which would be a foretaste of things to come.
Inkatha, the Progressive-Reform Party and the United Party have to
face political alternatives for the future.... When we severally consider
the future, we need to bring our different thoughts into a pool of
thinking....
The body I am thinking about could enable Inkatha members,
Progressive-Reform and UP members to meet for interchanges of
ideas so that the endorsement or modification of party blueprints can
become informed.
I am talking about talking to each other — not about mergers.... If I
am the hand that my people offer in friendship, I am also the hand
they will withdraw in their anger.

The response of sections of the White press and leadership showed
which way the wind had begun to blow in some White groups. In an
editorial, *The Star* commented:
There are two different routes to change available to South Africa today.... The first involves bringing South Africa's peoples closer
together, the principle behind Chief Gatsha Buthelezi's suggestion that
Blacks and Whites need to form what he described as an opposition
"shadow cabinet," committed to change and justice.
This is the peaceful road. It recognises that stability in South Africa
ultimately rests in joint action by Black and White. It is no longer
possible to impose White solutions on Blacks. The great irony is that
Chief Buthelezi's proposition is virtually illegal — the government has
legislated Black-White political entente out of existence. It is a policy
we may all live bitterly to regret.[5]

This cautious endorsement of Buthelezi's proposals for a political
alliance with the parties which oppose apartheid on the White side was
only a climacteric in a development that has become a marked feature of
South African politics. On March 14, 1976, Buthelezi had stood up in
Soweto and had demanded the establishment of majority rule as an alternative to apartheid. He had been one of the guiding spirits behind the
Umtata Conference's commitment to the ideal of the Federal Union of
the Autonomous States of Southern Africa. In less than two weeks after
the Soweto demand, Senator W. Sutton, the Natal Whip of the conser-
vative White United Party made these statements in an interview with *The
Star*:[6]
I believe the Black-White issue is very far along the way to an accommodation. I am convinced that it will be a federal arrangement. . . . If

our society . . . is going to survive, then we must involve the Black man totally in the free enterprise society for his personal advantage and the advantage of the group as a whole. This will provide the strongest support of the Western system. . . . If we can involve the Black man in that kind of system, then the future is absolutely assured for us.

We started by saying that at Union, the Africans, Afrikaners and the English were transformed into self-centred monoliths and that each became a system with its own social and economic stratifications. Each monolith had its own ideal of nationhood and each occupied a position in national life which was determined by the reserves of power it controlled. While the Africans had the labour and the numbers, they were too poorly organised at the time to force the Whites to respect their wishes. The Afrikaners were the largest community on the White side. In a closed or racial caste-society, numerical preponderance gave them a political potential which enabled them to have absolute control of the government, the army and the police and to dominate parliament. The English were the dominant factor in the economy.

In this setting, the Afrikaners presided over a power structure based, in the main, on the labour of the African monolith and the technological-financial know-how of the English. Apartheid was adopted partly to preserve the cohesion of the closed society and partly to keep the Afrikaner in political control. It is in this sense that the majority of Afrikaners regard apartheid as a guarantee of their survival.

The fundamental weakness in the Afrikaner approach was that Afrikaner hegemony was based on reserves of power controlled or likely one day to be controlled by antagonistic monoliths. The Afrikaner assumed that race could be transformed into a permanent bond of unity on the White side and used apartheid to create an unbridgeable chasm between Black and White and, in that way, isolate the English and maximise their dependence on Afrikaner political goodwill.

African Nationalism developed a dialectic of displacement and organised the Evolving Revolt largely in response to the fundamental weakness on the Afrikaner side. The Youth League's confrontation strategy was designed, among other things, to exploit this weakness and create a vacuum in the Afrikaner's thinking on the future of South Africa and to subject apartheid to internal tests which would expose its futility and absurdity; to entangle it in the contradictions within contradictions which it produced to enable the Afrikaner to occupy a position in the government which the Africans and the English could make increasingly untenable.

In Natal, the dialectic began to take shape about a hundred years ago, when King Cetshwayo tried to form a Black military alliance which would regard Southern Africa as a collective security area. Seme proceeded from where Cetshwayo had been stopped. Instead of relying on military power, which the disarmed Africans could not have, Seme transformed the race quarrel into a war of minds; into the clash between the "common fundamental sentiment" and what he called "the sins of civilization." This change placed the African in the position where he could fight on ground chosen by him, using weapons developed by him and move to his freely chosen goal at a pace set by him.

The dialectic was one of the weapons developed to deal with the peculiar and complicated relations which had emerged in South Africa's situation of conflicting monoliths. While it rejected race as a determinant of policy, the dialectic focused on power dispositions within each monolith. These, the Bloemfontein Unity Conference believed, changed in response to how economic and political forces were aligned. The task of the Africans in this setting was to develop techniques for creating the situations which could broaden the area of polarisation between the Afrikaner and English monoliths.

On the homefront, the Bloemfontein Ideal of Nationhood, the Umtata Conference's Geopolitical Alternative to apartheid, the Evolving Revolt, the dialectic and the Soweto Rebellion exposed the major points of weakness in Afrikaner thinking on nationhood while apartheid worked continuously for the extension of the area of conflict and instability. These weaknesses were given new dimension by the way apartheid closed Free African markets to goods of South African manufacture.

The apartheid regime found itself in the awkward position of having to ask foreign investors to sink their money in a country where the Differential Wage limited the internal market for goods produced by foreign investments mainly to the White fifth of the population while South Africa's racial policies shut Free African markets to most products made in the Republic.

Caught in the contradictions within contradictions and dilemmas into which apartheid had thrown South Africa, some supporters of the government on the homefront and some of its agents in Western Europe started a campaign of threats to seek investment capital in communist countries; to form a gold and uranium cartel with the Soviet Union, to control world marketing of the two minerals, and to have trading partners in the Eastern Bloc.

The seriousness of these threats emerged in some of the statements made in the South African parliament in 1977 by supporters of the apartheid regime. The international edition of the Johannesburg *Star* of April 16, 1977 reported that during his speech in the resumed debate on the budget, Dr. P. van B. Viljoen, the apartheid member for the Newcastle industrial city had:

> warned the West that it could no longer take South Africa for granted, and if it came to a matter of survival the Republic would turn to communist and socialist countries of the Eastern Bloc to raise capital. . . .

... it was time south Africa became less dependent on the West for raising capital. . . . South Africa could not go on ignoring the hostility of certain Western countries after all South Africa had done for the less fortunate people in South Africa. . . .

... the time had come to establish economic links with certain communist countries . . . so that South Africa could rid itself of its dependence on the West and the vulnerability that went with dependence.

Dr. Viljoen's threat is interesting, not because of its unrealism, but because it shows the depth and width of the vacuum which has developed in the Afrikaner's thinking on the future of South Africa. The November, 1973, Umtata Conference rejected the balkanisation of South Africa into racial states because, like the Bloemfontein Unity Conference, it regarded the racial, economic and other difficulties which face all the countries of Southern Africa as related, complementary and inseparable aspects of a larger Southern African Problem which called for a larger Southern African Solution.

The apartheid regime refuses to see the crisis in Southern Africa from this angle. The refusal landed South Africa in the Soweto Rebellion on the one hand and, on the other, drove big business to the Left of the government on a fundamental policy issue. In short, the refusal prepared ground for an alliance between the African majority which provides labour and big business which pays the taxes and manages the economy.

But the refusal must be seen for what it is. In the final analysis it is an oblique admission by the advocates of apartheid that they are incapable of giving constructive leadership in the crisis their racial policy has created. The wooing of communist countries is an important aspect of the admission when it is remembered that for many years now, the apartheid regime has claimed that it is a Western bulwark against communism.

Mention was made earlier of the element of impermanence in some of the positions the Afrikaner takes. The shifts in his positions and the way he makes these shifts is another point of weakness in the Afrikaner monolith which will influence his dealings with the opponents of apartheid, now that he stands alone in the world.

Most writers on apartheid believe that the Afrikaner will fight to the bitter end and will sooner choose the diaspora and the destruction of Afrikanerdom than share power with the African people. The government's own pronouncements and tactics make it clear that while Pretoria will do a little window-dressing here and a little juggling with "petty apartheid" there, the Afrikaner monolith is in no mood to share power with the majority. Inflexibility seems the state of mind the Afrikaner monolith is in.

This type of inflexibility is not unusual in situations of race or ethnic conflict. America's slave-owners eventually resorted to the arbitrament of arms to defend their right to own their fellowmen. The inflexibility turned out to be no guarantee of victory.

But, side by side with the inflexibility, is an inner logic in the Afrikaans experience which focuses attention on areas of congruence in African and Afrikaner thinking. The Afrikaner is often accused of leading South Africa with his head in the sand. More often than not, the accusations ignore the most important determinant of Afrikaner policies: The Afrikaner's *survival problem*.

At first viewing, the Afrikaner advocate of apartheid appears to be allergic to equality between Black and White. A closer view of his history or his *survival problem* shows that the allergy is *a variable which responds to the demands of survival.*

When the shortage of White women threatened the settlement which Jan van Riebeeck founded at the Cape on behalf of the Dutch East India Company in 1652, he encouraged his men to marry women of colour. The Dutch Reformed Church solemnised the marriages.

Eric Walker, the South African historian, tells us that:[7]

> Van Riebeeck . . . recommended mixed marriages, and Jan Wouter had duly wedded Catherine, a freed woman, daughter of Antonie of Bengal. Then van Meerhof, the doughty explorer, married Eva, a Hottentot. He was the first European to marry a Hottentot and received promotion to the rank of surgeon as a wedding present from the Company.

In 1815 Frederick Bezuidenhout defied a British court's order to appear before it to answer charges levelled against him by his Khoikhoi servant. His refusal to do this started the Slachter's Nek Rebellion. His brother, acting on behalf of the rebels, made two unsuccessful appeals to Xhosa King Ngqika for an alliance against the British.

The search for allies was still very much in the mind of Afrikaner leaders after the end of World War I. In July, 1921, General J.B.M. Hertzog, who later became a South African prime minister, included the following in a letter he wrote to Clements Kadalie, the Black leader of the militant South African Industrial and Commercial Workers Union (ICU):[8]

> It is for us by our common endeavours to make this country, that we both love so much, great and good. In order to do that we must not only ourselves be good and great, but we must also see that there is established between the White and Black Afrikander that faith in and sympathy with one another which is so essential for the prosperity of a nation. It is my sincere desire that that faith and sympathy shall exist and to that end I hope to exert all my influence.

186

Black Leaders at 1973 Umtata conference. (*left to right:* Matanzima of Transkei; Mangope of Bophuthatswana; Sebe of Ciskei; and at right Buthelezi of KwaZulu)

Capture of Cetshwayo (the Zulu King) by the British at Battle of Ulundi, August 31, 1879.

Dr. D. F. Malan has the reputation of being the father of modern apartheid. He led Afrikaner nationalism to power in 1948 on the slogan that *die witman moet baas bly* (the Whiteman must remain master). In 1921, he sent the following telegram of good wishes to an African political gathering in Queenstown:[9]

No race has shown greater love for South Africa than the Natives. Therein he, the Native, assuredly is a pattern of true patriotism and is entitled to take his place side by side with the (Afrikaner) Nationalists in the common political arena.

In the days when the White powers decided the destinies of the world, Pretoria accused the United Nations of interfering in the domestic affairs of a member-nation when the world organisation attacked apartheid. Apartheid, Pretoria argued, was something that had to be settled by South Africa only. The collapse of White power in large parts of the world and the emergence of African states forced the Afrikaner to change his tune. The imperatives of survival compelled him to recognise the goodwill of the Free Africans as one of his new guarantees of survival.

In the 1974 Security Council debate on the expulsion of South Africa from the United Nations, Pretoria's permanent representative in the world organisation addressed this open invitation to Free Africa in particular and all interested countries in general:[10]

. . . our participation in these proceedings, in so far as they relate to the internal affairs of South Africa . . . should be seen as flowing from our willingness to discuss our differences with other countries which are genuinely interested in a constructive solution to them and are prepared to talk with us openly and objectively. It is particularly to these countries that we address ourselves—and more especially to the states of Africa. For we are an African state. It is in Africa, where we live and where we belong, that our destiny lies. We have an important identity of interest with other states of Africa. It is with them that we must talk and we firmly believe that all of us in Africa can only gain by communication with one another. . . . My government stands ready to explore all avenues which may bring about an understanding amongst us.

The operative phrase is: *explore all avenues.* The realism is not a pose, as anybody familiar with the Afrikaner's history can affirm; it is a response to Afrikaner weaknesses in the context provided by given African actualities. The Afrikaner's political potential can remain the decisive determinant of policy only if African labour and English technology and financial know-how decide to remain docile and submit themselves to permanent Afrikaner hegemony.

The Africans transformed themselves into a monolith to challenge this hegemony and succeeded in isolating it on the international plane; in smashing the satellite system in which policy sought to force the English monolith and the Coloured and Indian sub-monoliths to orbit around the Afrikaner monolith for the purpose of forcing these communities to gang up with the Afrikaner to help him solve his *survival problem.*

Sudic diplomacy created the situation where the Coloured and Asian sub-monoliths were confronted with crucial choices. The government offered a destiny imposed from above by the Whites. Buthelezi offered them a destiny in whose shaping they would have as full a say as the African majority. The two sub-monoliths chose to line up with the Africans.

This isolation of White domination on territory where it thought itself invincible exposed one more area of weakness in the Afrikaner monolith.

The shift in internal African, Coloured and Asian attitudes created a new set of relations between the non-White majority, which provides the labour that sustains South Africa's economy and the English monolith which is still the dominant factor in the economy. This relationship forced Big Business to move into opposition to the government's racial policy; into advocating the abolition of race discrimination.

The advocates of apartheid took away the African peoples' political rights in the effort to drive a wedge between the Africans and the English on the political plane and succeeded in creating a new area of congruity in African and English attitudes to race discrimination. This happened because the Afrikaner concerned himself so much with his *survival problem* he defined himself and the other South Africans in terms which extended the area of his isolation.

The Africans, Coloureds and to a lesser extent Asians concerned themselves as much with the fundamentals of conflict—of which the *survival problem* is one—as with the operational aspects of race oppression. As a result, they paid as much attention to the Evolving Revolt as to residential segregation, the Pass Laws, the Differential Wage, etc. They set as great store by the Collective Will of the Africans on one hand and, on the other, of the non-Whites as they did on the abolition of race discrimination. They might be said to have regarded the meaning freedom would have after the overthrow of White domination as being equally important with the means for winning it.

The Afrikaner strove to smash the Collective Will—which will be discussed in a later chapter—while the Africans struggled to crack the foundations of the united front of White monoliths. The Soweto Rebellion, the Coloureds' identification with the Africans in Cape Town during the Rebellion, and the formation of the South African Black Alliance showed that the non-Caucasian peoples were winning the war of minds; that the African definition of the race problem was filling the vacuum in White thinking on the future of South Africa which had been created by White definitions of the quarrel between Black and White.

Some Afrikaners took note of these defeats and realised that a united African-Coloured-Asian front would have the potential to push all the Whites into the sea, simply by withdrawing its labour, paralysing the economy and creating conditions in which it would be impossible for the Whites to live in the affluence to which they are accustomed.

The English, the Jews and other Caucasians can emigrate to other countries where they have kinsmen. The Afrikaner has no kinsmen in foreign lands; he belongs to South Africa. If he were thrown out of the Republic his community would be destroyed.

The Jews survived the diaspora because they contributed towards the hegemony of Graeco-Romano-Hebraic civilisation in the days when it had the power to impose the Caucasian will on, and prescribe destiny for, the Third World. The Afrikaner has nothing to give the White race. He can give it the minerals of South Africa or guarantee the Cape sea route or remain a gateway into Southern Africa for Western manufactures only with the co-operation of the African-Coloured-Asian majority.

Thoughtful Afrikaners have faced these weaknesses and a few of them have begun to think of alternatives to apartheid; of exploring avenues for discovering alternative guarantees of survival. These searches for alternatives to the status quo have not been given the attention they deserve by Free Africa, the OAU and the United Nations. America, Britain, France and West Germany are spending a lot of money on efforts to have a clear view of what is going on in South Africa. Free Africa, the OAU and the Frontline States continue to mouth slogans about armed struggle when not a single African country manufactures arms; when, in fact, they do not have an internal political base to lead the armed struggle inside the country; when they continue not to co-ordinate internal and external campaigns against apartheid.

But the Afrikaner's weaknesses must be seen against developments in the African community; against African reactions to conquest.

It will shed more light on this exciting period in our history if we let the leaders of the African after Sharpeville tell us in their own words how they saw the position of their people then.

After the Sharpeville shootings, as already said, the government banned the main political organisations in the Black community and hoped to fill the leadership vacuum thus created with co-operative chiefs. The African people's answer was to launch two offensives, one to block the election of co-operative chiefs in some homelands and the other to isolate the Whites in South Africa. Chief Gatsha Buthelezi spoke for the first group while the Black Consciousness Movement led the campaigns of isolation. In an interview with DRUM magazine (November, 1971), Buthelezi said:

We will always be part of a greater South Africa whether we like it or not. . . . What concerns me is that my people must get equal opportunities. How they get this I am not concerned about. If there will be some improvement for my people, even if it is not exactly the ideal in terms of my own principles and beliefs, I have no option but to take advantage. . . .

I always believe that the interests of my people whether they are Zulus, Venda, Sotho, Shangaan, etc., are so intwined that it is impossible to separate them realistically. . . .

It seems that the role we are forced by circumstances to operate on (is) ethnic grouping, but I don't think people should be just paralysed from doing something for themselves merely because they are against ethnic grouping. . . . We should take advantage of this time to consolidate ourselves. As long as we know our goals it is not important to waste time bickering about whether ethnic grouping is bad or not. . . . We are aiming for nothing less than full human rights to which all our people are entitled. Nothing less can ever satisfy.

Buthelezi was feeling his way into the leadership suddenly thrust on him by events after the Sharpeville shootings. His mandate required him to rededicate the African people to the Bloemfontein Ideal of Nationhood, transform the bantustan institution into a revolutionary weapon against apartheid, build effective political power bases, co-ordinate internal and external campaigns against apartheid and make majority rule the issue in the quarrel on apartheid. Building a political base was the most difficult of his tasks.

The government was determined to crush every political party which operated outside of the homelands administrations. It would do all in its power to remove all political opposition to apartheid. At the time, many people, particularly the younger Nationalists, rejected the idea of forming a political organisation that could function within the law; they argued that to create such an organisation was indistinguishable from collaboration in operating apartheid institutions.

Another group of Nationalists urged that realism should guide African thinking on the turn events were likely to take. The Evolving Revolt had developed beyond a struggle for the extension of the area of liberty for the African and had become a struggle for power. The government would exploit every weakness on the Black side to crush this challenge to White leadership.

This called for a strategy which would be aggressive wherever the African was strong and for realism where he was weak. The end in view was not to collaborate; it was to challenge apartheid on every plane, including its own ground. These Nationalists listed the following as Buthelezi's priorities in the conditions created by Sharpeville setbacks: the seizure of power in the Kwa Zulu homeland to prevent co-operative chiefs from dominating the Zulu Territorial Authority; the rededication of all the African language-groups to the Bloemfontein Ideal of Nationhood which apartheid sought to destroy; the transformation of the Territorial Authority into a revolutionary weapon for use in the dual authority crisis to which apartheid was pushing Black and White; building a political power-base to fill the leadership vacuum which emerged after the bans on the ANC and the PAC in 1960; subjecting "self-government" to severe tests on every plane; creating a vacuum in White thinking on the future of South Africa; giving a unifying momentum to events in Southern Africa and confronting apartheid with a better and more satisfying alternative to the vassalage which Pretoria peddled as "independence" in unviable mini-states.

These priorities which are not in their order of importance, were designed to give the Africans a political weapon by which to fill the leadership vacuum created by the bans on the PAC and the ANC, to rally the people by showing that apartheid could be fought and defeated on its own territory, and to co-ordinate internal and external campaigns against apartheid for the purpose of moving all concerned to a political solution.

As one of those who actively influenced Buthelezi to stand for election, I can say what I had in mind. For ninety-one years after 1879, the Zulus had been a defeated, humiliated and fragmented people; for fifty-eight years after 1912, we had thrown our lot with the other African language-groups to form a new and stronger nation which would make it possible for all of us to free ourselves and all our people from continuing humiliation and restore to all our peoples that land and freedom which belonged to them.

Rising from defeat and humiliation was not a pleasant task; on the contrary, it was painful, unrewarding and often dangerous and ugly in the conditions which existed in South Africa. Nobody would lead us out of the situation of defeat and fragmentation; we and we alone had to do that. We would be misunderstood and called names; we would not be the first people to be so abused. To be thus called names was part of the challenge of freedom. We had to stand up and fight for that which belonged to us even when people burnt us on the stake or poured boiling oil over our bodies or murdered us in police cells.

Our commitment to freedom demanded that we should fight for that which belonged to us no matter what it cost us. Some of our people had been hanged in the bid to crush the commitment; some were serving life sentences on Robben Island while others were in exile. Our task as a people was to see to it that these temporary setbacks did not bring our struggle to a stop; we had to fight even inside the very institutions our oppressors set up to give permanence to our humiliation.

Buthelezi was not the type of man who would tremble at the thought, or be awed by the prospect, of fighting oppression on its own ground. He was the type of man who would lead the struggle from where it had been temporarily stopped after Sharpeville. Our people wanted him to lead them; he never offered himself for election and did not canvass for support. All the committed spent their time, money and energy canvassing Zulu voters to support Buthelezi's election.

Those of us who urged him to stand knew that he was the type of man who had no time for political heroics. Like us, he saw no point in attacking apartheid in the absence of a well-organised political base. His first step in building this base was to go to the Umtata Conference in November, 1973, and argue the case for rededication to the Bloemfontein Ideal of Nationhood.

He followed his success in Umtata with the establishment of the National Cultural Liberation Movement (Inkatha), which evolved from a Zulu association into a national organisation.

From platforms provided him by the homelands institutions he rejected White definitions of the race problem and laid down the terms his people wanted. He rejected the concept of Black integration in a White-dominated society and stated in terms nobody could mistake that his and his people's goal was majority rule. Before long, Prime Minister Vorster himself was forced to address himself to and talk about majority rule—attacking it, of course.

Buthelezi gave a lot of thought and time to the re-ordering of monolithal alignments. His strategy on this plane succeeded when the United Party began to split. Buthelezi signed a pact with Harry Schwarz which accelerated the United Party's drift toward final collapse.

In September, 1971, he addressed Afrikaner students in Stellenbosch University. Stellenbosch was not only the most important centre of higher learning in the Afrikaner monolith; it was the main centre of cultural power in the Afrikaans community.

Buthelezi was still feeling his way. The Zulus had given him an awesome mandate. He had been asked to adhere strictly to the law of the Whites and at the same time to make the fullest possible use of the contradictions in this law to challenge apartheid in particular and White domination generally; he had to use the law to attack apartheid. The complete disarming of the African community made it impossible for these people to talk of an armed struggle at the time; they could think in terms of political weapons and political solutions; this mandate required that he move Black and White to a political solution.

NOMINALISM

Buthelezi's role in African politics must be seen against the background provided by the decline in the influence of Nominalism.

Led by Clements Kadalie, who was later joined by Allison Wessels George Champion, the ICU threatened, from 1919 onward, to paralyse the economy with a general strike in protest against race humiliation.

General Smuts rushed to parliament with the Native Affairs Act (1920) which established the Native Conferences, a get-together in which government officials sat and listened to the "grievances" of the African people, without being bound to do anything after hearing these grievances.

The Native Conferences were abolished by the Hertzog government in 1929. The Nominalists lost an instrument by which they had conducted a futile dialogue with the government.

The abolition of the Cape African Vote in 1935 was the fatal blow which sent political Nominalism to its grave. With political Nominalism there also died the tradition of collaboration with the Whites which the Nominalists had upheld.

The Nominalist was a man of two worlds. He had turned his back on enchorialism and believed that the traditionalists were heathens. To associate with them was to live in evil. If he lived among them, he disorganised their society; he despised them; they were a condemned people; they were the enemies of Christ just because a few White men said this.

The irony in his position was that that White Christian world to which he belonged spiritually rejected him because he was not White. That left him floating somewhere between enchorialism and Christianity.

The state of not belonging to the nomarchy and the community of Christians placed the Nominalist in a situation of spiritual isolation and insecurity. His Sudic evaluation of the person had been a reliable anchor for his personality; it had been developed and tested continuously for thousands of years. It made him feel secure and at home in the cosmic experience; it harmonised his personality and his society.

Because Christianity was given one meaning in the relations between White and White, and another between Black and White, he doubted if it could give him that security which his Buntu philosophy had guaranteed him. Thus, thrown out of his traditional world while he was unwanted in the White Christian, he remained an enchorialist in his dealings with his Black neighbours and in his assessment of himself while adopting the ritual of the Christians. It is in this sense that he became a Nominalist Christian.

Belonging to two worlds gave him a two-dimensional or Bicipitous Mind; he saw things simultaneously from the enchorial and Christian perspectives. The change was often painful for him; it introduced painful disharmonies in his personality and made him a misfit in his community. He was often thrown out of his traditional society because his loyalty to Christ and his two-dimensional mind disorganised and destabilised his society.

If he was not thrown out, there always was the danger that he might revert to enchorialism. The missionaries in time established mission stations where the converts could be segregated to live out "Christian" lives.

A new lifestyle developed in the mission stations, which were under the watchful eye of the White missionaries. This was a synthesis of Sudic and Christian value-systems. It combined with other forces and developed into what Seme was to call "a new and unique civilization."

The Zulu gave the name *isikholwa* (the culture of the believers) to the lifestyle of the mission stations.

A parallel change was afoot among the Africans in the urban locations. Proletariatisation did not commit the African to any moral values. At the same time it changed his lifestyle; it forced him to subject himself to disciplines designed to serve best the interests of the Whites. He created a synthesis of disciplines which blended what he had brought over from his nomarchy or culture with what he took over from the White side.

The Zulus called his culture *isidolobha,* the culture of the towns.

The schools established by the missionaries and the government initially drew no distinction between one language-group and another or between Christians and enchorialists; it blended the two cultures and produced a synthesis of syntheses; "the new and unique civilization."

Like its constituent cultures, the new civilisation produced the person with a mind which perceived simultaneously from two angles. Every educated African today is the product of the synthesis of syntheses. For anybody to say the African's heart is in the tribe clashes with known facts. The overwhelming majority of the Black people were born into the synthesis; they see life, reality, men and events from perspectives developed by the synthesis. In simple language, they do not even have the mind of the tribesman.

But let us return to the Nominalist. If the mission stations produced the Christian Nominalist, the urban area brought the Cultural Nominalist into being. This person had been torn away from his nomarchy by pressures he had no power to resist. He was thrown into the industrial maelstrom which the White man had set in motion in the towns. Like the convert, White society rejected him. He developed a culture which was shaped by proletariatisation.

The communists hoped that the African so conditioned was a ready customer for the type of ideological goods they peddled as a creed of economic salvation. This was where they misread the African experience. The "new and unique civilization" was a Sudic response to a fundamental challenge; the Collective Will forged in Bloemfontein in 1912 was a fundamental answer to this fundamental challenge.

The answer responded to the environment which the Africans were forced into by conquest. As long as conquest prescribed destiny for the Africans they would continue to see in the Collective Will a guarantee of survival, victory and a better life.

The creation of the synthesis of syntheses was an integral part of nation-building; it was by no means easy. It led to bitter and prolonged fights inside the African community. Seme had scathing things to say against the Nominalists when he was president of the ANC:

. . . the missionaries came into this country to look after the heathen and to love them, but by a strange contrast, every "native" who got educated by these missionaries immediately became disinterested in the heathen and, in fact, despised his heathen brothers. The result has been that the greatest bulk of our people who are still heathen have no educated men to lead them amongst their own tribes. The Chiefs and their uneducated people are despised and forsaken by their own educated tribesmen.

This attitude of despising your own people has created antipathies between the new leaders and the old population, which are most regrettable. There is no reason why the educated Africans should throw away their tribal connections and so much desire to be regarded as being detribalised natives. I fear that in this sense the so-called "detribalised natives" have not properly considered their positions and their duties towards their own people. . . .

—Vol. I, Document 481

This gives but one aspect of the many, complicated tasks of nation-building which the Whites did not know or understand. With the advantage of hindsight, we might be tempted to pass harsh judgment on the Nominalists. But in our difficult situation, out of which there have never been easy ways, it is wise to regard the performance of each generation as a response to the challenge as the times presented it. Seme's scathing remarks were provoked by the individualism of the converts who had been taught that they lived for themselves and Christ and not for themselves and their neighbours.

MEDIALISM

Unlike the Nominalist, the Medialist was outraged by a Christian morality which was given one meaning in the White and another in the African community. He blamed the divalency on the immaturity of the Whites. Since the Whites did not want him in their world as an equal, he did not want them to lead him; he walked out of the White-led church to establish his own denomination where he would give to Christian values the meaning that would be valid in the situation of his people.

He had moved out of the enchorial experience when he became a Christian; he set out to create his own world, between the enchorial and White worlds.

Vittorio Lanternari gives this description of the beginnings of religious Medialism in South Africa.[12]

The messianic cults rose and multiplied in South Africa long before they developed elsewhere on the African continent. The Ethiopian

Church founded in 1892 by Mangena M. Mokone set the first example of autonomy. . . . Several isolated attempts at secession from establish- ed mission churches, poorly organised and scarcely influential, had been made by such earlier leaders as Nehemiah Tile and Kgantlapane. Nehemiah Tile, who left the Methodist missions under attack for his interest in native Tembu nationalism, created a Tembu church as early as 1884. The objective of the Tembu was to oppose the religious con- trol of the Europeans while also adapting the Christian message to native conditions; and since the Queen of England was the head of the Anglican Church, the Tembu maintained that their own Supreme Tribal Chief should be recognised as the bishop of their religious body.

Medialism was the third African response to conquest; it was a reaction of the ciliate human mind to a given challenge, just as Nominalism and Enchorialism were. The point to note is that these reactions were more or less contemporaneous. Tile worked among the Xhosa, about a thousand miles away from Mokone and Kgantlapane. Every major language group produced its crop of Enchorialists, Nominalists, Medialists and Mono- lithists.

The spontaneity and simultaneousness of these revolts in all the African communities show the dynamism of the Sudic mind in a situation of challenge; they show this mind responding to the challenge of its nature when confronted by the Graeco-Romano-Hebraic mind; they show how the Sudic Ideal performed when subjected to the harsh tests which came with conquest and the prescribed destiny. These responses were vindica- tions of the person as an individualisation of *NU* or *NTU*.

Like the Enchorialist, the Medialist rejected the prescribed destiny on some planes and accepted it on others. He rejected the leadership of the White man in the church but accepted the Christian teaching, which he tried to interpret in his terms. That produced problems to which we shall soon come. Before we deal with these, let us see how political Medialism functioned.

On October 4, 1904, Reverends Samuel Jacobus Brander, a Northern Sotho-speaking African, and Joshua Mphothleng Mphela and Mr. Stephen Nguato gave evidence before the South African Native Affairs Commission. The members of the Commission were all White. The answers Mr. Brander gave under cross-examination show the aspirations and dilemmas of the Medialists:

40,855. Do you think it would be a good thing for you Native races to run side by side with the white races in everything, just like the two rails of a railway line?—Not at present, but in the future I think so.

40,856. When?—In years to come; maybe after 50 years.

40,857.   Do you not think it will be better for you to keep always separate like the two rails on a railway line, so that you will not come into conflict, and perhaps into ill-feeling with one another, and so get into trouble with each other in some way?—No; I think when we are educated we can be united and we can be one with the white all over, and I think we will have peace later on.

40,858.   You think at the same time you should all have the same right to the franchise, the same political rights and the same social rights?—Yes, when our people are educated to such a standard.

40,859.   And you would also like in time by constitutional methods, that is by lawful measures, to get yourselves into the control and management of public affairs in the Government as you have done in the church?—Yes, I should think so.

40,860.   Mr. Thompson: And where would you end; would you like the races to amalgamate?—Yes.

40,861.   Would you like the White man to marry the Native Woman? —I should think so.

40,862.   And the Native man to marry the White woman?—I should think so.

40,863.   Did you quite understand that question about getting ultimate political control into your hands; do you mean that you want to govern the White people of this country?—No, it is not so. While we live together. . . . While we live together it would not be for us to govern the white people, but to be with them. . . .

—Vol.I, Document 8c

Two additional dimensions of Medialist thinking emerge from Brander's testimony. He envisaged the emergence, some time in the future, when the Africans were better educated in the ways of the Whites, of an open society based on race equality.

The key sentence in the second dimension is: "While we live together." In the Sotho and Nguni languages of South Africa to "live together" means to live side by side on the basis of consensus. Lions, zebras and hyenas live together in Tanzania's Ngorongoro National Park without any consensus, whereas people live together in a village, city or country on the basis of consensus; on the basis of the same attitude to the person.

Brander realised that the basis for a viable Black-White consensus on living together was still a long way off; that the African would have to be "educated" first before he could develop a meaningful formula for co-existence. When the African was ready to participate in the formulation of the basis for co-existence, there would be no need for him to "govern the White people" just as there would be no need for the White people to govern the Africans. "To be with them" meant that Black and White belong together and those who belonged together did things together; they governed together. This was the gravamen of Brander's testimony.

At the time, Brander was not interested in race equality; he wanted the right to use "constitutional methods" and "lawful measures" to prepare his people for the time when they would get themselves "into the control and management of public affairs in the Government."

His quarrel with the British government was that it was denying him the right to develop institutions which would enable him to use "constitutional methods" and "lawful measures" to ensure respect for the wishes of his people. The denial frustrated life's purpose for the person brought up on the Sudic evaluation of the human being; it defined the fundamental cause of conflict between Black and White.

The Medialists were dedicated to the creation of a synthesis of value-systems which would give valid meaning to life in the conditions created by conquest. Isaiah Shembe started by creating a synthesis of enchorial and Christian values and proceeded from this to establish a community, at Ekuphakameni, a few kilometres below the hill on which Dube had established Ohlange College, about fifteen miles to the north-west of Durban.

Shembe regarded the Old Testament as his source of enlightenment. He composed psalms and hymns for his followers. At first, he addressed himself to the Zulu

Lalela Zulu
Lalela abantu bengiphethe,
Ngezwe lethu.

Siyazizwa izizwe zivungama
Zivungama ngawe
Njengezinyoni.

Sisho izinyoni sisho amahlokohloko!

Acekezela insimu
Ka Dingana no Senzangakhona.

Ayiqedile mamo!

Sizwa ngo Mnyayiza
Ka Ndabuko.

Listen, O Zulu!

Listen; here are people who pester me;
About our land they bother me.

We hear the nations conspiring;
Conspiring [against] you;
They make bird-like noises.

When we talk of birds, We talk of amahlokohloko
Which consume the harvest in the field;
The field of Dingana and Senzangakhona.

Lo! See how they have laid it to waste!

Mnyayiza tells us they have;
Mnyayiza the scion of Ndabuko.

Like Tile, Shembe's message was at first addressed to his language-group; he spoke to it in terms which emphasised the indivisibility of the Zulu soul. This soul was in harmony with itself and that harmony was a blend of bitter humiliation, continuing pain, faith in the person and confidence in final victory.

The names he mentions in the psalm stir the deepest passions in the Zulu consciousness; they call to mind the wounds inflicted on the Zulu personality in the past and the present. The evocation creates a synthesis of passions which gives the Zulu experience its peculiar symmetry.

It should always be remembered that the other language-groups were producing their prototypes of Shembe; their own responses to conquest. All these responses had their roots in the Sudic evaluation of the person.

In time, Shembe realised that the indivisible soul of the Zulu was, in fact, only a fragment of a whole: the indivisible soul of mankind. He addressed himself to the mankind that surrounded him in his country. In Psalm 120, he cried out:

Arise O South Africa
Set alight your firewood;
Let all nations gather around,
From your fire to derive warmth!

Arise O South Africa!
Ignite the wood for your fire;
The fire your God gave you.

No other support exists
For you, O Africa:
Jehova alone ———
He is your light.

I am adequate;
I live in hope.
Whether or not they like it,
The dawn of your day shall come.
When the sun rises then,
All nations shall bask in it.

The logic of Medialism demanded that the Medialist should at all times respond to an ever-evolving challenge. It required that Shembe and other Medialists discover a *universal dimension* which would make Christianity simultaneously valid in the lives of all human beings. Shembe and the religious Medialists of his time created a synthesis of Enchorial and Christian values and saw this as the *universal dimension* they were looking for because it defined the person in positive and optimistic terms and recognised the simultaneous legitimacy of his community's self-definition.

To people brought up on the Sudic view of the human being, the definition of the person as a creature created catastrophic disharmonies in the person, as already pointed out. First and foremost, it forced the person to apologise for being human, when he had been taught all his life that to be human meant striving perpetually to discover more satisfying dimensions of being a self-defining value.

The Christian mandate and the dogmas it prescribed frustrated life's purpose for this type of person: they distorted his personality and sent him back to what he regarded as the childhood days of the human race. His ancestors had outgrown these days. Down the ages, they had developed a most challenging attitude to the person and had evolved a complex but readily recognisable social system to ensure that the person realised the full promise of being human.

People like Shembe and other leaders of the time set out to develop a philosophy which would not create catastrophic disharmonies in the person and in society. The *universal dimension* they produced sought to discipline the person and society and to create social rhythms which would guarantee survival in the conditions created by defeat. Any truly scientific analysis of African society in the urban and rural areas which ignored these rhythms would defeat its own ends.

The Medialist's Bicipitous Mind opened out simultaneously to Black humanity and to the larger humanity outside of the Black experience. The response issued directly from Buntu's emphasis on the primacy of the person and Christian humanism as understood during the first half-century after conquest.

The Buntu assessment of the person taught that the individual extended himself into the family, the nome, the nation and humanity. Shembe's response to the challenge the concatenation called for was Hymn 180 which he composed in 1931:

Come, all you nations;
The fire has been lit in the hearth;
All nations warm themselves before it;
Come, you who are in need.

Come, you who are invited
Your heritage is ripe (for your taking).
Why do you moan,
When your heritage is in your hands?
It is enough;
Enjoy it.

Only to those who do not like it
Is the heritage denied.
Come, you who desire it.
For you the gates are open,
You who desire the heritage.

For you the heritage has been preserved;
It has been preserved
From before the heavens and this earth existed.

Medialism's concern with "all...nations" was translated into informative political action. In the South African setting, all nations included the Africans, Coloureds, Asians and Whites. The common factor among all these was that the person was a value regardless of who his parents were. The person was above race, colour and ethnicity. In addition, the various groups were bound together by the fact that South Africa was their home.

Political Medialism took form mainly in the Xhosa experience. A group of African intellectuals, led by Walter B. Rubusana, John Tengo Jabavu and others fought a long war of words against race discrimination. Like Shembe, these men took the position that the common humanity all races had should be the determinant of policies and not colour. In 1909 the Africans of the Cape Province joined hands with Coloured intellectuals and decided to send a delegation to London. Apart from John Tengo Jabavu and other Africans, the delegation included Dr. Abdullah Abdurahman, a Cape Coloured leader and a White man, Mr. W. P. Schreiner. The plea of the delegates gets to the core of Medialism:

> Your humble Petitioners respectfully submit that the only practical and efficient means whereby fair and just administration and legislation can be attained, peace, harmony and contentment secured, is by granting equal political rights to qualified men irrespective of race, colour or creed....

> Your Petitioners apprehend that by the racial discrimination proposed in the aforesaid Bill as regards the qualification of members of the Union Parliament, the prejudice already existing in the Transvaal, Orange River Colony, and Natal will be accentuated and increased; that the status of the Coloured people and natives will be lowered, and that an injustice will be done to those who are the majority.

—Vol. I, Document 17

Aided by the Communist Party of South Africa and the all-White Labour Party, Hertzog's Afrikaner nationalist party captured power in 1924 and became the dominant influence in South African politics. It pursued aggressively anti-African policies and whittled away some of the rights enjoyed by the Coloured community. That stimulated African and Coloured interest in a non-White united front against race oppression.

At the 1927 conference of non-White leaders, Mr. I. P. Joshua, of Kimberley, made this statement:

> The Conference was called primarily to discuss and evolve methods of co-operation between non-Europeans.

—Vol. I, Document 44

At the Third Non-European Conference held in 1931, Dr. Abdurahman moved the following resolution:

> That as the want of unity was the greatest stumbling block to the improvement of non-European conditions in the Union of South Africa, this Congress resolves:

> (a)   that the various non-European industrial and political organisations should unite and present demands for the improvement of non-European conditions in the Union on economic, social and political lines to Conferences of Employers and the Government....

—Vol. I, Document 46

In his address to the Conference, Dr. Abdurahman said that "unity was the first and primary essential to controlling power." He told the delegates, who represented the African, Coloured and Asian communities that the non-Europeans:

> must first put their house in order before they could improve conditions. The time had arrived, in fact the rank and file were demanding that they should pool their brains and resources, unite the multifarious Non-European Organisations into one powerful body and direct and guide the enormous power that lay in the Non-European workers.
> Vol. I, Document 46

The Hertzog government's decision to remove the Cape Africans from the Common Roll of Voters in the Cape Province brought into being the All-African Convention which, under the leadership of Professor Don Davidson Tengo Jabavu, the son of John Tengo, sought:

(a) To act in unity in developing the political and economic power of the African people.

(b) To serve as a medium of expression of the united voice of the African people on all matters affecting their welfare.

(c) To formulate and give effect to a national programme for the advancement and protection of the interests of the African people.

(d) To assist in rehabilitating dormant and moribund African organisations and bringing together unorganised Africans into societies, communities or bodies affiliated to the All African Convention. Vol. II, Doc. 15

Like the ANC, the All-African Convention (AAC) was formed in Bloemfontein. D.D.T. Jabavu and Seme had together issued a call to the African to meet and agree on a joint reaction to the abolition of the Cape African's right to be on the Common Voters' Roll.

At this meeting, which was held in December, 1935, Dr. G.H. Gool, a Coloured delegate from Cape Town, urged the AAC to:

> lay the foundations of a national liberation movement to fight against all the repressive laws of South Africa. Vol. II, page 7

Moderate Medialism had brought the AAC into existence. Dr. Gool represented the radical Coloured intellectuals of the Cape who worked with radical Black intellectuals to transform the AAC into a militant organisation. Tension was rising in the African community because of the Hertzog government's policies for the rehabilitation of the Poor Whites and the re-imposition of the poll tax in 1925. This tax had been the immediate cause of Bhambada's rebellion.

At the January, 1926, annual conference of the ANC, Clements Kadalie, a leader of radical Medialism in the trade union movement, had angrily denounced the Whites in a speech and had warned:

We are dealing with rascals — the Europeans are rascals.
Vol. I, Doc. 48d

Kadalie had spent his younger years in Cape Town where he was exposed to the radical African and Coloured influences which emanated from the city. The labelling of the Whites as "rascals" reflected the changing mood of Medialism; it complemented Dr. Gool's demand for a national resistance movement formed by all the non-White people.

This rising anger reached explosion point in 1943 when the Smuts government created the Coloured Affairs Department. In the view of the Coloured Community, this act extended the area of segregation for the Coloured people. The Coloureds, who had formed the Anti-CAD Movement to oppose the establishment of the Coloured Affairs Department joined the AAC, which was coming under the control of Black radicals.

Events were galloping to a climax. On December 17, 1943, AAC and Anti-CAD delegates met in conference and issued a *Draft Declaration Of Unity* and the well-known *Ten-Point Programme*. The conference elected a Continuation Committee and in doing this brought the Non-European Unity Movement into being.

One of the ingredients of the new African-Coloured united front was the rejection of the Whites. In a speech to the AAC conference on December 16, 1941, Mr. I.B. Tabata had attacked the performance of the African people's White representatives in parliament and had added:

I maintain that one has first to be in the skin of the oppressed and suffer as an African does, if he wants to represent him.
—Vol. II, Document 62

At first reading, this sounds like a negation of the non-racialism which had brought together the AAC and the Anti-CAD in the Non-European Unity Movement. In actual practice this was a translation into action of the radical Medialists' policy of non-collaboration. The inner logic of non-collaboration worked for the systematic isolation of the Whites on every conceivable scale.

In its final form, the Unity Resolution passed by the January, 1931, Non-European Conference had read:

That this third non-European Conference hereby approves of the urgent necessity of establishing a central body of the constituent

Associations of Bantu, Coloured and Indian Organisations of South Africa and resolves that the time is opportune to form such an Organisation....

Volume II, Document 46

The synthesis of experiences which the communion of African and Coloured radical minds produced was to a large extent a southern development. A related, though different experience was under way in the northern provinces of the Transvaal, the Orange Free State and Natal. We shall come to it in the next section of this chapter.

Medialism was the half-way house between the African and White worlds. Its political form moved the Africans, Coloureds and Asians to a non-White consensus on attitudes to the united front of White monoliths. While the Non-European Unity Movement stated in its Ten-Point Programme that it was not against Whites, the logic of the solidarity for which it stood moved events to the isolation of the Whites.

The Medialists argued that the Africans, Coloureds and Asians controlled the labour which sustained the White man's economy; that if these communities could pool their resources they could use strikes and boycotts to paralyse the economy and bring the White united front face to face with disaster.

The commitment to boycotts and non-collaboration was the essential step which would set people of all races on the non-White side moving toward the withdrawal of non-European labour.

Compromises became necessary in order to give viability to the non-European consensus on final goals and strategy. The AAC and the NEUM campaigned vigorously for organisational federalism, to enable each of the racial groups to maintain its identity in its organisations while pooling the resources and co-ordinating the activities of all when it came to action. Here, they were laying the foundations for one more form of weapon against White domination: African-Coloured-Asian Unity.

BLACK MONOLITHISM

In the main industrial cities of the Transvaal, Natal and the Orange Free State the Africans did not have as close contact with the Coloureds as in the Western Cape. Besides, race prejudice was stronger in the northern provinces, where the Africans did not have the vote. In the economy, the discrimination which existed was more benevolently disposed toward the Coloureds and the Asians, sometimes at the expense of the Africans. If this created the distance between the Africans on one hand and, on the other, the Coloureds and the Asians, it set the Africans moving toward the creation of a Black monolith as an answer to monolithism on the White side.

Dr. Pixley ka Isaka Seme, about whom much was said on the evolution of the ideal of African unity in an earlier chapter, was the father of African Monolithism. The ideals he propounded were the main pillars of the philosophy he and his colleagues held out as the African people's creed of salvation.

Seme and his colleagues were based in Johannesburg, the political cauldron in which nearly all the main language-groups of Southern Africa were churned by segregatory laws into a new community. Since the philosophy of this community has already been dealt with, attention might be given to its strategy, the dilemmas it faced, the type of action it took and the results it produced.

Like all the moods of African Nationalism, Monolithism had two minds; it was aggressive where it was strong and conciliated when weak. Medialism had done this to a greater extent. The movement of the AAC from being a moderatist organisation to the laying of the foundations of militancy, which inspired the Coloureds to throw in their lot unreservedly with the Africans during the Soweto Rebellion, was a moment of glory for Medialism. But it took a whole generation to give viable focus to the revolt of the Africans, Coloureds and Asians as a group. It went through phases when it was conciliatory and moved step by step to militancy.

The Monolithists were not committed to racialism as their spokesmen were to repeat for more than half a century after 1912. They felt that the Whites attacked and punished them for being the children of their particular parents; that the punishment translated into action a given attitude to the person and that this attitude was antithetical to everything sacred in Sudic tradition.

The White attitude to the person did violence to the Black person in unique ways. This circumstance demanded that the Black man should react to the provocation in a unique way. Seme proposed the transformation of all the Black peoples of Southern Africa, many of whom were represented in the Witwatersrand, whose gold mines made this region the industrial hub of South Africa, into a co-operating economic and political community.

These communities came from different parts of the subcontinent and spoke different languages. All of them were committed to the Sudic evaluation of the person. Seme and his supporters argued that this commitment should be the bond of unity which would give character and form to the Black monolith.

Like the Medialists, the Monolithists regarded the African's labour as the most powerful weapon in Black hands. While they accepted the principle of co-operation across racial barriers if need arose, they did not feel as strongly about African-Coloured-Asian collaboration as the Medialists were to feel. They laid stress on African unity and argued that a strong and well-organised African community was the first prerequisite for an effective non-European united front.

Their priorities were: the building of the new nation; the development of the Evolving Revolt on the homefront, the systematic isolation of the united front of White monoliths on the international plane and the maximisation of Black power.

Building a nation under the conditions created by conquest was a complicated and trying task. Contradictions and conflicts arose within the new nation which called for complicated compromises and accommodations. The Nominalists and early Medialists were the most important leaders of the new nation during the first twenty-five years of its existence. Attacked by the White supremacists on one hand, the communists on another and living in constant fear of disruption of the nationhood they were developing, the founders of the new nation went to great extremes to avoid those conflicts with the Whites which could lead to the destruction of the Bloemfontein Unity Ideal. They dreaded violence and "extremism" as they did the plague and adored "constitutional methods."

The Bicipitous Mind was in action in all these developments. The aggressive side of this mind had brought the Africans to Bloemfontein in 1912, had enabled them to create the new nation and was responsible for the launching of the Evolving Revolt on the homefront and the campaign against White domination on the world plane.

The mood of conciliation found expression in the hostility to "extremism,"futile dialogues with the government and the Dutch Reformed Church, and the failure of the AAC to launch a massive resistance movement against the abolition of the Cape Vote—although people like Dr. Gool and others had talked about a stand at the formation of the Convention.

Conflict with the Whites was passing through its second phase. There had first been the era of the wars which came to an end with Bhambada's rebellion in 1905—06 and the subsequent imposition of White rule. The years of disintegration had followed the collapse of Bhambada's rising. The Bloemfontein Unity Conference had seen the dawn of the age of fusion, which produced the Congress Youth League and the Non-European Unity Movement in 1943.

Anton Mziwakhe Lembede, Ashby Peter Mda and Robert Mangaliso Sobukwe were the principal spokesmen of the League. They made it clear that they were committed, not only to the Bloemfontein Ideal of Nationhood, but also to a united Africa. While Mda and Sobukwe sometimes expressed socialist sympathies, both were uncompromisingly opposed to communism. Lembede, Mda and Sobukwe wanted all with ears to hear to understand that they belonged neither to the West nor the East, but only to Africa.

The Youth League proclaimed its commitments with a vigour and determination which threatened to frustrate the ends of Soviet policy. The influence of the League over the ANC was so great, the League overthrew the leadership of the Nominalists in Natal and from then onward, became the kingmaker in the ANC. Xuma was thrown out of the Presidency-General of the ANC by the League. In Natal, Mr. A.W.G. Champion was elected to the Natal presidency of the ANC and rejected, years later, by the League. Chief Albert John Lutuli was a Youth League protege.

The surrogates of Moscow took steps to curb the growing power of the League. An alliance of five organisations was formed, which included the ANC. It has already been said that this set-up gave the ANC, which represented the majority, the status of a minority in the alliance.

One of the tasks the Congress Alliance (as it was called) had was to issue a document redefining nationhood for all communities. The Freedom Charter was this document. It was designed to supersede the Bloemfontein Ideal of Nationhood and commit the ANC to a nationhood which would serve best the ends of the Communist Party. Its acceptance by the ANC meant that the Soviet Union thought it was in sight of the mass organisation described by Eddie Roux in an earlier chapter.

This drift to the Left was reinforced by visits to Moscow and other Eastern European countries by members of the pro-Left leadership of the ANC. Walter Sisulu and Duma Nokwe were among those who visited Moscow during these years.

Opposition to the Charter was labelled *Black Racism* and was given the character of the unforgivable sin of South Africa's race politics. The Left spoke of South Africa as a "multi-racial" or "multi-national" country.Massabalala B. Yengwa, who was secretary of the Natal branch of the ANC for many years stated during the Treason Trial that he thought:

> there will be a stage where I think the people of South Africa will realise that this inequality is wrong; they'll find a way, as a group—as a multi-racial nation—as a common nation they'll find a way of distributing this land.
>
> —Vol. III, Document 53

In earlier years, Yengwa had been one of the founders of the League in Natal. When the communist offensive got into its stride, he shifted to the Left. In so far as I know, he never became a communist at any time. In his testimony under cross-examination during the Treason Trial again, he observed:

> My lords, what I do know is that Russia for instance has always con-sistently supported the struggle of the people of this country; it has never failed at any time to support us; it has always expressed itself as supporting the struggle of the Colonial peoples. . . . And it was natural that as far as we were concerned Russia was committed to supporting our liberatory struggle in this particular country. But that did not in

any way mean that we supported the Russian. . . .

—Vol. III, Document 53

Yengwa's statements are important because he was Lutuli's principal adviser and right-hand man.

The drift to the Left combined with the acceptance of the Freedom Charter as a declaration of ANC policy to split the movement and brought into being the PAC.

This split is important; it resulted from a head-on collision between the Bloemfontein Ideal of Nationhood, which Moscow rejected as *racist,* and the *multi-racialism* of the Freedom Charter. To an outsider, the quarrel might look complicated. In the South African setting, however, it was easy to understand. The African Nationalists rejected the prescription of destiny behind the imposition of the Charter on the Black people and argued that the Charter was an involved way of guaranteeing "national rights" (minority rights) over which Black and White were quarrelling. The African's struggle for freedom was a waste of time if its goal was to guarantee "national rights." What African Nationalism was prepared to guarantee were human rights, regardless of race, colour, ethnicity, sex or creed.

I was involved in this quarrel; I was against the Freedom Charter. Our side has never been given the hearing it was shown by subsequent events to deserve.

At the time I was not interested in the ideological aspects of Communism. What I objected to was the involvement of any foreign power in what I regarded as a Black man's struggle. I would have objected equally strenuously at the time if Britain or the United States had interfered in the way the Soviet Union was doing in our politics. At this time, my quarrel with the communists was over methods and not their ideology. I did not want us to be involved in Caucasian ideological quarrels because these had the effect of splitting us and of weakening us in our fight against the united front of White monoliths.

I regarded our struggle as a collision of minds which we would resolve by creating a mutually satisfying synthesis of values as African, Coloured, Asian and White South Africans. I did not want any of our people to impose their self-definitions on the other groups. But since the other groups thrived on our humiliation, we would have to develop enough power by ourselves to guarantee respect for our wishes. It was only when we were strong that the other communities would be prepared to recognise us as equals; when they would sit down with us and hammer out a formula for existence which all could accept with honour.

I saw the Evolving Revolt as a weapon in a war of minds. The balance of Black and White power was heavily against us. We were disarmed, desperately poor and largely illiterate. That meant that we had to work very hard to build our power. I was prepared to take over power wherever the enemy yielded ground; to consolidate our position on this ground and to move from there to conquer new ground. Whatever victory we scored diminished the power of the enemy. I was prepared for the trials and disappointments all this entailed; that was what an Evolving Revolt involved.

Our position demanded that we should concentrate on power dispositions in our group and on the White side. My duty was to serve the ends of power-maximisation in order that we might one day speak as equals of the other groups. My concern with power dispositions and monolithal alignments made me a functionalist. I was prepared to work with Moses Kotane and Dan Tloome, who, I knew, were Communist Nominalists. Like the Christian Nominalists, the Communist Nominalists were converts whom the White community rejected as it rejected me. I wanted a united front of the rejected wherever this was possible. Thus, when Lembede demanded the expulsion of the communists from the ANC, I opposed him because that would upset our plans for the maximisation of Black power.

If men like Moses Kotane and Dan Tloome had been in charge of the Communist Party of South Africa; if Moscow had trusted the Africans and left them free to develop their synthesis of Sudic and Marxist values, I would have had no quarrel with the communists. But the Whites who controlled policy in the CPSA wanted no deviation to the right or the left; they were determined to prescribe destiny for us. As Malkenson had said at the 1930 annual conference of ANC, the communists would declare open war on African Nationalists if we did not line up behind the Soviet Union as Gumede had said we should.

The White Christians had divided us so badly the Black Roman Catholic priests did not associate with their Protestant brothers in Christ to discuss common problems when I grew up. The Whites were bringing their divisive ideologies into our struggle to weaken us further. In all this I saw only disaster for our side. Our problem was that wherever Whites came into our organisations, they prescribed destiny and split us. Soviet policies cracked the foundations of unity which we, in the League, had worked so hard to build.

The position might be put a little differently. The two dimensions of the African mind had developed two responses to challenges. These responses determined thought and action in the Black community.

Under the stimulus of race oppression the Southern Response, based mainly in Cape Town, shed its racial angularities and created an African-Coloured consensus on the overthrow of White domination. Under the same stimulus, the Northern Response, which developed in the Witwatersrand, abandoned narrowly ethnic loyalties and created an all-African consensus on crushing White domination.

Thinkers in the NEUM and the League looked forward to the emergence of a consensus based on the reconciliation of the determinative responses. At the December, 1958, conference of the AAC, Mr. W.M. Tsotsi described the Congress Youth League in these terms in his presidential address:

> Those whose politics consist of stereotyped slogans and cliches will no doubt raise their eyebrows when I say it is our duty to guide and not to condemn categorically the emergent African Nationalism. We have to recognise that, in so far as it is genuinely anti-imperialism and anti-colonialism, African nationalism is a progressive and political force. ...

—Vol. III, Document 34

Years earlier, the AAC and the ANC had met in conferences to try to hammer out a formula for creating a synthesis of the determinative responses. At the 1948 joint gathering, A. P. Mda had sent signals to the leaders of the Southern Response indicating that the Youth League, the militant vehicle of the Northern Response, realised that there was merit in the Southern Response's insistence on non-collaboration. This is what he told the conference:

> . . . there was much in what Convention said on Non-collaboration. There was also much weight in what Congress said. But we shall all be forced in time to accept Non-collaboration. The discussion should boil down to whether Congress was prepared to accept Boycott as long-term policy. In 1946 the African National Congress had resolved to boycott the N.R.C. and Advisory Boards. In 1947 there was a slight change in the attitude of Congress. They advocated the election of ''Boycott candidates.''

> Mr. Mda . . . proposed the acceptance of the boycott weapon on principle.

—Vol. II, Document 69

When there was nobody around to prescribe destiny, the Africans tended to move gradually in the direction of a synthesis of determinative responses. At the 1949 joint conference of the AAC and the ANC, Mr. Moses Kotane, who typified a Communist Nominalist, argued that it was wrong for anybody to imagine that the ANC wanted to collaborate with the race oppressor:

> Congress did not want to collaborate. The worker in production was operating the machinery of oppression, but he formed another instru-

ment whereby the same instrument could be overthrown through strikes and revolutions. Congress did not want to collaborate, but the people were not ready. We could not carry out "Non-collaboration." The AAC itself had not been able to carry out "Non-collaboration." In some cases non-collaboration might be possible, determined by the preparedness of the people at the particular time. Congress stood for Non-collaboration—when the people were ready. They went into the N.R.C. to abolish it from within. They could not accept an inflexible term.

—Vol.II, Document 69

Kotane's realism reflected the state of mind among those who were committed to the Northern Determinative Response. At the 1958 annual conference of the AAC, Tsotsi adopted a realistic attitude in his presidential address, to which reference has been made above:

To give the Ten-Point Programme a leftist interpretation, no matter how cock-eyed, is to bring the whole movement within the definition of statutory communism and to run the risk of it being declared an unlawful organisation within the meaning of the Suppression of Communism Act. It is difficult to resist the inference that this is a consummation which many of the revisionists would devoutly wish as offering an easy method of escape from the hazardous tasks which presently devolve on them as members of the liberatory movement.

Tsotsi spoke for those committed to the Southern Determinative Response. The realism in the two Responses issued from the logic of the Evolving Revolt; from the need to move the two minds of African Nationalism toward convergence and an alternative to apartheid which would be acceptable in the two wings of the Evolving Revolt.

Soviet policy dreaded this move toward convergence. Those communists with whom I was friendly told me that Kotane often warned the White surrogates of the Soviet Union that it would be disastrous for communists if they went too far to lay down the law for the African.

Apparently, the Marxists forgot about his warnings when he went into exile and conducted the struggle in ways which prescribed destiny for the Black people. Nobody gives a better view than Ben Turok of what happened thereafter.

The reader has noted by now that conquest forced the African people to make a fundamental re-assessment of themselves; that, as a result, their thinking evolves according to a clearly recognisable and self-defining pattern toward a clearly stated goal. This pattern is heroic or idealistic or militant on one plane and, on another, conciliatory, realistic or functionalist. In preceding chapters the reader has been given brief outlines of the ingredients which went into the emergence of each response.

In every African from South Africa, there is the Enchorialist, Nominalist, Medialist, Monolithist and Supermonolithist. The family into which he was born, the community in which he grew up and the rhythms which give uniqueness to his culture and harmony to his society are a synthesis of all these ingredients. The pattern is a total of all these elements.

As said above, every African is born into this pattern; he grows up, matures and fulfils himself in it and eventually dies in it. This pattern determines his habits of thinking; it creates harmonies and conflicts which hone his personality, give symmetry to his culture, balance his society, prescribe final goals and fix his priorities. In the Zulu language, this pattern is defined in the two principles of *ukuba ngumuntu* and *ukuma njalo.*

These principles have their equivalents in all the major African language-groups of South Africa; they give the African community of the Republic its peculiar perspective; they make it what it is; they give it its identity and this identity is neither Zulu, Xhosa nor Sotho; it is a synthesis consciously and deliberately built by all the language-groups; it is a self-guided process of moving from one form of existence to a more satisfying dimension of being human.

The reader has noted, also, that the logic of this pattern moves all the African people to a clearly stated goal; to the creation of "a new and unique civilization"; to a "civilization" in which nobody will ever again prescribe destiny for the African.

The Christian missionaries, like the communists, erred in one fundamental respect: they set out to force the African to define himself in terms which served White interests, at the expense of the Black people. The London Missionary Society would see no reason for the African to define himself in his own terms when Jesus Christ had already done this for him. The missionaries of Marxism, for whom Potekhin speaks, see no reason why Africans are "unwilling to accept the scientific theory of socialism, tested in practice, and instead engage in a search for some other kind of socialist society" when Karl Marx has prescribed destiny for them so clearly.

The Collective Will rejected these evaluations of the African and developed its own definitions. These new self-definitions bound the Africans into a new community both in Bloemfontein in 1912 and in the formation of the Congress Youth League and the Non-European Unity Movement in 1943. The communists did try to form a racially mixed organisation—the Non-European United Front. This Front, however, set out to prescribe destiny for the Africans and was manipulated by the Whites to serve the interests of the Soviet Union. This circumstance damaged the credibility of the Front.

Left-wing "interpreters" of the African experience write extensively in efforts to split and divide the African people as we move toward the moment of victory. During the first fifty years of the ANC, they fought its

leadership and called it names taken over from their European experience. After their success in splitting the ANC, they created new
classes: the rural bourgeoisie and the urban bourgeoisie. The rural
bourgeoisie was the leadership involved in the homelands administrations
while the urban bourgeoisie led the Black Consciousness Movement.

These people who claim to be our allies but systematically disrupt our
efforts to unite ourselves do all these things not because they are White;
they split, divide and categorise us because they are committed to a
divisive attitude to the person. It is this attitude which is the enemy of the
African committed to the Sudic evaluation of the person. It is to this attitude that we must at all times direct our attention. Seme did this and
came to the conclusion that the integration of the African peoples in the
civilisation built on the pessimistic and devaluative view of the human being, which was developed by the ancient Greeks, Romans and Hebrews,
did not suit African conditions and that since we were a conquered people
we had to face realities. We could not move at will out of the experience
of conquest; we therefore had to create a synthesis of values and on this
synthesis build "a new and unique civilization."

Seme and the delegates in the Bloemfontein Unity Conference told the
world that we Africans were the product of a particular historical experience and that the Whites were the products of a different historical experience. The Bloemfontein Unity Conference set out to build an open,
non-racial society based on a communion of like-minded African, Coloured, Asian and White minds. This gathering represented the Northern,
functionalist Response; its strategy was to maximise the power of the
African monolith as the first precondition for establishing African-
Coloured-Asian-White agreement on final goals.

The Southern Response had, at an early stage (1909) begun by creating
a communion of the like-minded when it sent a mixed delegation to London to protest against race discrimination in plans for the establishment
of the Union of South Africa.

These responses did not have anything to do with class; they translated
into political action the bicipitous mind based on blended African and
Caucasian perspectives. Christianity and apartheid are in difficulties
because they have not as yet studied the two-dimensional mind and have
not developed a satisfactory formula for dealing with it on its own terms.
The Soviet Union is in similar trouble; its philosophy is so rigid that it does
not recognise the simultaneous legitimacy of African self-definitions. It
wants the African to define himself as the Whites in Moscow define him.
Lt-General Obasanjo of Nigeria has a name for this; he calls it
"teleguidance." We call it prescribing destiny for the African.

A lot has been said about prescribing destiny. How does it affect the
African today? Let us take and compare the positions of the Jew and the
African in the world today. Both have been exposed to extremes of
humiliation which few races of men have known. The Jews were once

slaves drawing water and hewing wood for Black men. The Africans were once slaves of White people. In our own generation, Hitler whipped the Jews all over Europe and wherever he had the opportunity, he roasted them alive in his incinerators. Hitler was a White man; he did these things to fellow White men.

The Zulus have this saying: *Yizulu elisusa osemnyango, limphos' emsamo, lithathe osemsamo limjik' emnyango* (It is that type of lightening which flings a person at the door to the rear of the hut and throws the one at the rear to the door.) In this aphorism, the Zulus describe a cataclysm or holocaust. Both the Africans and the Jews have gone through different holocausts. The Zulu aphorism teaches that he who has been reduced to the depths of suffering will, if he disciplines himself accordingly, rise to be the teacher of mankind.

Max I. Dimont, who wrote *The Indestructible Jews*, lists the following achievements of the Jews in *Jews, God and History:*

> There are approximately three billion people on this earth, of whom twelve million—less than one half of one per cent —are classified as Jews. Statistically, they should hardly be heard of. . . . But the Jews are heard of totally out of proportion to their small numbers. No less than 12 percent of all the Nobel prizes in physics, chemistry, and medicine have gone to Jews. The Jewish contribution to the world's list of great names in religion, science, literature, music, finance, and philosophy is staggering. . . .

> From this people (the Jews) sprang Jesus Christ, acclaimed Son of God by more than 850 million Christians. . . .

> From this people came Paul, organiser of the Christian Church. . . .

> Another Jew is venerated by more than one billion people. He is Karl Marx, whose book *Das Kapital* is the secular gospel of Communists the world over, with Marx himself enshrined in Russia and China. . . . Albert Einstein, the Jewish mathematician, ushered in the atomic age and opened a path to the moon with his theoretical physics. A Jewish psychiatrist, Sigmund Freud, lifted the lid of man's mind. . . . three hundred years earlier, a Jewish philosopher, Baruch Spinoza, pried philosophy loose from mysticism, opening a path to rationalism and modern science.

> Through the ages, the Jews successively introduced such concepts as prayer, church, redemption, universal education, charity. . . .

In the case of the Jews, history has been that lightning which flings to the top that man who has been at the bottom. But this is precisely what history is doing in the case of the African. The Jew and the Hellene gave mankind the pessimistic and devaluative evaluation of the human being. The Sudic African evolved and has been developing in the last 10,000 years the Sudic definition of the person. That Africa is becoming increasingly free has brought the Black and White races to the crossroads. From here, the two might divide into two camps and march straight to a head-on collision. The fundamental issue on which they would quarrel would be the attitude to the person. On the other hand the two might work toward the creation of a global communion of minds; toward a synthesis of attitudes to the human being to which both sides would freely give and from which they would freely receive.

The African victims of slavery, colonialism and apartheid are building such a synthesis because they need it and believe that mankind needs it. This synthesis, as everybody knows, was built on the basis of a composite strategy; on negotiation or violence, depending on the challenge the Africans faced in every given situation.

Where the situation demands it, the victims of apartheid will continue to negotiate; and where the need is for armed conflict, nobody should be in any doubt about what they will do: they will lay down their lives and shed other people's blood.

These victims are determined to create for themselves the world in which it will not be a crime to be an African. They are establishing an order in which they will have their own equivalents of the Nobel Prize and win these prizes in large numbers because the civilisation they will have built will not have been developed by the Greeks, Romans and Hebrews. When the time comes for them to have their own prizes, the chances are that for an African to accept the Nobel Prize will be to commit cultural or political suicide.

This takes us back to Mda and Tsotsi, to their efforts to move the Northern and Southern Responses toward convergence. The Nothern Response attached maximum importance to the maximisation of African power because it believed that neither the Coloureds nor the Asians nor the Whites would agree to work with the Africans as equals as long as the Black people remained weak. Only when the African was seen to be strong would the privileged groups regard African goodwill as their guarantee of survival.

The Southern Response believed that if the Africans, Coloureds and Asians struggled together and co-ordinated policies and action, they would, through such action, learn the habit of working together against White domination.

As the quotation from Mda shows, the two strategies were not incompatible. Given the time, people would regard them as the two aspects of the mind of the new nation. The Evolving Revolt—from King Cetshwayo who wanted a military alliance, through the Bloemfontein Unity Conference, to the formation of the League and the Unity

Movement—directed events toward convergence. Enchorialism and Nominalism had been eliminated as factors of political significance; Medialism and Monolithism had become the dominant influences.

By 1960, the Northern Response, represented by the Pan-Africanist Congress, had swung over to non-collaboration and had launched the great anti-pass campaign which wrote the Sharpeville Revolt into the history of South Africa. The following year, Nelson R. Mandela sent a letter to Sir De Villiers Graaff, then leader of the now defunct United Party that was the Opposition in the all-White parliament, in which he warned:

> The country is becoming an armed camp, the Government is preparing for civil war with increasingly heavy police and military apparatus, the non-White population for a general strike and long-term non-co-operation with the Government. . . .
>
> Vol. III, Doc. 34

> We have called on the Government to convene an elected National Convention of representatives of all races without delay, and to charge that Convention with the task of drawing up a new Constitution for this country which would be acceptable to all racial groups.
>
> Vol. III, Document 58

The Freedom Charter and Moscow's will to prescribe destiny had split the ANC and had produced the PAC. The two organisations fought bitter ideological and other wars until they were both banned after the Sharpeville Shootings. The ANC-sponsored Consultative Conference of African Leaders passed a resolution in December, 1960, which said, *inter alia:*

> It is its (the Conference's) considered view that the situation is further aggravated by the efforts of the Government to muzzle the political expression of the African people by the banning of the African National Congress and the Pan Africanist Congress.
>
> Vol. III, Document 54

The government's intransigence was making it clear that confrontation could no longer be delayed. But before we discuss this period, let us draw attention to two important features of monolithism.

At the height of the Soweto Rebellion, White journalists in South Africa described the rebellious students as "a new breed of Africans." There is a marked tendency in sections of the White community, which has always opposed the Collective Will, to perpetuate the canard that every revolt against White rule is a new phenomenon. The intention here is to destroy the element of continuity in the struggle and to represent our fight for freedom as the work of stray agitators.

Between M.B. Yengwa and Ben M. Khoapa there exists the thinking of a whole generation. Yengwa was one of the earliest leaders of the Youth League in Natal. That was in the 1940s. He could by no stretch of the imagination be said to be one of the spokesmen of the Black Consciousness Movement, just as I cannot be. Testifying during the Treason Trial, he told the all-White apartheid court:

> The oppressor and the oppressed will always have a struggle; there will always be a struggle between the oppressor and the oppressed. . . . You will never find the oppressed merely sitting down and making no effort to liberate themselves.

—Vol. III, Document 53

Ben Khoapa was one of the ablest spokesmen of the Black Consciousness Movement. In an address to students of the University of Cape Town in June, 1972, he warned:

> This is a world of groups. A man's power depends ultimately on the power of his group. This means that oppressed individuals must recognise their common interests and create a group. The oppressor creates a situation from which the oppressed can only extricate themselves by a regroupment.

> From this sketch, it is clear that the oppressor and the oppressed must clash. Some men try to avoid the exigencies of the situation by preaching universal brotherhood in a situation of oppression.[10]

Yengwa was not the author of the idea that oppressed and oppressor must clash. Cetshwayo and Mvambo before him enunciated the doctrine. There was nothing wrong in Khoapa re-stating a truth for which Yengwa had gone to jail. The children who offered their lives in 1976 in the bid to make it clear that they were determined to rule their country were not *a new breed of people* as the "interpreters" of the African say. In February, 1857, Nongqauza urged her people to sacrifice everything they possessed; to scorch the earth itself and die in order to be reborn into a more satisfying destiny. In White textbooks, Nongqauza is described as a sick woman; her people are given the image of history's idiots for having accepted the challenge with which she confronted them. But those people would not have produced Steve Biko if they had not heeded Nongquaza's call.

Caught in a not dissimilar situation of challenge when Titus conquered the Romans in A.D. 70-71, the Jews behaved as the Xhosa did. Let Solomon Grayzel, a Jewish historian, tell the story himself:

. . . all that was left for the Jews to defend was the Temple area. . . . This was the last stand for Jerusalem. Here the Jews felt they would be invincible, since God would not permit His Holy Place to be destroyed. Regardless of war and famine the sacrifices in the Temple had been going on as usual, until there was nothing to sacrifice.

The history of the Africans in South Africa has yet to be written. Much of what passes for history is a vindication of the White man and no African in his senses will accept that as his history. The Jews who sacrificed everything they possessed until there was nothing to give up are hailed as heroes; and when we Africans do heroic things, people call us names.

But that is not the point pursued at the moment. What we are concerned with is the element of continuity in our struggle. One of the most remarkable issues on which the Northern and Southern Responses moved toward convergence was the federal or confederal structure of society.

The Constitution of the ANC stated that African Kings and Princes and people from the Territories (Transkei and Ciskei) and the Protectorates (Botswana, Lesotho and Swaziland) would be members. The peoples in these lands were committed to different cultures, spoke different languages and defined themselves in different terms. The Unity Conference had regarded them all as "children of one house-hold." They had accepted this new definition of themselves. They accepted this because the Unity Conference recognised the simultaneous legitimacy of their self-definitions; that is: it recognised their right to their different territories and lands. This recognition could be on only one basis: a federal structure for the united nation.

At first, the Northern and Southern responses favoured the division of the country into two states. Writing in *The Guardian* in 1922, Mr. R.V. Selope Thema, the first editor of *The World,* argued the case for *"The Principle of Self Determination"* in these terms:

this principle means the division of the country into two parts to be controlled respectively by Europeans and Africans. That is to say, each race will have its own sovereign rights to manage its affairs in its portion of the country without interference from the other.

—Vol. I, Document 41a

Professor D.D.T. Jabavu gave evidence before the Governor-General's African Conference in 1925. One of the points he made was:

If political segregation were contemplated, the Natives should have their own Magistrates and the machinery of self-government. . . .

Now the Natives had to go back to their own civilization and develop along their own lines. That was logical if territorial segregation was applied, for the land question overshadowed all other questions.

—Vol. I, Document 39c

Seme was, like other early federalists, prepared to challenge the Whites to follow the logic of the policy of segregation. He told the 1933 annual conference of the ANC:

If the advocates of segregation are sincere, let them come out and give the Natives enough land for all their reasonable requirements. Let them draw up a dividing line from North to South or from East to West. Then let the Government order every White man to cross the line and go to his own corner and the Native to go to his own likewise. I beg to ask, if there is any Government in this country which would dare to put such a policy into practice.

—Vol. I, Document 43b

After the abolition of the Cape Vote in 1936, the Southern Response openly advocated federalism, beginning with organisations in each racial group.

We have already shown that the Umtata Conference of Chief Executive Officers committed itself to the ideal of forming the Federal Union of the Autonomous States of Southern Africa.

Nobody expected the new nation to think alike and agree on everything from the beginning. The people who went to Bloemfontein belonged to language-groups which defined themselves in different terms. Some of them had fought each other before the coming of the Whites. It was natural that they should have a number of areas where they held divergent views. One of the main tasks of the Evolving Revolt was to extend the area of congruency.

Selope Thema and Seme represented the Northern tradition while Jabavu spoke for the Southern. Both traditions rejected segregation; both were ready, however, to discuss partition. If the land could be divided into Black and White states, they believed, they would tolerate no segregation in their state. The convergence of views on partition showed that the new nation was developing its own consensus on what meaning to give to South African citizenship.

Events in the African community were giving to the type of state toward which the Collective Will was moving South Africa the character of what we shall call a synarchy, which is a federal union based on economic integration, political mutualism and cultural autonomy.

This type of state seemed likely to accommodate the needs of all racial groups; it provided the kind of political structure which would enable them to pool their resources in matters vital to their security and, at the same time, maintain their different cultural identities and develop these as they thought best in their different states.

The question which the movement toward convergence raised was: If the Northern Response, which regarded the Collective Will, the commitment to the creation of "a new and unique civilization," monolithism and the maximisation of African power as guarantees of victory; if the Southerners preferred a strategy which brought together the Africans, Coloureds and Asians and enabled them to develop the poises of collaboration by working together—how could the two traditions be moulded into a single, national strategy?

The bans on the ANC and the PAC came on African Nationalism before the African dialogue on a national strategy had got into its stride.

This provides some of the context in which the quarrel between the functionalists and the militants, between Buthelezi's National Cultural Liberation Movement (Inkatha) and the Black Consciousness Movement (which is a school of thought and not an organisation), needs to be seen.

History sheds light on this quarrel. For many decades the Cape Province was more or less a liberal part of South Africa. Largely as a result, the Cape Africans developed attitudes of co-existence with the other races and techniques for collaboration with the others which made an African-Coloured-Asian united front the obvious weapon to use against White racism. This exposure to living and working closely with Coloureds and Whites in a city like Cape Town made cultural autonomy and organisational federalism readily acceptable to some Cape Africans.

The Whites in Natal, the Orange Free State and the Transvaal adopted more angular attitudes to the African. This maximised the appeal to the Blacks of monolithism, a distinct and unifying cultural identity, the Collective Will and a Black Ideal of Nationhood.

However, something more fundamental than debating strategy was involved in the great controversies from the 1920s to the 1960s. The new nation was clearing its mind on what to do with the Whites; it was making up its mind on where to fit the Caucasians in the *larger nation* which it was building.

The Southerners wanted this *larger nation,* which was distinct from the *new nation* built in 1912, to be based on a communion of like-minded Africans, Coloureds, Asians and Whites; they wanted South Africa to be ruled by a like-minded majority.

The Northerners saw South Africa from the perspective of conflicting monoliths and concentrated on building African political, economic and cultural power. While the Northerners, like the Southerners, were committed to the Sudic evaluation of the person, they were always exposed to situations of extreme race provocation. Their preference for Black monolithism responded to race provocation.

The bans on the PAC and ANC combined with the persecution of the NEUM and the AAC to stop the public debate on where to fit the Whites; they brought to a halt the movement toward a consensus on strategies for the creation of a larger South Africa in which it would never again be a crime for a person to be the child of his or her particular parents.

The bans focused attention on an extemely important aspect of the nature of the two Responses; it showed that the two Responses were complements. The bans created a political leadership vacuum which the government hoped to fill with co-operative chiefs. The militant Medialists at the head of the Black Consciousness Movement decided not to collaborate with the government in operating the segregated homelands administrations. This was precisely what the government had wanted the militants to do. By adopting an inflexibly rigid stance of non-collaboration they made it easy for the government to isolate them and crush them in ways which enabled Matanzima in the Transkei and Mangope in Bophuthatswana to march unhampered to the vassalage which Pretoria peddled as independence in unviable mini-states.

The functionalists took a diametrically opposed position. While they declared war on apartheid, they defined the crisis in South Africa as a situation of changing dispositions of power. The united front of White monoliths wanted to keep power in its hands for all time. To change this position the African monolith's first priority was to build African power. Whatever situation offered the Black people power, no matter how limited, had to be consolidated and added on to the Black power-structure. These accretions of limited power would in time place the African monolith in a stronger position to challenge the power of the White monoliths.

The functionalists were determined to make it as difficult for the government to impose "independence" on Natal as they could. This required that they should use the homelands administrations elections to place nationalistic chiefs in office. This strategy placed the functionalists in situations of advantage in the dual-authority crisis apartheid had created.

Conflict rationalisation was the strategy the functionalists used here. The strategy was to be used by the Zulu-speaking functionalists during the Soweto Rebellion. The Zulus in Soweto fought the imposition of Afrikaans as an additional medium of instruction in African schools and rebelled with the other language-groups. While they clashed with the Afrikaner monolith in the Transvaal, the Zulus conciliated the English monolith in Natal. This stance must be seen, among other things, against the fact that Big Business, which is still dominated by the English-speaking, has thrown in its lot with the Africans in demanding the abolition of race discrimination. This has brought Big Business to the left of the government on a major policy issue—which is unique in the capitalist world. The functionalists felt that they were in business to create problems for apartheid and not to act in ways which reinforced the united front of White monoliths.

The Sharpeville episode marked a turning-point in the relations between Black and White. The Africans asserted determined leadership initiatives to seize power from the Whites. The real importance of this event lies in the fact that after the collapse of the ICU, it was the first political move to assert the Collective Will for the purpose of evoking a nationwide response to similar provocations.

The Soweto Rebellion was a massive assertion of the Collective Will.

The point to note about Sharpeville is that it had taken the new nation nearly fifty years to enable the Collective Will to evoke a national response to similar provocations. The Sharpeville stand hurled Black and White headlong into the era of confrontation.

That one wing of the African political world worked tirelessly for nearly fifty years to give unifying momentum to the Collective Will in the Black community, while its other wing moved events toward African-Coloured solidarity, goes beyond explaining the difficulties of nation-building; it explains the nature of the Evolving Revolt; it tells us that this Revolt is a process. In this process, different forces, disciplined by similar provocations and motivated by the same aspirations, move on different planes to the same goal.

The logic of the Sudic view of the person moves the African victims of race discrimination to the most important point of convergence with the Coloureds and Asians in the conditions created by apartheid. When the South African Students Organisation (SASO) came into being, it opened its doors to Coloured and Asian students as well. The durability of the bonds which SASO and other Black Consciousness Movement organisations developed was tested harshly during the Soweto Rebellion, and the young Africans and Coloureds came out of it all covered in glory.

People offer their lives, not for abstractions, but for vital things, for concrete beliefs which give meaning to their lives. The young Coloured men and women who chose to die by our side demonstrated their commitment to the Consensus on Nationhood whose foundations had been laid by the Medialists.

The consensus expressed a spirit of the times. African functionalists, leaders of the Coloured Labour Party and of the Indian Reform Party, met in Cape Town in January, 1978, where they formally launched the South African Black Alliance.

In 1912, the African monolithists had gone to Bloemfontein where they united the various language-groups into a new nation. In 1978, this nation felt strong enough to join hands with the Coloureds and Asians in order to build the larger nation. In 1935, the leaders of the Southern Response went to Bloemfontein to lay foundations for the larger nation. In 1976, the shedding of African and Coloured blood showed how solid and deep the foundations of the larger nation were. These are the events which determine thought and action in the African and Coloured communities and not class conflict.

A people involved in an Evolving Revolt that is inspired by a universally valid ideal is like an avalanche; it gains magnitude and momentum as it rolls down a mountain-side. The Evolving Revolt makes provision for and accommodates all adaptations to a constantly changing situation. Because it focuses on the fundamentals of conflict, the Evolving Revolt does not take rigid positions on the operational aspects of apartheid.

The advocates of apartheid, like the Marxists and the Christians, define the person in terms so rigid that they make themselves largely irrelevant in the Evolving Revolt. The exponents of these terms avoid the fundamentals of conflict because if they face them, they know on which side most Africans will go. Largely as a result, they concentrate on the operational aspects of White domination; they focus on race discrimination, pass laws, etc., when Black and White quarrel on the meaning given to South African citizenship and the attitude to the person on which this meaning is based.

But let us not digress too far from the Consensus on Nationhood. On their own, the Africans, Coloureds and Asians brought into being, after nearly 70 years of trying, a representative Black Alliance. Unlike the communist-sponsored Non-European United Front, the Black Alliance is not a front for any group of Whites who manipulate the non-Whites to serve the ends of Soviet foreign policy.

The logic of events on the African and Coloured sides points to a non-racial state as the only choice for South Africa. To say, against this background, that Black racism is the greatest danger in South Africa is a cover-up which the surrogates of Moscow use to disrupt African, Asian and Coloured movement toward a truly non-racial state.

This does not mean that there are no African or Coloured racists. Something would be wrong in these communities if there were none in a state based on racism. But we shall soon come to these.

For the present, let us have a look at the relations between the functionalists and the militants. It has been shown that the Black community is of one mind on the need for a viable form of unity both within itself and with other racial groups and on a non-racial society based on federalism. Medialism steadily developed into a radical movement under pressure from White domination. This increasingly was the case after the abolition of the Cape Vote.

The Natal functionalists decided to extort maximum advantage from the homelands administration which gave them legal platforms to commit illegalities like defying the government's ban on the NCLM's *Inkatha* magazine.

The quarrel on "collaboration" has been allowed to develop without adequate attention being given to it. The commitment to non-collaboration among the Xhosa-speaking Africans in the main conflict rationalisation also has its roots in the history of Zulu-speaking Africans. If the problem is seen in this light, we all can move a step or two nearer a consensus on strategy as well.

Functionalism was not invented by Buthelezi; it has its origins in Seme himself. The Zulu aphorism on which it is based states:

Inja iwaqeda ngolimi amanzi.
The dog finishes water not by drinking, but by lapping it.

This means that the ciliate mind has many ways of solving a problem; that one should not cease to struggle for the realisation of one's hopes simply because one does not have the tools one would like to have.

Seme did not make a great President when he led the ANC. He was too concerned with building the nation he and his contemporaries had founded, to turn it into an effective monolith, so that in the face of challenges from the White side, some of his schemes were bound to fail. He advocated the establishment of African Congress Clubs, one of whose tasks was to:

bring to the door of every African home the messages of Hope, Cooperation and Good Will from every corner of South Africa, . . . cater for all economic needs of our people, in towns as well as in the country....

The African must be taught to build himself up and not to expect all other people to get out of his way and give him an open road to progress. He has to fight for his freedom so as to learn its great value. . . .

[The African Congress Clubs institution] is a great national insurance system against unemployment and it should ensure the steady progress of the African nation. For this reason we must take every precaution to make it a success and to avoid all chances of failure. Therefore I shall propose that we start by employing the very best and most reliable Europeans to assist us in managing the Congress's business undertakings. The Revenue Department for instance should be placed under an ex-senior officer of the Native Affairs Department, who shall enjoy the full confidence of the African National Congress. . . .

—Vol. I, Document 48

Seme was a realist. He was aware that the inferior education given the African (at the time and at the present) made it impossible for the Black people to acquire given skills. The building of "a new and unique civilization" demanded these skills. Seme was not going to sit down and fold his hands until the day came when the Africans had the required skills; he was going to buy these from anybody who had them, even from the White side.

THE SUPERMONOLITHISTS

By the beginning of the 1960s, the Collective Will of the African monolith had become enough of a determinant of attitudes to draw in sharp outlines the character of the Evolving Revolt.

A brief recapitulation of the salient points in the evolution of the Revolt will provide the background against which the emergence of the Supermonoliths must be seen.

Contact with the Whites destroyed Enchorialism and political Nominalism and gave the Africans a Bicipitous Mind which developed a Collective Will. This Will spearheaded the revolt against White domination and set events moving toward the restoration to the African of his land and freedom.

The Collective Will was opposed by the will of the united front of White monoliths. The two wills derived inspiration from two diametrically opposed attitudes to the person. The clash between them was fuelled by race.

The performance of the Bicipitous Mind in this setting sheds light on the turn the crisis is taking in South Africa.

Whenever the Africans faced a fundamental challenge, the Bicipitous Mind responded in predictable ways; it simultaneously asserted conciliatory and aggressive leadership initiatives. Its first response to Union was the despatch to London in 1909 of a racially mixed delegation to oppose race discrimination in the constitution of the new Union. The tone of the delegation's representations was conciliatory. Its other answer was the decision to form a new nation whose destiny was to create "a new and unique civilization."

World War II confronted the African monolith with another fundamental challenge. It responded with radical monolithism in the form of the Congress Youth League and radical medialism in the form of the Non-European Unity Movement in 1943.

The Sharpeville Shootings and the bans on the PAC and the ANC created a political leadership vacuum which the Bicipitous Mind promptly filled with the Black Consciousness Movement and the National Cultural Liberation Movement. The Black Consciousness Movement's doctrines were vindicated when African and Coloured students died together in Cape Town during the Soweto Rebellion. The teachings of the Northern tradition were vindicated when the students from all the African's language-groups fought apartheid together and died together to establish their point.

The vindications showed that the radical Medialists and advocates of the Northern tradition were moving toward a convergence of minds when it came to tactics in given situations. One weakness remained: Radical Medialism, which was committed to non-collaboration, had not reached the point where it could recognise functionalism as another aspect of the Bicipitous Mind; where it could recognize the logic of events as moving the African, Coloured and Asian opponents of race oppression toward agreement on a national strategy against apartheid.

Dr. Gool had pleaded as far back as 1935 for this type of strategy. White South Africa's strategy of setting one non-White group against the others complicated movement toward agreement on this strategy. The decision of the Coloured students to die by the side of their African comrades made mincemeat of White attempts to set the Africans and the Coloureds against each other.

Bonds cast in blood cannot be legislated out of existence. What happened in Cape Town and elsewhere during the 1976 rebellion created the need for a quality of leadership which would translate into political action the consensus on final goals which, in the main, Africans and Coloureds and to a lesser extent the Asians, had established before and after the Soweto Rebellion.

As should have been expected, the Bicipitous Mind acted in characteristic ways. In an interview with the *Sunday Express* (Johannesburg, July 16, 1972) Jerry Modisane gave this glimpse of what is going on in the minds of many young Africans:[14]

> We do not need the co-operation of the White man any more—and we do not want him. We can find liberation from perpetual servitude on our own.

In 1919 the monolithists had gone to Versailles to set in motion the process of isolating the White supremacists on the international plane. How successful they had been was shown by the fact that in the 1970s even Pretoria's Western friends lacked enthusiasm for being seen to identify themselves with the apartheid regime.

From the early 1970s, the Black Consciousness Movement had worked systematically for the isolation of the Whites on the homefront. How far it succeeded was shown by the ways the Coloured community identified itself with the Africans.

In these changes, events were developing a mould in which to create a new consensus of like-minded Africans, Coloureds, Asians and those Whites who rejected the Caucasian will to prescribe destiny for the peoples of colour. Chief Gatsha Buthelezi, who led the all-African National Cultural Liberation Movement, Mr. Sonny Leon, the head of the Coloured Labour Party and Mr. Y.P. Chinsamy, the president of the Indian Reform Party met in Cape Town in March, 1978, and formally established the South African Black Alliance to create the new consensus.

In 1909 the Medialists had sent a mixed delegation to London. Their successors had gone to Bloemfontein in 1935 and argued the case for an African-Coloured-Asian united front against the united front of White monoliths. Their grandchildren had brought into being the Black Consciousness Movement which drew no distinction between Africans, Coloureds and Asians.

These areas defined another area of congruity in African thinking on the quarrel with the Whites; they showed that the so-called "moderates" in the African, Coloured and Asian groups were moving toward a consensus on an African-Coloured-Asian stand against apartheid; they showed, also, that the militants were moving toward the same consensus.

If the two sides finally created a consensus on strategy, they would force South Africa into a collision which would be a war of minds on the first plane, a race war on the second and an ethnic conflict on the third.

It is at this point that Modisane's words assume the harshest possible significance for Black and White in South Africa. When they were powerful in 1910, the Whites rejected the African. During the first half of the 1970s the African staged strikes in the major industrial areas of the Republic which the government could not suppress with the armed might at its disposal. If this established the relativity of White power, it placed Modisane and the South African Students Organisation, which he led, in a position to draw attention to the expendability of the Whites. The African was becoming strong, and when he was strong there were indications that he would reject those Whites who rejected him. The mutual rejection would produce one simple consequence: it would reduce South Africa to ashes.

The mood of counter-rejection must be seen in the context provided by history. This mood is important because it suggests that South Africa is moving toward an explosion which will simultaneously be a war of minds, races and ethnicity. The Sudic Ideal will be at war with the Caucasian Ideal; Black will fight White; Capitalists will clash with Communists while Enchorialists will march barefooted against each other.

History lists the provocations which produced the counter-rejection; at the same time it shows how African attitudes stiffened to the point that some Black people had to regard the Whites as expendable. To understand the development of mutual rejection, let us go back to the wars during the second half of the nineteenth century. This is a long and complicated story. Here we shall outline it only to the extent to which it sheds light on the rejection of the Whites by the non-Whites.

As already pointed out, the Nominalists regarded Christianity as a philosophy that would unify peoples and races. This belief developed a commitment to collaboration which had deep roots in all language-groups. The Africans so committed were given the status of "civilised Natives,"and could vote in the Cape and own land in Natal.

The monolithisation of the Afrikaners and the English called for the drastic modification of the policy which had rewarded the "civilized Natives." Modification led events in a straight line to a crisis of survival for the African. Let us have a good look at what happened.

After the Anglo-Afrikaner war of 1899-1901, the "civilised" Africans expressed their attitude to English pressures to unify the various provinces of South Africa in a statement the executive committee of the South African Congress sent to the British in about 1903. Among other things, the Africans declared that:

> The black races are too conscious of their dependence upon the white missionaries, and of their obligations towards the British race, and the benefits to be derived by their presence in the general control and guidance of the civil and religious affairs of the country to harbour foolish notions of political ascendancy. The idea [of African unity and independence as preached by Ethiopianism in the 1880s] is too palpably absurd to carry weight with well-informed minds, and tends to obscure the real issues and to injure the people as a class. The common law of the country is amply sufficient to protect the rights of the individual or the Church.
>
> Vol. I, Doc. 7

The bias for collaborating with the English is important not only because it extended the area of isolation for the Afrikaner, but also because when the English betrayed the Africans when the Union of South Africa was formed, there developed a bitterness against collaboration with the Whites which today finds expression in the hostility of the present Black Consciousness Movement, of which the South African Students Organisation (SASO) is one of the leaders, to given forms of cooperation with the Whites. This hostility has traditionally been strongest in the Cape where the Africans had made the greatest strides in education and political advancement. For these reasons, let us pursue the pro-English bias a little.

The South African Native Convention, the "civilised" equivalent of the White Convention which approved Union, met in conference in Bloemfontein from the 24th to the 26th of March, 1909. In its first resolution the Convention made this declaration:

1. This Convention recognises the principle of Union amongst all His Majesty's subjects in the South African colonies to be essential, necessary, and inevitable, the ultimate object of which seeks to promote the future progress and welfare of all.

2. The Imperial Government, of which we are now all loyal citizens, interested in, and sharing alike its responsibilities, is bound by both fundamental and specific obligations towards the natives and coloured races of South Africa to extend to them the same

measure of equitable justice and consideration as is extended to those of European descent under the law.

Vol. I, Doc. 15

At first reading, these professions of loyalty to the English might illustrate the extremes to which the "civilised" could go to accommodate the English. But any scholar or journalist who has familiarised himself with the attitudes of the Africans as expressed in newspaper writings of the times will have noted that the Africans were forging the dialectic of displacement as a weapon with which to crack the foundations of the closed society and neutralise the united front of White monoliths; it was a weapon developed for use in a situation of conflicting monoliths. It is this weapon that the students used to tear off the community of mixed blood from the Whites during the Soweto Rebellion in 1976 and to isolate the Whites.

British greed for diamonds and gold ignored the hand of friendship offered by the African side. Ignored, also, was the potential of the dialectic for changing the course of events when used as a weapon in a situation of conflicting Black and White monoliths.

The British eventually agreed with the Afrikaners to establish the Union of South Africa; to give it the character of a closed society in which the White skin was the definitive qualification for citizenship; to monolithise South African society, create a united front of the White monoliths and form a power-structure based on African labour, the Afrikaner's political potential, and English economic power. The English and the Afrikaner would function as a consortium of resident colonialists, guiding the destinies of the closed society and the conquered Africans.

The Afrikaners wasted no time in translating their political potential into action. Divided into conciliators, led by Louis Botha and Jan Christiaan Smuts, and the nationalists, who followed James Barry Munnik Hertzog, they threw in their lot with the English and sat in the first cabinet of the Union. Two years later, however, the Afrikaner monolith was making it clear that it would be satisfied with nothing less than the displacement of English as the main official language of South Africa. Hertzog, then in charge of schools, gave orders to the effect that Dutch should be the main official language in his province, the Orange Free State.

That moved the conciliators and the nationalists to a head-on collision. Botha dissolved his cabinet and reconstituted it without Hertzog. The latter went to De Wildt, a rural settlement in the Transvaal, where on December 12, 1912, he defined the destiny of the Afrikaner as the establishment of an Afrikaner-type of republic and committed Afrikanerdom to apartheid by insisting on the segregation of every community from every other. The Afrikaners, the English and the Africans were each to develop along their own separate lines.

Less than two years later, the Afrikaner's Nationalist Party, which is basically the group in power today, was formed in Bloemfontein. That gave the Afrikaner monolith a distinctive identity and set it moving in a straight line to conflict with the English monolith.

The moment of decision came in 1922, during the disturbances resulting from the discontent of White workers with conditions in the gold mines around Johannesburg. Smuts suppressed the revolt with a ruthlessness that led eventually to his downfall in 1948.

Afrikaner nationalism first set itself the goal of displacing the English from the position they occupied in the government. In the 1924 elections, Hertzog allied himself with the predominantly English-speaking Labour Party and overthrew the Smuts government. (Smuts had become prime minister after Botha's death in 1918.)

Hertzog was a man with an appointment with destiny. He wasted little time in dislodging the English from their positions of power in the state. The following list of the steps he took and their dates summarise the way he used the dialectic of displacement:

Date	Event
1925	Afrikaans recognised as the second official language.
1926	Under pressure from Hertzog, the Imperial Conference grants constitutional equality with Britain to the Dominions.
1927	The flag agreement with Britain recognises South Africa's right to have her own flag, side by side with the Union Jack.
1930	White women given the vote.
1931	The Statute of Westminster gives South Africa full freedom to administer her own affairs.
1938	*Die Stem van Suid-Afrika* becomes the second national anthem, next to *God Save The King*.

From *This Is South Africa,*
issued by the Department of
Information, Pretoria, S.A.,
Dec. 1971, pp. 68-71.

232

1976 South African Yearbook

General J.B.M. Hertzog, Prime Minister from 1929-1939.

General J.C. Smuts, Prime Minister from 1919-1924 and from 1939-1948.

Dr. D. F. Malan, Prime Minister from 1948-1954.

Hertzog's successors continued the process of displacement after the collapse of his government in 1939 by abolishing appeals to the Privy Council (1950); the cession to South Africa by Britain of the Simonstown Naval Base, the recognition of the South African flag as the only flag of the Union and the recognition of *Die Stem* as the only South African anthem, in 1957; the transformation of South Africa into a republic (1961).

Side by side with these moves were vigorous leadership initiatives asserted by the Afrikaner government to break Britain's stranglehold on South Africa's economy. The government nationalised the ownership of the most important primary resources and set up commissions and parastatal agencies to exploit and control the exploitation of these. The Afrikaners also embarked on a global policy for attracting foreign investments to South Africa, to reduce dependence on the English.

The Afrikaner monolith felt threatened not only by the English but also by the Africans who were owners of the land and had the advantage of numbers on their side. It set out to dispossess the African of whatever bits and pieces of land he still owned, crowded him into rural reserves which he did not own and forced him to sell his labour on the cheapest terms possible. How it did this is the subject of the rest of this chapter.

The dispossession as it took place in the land of the Zulus will be our model because the present author is most familiar with the history of this part of South Africa. There certainly were variations in the techniques used, but all these derived from one fundamental attitude to the person.

The case of the apartheid regime on the land issue is stated in the following quotation from *State of South Africa*[17]

The European settlers moved into areas not yet reached by the Bantu invaders or, as was the case in the Northern Provinces, deserted by them. At no time did European settlers deprive the Bantu of their lands....

The areas chosen by Bantu 300 years ago are still in Bantu hands and they were made inalienable Bantu areas by the South African government in 1913....

The official argument used by the advocates of apartheid is that "South Africa has never been exclusively a Black man's country.... Bantu tribes from Central and East Africa invaded South Africa at the time when Europeans landed at the Cape...." We are all familiar with the distortions of the truth used down the generations to justify the transfer of 87 per cent of African land to White ownership and to set aside only 13 per cent for the majority. The "evidence" of history is adduced selectively to prove that the Africans came to South Africa at about the same time that the Whites were settling down at the Cape. Science is placing at the disposal of all concerned techniques for establishing the antiquity of the African experience in South Africa.

Before we get to these techniques and what they tell us, let us make one point clear. While the White man's bias for categorisation divides human beings into groups and classes and inflates racial differences into determinants of policy, the Sudic evaluation of the person insists that the human value which metamorphoses into the human being belongs to no race; it defines the person regardless of where he is born and who his parents were.

The Khoikhoi and the Ba-Twa (the so-called Bushmen) belong to Africa; they are children of Africa and are as precious as any other. Our quarrel with the Whites is not that they dominate the Africans of Buntu origin; we oppose their rule because their bias for categorisation distorts the human personality regardless of who the person is. The important issue for us is the person; we emphasise the primacy of this person regardless of whether or not the person has Buntu, Khoikhoi, Bu-Twa or White or Asian origins.

The Khoikhoi and the Ba-Twa the Whites found beyond the Kei River were Africa's own children; what happened to them when the Whites landed in South Africa set precedents for what the Whites were to do to the Sudic Africans. It is the element of continuity in the White approach which deserves attention. They behaved the same way toward all the children of Africa.

Now for the antiquity of the African experience in South Africa. Colin Legum, the South African journalist who distinguished himself by writing for the London *Observer* on Africa, quotes [18] Monica Wilson, a White South African anthropologist, as saying:

The Portuguese records show that from 1554 there were people "very black in colour" south of the Mtata river [in the Transkei and a little further north] "the country was thickly populated and provided with cattle." From 1593 there is evidence that the people *south* of the Mtata spoke a Nguni language [Zulu], and from 1686 we can place the various Xhosa—speaking tribes known today; they occupied the country from the Buffalo River [East London] northwards. Traditions indicate that the Xhosa, Pondomise, and Thembu were living on the tributaries of the (M)zimvubu near the mountains, before they came to the coast. They may have been there for many generations: we do not know. There is nothing in the recorded traditions to indicate any substantial movement of Nguni [Zulu] people from north of the Drakensberg—much less the Limpopo— within the period covered by the genealogies, *i.e.* since 1300, and it may well have been centuries before that. None of these facts is new; all have been published at one time or another; but their implications appear to have been overlooked by the myth-makers of this generation'; Professor Monica Wilson: The Early History of Transkei and Ciskei, *African Studies*, Vol. 18, No. 4, 1959.

Jean Hiernaux, the distinguished French physical anthropologist, tells us in *The People of Africa*[19]:

The Iron Age, presumably introduced by Bantu peoples, has been dated back to the fifth century A.D. as far south as Swaziland, and to the ninth century A.D. in the north of South West Africa.... p. 179.

On page 177, Hiernaux notes that "at all the Early Iron Age sites (the region broadly from the Cameroons in the west to Kenya in the east and South Africa in the south) pottery belongs to the same (iron-metallurgical) industrial complex; its regional variants clearly derive from a common tradition." Such sites, he observes, have been found at different points in Southern Africa:

Country	Site	Earliest Carbon 14 Dating
Rhodesia	Mabveni	A.D. 180
Zambia	Kalambo Falls	A.D. 345
	Kalundu	A.D. 300
	Kangonga	A.D. 340
Uganda	Chobi	A.D. 290

Kenya	Urewe	A.D. 270, 320, 390
	Hills Behind Mombasa	A.D. 120, 160, 260, etc.
Tanzania	Bombo Kaburi	A.D. 220
	Uvinza (Pagwa)	A.D. 420

If Bantu or Sudic communities were settled in the Rhodesia-Zambia-Uganda-Kenya-Tanzania region between the years A.D. 180 and A.D. 420, it requires a particularly imaginative reading of history to argue that the Sudic peoples, to the south of the region under discussion, reached South Africa about 300 years ago. Whatever the shortcomings of the apartheid mind might be, it is certainly not unimaginative.

This background provides the framework in which we must view other developments in South Africa; developments which destroyed the African peoples' confidence in the leadership of the Whites in religion. The seizure of African lands was one of these. Defending the ratio of land held by the White minority to that reserved for the Africans, the *Year Book* argues that the Whites did not at any time seize African lands. The records of history tell a different story.

On May 12, 1843, Napier, the British governor of the Cape of Good Hope, announced that Queen Victoria planned "to adopt Natal as one of her colonies." He conferred the title of High Commissioner on Cloete, a Cape Town barrister of Dutch descent, and instructed him to travel to Natal to prepare ground for the take-over of Zulu land. Cloete cut up Natal into British territory to the south of the Tukela River while he expected the Zulus to be satisfied with the portion to the north of the river.

He then proceeded to Zululand where he forced Mpande, the Zulu King, to cede St. Lucia Bay to the British, "although it was obvious that the area could never be turned into a commercial harbour." By October 5, Mpande was left with no alternative other than to sign the treaty in which he was forced to recognise British sovereignty over land seized from the Zulus.

Cloete then returned to Durban where he considered the claims made by various White people on the land he had taken from the Zulus. Donald Morris, the American author of *The Washing of the Spears,* travelled to South Africa and spent some time in Natal where he had access to White records on the events under discussion. He reports that: [20]

Although only 365 emigrant Boer families were living in Natal, and most of these were in townships, no less than 760 individuals had submitted claims—most of them more than one. A Commandant Rudolph, who had done little farming but a considerable amount of commando riding, laid claim to forty farms totalling 400,000 acres;

Pretorius himself (the leader of the Natal Boers) wanted ten farms. A Mr. Aspeling in Cape Town, who had never lived in Natal, outdid them all by claiming 3,500 square miles. . . .

Cloete ruthlessly disallowed all these claims and gave some 200 families who were able to prove they had occupied the land for at least a year farms of 6,000 acres each. Smaller grants were made to families that had been farming for less than a year.

Sir Harry Smith, governor of the Cape Colony, annexed all the lands between the Orange and Vaal rivers and brought them under British rule as the Orange River Sovereignty on February 3, 1848. This seizure of African lands was in line with a long-established tradition. Jan van Riebeeck had laid down the Liesbeeck River as the boundary between White Africa and Black Africa. In 1778 van Plettenberg had fixed the boundary on the Fish River. During the Great Trek, the ancestors of the Afrikaner had descended on Natal and had occupied Zulu territory in the Weenen area without authorisation by the Zulu government.

These and similar precedents established minority "rights" at the expense of the majority. These "rights", most of which were established illegally, are today what the surrogates of Moscow, Dr. Kissinger and President Carter, want guaranteed by the dispossessed majority. This superpower consensus on guarantees for minority rights is indistinguishable from a demand for the legitimisation by the African people of White larceny.

If minority rights are to be guaranteed, it stands to reason that majority rights, too, must be secured. In the conditions which exist in the Middle World, however, to speak of group rights is to create unnecessary polarisations. The only rights that need to be and should be guaranteed in pluralistic societies are the rights of the individual regardless of race, colour, sex, station in life, class or creed.

The revolt of the converts was a protest against a system of values which connived at or permitted the dispossession of human beings if they happened to have the wrong type of skin complexion.

The divalent morality was to go beyond encouraging dispossession; it was to define final goals in terms which reduced the Africans to the status of the permanently deprived in their own land. The *Year Book* continued:

The South African government has accepted the desire of colonial people for self-rule as a natural right. In contradistinction with colonial powers in Europe, South Africa has its dependent people within her own borders. The granting of independence can, therefore, not follow the political pattern worked out by the colonial powers of Europe. For good reasons colonial people were not represented in the parliaments of the European mother countries. These reasons also hold good for

South Africa. Most multi-national states created in Europe were not a success, but led to friction and the fear of domination.

—pp. 70-71

Every eighth grade schoolboy who does his history homework almost anywhere in the world knows that by 1914 an African deputy from Senegal had been elected to the French National Assembly. Black men were officers in Napoleon's army. Men of African descent sat in French cabinets and were mayors of French cities. The *Year Book* than proceeds to justify apartheid:

It is well-nigh impossible to create one nation out of the different population groups inhabiting the Republic of South Africa. Each group clings to its own culture, language and traditions. This natural trend must be respected. The integration of all population groups in one body politic would have to start at school, but there is no single medium acceptable to all national groups. Western democracy is foreign to Bantu tradition. All over Africa the tendency is towards a one-party state under a black dictator. To adopt the principle of One-Man-One-Vote in South Africa would hand over the culturally advanced groups, *i.e.,* the Whites, Coloureds and Indians, to the mercies of a Bantu leader who might well have communist affiliations. The problem which South African statesmen have to solve is to protect the position of each population group and to give them full opportunities for political, economic and cultural development without doing injustice to or hampering the development of the other population groups. It is a unique problem for the solution of which no precedent exists in the world. The solution is being sought along the lines of parallel development, *i.e.,* each population group should manage its own affairs and, wherever practical, develop into self-governing states which will form a South African Commonwealth. South Africa's policy could rightly be described as Nation Building.

"Nation Building" is closely related to the economic set-up in South Africa and for this reason needs to be seen against the background provided by what the Minister of Bantu Administration and Development called "the basis on which we organise our labour policy for the Bantu." In actual practice "nation building"and the organisation of African labour are synonymous.

"Nation building" is one of apartheid's holy words. South Africa, every spokesman of apartheid will start by saying, is made up of a number of nations. Apartheid seeks to allow each of these nations to develop along its own lines.

Two snags immediately come to the fore. If the idea is to guide the evolution to nationhood, why is it that there is no African input? Nationhood is defined for the Africans by the omnipotent Afrikaner monolith. The land set aside for the African nations is demarcated by the Whites to serve White interests.

The use of euphemisms to conceal the evils of any given system of tyranny was not invented by the White supremacists in South Africa. It was resorted to over and over again by the slaveholders in the United States and the traffickers in human beings in Britain. More than two hundred years ago Malachy Postlethwait wrote[21] that the enslavement of the Africans was "a Melioration of their Condition; provided living in a civilised Christian Country is better than living among savages. . . . Their Condition," he continued, "is much better [compared] to what it was in their own Country." The areas of "betterment" are examined in the light, not only of the meaning "nation building" gives to the day-to-day lives of the Africans but also of the peculiar economic and quasi-military relationship that apartheid seeks between South Africa and the United States.

Land is the most important area in which "nation building" might be seen at work. South Africa has a land area of 472,359 square miles and is larger than "Germany, France, Italy and Portugal put together," to quote the *Year Book* again. This area is divided into four provinces as follows:

Province	Area in Square Miles
The Cape	278,465
The Transvaal	110,450
The Orange Free State	49,866
Natal	33,578

Like the United States, South Africa has a mixed population whose components are drawn from almost every continent in the world. In 1970 the figures for the main sections of the population stood at:

Group	Population Size
Africans	14,893,000
Whites	3,779,000
Coloureds	1,996,000
Asians	614,000

Each of these groups is divided into two or more ethnic sections. The Africans separate into the Zulu, Xhosa, Sotho and Shangane-Tonga-Venda sections, while the White community is made up mainly of the Afrikaners (the descendants of the Dutch, French Huguenot and German settlers), the English and the Jews. There are also Hollanders, Germans, French, Portuguese, Italians, Greeks, etc. The Coloureds, or people of mixed blood, are made up of the Cape Malays or Cape Coloureds, whose ancestors originally came from the East Indies and served the Dutch as slaves in the Cape of Good Hope, and the Coloureds Proper. The Asians include the dark-skinned, mainly Hindu, Indians, Arabs, Chinese and a handful of Japanese. The Coloureds live mainly in the Western part of the Cape Province, where the Dutch first established their settlement, while the Asians, in particular the Indians and the Arabs, are concentrated in Natal. Like the Africans, the Whites are scattered all over the country though each of the main language groups in each community tends to be dominant in some provinces:

Group	Area Of Preponderance
Zulu	Natal and Transvaal
Xhosa	Cape, Transkei and Ciskei
Sotho-Tswana-Pedi	Orange Free State and Transvaal
Shangane-Tonga-Venda	Central, East and Northern Transvaal
Afrikaans	Orange Free State and Transvaal
English	Natal and the Cape.

The total area reserved for African occupation is about 59,338 square miles or 13% of the total land area of the country[22] while the so-called White areas constitute about 87% of the land. The following table shows the distribution of the African majority's 13% of the land in 1971:

Ethnic Group	Population Size	Area Inhabited	Living Space (in morgan	Number of Reserves
Zulu	3,970,000	Natal	3,585,212m	29
Xhosa	3,907,000	Transkei-Ciskei	5,016,550	19
Tswana	1,702,000	W. Tvl, N. Cape, OFS	4,330,135	19
BaPedi	1,596,000	N. Transvaal	1,947,277	3
Southern Sotho	1,416,000	N. Cape, OFS	50,000	1
Shangane	731,000	N. Transvaal		4
Swazi	487,000	E. Transvaal	519,057	3
Venda	360,000	N. Transvaal	935,800	3
Tonga	—	NE. Transvaal	890,716	—
South Ndebele	230,000	N. Transvaal	—	—
North Ndebele	180,000	N. Tvl, Rhodesia	—	—
Other	314,000	— —	—	—

The Africans live in the reserves, on White farms and in the urban areas. In 1970 they were distributed as follows:

Area	Numbers	Percentage of Total
Rural Reserves	4.5 million	41.7
Urban (White) Areas	3.1 million	28.7
White Farming Areas	3.2 million	29.6

For many years White policy aimed at making the reserves a vast reservoir of cheap Black labour for the White man's mines, farms, industries and homes. Apartheid set out to stop the influx into the White areas. In spite of intensified control of the movements of the African people the number of Africans in the so-called "White areas" rose from 6,827,000 in 1960 to 7,975,000 in 1970. During the latter year there were about 6,918,000 Africans in the reserves. The increase in the number of Africans in the urban areas constituted one of the earliest defeats of the policy of apartheid. The figures which follow tell how this happened:

Year	Urban African Population
1936	1,245,000
1946	1,856,000
1951	2,328,000
1960	3,192,000
1969	4,000,000(Estimate)

Behind these figures lies a revealing story of life in the reserves or "bantustans." In 1969, for example, South Africa had 1,029,000 workers from the Transkei. In other words, nearly all the reserve's most productive manpower was working in South Africa on a more or less permanent basis. In 1970 the South African Institute of Race Relations reported that the density of population in the African reserves averaged 117.2 per square mile as against 34.8 per square mile in the so-called White areas. The overcrowding combined with the exportation to South Africa of productive manpower to create the following position at the food production level [23]:

Item	Area	Production Figures	
		1947-48	*1967—68*
Maize	White	30.4	105.2
(per million bags)	African	3.8	3.7
Sorghum			
(per million bags)	White	1.8	9.5
	African	1.2	0.7
Livestock	White	8.8	7.5
(per million units)	African	3.6	4.0

The results of the type of nation-building which the apartheid regime seeks to impose on the African people was best described in a statistical summary made by concerned Americans in the late sixties or early seventies:

Item	Africans	Whites
Population (millions)	14.9	3.8
% of population	69	18
% land reserved	13	87
% of income received	18.8	74
Average income/head/year	$188	$1,596
Average annual wage in mining (cash only)	$302	$5,275
Average annual wage in manufacturing	$828	$4,032
Minimum cost of living for family of 5 in city	$1,075	$1,075
Life expectancy	35-40	64-70
Infant mortality per 1,000 births	200-250	2-4
No. of pass arrests/year	7-9000,000	0

Comment on the story told by these figures would be superfluous. The only addition one can make is that in a parallel though different situation of deprivation, the Americans in the colonies took to arms and proclaimed themselves a sovereign independent people. The Evolving Revolt, the Sharpeville Shootings and the Soweto Rebellion are moving the Africans in the same direction.

Let us see another aspect of African responses to conquest.

The course of dispossession of the African on which the united front of White monoliths embarked exposed Christianity as a soporific for dulling African reactions to conquest and deprivation. The loss of the Cape Vote produced the commitment never again to collaborate with the Whites.

By slow degrees, the Africans of Natal lost most of their rights to own land.

In these changes, the White power-structure destroyed the nascent Black middle class, the class which had been a moderating influence in the Black community; the class which had a vested interest in collaborating with the Whites. Moderatism began to be rejected as a political approach. Everywhere, clamours were raised demanding that the Africans should not collaborate with the Whites in given areas.

One point should be made before tracing the evolution of non-collaboration. Reference has been made to the Southern Response and the Northern Response. These had nothing to do with Xhosa or Zulu or Sotho experiences. It is true that in the South the Xhosa were the dominant community, just as it is true that in Cape Town the Coloureds were the dominant community. The Southern Response was a synthesis of African and Coloured attitudes.

It would be wrong to regard the Northern Responses as a Zulu approach. Johannesburg was the melting-pot in which all language-groups were forced by race humiliation to see salvation for themselves in a rebirth into a new destiny.

Some of the most distinguished names in the evolution of the Northern Response were Xhosa-speaking. The history of the new nation would be incomplete without the names of Dr. A. B. Xuma, A. P. Mda, Nelson Mandela, Walter Sisulu, Oliver Tambo and others, while the history of the Southern Response has Northern names like Martin L. Khumalo, Dan Khoza, Gaur Radebe, etc.

When we speak of responses, we refer to movements of ideas in a constantly changing or Evolving Revolt.

But let us return to the clamours for non-collaboration. These clamours were loudest in the Cape, where the Africans suffered the greatest political losses. It was in the midst of these rejections of collaboration that the Congress Youth League came into being to develop a strategy for confronting White domination with "the reality of disaster."

Formed in April, 1944, the League laid great stress on the ideological aspects of the fight against White domination. In the same year, it issued its "Manifesto" which contained the following:[24]

The Ideal of National Unity Must Be the
Guiding Ideal of Every Young African's Life

Our Creed

a.)   We believe in the divine destiny of nations.

b.)   The goal of all our struggles is Africanism and our motto is "Africa's cause must triumph."

c.)   We believe that the national liberation of Africans will be achieved by Africans themselves. We reject foreign leadership of Africa.

d.)   We may borrow useful ideologies from foreign ideologies, but we reject the wholesale importation of foreign ideologies into Africa.

e.)   We believe that leadership must be the personification and symbol of popular aspirations and ideals.

f.)   We believe that practical leadership must be given to capable men, whatever their status in society.

g.)   We believe in the scientific approach to all African problems.

h.)   We combat moral disintegration among Africans by maintaining and upholding high ethical standards ourselves.

i.)   We believe in the unity of all Africans from the Mediterranean Sea in the North to the Indian and Atlantic Oceans in the South . . . and that Africans must speak with one voice.

Vol II, Doc. 48

I was secretary of the subcommittee set up to draft the "Manifesto." The draft which we finally presented to the conference of African youth which met in the Bantu Social Centre on Eloff Street, Johannesburg, reflected the thinking of the more important members of the subcommittee. Anton Mziwakhe Lembede, who was eventually elected the first president of the League was an ascetic idealist; an uncompromising partisan for what he called Africanism. The strong emphasis on moral rectitude which characterises the early pronouncements of the League are to a large extent attributable to his thinking. Ashby Peter Mda, the most perceptive political leader I knew in the forty years of my involvement in African politics was the consistently realistic and anti-racist theoretician of the League. Walter Max Sisulu, for whom I had a high regard and whom I continue to respect in spite of his defection to the Left, was always concerned with the realities and practicalities of race conflict. My own concern was the ideological aspect of the quarrel between Black and White.

The League contributed a new factor to the evolution of the dialectic: the confrontation strategy which could, in Mda's letter[25] to G. M. Pitje dated August 24, 1948, "in clear terms set a new pace to the politics of South Africa."

Mda's thinking, which most young men and women in the League shared, set out to corrode the leadership provided by the Old Guard which believed in collaboration because of the voting rights enjoyed by the Africans in the Cape and the land rights the English extended to the Africans in Natal. The generation to which Mda and I belonged had been born into dispossession; we grew up in dispossession; our thinking and behaviour were influenced by the temper of the dispossessed. Our first priority was to destroy the leadership which believed in collaboration on terms dictated by the Whites. Mda expressed our viewpoint in the letter referred to above in these terms:

> The clash is inevitable, because the Congress senior leadership reflects the dying order of pseudo-liberalism and conservatism, of appeasement and compromises. The Youth League reflects the new spirit of a self-conscious Africa, striving to break age-old oppression and liberate the national forces of progress.
>
> Vol. II, Doc. 55

The League set out to move events to the moment of decision; to redefine the race problem and make majority rule the central issue in the quarrel between Black and White. The League's first priority was what Mda called the *politicisation* of the African people. This meant that as a people we should draw the distinction between the fundamentals of conflict and the operational aspects of race oppression; that we should concentrate on fundamentals and refuse to waste time on the functional aspects of White domination. To spend all our energy and time on these aspects was to accept White definitions of the race problem and to collaborate in our humiliation.

Up to the formation of the League the Old Guard had regarded the operational aspects of White domination—the abolition of the Cape Vote, residential segregation, the Pass Laws, the Differential Wage, etc.,—as the issues on which Black and White quarrelled. This departure from the spirit of the Bloemfontein Conference of 1912, this collaborationist approach, surrendered the initiative to influence events to the Whites. The Whites would do the thinking for the African as long as the latter defined the race problem in operational terms. The African would continue to be oppressed by consent.

The League rejected the emphasis on the operational aspects and concentrated on fundamentals. The December, 1949, annual conference of the ANC discussed a statement to be issued on the preparations made by the Whites for the tercentenary anniversary celebrations of the landing of Jan van Riebeeck at the Cape in 1652. The Old Guard adopted positions which Ntsu Mokhehle, the Youth League leader from Lesotho, characterised as being "inclined towards the Whiteman's point of view." Mda agreed with Mokhehle and rejected references to the anniversary which suggested collaboration. He drew attention to the fundamentals of conflict and indicated that a statement of the African position in non-collaborative terms would signify[26]

> not only our challenge to the Whiteman's point of view but also an inflexible determination on the part of the African to struggle for National Freedom. . . . in spite of the odds heavily loaded against the African by an enemy highly organised and armed with a perfected technique of domination.   Doc. 47

Concentrating on the fundamentals of conflict was designed, among other things, to create a vacuum in White thinking on the future of South Africa. The League planned to fill this vacuum with an African alternative to apartheid; with a translation into geopolitical terms of the Bloemfontein Ideal of Nationhood.

The creation of the vacuum led to a violent clash between the League and the Communist Party of South Africa (CPSA). Lembede even demanded the expulsion of the Black communists from the ANC. But Lembede missed one vital point: the communists were, like the Christians, products of the Graeco-Romano-Hebraic evaluation of the person. One could not throw them out of the ANC without expelling the Christians.

I opposed the expulsion of the communists because it seemed to me a tactic for dealing with the operational aspects of what I was to call albification. If we were to deal successfully with the communists, we had to straighten out our thinking on the conflict between the black and the White attitudes to the person. I was certain in my mind that at the time our people were not ready for a decisive stand against the Christian assessment of the human being. Where our first priority was to politicise them for the purpose of creating the vacuum in White thinking, we had to avoid making too many enemies on the African side.

By the middle of the 1950s the communists were strong enough in the ANC to be able to impose the Freedom Charter on the African organisation. This document, which was first adopted in Kliptown, near Johannesburg, on June 26, 1956 set out to supplant the Bloemfontein Ideal of Nationhood and, in its place, to give the Africans a goal which provided for guarantees for minority rights. The Charter did not say a word on the 1912 Ideal of Nationhood; at the same time it said a lot about minority rights which it regarded as "national rights."

The adherents to the Bloemfontein Ideal rejected the Charter's definition of nationhood and argued that by adopting the Charter as a statement of policy, the ANC had renounced its position of custodian of the 1912 Ideal. They broke away and formed themselves into the Pan-Africanist Congress (PAC).

BLACK CONSCIOUSNESS MOVEMENT

The statements of the leaders of the Black Consciousness Movement shed light on the situation of ungovernability.

The emergence of the Black Consciousness Movement was an important turning-point in the crisis in South Africa; it showed the Bicipitous Mind giving fundamental answers to a fundamental problem.

On March 21, 1960, the PAC led the Africans in the main industrial areas in a nation-wide demonstration against the Pass Laws. The government's answer was to write the Sharpeville Shootings into our history and to ban the PAC and the ANC.

The bans created a political leadership vacuum on the African side which the government hoped to fill with co-operative chiefs. The Africans countered with a two-pronged offensive which aimed at making it difficult for the government to bring all the homelands institutions under the control of the surrogates of Pretoria. In Natal, the Zulu-speaking Africans persuaded Chief Gatsha Buthelezi to stand for election as chief executive officer of the Zulu Territorial Authority (ZTA), not only to make it impossible for collaborative chiefs to endorse apartheid, but also to use the ZTA to build a new political power-base and rededicate the Natal Africans to the Bloemfontein Ideal, which the apartheid regime sought to destroy.

At about the same time—the last years of the 1960s—a ferment developed in African student organisations which led to the severance of African links with the White National Union of South African Students (NUSAS) and the formation of a non-White South African Students Organisation (SASO). SASO developed into the spearhead of what came to be known as the Black Consciousness Movement (BCM).

The BCM was not an organisation; it was a school of thought and reflected the climate of thinking in the African community in the 1960s. It laid stress on self-reliance in the African community, collaboration among the Africans, people of mixed blood and the Asians, and the isolation of the Whites on the homefront. At the same time the BCM asserted vigorous leadership initiatives to deepen the vacuum created by the League.

The Black Consciousness Movement influenced behaviour in many departments of African life. The Black Theology school of thought came into being to give to Christianity a meaning that would be valid and satisfactory on the African side of the colour line. The government believed that the Federal Theological Seminary in Alice produced the theological agitators who gave to Christianity an English-oriented meaning which was designed to destroy the political power of the Afrikaner. The government denounced the Black Theologians as "communists" and eventually closed down the Theological Seminary.

On the economic plane, Black traders organised themselves into the National African Federation of Chambers of Commerce (NAFCOC) which set out to use the African's purchasing power as a weapon for the establishment of a satisfying place for the Africans in the economy. NAFCOC was instrumental in establishing the mainly Black-owned African Bank of South Africa to challenge White dominance in the economy.

Workers' organisations were formed in the major industrial areas of the country. Some of these were involved in the wave of strikes which swept Natal in particular and South Africa generally from 1971 to 1975.

These strikes have a special importance. In terms of South African law, it is a crime for Africans to stage a strike. The law is so bitterly hostile to African strikes that the police do not always draw the distinction between the strike as an economic weapon and the strike as an act of treason. In spite of this, the Africans were able to organise demonstrations for higher pay and improved working conditions which have important political implications for the future of South Africa.

During the 1974 budget debate on the Labour Vote Dr. A. Boraine, then the Progressive Party's spokesman on Labour, quoted the following from figures supplied by the Department of Labour:

Year	Number Of Strikes
1973	246
1974	374

Another dimension of the dialectic was emerging here. The unification of the traders' organisation and the formation of the African Bank threatened to displace the Afrikaner from the positon he was establishing for himself in the economy. The two developments laid the foundation for an economic alliance between the Africans as workers and consumers and big business, which was mainly English. The strikes showed that the dialectic had pushed the African to the point where he had begun to experiment with the use of the strike as a political weapon.

That in 1974 alone, strikes averaged more than one work-stoppage per day—the majority of the strikes were organised by the Africans—brought to light an extremely important feature of the dialectic. The strikes were damaging to apartheid; they tarnished South Africa's reputation as a paradise for foreign investors. The government went to known extremes to suppress them. The fact that in spite of everything it did, it failed to stop them brought to view a new point of weakness in the White power-structure: the government had begun to lose some of its ability to impose its will on the Africans.

This weakness was drawn in the sharpest outlines possible by the Soweto Rebellion which continued for more than a year in spite of unprecedented shootings of the Africans to suppress it. The mood of ungovernability which the rebellion expressed paralysed the authority of the Whites in Soweto and forced the government to withdraw its order imposing Afrikaans as a second medium of instruction in Transvaal schools for the Black race.

The dialectic had displaced White authority in the church, isolated the White supremacists on the international plane, driven a wedge between the people of mixed blood and the Whites, and brought the African to the point where he began to launch economic offensives to displace Afrikaner power at this level and, finally, to rebel and create a situation of ungovernability.

Those sections of the White press, like some White authors who specialised in "interpreting" developments on the African side, rushed to see in the ungovernability, the mood of "a new type of African." The statements of the leaders of the "new type" told a different story; they told mankind that the Evolving Revolt had taken one more step toward majority rule and that the Africans were determined to reach their goal no matter who opposed them; that they were rejecting all forms of collaboration with the Whites. In 1972, Mr. Jerry Modisane was elected president of the South African Students Association, whose approach to the race quarrel has had a profound effect on the thinking of Black students. In an interview with the Johannesburg *Sunday Express* (July 16, 1972) Mr. Modisane is reported to have said:

> We do not need the co-operation of the White man any more—and we do not want him. We can find liberation from perpetual servitude on our own.

Writing in *Creativity and Black Development,* a South African Students Association publication, Mafika Pascal Gwala made this angry protest against the distortion of African history by the Whites:

> We are commonly told of our barbaric aggressions, of intertribal friction and of the need to christianize and civilise us. This White attitude towards the Black man's past impels that a struggle against White interpretation of history become an absolute necessity. [27]

Gwala's rejection of White interpretations of African history did not stop at the above. He condemned those Africans, particularly in Francophone Africa, who accepted French cultural inspirations. He continued:

> With the regaining of freedom the leadership sector that only yesterday had been talking of Negritude looked up to Paris for all its cultural needs; French ways of thinking and behaviour were enhanced. Corrup-

tion and scandal mongering thrived while the people starved and suffered. The rebels of yesterday have become the good boys of today's Paris.

Gwala consistently exhorted his readers to guard against

the deviating tendency of judging reality through a distorting mirror of the White world. . . . A truly conscious student will thence fight for his human dignity too. He will stand against White preaching of free enquiry while they [the Whites] enforce obscurantist outlook[s) on the university campus. He will expose the danger of those books in which equality is made synonymous with privilege. He will not accept lies and inverted truths that are expounded in the name of democracy. Let me add, an abstracted democracy. . . . Some of our [South African] Blacks are not innocent of the crime of fostering White attitudes in their contact with other Blacks. We can no more tolerate. . . . Black selling whiteness to fellow Black.

To Ben J. Langa, then editor of the volume of essays under discussion, the humiliation of the Africans called for "a new spirit of human-beingness" in the Black people's "struggle for identity." Turning his back on White culture, Langa continued (page 63):

Black people now need . . . evolvement of a new Culture—a Black culture that will want to liberate them [from] the shackles of perpetual servitude and subordination. In so many ways have they clearly demonstrated their total abomination of the system that deprives them of a decent living when they so deserve it.

All this and our common oppression should be enough reason why we should come together and found our new Black culture. We don't seek another europe, one europe is enough. . . .

Art by Blacks must be for Black people. It must not be for White consumption and be meaningless pieces of irrelevant "art" hanging in Parktown North,[28] Berea or Houghton. . . . Our art . . . must derive its life in the communes and ghettoes where there are no Rembrandts, Picassos or Da Vincis. Black artists must expose the ills of the world, reflect answers to these ills. . . . We must reach for a true new Black culture and true humanity will be our reward.

One of the features of the revolution in African thinking as revealed in the writings of youth leaders is the element of ruthless self-criticism.

Another voice from the ranks of the Black Consciousness Movement was raised. Barney Pityana was president of SASO at the time of Biko's speech in Cape Town. He was thinking in terms of a functional monolithism which would work for Black disengagement from the White cultural experience.

> The Black person must realise that he is on his own. . . . In order that a group of people can bring about a change there must be an identity of interests. . . . Any identical interest between Black and White is effectively blurred by the colour question. The Blacks . . . must be deeply rooted in their own being and see themselves as a functional monolithic structure. This means that Black people must build themselves to a position of non-dependence on Whites. They must work toward a self-sufficient political, social and economic unit. . . . The way to the future is not through directionless and arrogant multi-racialism but through a purposeful and positive unilateral approach. Black man, you are on your own. . . .

Functional monolithism was no longer interested in concessions and reforms or in integrating the African in the White man's economy. It set itself the goal of destroying the power-structure itself and to replace it with a new society based on an ideal of fulfillment and nationhood which had its roots in the African experience. If the White man felt he could not accept this, there always were the American, British and other Western air forces to airlift the Whites out of South Africa as happened in the crisis which developed after the independence of Zaire. Nixon's threat that his administration would not condone violence in Southern Africa thus did not address itself to the realities of the Black-White crisis.

A commentator in the September-October 1972 issue of the SASO *Newsletter* expressed the African mood in these terms:

> ...We Black people should all the time keep in mind that South Africa is our country and that *all* of it belongs to us. The arrogance that makes White people travel all the way from Holland to come and balkanise our country and shift us around has to be destroyed. Our kindness has been misused and our hospitality turned against us. Whereas Whites were mere guests to us on their arrival in this country they have now pushed us out to a 13% corner of the land and are acting as bad hosts in the rest of the country.

The answer to the White problem, the commentator proceeded, was "to provide our own initiative and to act at our own pace and not that created for us by the system." This expressed a mood shared by increasing numbers of people in Free Africa. As the area of freedom widened on the continent it became increasingly clear that the circle of hostility to the White man was growing.

The will to isolate the Whites found expression in the formation in 1971 of the Black Peoples Convention which set out to unite in action Africans, people of mixed blood and Asians behind this programme of principles:

- to liberate and emancipate Blacks from psychological and physical oppression;
- to create a humanitarian society where justice is meted out equally to all;
- to co-operate with existing agencies with the same ideals;
- to re-orientate the theological system with a view of making religion relevant to the aspirations of the Black people;
- to formulate and implement an education policy of Blacks, by Blacks for Blacks.

Ben A. Khoapa became one of the ablest exponents of the philosophy of the Black Consciousness Movement. In an address to students of the University of Cape Town in June, 1972, he defined[29] himself as one of those

people who are seeing increasingly the futility of devoting a major portion of their time to talking and intellectualising about things that prove unhelpful to both sides because we see things differently. . . .

The Black people, he continued, must

do whatever they conceive they must do as if Whites did not exist at all. . . . The question of the presence or absence of White people is a tactical matter which can only be answered in a concrete way by reference to the long-term and short-term interests of Blacks. . . . We are caught just now in an impossible historical situation, and that fact, which terrifies some and leads others to despair, gives our struggle a grandeur, a nobility, and a certain tragedy which makes it of moment to the world. . . . Blacks must organise and use their group strength to wrest control of every organisation and institution within reach. . . . This is a world of groups. A man's power depends ultimately on the power of his group. This means that oppressed individuals must recognise their common interests and create a group. . . . that the oppressor and the oppressed must clash. Some men try to avoid the exigencies of the situation by preaching universal brotherhood. But it is a mystification to preach universal brotherhood in a situation of oppression. Paradoxically, a prerequisite for human solidarity is a feeling of non-solidarity with men who stand in the way of solidarity. . . . The oppressed can only bring about a future of universal brotherhood in proportion as they feel and exhibit group solidarity among themselves and cease to feel solidarity with the enemies of human solidarity. . . . History has charged us with the cruel responsibility of going to the very gate of racism in order to destroy racism—to the gate, not further.

Those with whom Khoapa belonged, the Sharpeville Generation, took pains to point out why they had turned their backs on the White man:

Preoccupation with the White man leads to blunders, confusion in the ranks and demoralisation; it obscures the issues. It is possible for example to be free, creative and happy without being in the presence of White people. It is also possible to be free, creative and happy in groups which are not all Black. Neither separation nor integration confronts the system in its totality for both share the same root postulates. In one way both deplore the fact that White people do not love Black people. But love is irrelevant. History is a struggle, not an orgy.

The crucial factor responsible for marching to "the gate of racism" was the value-system to which the Whites, both the liberals and the advocates of apartheid, were committed. "One of its most shattering characteristics,"[30] wrote Njabulo Ndebele, a perspicacious spokesman of the Sharpeville Generation, was that it "tends to be extremely acquisitive." It transforms people into prisoners of possessions. Ndebele continued:

The urban Blacks have joined this acquisitive world. . . . People do not matter; it is things that matter. Things make people; people no longer make things. . . . People no longer approach work and matter with a creative bent, because their handling of matter is no longer a means of self-expression, it is now a barren conformity to an impersonal acquisitive norm. An acquisitive society is also characterised by its purposelessness. There is no intrinsic purpose behind this blind acquisition of material things; indeed, acquisition is an end in itself. That is why after having acquired out of conformity, one has no value for that which one has acquired, because it has no intrinsic value for one: . . . the Whites cannot help but acquire, and in doing so, these Whites may be ignorant of the injustices they perpetrate, having been rendered feelingless by the blind urge to acquire. The Blacks must assert their human dignity and rebel against an institution which relegates them to the status of things.

The "rebellion" must be a gigantic and all-embracing leap into the future; a bid to seize the moment that will carry the Black people to a satisfying destiny. Its priorities range over every department of African life. J. Dumo Baqwa, another member of the Sharpeville Generation, lists them in the following quotations from Robert Williams, a black American theologian:[31]

The will to leave the ideals and standards of Western culture behind and the courage to risk the creation of new modes of thought and new institutions based on the Black experience; a return to the songs and dances and rituals that speak of solidarity and survival and hope; a thorough-going re-evaluation of the moral and spiritual values of the African past; an astringent reassertion of the life-force and wisdom of the elders and ancestors; a resolve to re-establish and sustain those family ties and communal bonds that form the basis of Black humanism and dignity; the forging and reshaping of an idiom of expression, a form of effective communicating that will lead to a representation of the life and reality characteristic of the Black experience.

The quotation from the Black American theologian is of interest for two reasons. Williams was invited by SASO to deliver the keynote address to its third Students' Council Conference at Hammanskraal in 1972 but was refused a visa by the South African government. His address was nevertheless presented to the students.

The invitation must be seen as an African bid to establish effective bonds with the Black Americans for the purpose of reinforcing the "rebellion." While the Sharpeville Generation emphasised its commitment to Black Consciousness, its spokesmen took pains to deny that there was a "close parallel" between it and the Black Power movement in the United States, for example.

The denial must be seen in perspective. While there were striking similarities in the positions of the Black people in South Africa and the United States in given directions, elsewhere there also were fundamental differences. Apart from the differences in historical backgrounds, the two communities moved into the future at two different levels. In South Africa, the main inspiration against White domination was the *uBuntu* ideal of fulfillment whereas the Black American saw his future largely in terms defined by the White experience.

Thus, while at given levels the daishiki revolution laid stress on *re-africanisation,* in South Africa the quest was for a satisfying meaning of *regeneration.* Policy among the Africans in South Africa sought to give a valid meaning to *uBuntu* in situations of Black-White conflict. The Black Americans were still searching for a satisfying definition of the ideal which they translated into experience. Some Afrikaners took advantage of this difference to stress the importance of closer links between the Black Americans and the Afrikaners, and not the Africans. One assumption was that the Afrikaner and the Black Muslim, for example, were committed to a brand of race exclusiveness which the Africans reject; and that this exclusiveness moved the Afrikaners and some Black Americans to a future not without identical goals. The Sharpeville Generation countered this interpretation of the Black American's position by making it clear, as Khoapa did, that racism as such was not an end; that it was a vehicle for the creation of a world based on values with a universal meaning. Ndebele supported Khoapa by adding that:

It is important . . . . that the Blacks cultivate and develop a philosophy of nature and of life that will centre around the concept of human worth and human dignity. . . .

Ndebele went out of his way to explain that the Black Consciousness revolution searches "for a new culture" which will

. . . explore intellectual avenues and channel them towards the realisation of our aspirations thereby bringing about a new way of life that is more human and humane.

For this culture to thrive, the African had to be ready for drastic changes in his outlook on life; he should re-evaluate the religious experience forced on him by the White conqueror. This is how Ndebele approached the problem:

. . . the Blacks must turn their backs on all the Western Churches; they have been shorn of all emotional content. A genuine religion will spring out of the Blacks' own circumstances, just as a genuine philosophy of life should. It should be a religion that will find God through man; and not man through God. . . . If the Whites do not want to change their attitudes, let the Blacks advance and leave them behind; and when they have been left behind, let them be waited for on the day they realise the value of the change. The important thing to realise is that what the Blacks are striving for is more valuable than racial hatred.

The attacks on the Christian Church were a rejection of the divalent morality which had one meaning in dealings between Black and White and another in relations between White and White. The Africans wanted a mature morality which would be simultaneously valid on both sides of the colour line.

The leaders of the Christian church in Africa had set out to discover a *universal dimension* because the White-led church did not have it; the church failed because it did not define the person in universally valid terms. It said he was a creature when the Sudic experience regarded him as a self-defining value.

A crisis of disenchantment with Christianity was emerging in the search. But the All-Africa Church Conference would not find the *universal dimension* so long as it refused to face the fact that the Sudic and Graeco-Romano-Hebraic evaluations of the person were polarities; that the African Christian is a contradiction in perspectives and that the Christian Nominalist is a product of conflicting perspectives.

The crisis of disenchantment was an evolving process. In 1975, the All-Africa Church Conference was casting around for a *universal dimension*. By 1977, the outlines of the crisis had emerged most clearly in the church in South Africa. Black Protestant leaders had embraced the philosophy of the Black Consciousness Movement and had brought into being the Black Theology school of thought which set out to give to Christian values a relevant meaning on the African side of the colour line.

A particularly significant feature of the crisis in the land of apartheid was the "identity" quarrel inside the Roman Catholic Church. The roots of this quarrel could be traced to Roman Catholic teachings on authority and the person. Writing in *The Washington Post* of December 30, 1977, Pierre Haski of Agence France-Presse made this report:

> JOHANNESBURG—A crisis is brewing within the South African Roman Catholic Church between the bishops, most of whom are White, and Black African priests who support the philosophy of Black Consciousness. . . .
>
> The conflict has reached such proportions that some Black clergymen are considering training their own Black priests outside the authority of the bishops, according to well informed church sources. . . .
>
> The Black church leaders wanted an Africanization of teaching so they could "recover their identity."

The crisis of disenchantment set out to discover a *universal dimension* which would enable the Africans to *recover their identity*. In other words, the crisis of disillusionment was a collision inside the Catholic Church, between interpretations of the Christian philosophy which clashed because they were based on diametrically opposed evaluations of the person.

The collision produced the Christian Nominalist whose mind was cast in a Christian mould while his psyche was shaped by his Sudic view of the person. Forced by conquest out of his Sudic environment and rejected by the Whites, he turned inward, to himself, for the fundamental inspiration which would enable him to build for himself and his people the world after their design; the world in which they would realise the promise of being human.

The point to be noted about the Nominalist is that he is a product of conflict between a civilisation which lays emphasis on the primacy of the person and recognises the simultaneous legitimacy, validity and importance of all cultural self-definitions, and another, which defines the person in devaluative terms and works for the diminution of his worth as a human being. Nominalism sets out to bridge the chasm between the two outlooks by creating a synthesis of perceptions which will have universal validity.

The Nominalist emerges in all situations of contact and conflict between Black and White in Africa. Up to now, the Christian Nominalist has featured prominently in the clash of colour because Christian missionaries arrived in Africa before the Marxists did. The search for a *universal dimension* and the commitment to the recovery of the African people's *identity* have begun to establish the irrelevance of the White missionary in Africa. Christianity is on the defensive because it used a divalent morality to destroy the African's *identity*.

Like Christianity, Marxism is a product of the devaluative, Graeco-Romano-Hebraic evaluation of the person. Where Christianity discovered the African "savage" generations ago, Marxism is beginning to discover the ideological "heathen" in our time. Marxist missionaries overwork themselves making converts from the ideological "heathens" and proselytes from the Christian Nominalists.

Unlike the other spokesmen of the Black Consciousness Movement, whose thinking has been influenced to a large extent by SASO, Njabulo Ndebele goes out of his way to castigate not only the educated Africans who have accepted albification—the imposition of Caucasian values on the African— but also the largely unschooled in the separatist churches. These people reject albification at the level of church leadership but accept the Christian evaluation of the person to which they try to give a Sudic meaning. The syncresis works for the continuous extension of the area of fragmentation in the African community. Ndebele reacts to this by proposing an alternative religion:

> We have seen how religion has seemingly been used as a substitute for political expression. In being thus, religion in the Black community has become barren, because it has no intellectual content to it. Thus, the many sects we see are a perpetuation of bondage. The Blacks must obliterate all these sects. On the other hand, the Blacks must turn their back on all the Western Churches; they have been shorn of all emotional content. A genuine religion will spring out of the Blacks' own circumstances, just as a genuine philosophy of life should.

Black theologians are as vehement in their attacks on Christianity's pessimistic evaluation of the person as are the theoreticians of the Black Consciousness Movement. The Reverend Sabelo Ntwasa attacks albification in the Christian church in these terms:

Now traditional Christianity, as taught us by our know-all White tutors, has set out to teach us a lot about our shortcomings and little about the positive and essentially good nature of man....

We must also remember that the individualistic approach of the missionaries is due to their having come from an individualistic society; hence their failure to understand our communal- and man-centred society, which is the hallmark of the black world....

And all the White, imbibed values in our life-style as Black people will never die unless my brothers will sit up and heed the call of Black Theology and just for a moment forget the vulgar fish-and-chips and Coca-Cola way of life we have inherited from the White world....

Blacks, therefore, with their tremendous sense of community in their culture, have the responsibility of building this into the very fabric of the life of the Church. [32]

The government conveniently ignores the fundamental criticisms of the Caucasian evaluation of the person which guide the African people's Evolving Revolt and blames all attacks on White domination on communist instigation. The Reverend Mokgethi Motlhabi, also writing in *Black Theology*, starts by tracing the origins of racism in South Africa which, he says, arose from quarrels over land. The Africans, he continues, lost on the battlefield because of their poorer technology. This leads him to the following conclusion[33]:

If racial prejudice exists as a myth to preserve a structure in which a few have a monopoly of power and wealth, then it is the concept of a few having a monopoly of power and wealth which must be attacked....

In every instance the structure is supported by a myth. In the political power structure the myth of racism is crucial, as is also the myth of communism—*i.e.* every person who questions this political structure is labelled a "subversive communistic agitator."

...God is neither our servant, to be treated as we choose, nor our master, to treat us as he chooses, but our comrade and friend in the struggle for freedom....

Africa has a value system which makes people more important than time and speed. The West has a value system which makes speed more crucial than people....We cannot have the authoritarians who try to tell us what we believe or what to believe and who have the power to reward or punish us.

The situation of ungovernability is the most remarkable development in South Africa's crisis of colour. It shows that the Evolving Revolt organised in 1912 has developed enough momentum to make a frontal attack on White domination. The attack cracked the unity of the White monoliths and forced Big Business to oppose race discrimination and to come out in support of the Africans on this issue. At the same time it exposed the gravity of one of the fundamental weaknesses in the White power-structure: the paucity of White numbers. Up to the time of this writing, fifteen months after the first eruption of violence in Soweto on June 16, 1976, White authority has not been fully restored in Soweto where riots erupt on the slightest provocation. The government's failure to pacify the township shows that there are limits to White power; that the gun is no guarantee of White dominance or security when opposed by a determined Black majority.

Of especial importance in considering ungovernability is the evolution of the student revolt. The students did not defy White authority for the first time on June 16. For more than five years before this date they had been rebelling and rioting in different parts of the country. The government failed to suppress these revolts, many of which were violent.

In 1976 the Black Peoples' Convention issued *Focus On South Africa,* a bulletin in which it expressed its attitude to the crisis in South Africa. The Convention, which worked in close collaboration with the South African Students Organisation, was the leading political organisation in the Black Consciousness Movement. Among other things, the bulletin said:

> Violence in Black schools has been reported to be caused by a number of factors, listed as follows: dissatisfaction with food, draconian rules and regulations, teaching, the lack of books, the behaviour of the masters, etc.

> The above expressed factors are however not the fundamental factors. These are just secondary factors which emanate from deep resentment of the system of education dictated to Blacks, without their prior consultation, by the fascist and racist White-minority regime in South Africa. This deep resentment and rejection of this oppressive and slave educational system has brought about confrontation between the designers of the system and the consumers of the evil system. The events listed below are but a few.

- May, 1972—University of the North students walk off the campus after a speech given during a graduation ceremony against the type of education given to Blacks. The walkout is joined by students from the University of Zululand and Fort Hare University. The struggle is also joined by students at the University of Western Cape (meant for so-called Coloured students).

- April, 1975—All boys at Nchawe High School at Hammanskraal near Pretoria were detained by police after buildings were damaged during a protest against inadequate food and sleeping facilities. Later 122 were found guilty of public violence and 87 were to receive cuts (lashes).

- May, 1975—The Nathaniel Nyalusa (High) School, Grahamstown, came to a halt for several weeks. The trouble was started by students' protest(s) against staff misconduct, inferior education and shortage of textbooks. Nineteen teachers who left the school were dismissed.

- September, 1975—About 500 students at Blythswood School in the Transkei went on a rampage after complaining that their food smelt of oil. They cut off the power, assaulted a teacher and broke windows. After an inquiry 56 pupils were suspended.

- October, 1975—Nearly 350 boys at the largest African high school in the Cape, Healdtown High School, near Fort Beaufort, walked out after a week of violence.

- October, 1975—In a revolt at a vocational school at Nongoma, Zululand, a pupil was shot in the stomach by police, a vehicle was overturned and one had its tires slashed.

- November, 1975—Thirty pupils from Moroka High School, Thaba Nchu, were treated in hospital after a "disturbance" caused when girls refused to attend a Sunday Service.

- April, 1976—A high school at Waterval in the Eastern Transvaal failed to re-open after the holidays following boycotts and strikes by students and staff in sympathy with 142 boys expelled during the first term.

- May, 1976—400 African students stoned two Security Police cars and two teachers have since been arrested under (the) Terrorism Act. This happened at Siyamukela High School, Madadeni, Newcastle.

- May, 1976—More than 200 students at the University of Zululand stoned Chief Gatsha Buthelezi's car during a graduation ceremony at the campus. The students carried placards which read: "We reject Vorster's puppets." This was clearly the students' rejection of Vorster's government's policy of separate ethnic homelands.

- May, 1976—More than 120 boys were suspended from Lourdes High School near Umzimkhulu after a fight at the school.

- June, 1976—The burning of a police vehicle in Soweto and other acts of violence, culminating in growing strikes against the enforced use of Afrikaans as a medium for instruction.

An unpublicised cause of ungovernability was the government's contradictory translations of its own policies into action. Apartheid had insisted all along that it set out to enable the African to *develop along his own lines*. These lines were laid down by Afrikaner cultural leaders in Black universities; by a system of education developed and applied by Afrikaners for the purpose of afrikanerising African thought.

When the Africans tried to show that Afrikaner definitions of the African were as irrelevant as the lines laid down by the advocates of apartheid, the police moved in. In June, 1976, the Black People's Convention held a seminar on economic policy. Its members met at St. Joseph's Catechetical Centre, in Mafeking. The seminar resolved that the policy of the Convention would be Black Communalism which it defined as "an economic system based on the principle of sharing, laying emphasis on community ownership of land and its wealth and riches."

In approving the policy, the seminar noted:

- That Black Communalism, as defined, is a modified version of the traditional African economic lifestyle, which is being geared to meet the demands of a highly industrialised and modern economy;

- The sharing envisaged will not necessarily be monitored by the state, but may well be either between groups of individuals or specific communities within the state, or all the communities comprising the state.

- As in the traditional outlook, sharing should imply not only the sharing of property and wealth, but also of services, which would result in the systematic division of labour. This would manifest itself in the economic system of the country.

This perfectly harmless junior high school attempt to develop economic theory in response to the challenge that the African should develop along his own lines is regarded as proof of Marxist indoctrination and punished accordingly.

At this writing, the government has not banned the Convention. What it has done has been to use a wide variety of stratagems to destroy the leadership of this mainly young people's organisation.

The National Cultural Liberation Movement which, according to White press reports, had a paid-up membership of over 120,000 in 1976-77, proclaims in its constitution that:

> we have many things to copy from the Western economic, political and educational patterns of development and [strive] for the promotion of African patterns of thought and the achievement of African Humanism otherwise commonly known in Nguni languages as *ubuntu* and in Sotho languages as *botho*.

The Nguni and Sotho words have one and the same meaning. Literally: the art or practice of being human; virtue. The philosophy which the Nguni and Sotho experiences translate into action teaches that highest virtue consists in the person identifying himself with his neighbour; in regarding himself as the obverse side of a reality to which his neighbour is the reverse; it insists that the person is a self-defining value which is above race, colour and ethnicity.

For the Zulu, Sotho and Xhosa to live together, work together and pool their resources to solve common problems is what *Buntu* and *Botho* regard as the moral things to do; to act as Buntu and Botho teach is, in African eyes, to develop along their own lines.

In spite of this, Police Minister Jimmy Kruger summoned Chief Buthelezi, the president of the National Cultural Liberation Movement, to Pretoria in September, 1977, where, according to a report in the international edition of the Johannesburg *Star* (September 24, 1977), the minister warned Buthelezi that "there will be trouble if Inkatha (the National Cultural Liberation Movement) continued to accept non-Zulus as members."

Government policy here seeks to force the Africans to segregate themselves from each other even when this is in conflict with their system of morality or lines of development. The same government rejects the Judaeo-Christian teaching on the brotherhood of Man on the score that the Black man cannot be the brother of the White man.

The contradictions in which apartheid is caught here need to be seen from the perspective of history. The Crusades set out to conquer the pagan world for Christ and, as subsequent events were to show, collect the goodies of this world for the Europeans. The age of discovery extended the area to be conquered. Colonialism imposed the European attitude to the person on peoples of non-European descent.

But this attitude could not give a satisfying meaning to life among all groups in a racially and culturally mixed world; it could not cope with the imperatives of co-existence in pluralistic societies. The demands of co-existence strained and cracked it and led to the eventual expulsion of the White conquerors from many parts of the non-European world.

The Whites could not be expelled from the Middle World for a number of reasons. In America they were in the majority. Although a minority in South Africa, they were armed in such a way as to make their expulsion costly.

The Americans tackled the problems of racial and cultural co-existence by rejecting race as a determinant of public policy; they recognised the validated principle as the truth. This was an important development in the evolution of the American commonwealth; it opened doors to the accommodation of Black self-definitions if the Black people wanted to define themselves in their own terms.

The Whites went to the opposite extreme in South Africa. They rejected the logic of their religion's teaching on the brotherhood of Man on one side and, on the other, rejected the logic of the Buntu or Sudic evaluation of the person. That created a vacuum in their thinking on co-existence which produced the contradictions under discussion.

The vacuum raised the spectre of the Whites being eventually expelled from South Africa, not by force of arms but, as some militants say, by a scorched-earth policy which would starve them out of the country; by wrecking the economy in ways which would make it no longer worthwhile for the Whites to live in South Africa.

Newsweek

Schoolboy killed in Soweto rebellion, June 1976.

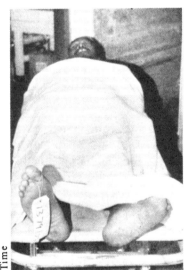

Time

Steve Biko's body after autopsy.

A COLLECTIVE RESPONSE

While the Southern and Northern approaches developed different answers to the challenge of conquest, they were the reactions of the same bicipitous mind to the same provocation. In the South, the clash between Sudic and Caucasian civilisations moved the Coloureds and the Africans toward the ideal of a *Larger Nation* while it drove the various Black language-groups in the North toward the ideal of a *New Nation*.

The two ideals responded to rejection of the Africans, Coloureds and Asians by the Whites. The side committed to the establishment of the *Larger Nation* believed that the answer to the situation created by conquest was the establishment of a consensus of the like-minded which would transcend race and colour.

The Whites rejected this ideal when they formed the Union of South Africa and brought into being a closed society in which the White skin became *the* qualification for citizenship. The African answer to this was the rejection of destiny as prescribed by the Whites. The various language-groups in South Africa, the Protectorates, the Transkei and the Ciskei welded themselves into a *New Nation* on the basis of a clearly stated philosophy. The destiny of this nation was to create "a new and unique civilization," a civilisation in which the person of African descent would never again be punished for being the child of his particular parents.

It is not without significance that in 1943 the advocates of the two ideals reacted in identical ways to the challenge of World War II, when they formed the Congress Youth League and the Non-European Unity Movement. Equally significant were Mda's and Tsotsi's efforts to move the two wings toward convergence.

By crushing radical Monolithism and militant Medialism from 1960 onward, apartheid drove the main anti-apartheid organisations underground where violence was the only political argument they could use. Each political organisation produced its official or related underground. *Poqo* was associated with the PAC while the ANC had the Spear of the Nation. The more radical members of the Liberal Party of South Africa banded themselves with other radicals to form the African Resistance Movement which had the distinction of producing the first anti-apartheid martyr on the White side. John Harris was hanged by the apartheid regime for his direct attacks on the White power-structure.

The government crushed all resistance groups and created the political leadership vacuum which has frequently been mentioned in this discussion. The bicipitous mind accepted the challenge. Its isolationist aspect took its stand on non-collaboration while the Monolithists attacked on the basis of functionalism. The non-collaborationists failed to stop the Transkei and Bophuthatswana from accepting "independence"; the functionalists stopped Chief Charles Hlengwa in Natal from accepting "independence."

It has been said that the non-collaborators reached their moment of glory in the Soweto Rebellion. It must be said that the functionalists reached their moment of glory on November 7-8, 1973, when the chief executive officers of the main homelands administrations met in Umtata and committed themselves to the ideal of establishing the Federal Union of the Autonomous States of Southern Africa.

A day or two later, Buthelezi spoke in East London (November 10, 1973) and defined functionalism's goals in these terms:

> We no longer think we should be preoccupied with begging for more reforms. . . . We dream now of . . . an alternative to what our White rulers have propounded so far. . . . This means a nonracial society in which every human being will have the right and opportunity to make the best possible use of his life. . . . Only through a Federal Union of the Autonomous States of Southern Africa can the Black man, the White man, the Brown man, each translate the great principles handed down to each one of them by their ancestors into satisfying social, economic and cultural action. The Federal Union of the Autonomous States of Southern Africa will guarantee the identity and cultural autonomy of every racial, ethnic or cultural group. . . .

Buthelezi wanted an internal, all-inclusive dialogue to hammer out a formula for co-existence which all races could accept with honour. The vehicle that could produce such a formula was a constitutional conference, which Buthelezi asked the prime minister to convene.

Again, the Whites rejected the African people's demand. Buthelezi warned that the Africans would withdraw their labour if White South Africa did not listen when the Black people spoke. A few months later, the Soweto Rebellion broke out.

Every African language-group was involved in the rebellion as the lists of the dead and the jailed testify. The Coloureds joined in this fight and laid down their lives as freely as the Africans did. Young Asians had gone to jail with our young people. In these events, a Collective Response was developing which was an African, Coloured and Asian answer to race humiliation.

The Collective Response was a part of a larger response; it was part of the Black world's answer to the peculiar relationship which emerged in situations of contact and conflict between the peoples of African and Caucasian descent. This larger Collective Response set out to create the world in which the peoples of African descent would be equipped, enabled and seen to discover more satisfying dimensions of being human.

The Black Writers Conference which met in Rome set out to discover this dimension. So did the African Students' Conference which met in Ghana in the 1960s. The satisfying dimension was the "universal dimension" for which the All-Africa Church Conference said it was looking at its Nairobi sessions in 1975. It was this dimension also which Lt.-General Olusegun Obasanjo was looking for when he rejected teleguidance at the Khartoum conference of the OAU in 1978.

These searches were rejections of the prescribed destiny. This gave to the crisis in South Africa the character of a war of minds and a conflict of wills; a collision between the Black World's Collective Response and the Caucasian World's bias for prescribing destiny for others.

South Africa's crisis was the decisive battle of the long-drawn war of minds. The relations between Black and White in the world would change after the collapse of apartheid, for, in the final analysis, the war of minds is a collision between conflicting attitudes to the person and not between classes. There is a positive side to the collision. The Africans who were forced out of the Sudic World created a synthesis of outlooks in order to survive in the situation of Black-White conflict. The Afrikaners' ancestors developed a parallel synthesis. The existence of these syntheses is an important area of congruity in the experience of the African and the Afrikaner. It means that the African and the Afrikaner who walked out of their worlds to create new worlds for themselves need to develop a unifying relationship which will transform Southern Africa into a co-operating economic and political community, which will include all races.

History confronts the Afrikaner with a momentous choice. If he wants to, he can join hands with the African in leading Africa in the new experiment with freedom which she has launched. That would guarantee him a permanent place in the African sun.

If he wants to, he can spend the rest of his life planning to build separate lavatories for Blacks and Whites. As the history of Caucasian civilisation shows, this will eventually destroy him.

His answer must of necessity be the creation of a synthesis of syntheses which, as Shaka taught, will be based on political self-determinism, economic integration and cultural autonomy which, as our history teaches, will draw the difference between the fundamentals of conflict and the operational aspects of conquest—between opposing attitudes to the person and vehicles like race discrimination, political oppression, economic exploitation and cultural asphyxiation.

The problem we are dealing with here is no longer one of race oppression or colour prejudice; it is one of building a nation; it is one of re-aligning forces for the purpose of moving to majority rule. Our problem is to identify the forces involved in the war of minds, to attain clarity on their interactions and to re-align them for the purpose of creating a national identity which will be acceptable to the Africans, Coloureds, Asians and Whites who have made Southern Africa their home.

The African must give leadership in moving events to the above goal. For good or for worse, the White man must effect a revolution in his thinking; he must teach himself the habit of playing a supportive role in the prescription of final goals if he wants to secure his position in

Southern Africa. The evil days when we were taught that we were savages and ideological heathens who had to be saved by Jesus Christ and Karl Marx are gone never to return. This is an important index of changing power dispositions.

The main submission made in what has been written up to now is that the pessimistic or devaluative attitude to the person guarantees its own failure in racially or culturally mixed societies; that apartheid, which translates this attitude into action in South Africa, creates the conditions which have begun to destroy White rule.

This setting gives to the crisis the character of a war of African and Caucasian minds which the African is now winning. The first round of decisive battles he fought and won were on the ideological plane. He rejected the prescribed destiny, set himself the goal of establishing "a new and unique civilization," created a vacuum in White thinking on the future of South Africa, and set out to fill the void with the ideal of the Federal Union of the Autonomous States of Southern Africa.

He proceeded from these victories to make strategic conquests. He cracked the foundations of the united front of White monoliths, forced Big Business to move to the left of the government on the abolition of race discrimination, sealed in blood the unity of the African and Coloured communities, established the relativity of Afrikaner power and effected the isolation of the White supremacists on the international plane.

The third battle the African has won is the psychological one. He has emerged victorious in the conflict between the psychology of prescribing destiny and the psychology of "creating a new and unique civilization." This change is of fundamental importance for all involved or interested in the crisis in South Africa. On the African side it means that the psychology based on the Sudic evaluation of the person has created a new psychology of survival in the conditions created by conquest: it has brought into being a synthesis of carry-overs from Sudic psychology and the psychology of proletariatisation.

The synthesis is essentially a psychology of rising from a fall. Conflict rationalisation is the philosophy of rising from a fall.

When opposing psychologies collide, the irresistible momentum of numbers in a race-conscious society gives the many, first, the potential and, later, the capability to expel the few. African numbers place the African on the winning side.

The failure of the White minority to impose its will and stop the strikes in 1973-74, which created a bad impression among foreign investors, was followed by the Soweto Rebellion, which continued for nearly two years in spite of determined government efforts to suppress it.

Reference was made in an earlier chapter to the rise in the numbers of Whites fleeing South Africa. There is also a fall in the numbers of White immigrants. This has created a crisis at the level of skilled work which has forced the apartheid regime to do some fundamental thinking on the use of African labour to fill the vacuum caused by the stoppage of the influx of skilled workers from White countries.

The international edition of the Johannesburg *Star* (October 14, 1978) reported that the Department of Education and Training planned to spend about R 40-million over two years to build more educational institutions for the Africans. The following was of particular interest in the report:

> The technical college [to be established by the plans] is scheduled to be opened in January, 1980 with a projected cost of R 30-million. . . . Engineering training for an enrollment of 5,000 is being offered.

One of Big Business's main concerns was the collapse of the policy of importing skilled White labour. The government offered attractive terms to would-be White settlers. Internal and external attacks on apartheid have combined with the Evolving Revolt to convince Whites who would want to emigrate to the Republic that South Africa is the wrong country to settle in at the moment.

The Associated Chambers of Commerce faced the implications of these realities at their annual conference held in Pietermaritzburg in October 1978. The conference demanded "an end to the subsidisation of White immigration."

The admission into skilled jobs every year of about 5,000 African technicians will place the Black populaton in a more advantageous position to use its labour as a political weapon.

That increasing numbers of Whites have begun to flee the country or avoid emigrating to the Republic is evidence that the African has created conditions on the homefront which increase White uncertainty about the future of South Africa.

The Afrikaner's reactions to these changing dispositions of power are informative. In the southern winter of 1978, the chairman of *Die Broederbond,* one of the groups which make policy in the Afrikaner monolith, joined hands with the editor of the pro-apartheid Johannesburg daily, *Die Transvaler,* to find an alternative to apartheid which would be based on "maximum consensus." This decision was supported by another Afrikaner organisation, Die Rapportryers. [34]

> Members of the Afrikaans cultural body, the Rapportryers, have come out in favour of contact with Africans, Indians and Coloured people—subject to certain conditions.

A week later *The Star* reported that the Afrikaanse Studentebond—the Afrikaner students' organisation—had decided to launch a programme for establishing contacts "with other races and groups which hold opposing views."

These developments do not indicate that the walls of Jericho are falling. What they show is that the crisis in all South Africa now confronts the Afrikaner monolith with a fundamental challenge which calls for a fundamental answer; they show, also, that groups are emerging in the Afrikaans community which seek to extend the area of contact between Black and White.

This development calls for the introduction of additional dimensions to the strategies adopted on the homefront and in foreign lands against apartheid. Political offensives should be launched to encourage Afrikaner rejections of apartheid and to fill the vacuum thus created with a clearly stated alternative to the status quo.

It calls, also, for the realisation that African victories on the ideological, strategic and psychological planes draw in sharper outlines the last battle the African has to win: the political battle; the battle for the establishment of majority rule—for the transfer of political power to the majority and the establishment of a society in which no person shall be punished for being the child of his or her particular parents. In this society, the person will be equipped, enabled and seen to realise the promise of being human regardless of race, colour, ethnicity, sex or creed.

This brings us to truly crucial points in the crisis. In historical terms, the Soweto Rebellion brought the era of race politics to an end and forced South Africa into the politics of confrontation. In the new dispensation, Black and White might be involved in a confrontation of minds or a confrontation of arms.

Ideology and power dispositions will be key factors in the politics of confrontation. Ideology will define purpose and prescribe final goals while power will give impact and momentum to movement toward these goals.

Ideology and power are inseparable complements in a monolith. For a monolith or combination of monoliths to be able to impose its will, it must have a clear vision, singlemindedness of purpose, and control of decisive power.

Afrikaner power remained invincible as long as it guaranteed profits to English entrepreneurs and had an absolute capability for crushing any African rebellion against White rule. Since the beginning of the 1970s the African's bicipitous mind organised the strikes which demonstrated that the government had a limited ability to discipline African workers and in that way guarantee profits. The **Soweto Rebellion** showed that the government's capability for suppressing rebellion is relative.

These developing weaknesses must be seen against conflicting psychologies of fulfillment on the White side. Our model will be the strategies used by Afrikaner and English churches. During the early years of the armed struggle on the borders of South Africa, the English-oriented Protestant churches announced that they would not encourage their followers to enlist for service against Black guerrillas. From then on, they moved away from policies which reinforced apartheid, toward a more or less central position in the clash between Black and White. They even established a united theological training centre in Alice which developed into a fount of the Black Consciousness Movement's Black Theology.

The government eventually closed down the seminary, which found a home in the Transkei for a while. It quarrelled with the Matanzima regime and ended up in Edendale, in Natal.

Here, the English Protestant churches were in effect using their resources to reinforce the African's psychology of creating "a new and unique civilization." Their flexibility contrasted sharply with the rigidity of the Dutch Reformed Church in the Afrikaans community.

Younger members of the Coloured community had intensified their attacks on the Immorality and Mixed Marriages Acts which gave to the Coloureds the identity of a community born in sin. The slur had always been bitterly resented by the Coloured community and played no small part in enabling the Coloured students to throw in their lot with the Africans in the Soweto Rebellion.

African and Coloured theologians intensified their attacks on Afrikaner cultural organisations, including Die Broederbond, for their support of racism and demanded the re-unification of the Black and White sections of the Nederduitse Gerevormeerde Kerk, the largest of Dutch Reformed Church denominations. The Afrikaner monolith would not tolerate this. NGK endorsement of re-unification would be tantamount to acceptance of race equality and recognition of the African's right to create "a new and unique civilization."

From the above, the predominantly English churches can be seen moving in directions which are different from those taken by the DRC. If this does anything, it shows the spiritual leadership echelons in the two monoliths drifting toward divergence on race discrimination. Big Business is rejecting racism.

In October, 1978, the Progressive Federal Party announced that it would call a national conference to consider plans for the transformation of South Africa into a federal state.

These splits together constitute a fundamental weakness in the united front of White monoliths; they give to the force of White unity the character of a variable which responds to changing dispositions of Black-White power, and damage the White side's capability for giving meaningful leadership in the conditions created by the relativity of Afrikaner power.

All these problems which the united front is having are overshadowed by blows to the Afrikaner self-image which threaten to shatter the psychology of *kragdadigheid*. The Afrikaner was taught and believed that his leaders were paragons of human excellence; that they were God-fearing, unwavering in their loyalty to their Afrikaner people, and unshakeable in their faith, and that they were morally unimpeachable patriots and patriarchs who could not be bought with wine, money or women.

The corruption and thuggery associated with the scandal which rocked the apartheid regime in 1978 shattered this image. The Afrikaners had largely condoned the murder of politically committed Africans detained by the police; they were outraged when murder seemed likely to be used in circumstances which suggested that it might become a political weapon against fellow Afrikaners.

The exposure of what the power-drunk incarnations of virtue did behind the scenes hurled the Afrikaner headlong into a crisis of self-definition which brought him face-to-face with the lie in his soul which had brought about the collapse of the Outward-looking Policy, the failure of the satellite system, the defection of Big Business, the drying up of the flow of immigrants, the diplomatic isolation of the apartheid regime and the establishment of the relativity of Afrikaner power.

A familiar pattern was unfolding in these events. From the beginnings of Caucasian civilisation, the definition of the person in devaluative and pessimistic terms had been an historic error which created catastrophic disharmonies in society and the human personality. These disharmonies had emerged in the Afrikaner monolith to crack the psychology of *kragdadigheid* and corrode the Afrikaner's sense of realities.

The offer of vassalage in mini-states which could not maintain themselves went beyond being an unrealistic pipedream; it was the product of a mind which had lost its sense of realities. It defined one dimension of the vacuum in White thinking on the "race" problem on one plane and, on another, demonstrated that the united front of White monoliths had lost the war of minds.

The relevant conclusion in this setting is that while the logic of White rule leads Black and White to an appointment on the battlefield, the victories scored by the Collective Will and the Evolving Revolt in the last sixty-six years give the political option the nature of a viable shortcut to majority rule and the stabilisation of conditions in South Africa.

One other fact must be noted. The splits developing in the White monoliths—Buthelezi has his own troubles with the Black Consciousness Movement—respond mainly to the demands of adnation. Neither *kragdadigheid* nor economic necessity can stop natural growth. Each monolith is dividing into diehards who reject race equality or collaboration and the advocates of accommodation across the colour line.

The accommodationists are the raw material out of which to build a like-minded majority of Africans, Afrikaners and English in the first instance. This majority would have the power to develop a viable alternative to the status quo which White liberals were never able to do because they came mainly from the English side.

Today's accommodationists are a different political breed. Their

Afrikaner section is not made up of individual do-gooders who hope to atone for Afrikaner injustices against the Blacks by joining racially mixed groups. They are members or leaders of important, opinion-forming organisations in the Afrikaner monolith; they are loyal Afrikaners who have been forced by the logic of events to realise that majority goodwill is the only reliable guarantee of Afrikaner survival in South Africa. Their existence is a relatively new development in the crisis and is one more argument for a political solution based on a consensus of the like-minded of all races.

The value of this consensus cannot be over-emphasised. By giving the like-minded a single goal, it could be made to impart a unifying momentum to events which could at least narrow down the area of bloodshed if the crisis got out of control.

The prospects of narrowing the area of bloodshed are underlined by the monolithistic stratifications of South African society and the fact that, on the important question of abolishing race discrimination, the Afrikaners and English have begun to have two minds. South Africa is unique in having a ruling race with two divergent minds on a major policy issue. It is to this unique situation that the political option must be addressed. The development of a viable political solution and strategy together might be said to be a short-cut to majority rule in the conditions which exist in the political battle.

As has been stated throughout the present discussion, the stress on a political solution must not be construed to be a condemnation of the military argument. It is an attempt to draw attention to the need for a strategy which will focus attacks on points of maximum vulnerability in apartheid. The angularities in the imperatives of monolithal survival on the White side are one such weakness.

The difficulties discussed in this chapter must be seen in context. The Afrikaner's problems spring partly from the fact that he wants to be a child of Africa on one hand and, on the other, to retain a European identity which hurts the Africans. This gives his people the character of political Siamese twins whose brains function in opposite directions. It is to this political dualism to which we must address ourselves in dealing with the "independent" homelands.

Free Africa and the rest of the international community need to see the peoples who "accept independence" as victims of political Siamism, as communities caught in a situation of tragic contradictions. If they were seen in this light, international policy would note that the Africans were not a party to the unitary state established by the British and that it is no crime for them to tear down the Westminster type of structure in any way which might suit their peculiar situation. This policy would proceed to lay down clearly stated conditions for the acceptance of the "secessionists" by the international community. One of these conditions would be commitment to a larger union of peoples which would create a new balance of

Black and White power on one hand and, on the other, form a united front of Black states which supply labour to "White" South Africa. The other could be the commitment by the "secessionists" to withdraw their labour from South Africa if and when the Black South Africans staged a national stay-at-home strike.

The most effective weapon the African controls in the political battle is a stay-at-home strike which would paralyse South Africa's economy, immobilise the seaports on the Cape sea route, and stop the production of strategic minerals for the West. The strike could be reinforeced by a crisis of dual-authority conflict in the homelands—to wreck the satellite system and destroy its ability to supply cheap labour to the master-state.

The changed dispositions of power argue the case for a multiple strategy which will address itself to the weaknesses which have emerged in the united front of White monoliths and, at the same time, provide scope for the simultaneous use of political, economic, military and other weapons against apartheid. Such a strategy would also provide for the co-ordination of internal and external campaigns against racism and for clarity on the goals the majority has set itself.

The point to note about the changing dispositions of power is that the Northern and Southern aspects of the African's bicipitous mind converge, first, at the point of isolating the White supremacists and, second, on the use of African, Coloured and Asian labour as a political weapon.

The convergence is the matrix in which the will to expel the Whites will continue to grow as long as the Afrikaner monolith makes it a crime for the African to be the child of his or her particular parents.

The fundamental question raised by the ideological outlooks described in the first two chapters and the mutually exclusive strategies outlined in Chapters Three and Four is whether or not there is room in South Africa for an ideal of fulfillment which has one meaning in dealings between White and White and another when it comes to relations between Black and White.

For sixty-six years, the African majority has been saying there is no room for such a divalent philosophy. They have since been joined by a growing number of Coloureds and Asians.

The evidence of these changes is that the Graeco-Romano-Hebraic attitude to the person is incapable of giving a satisfying meaning to life for all races in a mixed society; that it cannot cope with the demands of co-existence in the conditions which exist in Southern Africa; that the vacuum it has created calls for a vital African-Afrikaner relationship which will transform all the peoples, nations and races of Southern Africa into a co-operating economic and political community.

Constructive involvement in the creation of this community is a challenge of belonging to Africa which the Afrikaner must face in his own interest. The next chapter describes this involvement.

NOTES ON CHAPTER IV

1. Johannesburg *Star*, February 10, 1975.
2. Ibid., October 23, 1976.
3. Ibid.
4. Ibid., October 9, 1976.
5. December 6, 1976 (national edition).
6. International edition, March 27, 1976.
7. *The History Of Southern Africa*; Longmans, London, 1968; new impression with corrections; Pp 42-43, 153-4.
8. Quoted by Edward Roux: *Time Longer Than Rope*; University of Wisconsin Press, second edition, London, 1972, Pp 183-184.
9. Ibid., P 184.
10. DRUM, Johannesburg, December 22, 1974.
12. *The Religions of the Oppressed*; tr. Lisa Sergio; New American Library, New York, 1960; 3rd Printing; Pp 39-40.
13. Black Viewpoint; ed. Ben A. Koapa; Spro-Cas Black Community Programmes; Durban, 1972, P 64.
14. Quoted by *A Survey of Race Relations, 1972*, S.A. Institute of Race Race Relations, Vol. 26, 1973, P 30.
15. Ibid., Pp 18-19.
16. Ibid., P 53.
17. Year Book, 1970; Da Gama Publishers, Johannesburg.
18. South Africa: *Crisis for the West*, Frederick Prager, New York, 1964, Pp 264-65n.
19. Charles Scribner's Sons, New York, 1974-75.
20. Donald R. Morris: *The Washing of the Spears*; Simon and Schuster, New York, 1965; Pp 178-83.
21. In *Chronicles Of Black Protest*; ed., C. Eric Lincoln; The New American Library, New York, 1968, P 31.
22. Compiled from *A Survey Of Race Relations*, South African Institute of Race Relations: 1970, 1971, 1972, 1973 issues.
23. Quoted from *Financial Mail*, October 4, 1968, by Brian Bunting in *The Rise of the South African Reich*, Penguin African Library, Baltimore, 1969, P 499.
24. Ibid., Vol. II, P 308.
25. Ibid., P 320.
26. Ibid., P 292.
27. Editor: Ben Langa Saso Publications, Durban, 1973, P 42.
28. White suburbs.
29. Bennie A. Khoapa, *The New Black*, an essay in *Black Viewpoint*, published by Spro-Cas Black Community Programmes, Durban, 1972, P 61 *et seq*.

30. In *Black Viewpoint* and *Creativity and Black Development*, the former published by Black Community Programmes and the latter by Saso, in Durban.
31. In *Creativity and Black Development.*
32. *The Concept of the Church in Black Theology* in *Black Theology*, ed., Basil Moore, C. Hurst Co., London, 1973, Pp 112, 113, 117.
33. Ibid.
34. Johannesburg *Star*, (international edition), October 14, 1978.

V. An African Alternative
to Apartheid

BLUEPRINT FOR FREEDOM IN SOUTH AFRICA

Much has been written, first, on the conflict between the psychology of creating "a new and unique civilization" and the psychology of prescribing destiny and, second, on the changing dispositions of power produced by the conflict. Attention will now be given to the type of formula for co-existence which could be a basis for moving like-minded Africans, Coloureds, Asians and Whites to a consensus on final goals.

It has been said that South Africa is unique in that the African majority is oppressed by a united front of White monoliths which has its own unsolved identity problems. In this setting, White unity is a fragile plant which responds to changing dispositions of power in the African community. It was to this circumstance that the Bloemfontein Unity Conference addressed itself; it was this fact, also, which those Blacks, who rejected the destiny prescribed for the Africans in the Freedom Charter, had in mind when they broke from the ANC and formed the PAC.

The men and women who met in Bloemfontein in 1912 thought in terms of launching an Evolving Revolt which would in time make it impossible for the White minority to impose its will and rule on the majority. To complement the internal revolt, they launched an external campaign from Versailles in 1919 to effect the isolation of the White united front on the international plane. The Afrikaner and English monoliths are now caught in the grip of these pincers.

Their behaviour in this situation demands a recasting of African strategies and tactics.

In general terms, the industry-oriented English are moving away from the united front of White monoliths toward a consensus of the like-minded which will effect the minimum of dislocations in the economic status quo.

While the economic leaders of the English are sending signals of conciliation to the Africans—Natal's Chamber of Commerce is giving effective support to the province's African Chamber of Commerce—a substantial proportion of English in lower echelons voted for the Nasionale Party, which advocates apartheid, in the November, 1977, general elections.

This "contradiction" needs to be seen in perspective; it has its origins in the political impotence of the English. Constituting roughly about a third of the White population, they stand no chance of ever succeeding in using the ballot box to unseat the apartheid regime.

Those among them who do not believe Big Business speaks for them accept political integration with the Afrikaner. Whether or not this means that they are ready for absorption by the Afrikaner is another matter.

What everybody is certain about is that they have joined the White, political united front on terms laid down by the Afrikaner monolith. In a race-conscious society, they do not have much of a choice.

For the African, the united White political front means that the Black monolith does not need to speak to some of the English in one set of terms and to the Afrikaners in another; it means, in other words, that the day might come when an African-Afrikaner agreement on final goals would enable the Afrikaner to impose this agreement on at least a section of the English.

Our main interest at the moment is the economic status quo. In preceding chapters, it was shown that there are fundamental shifts in the centres of power in the White monoliths. Big Business works in close collaboration with the West to establish a Black middle class which would co-operate with similar classes in the Afrikaner and English monoliths and eventually join hands with these in forming a united front of African, Coloured, Asian, Afrikaner and English middle class people.

These would eventually gang up against the masses of the poor, hoard the wealth of South Africa and pass some of it to the West.

Two problems arise for the African and the Afrikaner from this. Both communities are dispossessed in different ways; both are victims of cultural, economic and pychological deprivation on different planes. These hurts have developed in them a response which might be called the temper of the dispossessed—a preoccupation with considerations of destiny which often downgrades economic necessity as a determinant of policy.

The temper of the dispossessed has, in the last sixty-six years, been moving both groups away from the English or Westminster or unitary type of state, toward different goals. The African set himself the ideal of a Federal Union of the Autonomous States of Southern Africa while the Afrikaner chose a satellite system.

The Afrikaner monolith made grave misreadings of African history and proceeded from this to commit one political blunder after another. He made himself believe that apartheid was his guarantee of survival and security. That made his community the most hated White community in the world; it left him isolated on the homefront and on the diplomatic plane.

He spent large sums of money attracting White immigrants when he should have known that the large number of African (and some White, Coloured and Asian) exiles he drove out of the country would organise, write, speak and act against apartheid in ways which would combine with the Evolving Revolt one day to frighten off immigrants to the racial dictatorship he established.

He did all he could to attract foreign investments but made no provision against the possibility that he could one day be caught in the tangles of his own errors. The stoppage of the influx of immigrants is forcing him to build a technical college to produce about 5,000 skilled African workers a year. This has political implications which call for an identity which all races and peoples can accept with honour.

South Africa does not as yet have this identity. Buthelezi's diplomacy seeks to establish this identity via a political solution.

In their search for it, the English established a unitary state which degenerated into a crude racist one. The Afrikaner monolith crushed the unitary state when it gave "independence" to the Transkei and Bophuthatswana and created its satellite system.

Numbers eventually describe the course history takes in the clash between Black and White. As has been shown, the satellite system is under attack from the African people. To take two instances: the strikes by African workers during the first five years of the 1970s combined with the Soweto Rebellion to establish the relativity of White power. At the same time, the Evolving Revolt drove a wedge between Big Business and the government in Pretoria on the issue of abolishing race discrimination. The Africans had no guns then.

The growing unity of the Africans, Coloureds and Asians will in the end destroy the satellite system, as the quarrel between the Transkei and Pretoria has begun to show. When Matanzima and Mangope accepted the vassalage Pretoria offered, they made it known that they had their eyes on the eventual establishment of the Federal Union of the Autonomous States of Southern Africa. If we put their opportunism aside for a moment, it will be seen that they moved out of South Africa in order to regroup and unite in a federal union formed on bases laid down by the Africans. When the homelands leaders committed themselves to the eventual formation of the federal union, they sealed the fate of the satellite system.

This definition of the "race" problem brings into view another dimension of the crisis; it shows the Black and White quarrel to be a clash between a narrow national identity which is valid only in the Afrikaner experience and a larger national identity which accommodates Africans, Coloureds, Asians and Whites and seeks to stabilise economic and political conditions in Southern Africa.

But the united front of White monoliths is on the defensive on other planes. Pretoria's policy of building buffer states on South Africa's northern borders has become a dismal failure. What the Whites dreaded most has become a fact of South African life. The crushing of White domination has given South Africa contiguous borders with Free Africa and created the situation in which arms, hostile propaganda, etc., can be taken into South Africa virtually at any point along its 4,500-mile border in the north.

An important aspect of the length of the border is that it thins out South Africa's line of defence and ties down productive White manpower to unproductive military duty on the front line. If this lowers production at a critical time in the economy, it combines with the instability which followed the Soweto Rebellion to shake external confidence in South Africa as an investment paradise; it shows the Whites failing to give leadership in a situation of challenge.

These defeats for apartheid must be seen as dimensions of its isolation. These dimensions combine with the Evolving Revolt to change the complexion of the crisis. Race ceases to be the basic cause of conflict and becomes a vehicle used in a quarrel at the level of fundamentals. The abolition of race discrimination or "petty" apartheid ceases to be the problem at issue, just as Black majority rule does. The problem becomes: what is the meaning which freedom and citizenship must have in South Africa? Must the Whites whose minds have been poisoned by racism be expelled to provide room for other Whites who will enter South Africa on terms dictated by the majority?

The Sudic answer is clear and uncompromising. The Whites in South Africa are human and are, for this reason, entitled to a place in the African sun if they seriously want it. Seriously is the operative word. If they want to belong to Africa, they must do the things which are done in Africa; they must stop punishing the African for being the child of his African parents in his own Africa and join hands with him in creating a society in which the person will be equipped, enabled and seen to realise the promise of being human regardless of race, colour, ethnicity, sex and creed. They must, in other words, be constructively involved in the development of a national identity which the like-minded majority of Africans, Coloureds and Asians desire.

If they cannot do this, if they cannot survive in South Africa without prescribing destiny for Black people, then they must be expelled so that the African can be free to invite other Whites from other parts of the world to settle in South Africa with their skills and capital.

No African in his senses expects the South African Whites to abandon their personality-distorting definition of the individual. No White man in his senses should expect Black South Africans to reject the Sudic view of the person—the All-Africa Church Conference has already warned that it is searching for a new dimension of Christianity which will satisfy African conditions—or to dissociate themselves from the Black World's Collective Will. As Seme put it, the best that the African can do is to be involved in the creation of a "new and unique civilization;" to contribute positively to the enrichment of the synthesis of values which sooner or later emerges in situations of Black-White contact and which gives meaning to life in the conditions created by conquest.

If the Afrikaner had something to give, he would co-operate with the African to create the civilisation in which it would not be a crime for a human being to be the child of his or her particular parents. As things stand, the Afrikaner is making himself the most hated White group in Africa; he has given his name an ugly odour in Africa. If this makes him expendable, his greed gives to his expulsion the character of an ideal young Africans who grow up in the shadow of the Sharpeville and Soweto massacres can live for.

The prospect of expulsion must, however, be also seen in light provided by global power rivalries. Oil and minerals are the main strategic resources over which the great White powers will be quarrelling in the twenty-first century. Africa's mineral potential has barely been touched. This makes Africa the continent of the future. Since her minerals appear to be concentrated in the South, Southern Africa in general and South Africa in particular seem destined to be the main fields on which World War III's fiercest battles will be fought.

The Soviet Union is steadily digging in its feet in Mozambique in readiness for the final showdown. West Germany balances this with nuclear installations in Zaire.

German strategy in Southern Africa complements German activity in South America. Large German communities have emerged in South America which have close connections with the fatherland. If World War III broke out, the United States and the Soviet Union would be the principal combatants. Germany would let them bleed each other to the point where, like Britain and France after World War III, they became second-class powers. During the war the West German economy, which could be paralysed by Soviet power, would be reinforced by Germany's satellite settlements in South America and possibly in parts of South Africa and Namibia. The German satellite system would enable Germany to recover swiftly enough after the war to become the dominant power in the world, with the possible collaboration of Japan.

The two countries would form a new axis which could, with the United States and the Soviet Union out of the way, prescribe destiny for Africa in general and Southern Africa in particular.

It must be understood that Germany here refers to West Germany. The framework in which German policy unfolds is informative. Germany continues to be a member of the United Nations. In the world organisation, Japan continues to be treated as a small boy in international affairs in spite of her tremendous economic achievements. While one understands the hostility of the Frontline States, the OAU and the United Nations to chief Kaiser Matanzima's and Lucas Mangope's acceptance of the vassalage which Pretoria peddles as independence, the three organisations have reacted in ways which ignore the internal power dispositions which fix priorities in the African community of South Africa at the moment. Chief Gatsha Buthelezi's Inkatha (National Cultural Liberation Movement) continues to be treated by these organisations as a pariah movement in spite of the fact that it could very well provide South Africa with her first Black government.

The pressure to push peoples rigidly to the left or the right could create a new bloc of nations: a coalition of African, Asian and European nations which would be bound together mainly by the circumstance that they were rejected by the left and humiliated by the right.

Black South Africa, the Transkei, Malawi and some French-speaking countries in West Africa belong to this category; so do Germany, Japan and some South American countries.

Let us have a closer look at this scenario because it has important implications for the crisis in South Africa. Germany's activities outside of the United Nations are ultimately a vote of no confidence in the world organisation's ability to create the disciplined global order which would give satisfying meaning to life for all the peoples of the world. The Germans realise that from the days of the Holy Roman Empire, Europe tried to discipline herself and, subsequently, the world, on the basis of the Graeco-Romano-Hebraic evaluation of the person. The result was that this philosophy moved Europe in cycles of conflict to the first and second world wars.

Germany's defeat in the last two conflagrations raised a fundamental question for the Germans which called for a fundamental answer. Was it worthwhile for Germany to strive to create the global discipline she desired on the basis of a *herrenvolkism* discredited by history, rejected by contemporary mankind and doomed by the proliferation of Black, Brown, Yellow and White nations?

So long as Germany did not have the answer to this question, she could not play a constructive role in the United Nations. For the Germans to regard themselves as a "chosen people" and to proceed from this to prescribe destiny for mankind was a proven invitation to disaster. Western-style democracy was not the answer. It had given the United States the schizophrenia which made it difficult for America to think at the level of fundamentals when it came to stabilising the crisis in Southern Africa.

Democracy was giving the United States a mind which elevated ignorance to the status of a determinant of policy in Africa.

The result was that the mass of the great American people were losing their sense of direction; everywhere, the values on which the United States was established seemed to be caving in; in every walk of life, the person was insecure; he felt threatened and could neither be certain about himself nor organise his personality in ways which gave a satisfying meaning to his life.

These weaknesses had disastrous effects on those aspects of American policy which dealt with Asia and Africa.

The humiliation of American arms in Southeast Asia was not accidental, just as the calamitous handling of the Rhodesian crisis was not. A vacuum had emerged in Caucasian thinking on relations with the Third World which moved the West inexorably to disaster. The West based its policy for dealing with the non-Caucasian peoples of the Third World on the cash value of the person which had produced successful nationalistic revolts against colonialism. Africans, Asians and South Americans were determined to create societies in which the person could make the best possible use of his life, no matter who he was.

In the ten years I was in the United States, Americans allowed me access to practically any department of their lives I wanted to see. One of the problems I came across was that American foreign policy was based on two unresolved and conflicting minds when it came to Africa, Asia and South America.

The side committed to the use of the cash value of the person as a criterion by which to judge human worth refused to see Third World problems from any angle other than perspectives dictated by East-West rivalries. All that was needed to establish the positions of these men was to mention the word *Communism*.

Opposed to these were those who wanted policy to respond to changed power dispositions in Africa, Asia and South America.

The two minds clashed so seriously in the ten years I was in America that it was not unusual for me to talk to a State Department official who would give me one version of the situation in South Africa and meet another, from the CIA, who would describe the same situation in diametrically opposed terms.

Concerned Americans told me that this schizophrenia had led to the humiliation of United States arms in Southeast Asia. I saw no possibility for removing the dangers of the split mind, except by effecting radical changes in America's attitude to the person.

A nation with the mind described above created the disharmonies in the individual personality which guaranteed the humiliation of American arms in Southeast Asia.

Germany was finding, also, that Marxism provided no answer to German problems. Like democracy, it led the world in cycles of conflict to ultimate catastrophe. It had joined hands with the West to split Germany from head to foot; to subject the Germans to a greater humiliation than defeat in two world wars.

The basic weakness in communism was that like the Roman Catholic Church, it elevated dogma into a prison of the mind. Its rigidity was such that it moved those who had been born outside of the Graeco-Romano-Hebraic experience in a straight line to evolving revolts. The logic of these revolts was the expulsion of the Whites from those areas whose resources the Whites needed most.

What this called for was a new and relevant political concept, a democracy of minds. Pessimistic and devaluative definitions of the human being would not produce this approach. What the times called for was a positive and optimistic attitude to the person which would reject the *herrenvolkism* that led to the humiliating fragmentation of Germany, and encourage an approach which would recognise the simultaneous legitimacy of different self-definitions in different environments. This attitude and the recognition are the only satisfying and reliable guarantees of a truly civilised and disciplined world.

In the years after World War II, Germany devoted more attention to Sudic Africa in order to discover the inner truth which had given durability to the African experience. This attention extended to South Africa, with its minerals on one side and, on the other, the complicated assortment of problems created by White *herrenvolkism*.

The Arnold-Bergstraesser Conference on South Africa was an important climacteric in the endeavour to obtain greater clarity on both the quality of mind which gives durability to the African experience on one plane and, on another, the dispositions of power in the Black community.

The Arnold-Bergstraesser Institut conducted a survey of African attitudes between 1974 and 1977 and concluded:

> The outstanding political phenomenon in Black urban politics is without a doubt Gatsha Buthelezi. Without doubt he is the leader of his own group, but the support he enjoys goes far beyond that. Altogether 40.3 percent of his supporters among urban Blacks are not Zulus. . . .

> . . . the political direction advocated by Buthelezi represents a force in South Africa as a whole beyond its regional and ethnic concentrations.

These conclusions were described in statistical terms as follows:

Leader or Organisation	Total Support
Buthelezi	43.8%
Nelson Mandela	8.5%
Robert Sobukwe	7.4%
ANC	21.7%
Black Consciousness Movement	5.6%
Chief Kaiser Matanzima	3.6%
Chief Lucas Mangope	2.7%

The report of the researchers, which was presented at the Conference, concluded:

> The results of the inquiry show not only that he alone (Buthelezi) of all homeland leaders is a national political figure but that over and above this he is *the* political figure of Black South Africa....

More important is that he is shown not to be a mere tribal leader. Without doubt he is the leader of his own group. But the support he enjoys goes far beyond that. Altogether 40.3% of supporters among urban Blacks are not Zulus.

The report paid attention to the influence of Inkatha in urban African politics. Its findings are informative because liberal circles in the United States take the position that Buthelezi leads rural, Zulu-speaking Africans and that he does not speak for the urban Blacks:

[Inkatha] represents by far the strongest organised political tendency among urban Blacks—the organised core of a much larger body of support for Buthelezi.... Inkatha occupies a key role in the future orientation of the urban black population.

These extracts from *The Natal Mercury* and *The Rand Daily Mail* at about the time of the Conference in June, 1978, give an image of Buthelezi which contrasts sharply with the quality of leadership some Black churchmen offer their people in South Africa. *The Natal Mercury* (July 21, 1978) published this report:

LONDON—The threat of a five-year jail sentence under the Terrorism Act stopped many South Africans from calling for world disinvestment from the Republic, Bishop Desmond Tutu, secretary-general of the South African Council of Churches (SACC), told an appreciative audience at the Royal Commonwealth Society here yesterday.

"That is why you won't hear anyone saying 'no investment,' " he said. "We would like to go to prison for something slightly better than that."

His lordship split hairs a little too finely to explain his fear of going to jail. The disinvestment issue is an integral part of the fight against apartheid. The truly committed would go to jail in protest against investments from abroad. The jail sentences would be as harsh as any passed against other offenders against apartheid's laws. What his lordship has never explained is why he did not go to jail in protest against Biko's murder, which was "something better" than going to prison for demanding disinvestment.

The logic of the report under discussion suggests that the Germans view dependence as one of the factors which works against the emergence of a disciplined world order. Here we get nearer a significant turning-point in the relations between Black and White.

The constructive element to which the German report draws attention is that Germany seems to be moving away from the Western liberal habit of concentrating on the operational aspects of the crisis in South Africa, toward giving informed attention to the fundamentals of conflict. The Collective Will of African victims of apartheid is one of these fundamentals; the Evolving Revolt is another.

Buthelezi's leadership translates the Collective Will into action. This gives it the character of a third fundamental. The massive urban and rural endorsement Buthelezi continues to receive are evidence that the Evolving Revolt is now a factor to be reckoned with in the crisis. The German report drew attention to this important point. To the extent that it did this, it was both a constructive contribution to the international debate on apartheid and a step toward the co-ordination of internal and external campaigns against apartheid.

The contribution, however, is at best a first step; it identifies a dimension of the crisis which White liberals in South Africa and the West—like the Frontline States, the OAU, the United Nations and the Soviet Bloc—continue to ignore. It does not offer a solution.

This sheds light on other aspects of the role Buthelezi and P. W. Botha can play in the crisis. Buthelezi's first priority is the liberation of his people. Botha's is the security and survival of the Afrikaner. The Africans and the Afrikaners are South Africa's key communities; they hold the secret to the resolution of conflict in South Africa.

The source of Buthelezi's strength in the rural and urban areas is that he defines the quarrel between Black and White in terms which are related to the African's day-to-day struggle. When he tells masses of humble Zulu, Xhosa, Sotho and other Africans that White domination is evil because it does violence to their *buntu* or *botho*, everyone of his hearers understands precisely what Buthelezi is saying and where he is leading them. He tells his people that government policy demands that the Africans should *develop along their own lines* and proceeds from this to ask the Zulus to gather at Ulundi in July 1979, to see where *their own lines* were set on fire by the British. Even the most illiterate Zulu knows precisely what happened when the British set Ulundi, the Zulu capital, on fire on July 4, 1879.

Against this vast background, we might be seeing a pattern emerge. The Germans in Europe whom defeat and fragmentation humiliated, the Africans in South Africa whom defeat and fragmentation humiliated, and the Japanese who are humiliated by being treated as the small boys of the international community are being given a vested interest in ganging-up to create a united front of the fragmented and the humiliated.

This gives added significance to the Bergstraesser Conference's focus on Buthelezi. The report under discussion showed that South Africa, as a racially mixed nation, had two wills: the Collective Will of the Blacks and the Uncertain Will of the Whites. The Collective Will has survived sixty-six years of brutal attacks by the united front of White monoliths and emerged strong enough to split this united front, disorient the satellite system, create the united front of African, Coloured and Asian victims of apartheid and—through the strikes in the early 1970s, the rise of Inkatha and the Soweto Rebellion—to establish the relativity of White power. That opens the way to a political solution, via a crisis of dual-authority conflict.

The White community's Uncertain Will has lost the war of minds. The absurd offers of vassalage in unviable mini-states led Matanzima to a head-on quarrel with the apartheid regime. Mangope stated publicly that he was leaving South Africa as the first step toward the formation of the Federal Union. Big Business has shifted significantly to the left of the government. The Afrikaner monolith has admitted, through its request to the Africans, Coloureds and Asians to join the South African army, that the united front of White monoliths can no longer defend South Africa. The fundamental weakness which emerges from all this is that the apartheid regime lied to the Afrikaner people when it said apartheid would guarantee Afrikaner security and survival. What proves it lied is the fact that Whites emigrate from South Africa at the rate of three to four thousand a year.

The problem before Buthelezi and P.W. Botha emerges in clearer outlines at this point. Buthelezi has no voice in the United Nations. While Botha's government is a member of the United Nations, it is treated as a polecat of international politics. Buthelezi and Botha have a vested interest in seeing to it that South Africa is not reduced to ashes; their duty is to evolve a quality of diplomacy and statesmanship which will enable all South Africans to stand shoulder to shoulder to prevent superpower rivalry from transforming South Africa into the main battlefield in the war for South Africa's minerals.

Germany is in the position to play a key role in the development of the diplomacy just described. She has access to Buthelezi, just as she has access to Botha. The Arnold-Bergstraesser Institut report prepared ground for what one might call an African-German-Afrikaner confrontation of minds on alternative guarantees of Afrikaner survival, on differences in majority rule in a unitary state, a federal union and a racial dictatorship and on a Black-White defence policy. Germany's role here could be that of a catalyst, helping to move events toward both a Black-White consensus on final goals and the creation of a like-minded majority of Africans, Coloureds, Asians and Whites.

Buthelezi's and Botha's peoples are not friends. For this reason, we cannot dream of a conversation of two minds between the two men. For some years Buthelezi had been making appeals to Vorster to convene a constitutional conference where all races together could hammer out a formula for co-existence which all could accept with honour. The Afrikaners have rejected these appeals and relied on shooting the Africans into submission. But the point has now been reached when no power on the White side can stop the momentum of the Evolving Revolt;

the African rejects the abolition of "petty apartheid" and wants to determine his life in his own country.

This aspiration sets the spotlight on the fact that the Black-White quarrel has deeper origins than the history of African-Afrikaner relations; it has its roots in values which determine the destiny of the person regardless of whether he is an African, an Asian, a Caucasian or à Coloured.

While the quarrels which embitter relations between the African and the Afrikaner are real and deepseated; while the wounds history cut into the psyche and personality of the two groups continue to fester, neither the Africans nor the Afrikaners can afford to become appendages of the West or the Soviet Bloc. To be enemies with both or either would be suicidal.

Graeco-Romano-Hebraic civilisation is in serious trouble. A *Washington Post* report gave a masterly diagnosis of the trouble when it publicly expressed distress over Christianity's failure, after 2,000 years, to persuade the human race that love for neighbours should be accepted as a guarantee of peace.

The teaching cannot and will not prevent men and events from moving in cycles of conflict to final disaster as long as it is based on a pessimistic and devaluative attitude to the person. As the Inquisition, slavery, colonialism, Nazism, apartheid and the drift to global wars show, Christianity itself might one day destroy Graeco-Romano-Hebraic civilisation because it defines the person in terms which transform this civilisation into a prison of the mind.

What happens when a civilisation becomes a prison of the mind might be seen in the United States and the Soviet Union. The United States was founded on a clearly stated moral ideal. This concept of nationhood went side by side with the commitment to the cash value of the person as a criterion by which to judge worth.

The schizophrenia which developed from this was one of the basic reasons for the humiliation of American arms in South Vietnam; it made it impossible for Washington to interpret the crisis in Southeast Asia in terms that were valid in the Vietnamese experience.

What the above situation calls for is the exertion of informed pressures on points of maximum weakness in the apartheid structure to encourage movement toward a constructive confrontation of African and Afrikaner minds—toward a face-to-face confrontation between Buthelezi and Botha on a Black-White defence policy, majority rule and alternative guarantees of survival for the Afrikaner.

Western economic pressures could be used to persuade Botha to do the statesmanlike thing and meet Buthelezi, either by himself or together with those leaders of the African people on the homefront who are committed to a political solution.

1976 South African Yearbook

Kissinger meets Vorster in South Africa in 1976.

This meeting, in itself, would not solve the "race" problem; it would at best be the beginning of an unfolding process. The meeting would be an announcement to the world that statesmanship had taken control where the politicians had failed.

The Americans enter the picture here. Their mood at present is to tell the victims of apartheid that they have limited power.

Not much importance should be attached to talk of the United States as the mightiest nation on earth. In terms of material power, the United States is the most powerful nation on earth at the moment. But America also has fatal weaknesses. One of these is that her mind is split by the demands of the moral ideal on which the United States is founded and the commitment to the cash value of the person on which the American economic system is based.

The schizophrenia was one of the basic reasons for the humiliation of United States arms in South Vietnam; it made it impossible for Washington to interpret the war in South Vietnam in terms which were valid in the Vietnamese experience. Defining the problem in Vietnam in American terms was a sure invitation to disaster.

The same mistake is being made in South Africa. Option 2 of the *Range of Policy Options* in the *Kissinger Study of Southern Africa* (National Security Study Memorandum 39) made these observations:

The Whites are here [in Southern Africa] to stay and the only way that constructive change can come about is through them. There is no hope for the Blacks to gain the political rights they seek through violence, which will only lead to chaos and increased opportunities for the communists. We can, by selective relaxation of our stance toward the White regimes, encourage some modification of their current racial and colonial policies and through more substantial economic assistance to the Black states [a total of about $5 million annually in technical assistance to the Black states] help to draw the two groups together and exert some influence on both for peaceful change.

In 1977, the Carter Administration sent Vice President Mondale to meet South African Prime Minister John Vorster in an effort to set in motion the process which would move Black and White visibly toward a political solution. In the American view, the natural thing was to engage in talks with Vorster since he was in power. This was based on a grave misreading of the South African situation.

Vorster was not the master of the Afrikaner monolith. He derived his power from the policy-making stratum of Afrikaner society who, in turn, think, act and formulate policy in the name of the Afrikaner people.

This stratum is made of people like John Vorster himself and the institutions they control. The latter include Afrikaner universities, churches, cultural organisations, banks, insurance companies and other financial houses, chambers of commerce and industry, the press, political organisations, etc.

The people involved in these institutions number approximately 12,000. Regardless of their number, they are important because they speak effectively in the name of the Afrikaner monolith. Like the monolith, they see everything in South Africa from the perspective of survival; they regard themselves as a threatened people; they live in fear of being crushed by the Africans and the English.

To ask Vorster to initiate movement to a political solution without saying anything or much about the Afrikaner's *survival problem* guaranteed a negative response from Vorster, his government and the leadership stratum in the Afrikaner monolith. To impress this stratum, there at least had to be corresponding moves to pin down the leaders of the Africans, Coloureds and Asians. Pretoria does not trust Washington any more than she trusts London.

The assumption that Vorster would respond to the dangling of carrots by the West was wrong; that was why the Mondale mission failed.

The schizophrenia has brought the American mind to virtual paralysis when it comes to thinking on South Africa. The United States cannot assert vigorous initiatives to reinforce African revolutionaries committed to the observance of human rights because the multinational corporations regard that as bad for business on one plane and, on the other, America's allies will scream: "Jackal diplomacy again!"

America's political name is not very good in Africa. The United States asserted vigorous initiatives to stop the admission of Maoist China into the United Nations. The Free Africans, many of whom survived on American aid of some form or another, used their vote to admit China. The message they sent to the United States in particular and the West generally was that in the view of the ex-colonial peoples, there was no relationship between aid and opposition to race humiliation.

The United States has not faced the implications of this African attitude; it has not developed a viable philosophy for dealing with the problems the implications create, and is therefore not ready for coping with the crisis in South Africa as it moves toward World War III.

In blunt language, the schizophrenia in the mind of the United States incapacitates this great nation for leading events effectively toward a political solution where the Africans—like Free Africa, Coloureds and Asians—are strongest.

Graeco-Romano-Hebraic civilisation is in trouble also in the Soviet Bloc. Eurocommunism is the product of a fundamental split in the mind of the Marxists on the transformation of Communism into a prison of the mind.

This transformation forced Maoist China to reject the destiny the Soviet Union prescribed for her. President Neto of Angola had no sooner assumed control of his country than he made it known that he did not think a mixed socialist-capitalist economy was a bad thing for Angola.

If the weaknesses in the West and the East require that the African and the Afrikaner should tie themselves to neither side, they also require that there should be a revolution in the Afrikaner's thinking on South Africa and the West.

The West created the crisis in which South Africa is caught; it kicked Paul Kruger in the teeth in his moment of humiliation after the 1899-1900 war; today it does not matter how many genuflexions the Afrikaner makes to prove that he belongs to the West, the Occident uses one criterion in judging him: the cash value of the person.

This criterion, and not the White skin, demands that the West, like the Soviet Bloc, should prescribe destiny for the African and the Afrikaner. But these communities have shown throughout their history that they will allow nobody to prescribe destiny for them.

If this defines another area of congruity in African and Afrikaner experiences, it is one more argument for a consensus on final goals; one more demand for a fundamental answer to a fundamental challenge; one more reason for a multiple strategy, and one more justification for moving events to a political solution.

The ideological, strategic and psychological wars won by the African require that the Afrikaner monolith should be confronted with clearly stated alternatives on every conceivable plane both to give constructive purpose to the polarisations emerging in this community and to reinforce movement toward a unifying national identity.

The United States re-enters the picture at this point. There are indications that the United States would like to involve itself constructively in the normalisation of the situation in Southern Africa. Instead of asserting uninformed leadership initiatives that—like the defeat in South Vietnam, the Chinese admission into the United Nations and the Mondale interview with Vorster in Vienna—eventually prove abortive, the United States seems to be accepting a supportive role in Africa. Emphasis in Washington is coming to be laid more and more on African solutions to African problems. This could very well be another step in the co-ordination.

Co-ordination in this direction would mean that United States investors in South Africa would band together to create a controlled economic crisis there. They would tell Big Business in the Republic that they would withhold credits against gold, diamonds and other commodities for a given period until Botha listened to Buthelezi's case for the convention of a constitutional conference to hammer out a formula for co-existence which all races could accept with honour. This is the only course open to any serious Western advocate of a political solution; it is the only way of averting the tragedies we see in Rhodesia.

The United States could use the temporary, credit-withdrawal weapon in another way. Washington could make it clear to Pretoria that if the apartheid regime fired on Africans demonstrating peacefully against race humiliation or in support of calls for a constitutional conference, the United States, and possibly the West as a whole, would suspend credits as a deterrent against government violence.

For, as we have tried to show, the African's Evolving Revolt is a struggle for the right to develop and operate legal institutions by which to transform Southern Africa into a stable and co-operating economic and political community. Apartheid opposes this intention and advocates a fragmentation of Southern Africa which can only extend the area of conflict and instability in the region.

FORMULA FOR CO-EXISTENCE

What the African has been saying in the last hundred years covered in the present analysis of his thinking is that the prescribed destiny humiliates him as much when it is imposed by the West as when it is imposed by the East; that the stratification of the Afrikaners and the English into monoliths is a weakness in the White power-structure which argues the case for accelerating movement toward a political solution; and, finally, that the Evolving Revolt has brought the Whites to their moment of decision; to the point of no-return in their drift to disaster.

What the Africans want can be stated in a few words. The Collective Will seeks to re-structure South African society in such a way that the person can be equipped, enabled and seen to realise the full promise of being human regardless of who his parents were.

The war in Rhodesia and uncertainty about the future in Namibia have opened South Africa's 4,500-mile border with Free Africa to attacks from virtually any point. Five million Whites are incapable of defending this border and manning the country's industries. Apartheid deceived the White people when it said it would enable them to secure borders and run industry.

To produce the desired results, re-structuring has to take place simultaneously at the economic and political levels. The temper of the dispossessed will not accept anything less.

Included in the redistribution of wealth are: extending the area of nationalisation, co-ownership of the vehicles for transforming primary resources into wealth, reparations for dispossession in order to create a satisfactory relationship between Black and White, and a Black-White consensus on the establishment of the Federal Union of the Autonomous States of South Africa.

It has been said that the movements of a monolith to its goal constitute a process. This gives the crisis the character of a clash between conflicting processes. The answer to this clash is a counter-process which will redefine the "race" problem and use diplomatic, political and economic pressures to speed up the establishment of a satisfactory balance of Black-White power.

The main ingredients of the counter-process have begun to emerge in clearer outlines in the crisis. Monolithal conflicts on the White side have been complicated by the circumstance that the Afrikaners and the English cannot reconcile the clash between economic necessity and the imperatives of Afrikaner "survival."This surrenders the initiative to influence events to the African.

But to extort maximum advantage from the initiative, the African has to launch a political offensive to create new monolithal alignments.

The formula for co-existence which follows is not a solution; it is a list of starting points in organising and launching the counter-process:

i. *The redefinition of the "race" problem.*

The crisis in South Africa needs to be recognised as a war of minds which can be resolved by a multiple strategy which allows for the use of every weapon available to the African.

ii. *The creation of a state based on the primacy of the person.*

Southern Africa is inhabited by peoples with different racial and cultural identities. Most of these define fulfilment in their terms and want to do this for as long as they live. They all have the right to define themselves in their terms. But individually, they are too small to establish viable communities. Getting any blocs to combine to impose destiny on others is unthinkable. The only viable basis for a unifying national identity is emphasis on the primacy of the person.

This basis rejects the principle of "separate freedoms," which is apartheid in a new guise, and limits the Afrikaner's role as oppressor in a larger federation of Southern African states.

Where the intention is to build a larger and stronger nation, whatever limits any community's ability to contribute constructively to the new experiment should be rejected.

The argument and propaganda for armed struggle are skilfully forged weapons for use in forcing the Africans, Coloureds and Asians to fight apartheid, not on political and diplomatic planes where they are stronger, but on ground where they are most vulnerable and where they will always be dependent on the West, the Soviet Union or Cuba for arms and expertise.

This point is so important for South Africa and the rest of the subcontinent that it needs to be stated in different terms. It is clear from African history in the last hundred years and the logic of events from this key community in the years since 1912 that the unitary state is no guarantee of security for anybody. The British imposed the unitary state on South Africa in 1910 and, by doing this, incited the Afrikaner to work for its destruction, as the existence of the Transkei and Bophuthatswana as "independent" states shows.

The Afrikaner monolith is trying to fill the power-vacuum created by the collapse of the unitary state with a satellite system in which a multiplicity of unviable Black mini-states will forever orbit around a central Afrikaner state to give permanence to Afrikaner domination.

The satellite system will be crushed by the African majority for obvious reasons. It is conceived in dishonesty and greed. The Afrikaner monolith lies to the world when it says it wants to give the African what it wants for the Afrikaner. The Afrikaner wants security for himself; security involves owning enough territory and resources to support a growing population. None of the plans published by the government and Afrikaner intellectuals give the African a fair proportion of land and resources to support a growing population.

Take the distribution of land and resources in Natal as an example. Durban has always belonged historically and geographically to Natal and the Zulu people; the latter have all the qualities of nationhood—an ideal of nationhood, a distinctive national identity, a well-known pattern of government, a culture of its own, territory with clearly drawn boundaries, a philosophy for defining the person, an established diplomatic tradition, a national will and a capacity for resisting attempts to destroy its nationhood. In spite of this, the Afrikaners excise Durban and Pietermaritzburg, the railway corridor from Durban to Charlestown and Southern Natal from Kwa Zulu and reserve these for the White minority.

Parallels of the excision exist in virtually every homeland. The idea behind it is to give a meaning to the Afrikaner ideal of *die wit man moet baas bly*, which will impress the uninformed in the conditions created by the extension of the area of freedom in Africa and the emergence of the Third World as a factor to reckon with in international politics.

Substance is given to this dishonesty by the fact that the Africans in the so-called Black homelands have no say in the delineation of boundaries for their "states." Everywhere, the rule is to prescribe destiny for the Black man, who is expected to prostrate himself before the Whites in gratitude for what is a standing insult to the Black race as a whole.

A fact which has to be faced is that whatever the Afrikaner says, he does not want the Africans to have that security which he wants for himself. As long as the dishonesty on this plane remains, Black and White will continue to move in different directions; they will be powerless to stop the reduction of South Africa to ashes.

If the unitary state and the satellite system are invitations to disaster; if they give the majority a vested interest in working for the expulsion of the Whites—Ian Smith said there would be no majority rule in Rhodesia in a thousand years; in less than a thousand days, Whites were fleeing the country by the thousand—the answer which events call for is not moving in circles to perpetuate the dishonesty of the Afrikaner; it is to take note of the fact that the Soweto Rebellion established the relativity of Afrikaner power. In doing this, the Rebellion cracked the foundations of

White power and demonstrated that the irresistible momentum of majority power, fuelled by Sudic anger, will eventually destroy the satellite system.

In short, the Rebellion created a power-vacuum which neither the Afrikaner monolith nor the united front of White monoliths can fill, without the consent of the African people. In simple language, this means that the Afrikaner monolith has lost the decisive battles of the war of minds; that the centre of gravity in the dispositions of Black and White power in South Africa has shifted from the Afrikaner monolith to the Black majority.

This situation focuses attention on two aspects of Black-White relations. Whites cannot stop the reduction of South Africa to ashes if the Collective Will rejects prescribed destiny. The Soweto Rebellion showed that there now are limitations to White power. The Africans asserted the Collective Will for more than a year and, in doing this, gave expression to the mood of ungovernability which apartheid had produced among them.

On the White side, Big Business, which had no love for the African, moved significantly to the left of the government on the crucial issue of race discrimination and reinforced this movement by asserting leadership initiatives in abolishing race discrimination in given areas of employment, home ownership, entertainment and eating.

While the 1978 East London conference of the Cape division of the ruling party was suppressing a Stellenbosch University motion for a recasting of government policy for urban Africans, Dr. Gerrit Viljoen, chairman of the largely anti-African organisation in the Afrikaner monolith, *Die Broederbond* (The Brothers' League), and Mr. Willem de Klerk, editor of the pro-government daily, *Die Transvaler,* which is published in Johannesburg, were planning to meet or were meeting African leaders of Soweto like Dr. Nthato Motlana and Dr. Maurice Nyembezi in efforts to bridge the chasm that divides the Africans and the Afrikaners.

In 1977 Police Minister Kruger had warned Buthelezi against admitting non-Zulus into the NCLM. Buthelezi made it known that he would ignore the warning.

The significant fact these developments draw attention to is that a crack, possibly invisible to those who see the crisis from Caucasian perspectives, has developed in the White community's ability to impose and enforce its will; a vacuum has emerged in the Afrikaner monolith's thinking on the problems created for the Afrikaner by apartheid.

The vacuum changes the character of the quarrel between Black and White on this plane. If the Viljoen and de Klerk initiatives mean anything, they tell us that sections of the leadership stratum in the Afrikaans community are now ready to exchange views with some Africans. This does not mean that an open split has developed in the Afrikaner community; it means that some Afrikaners have begun to give thought to alternative guarantees of survival for their people; that these Afrikaners are concerned over the prospect that South Africa might one day be reduced to ashes because of the evils of apartheid.

The incipient uncertainty about the efficacy of apartheid as a guarantee of survival calls for an African offensive which would be directed at the mind of the Afrikaner to enable him to see in the creation of a new balance in the dispositions of Black and White power the only reliable guarantee of survival for Afrikanerdom.

Armed struggle will not create this balance for the present; talking to the Afrikaner, negotiating with him if necessary and at all times moving events visibly to a political solution might create it.

Military and political weapons are not incompatibles in the conditions created by apartheid; this book argues that they are complements and shows that moving events to a political solution is as courageous, legitimate and honourable a course of action as armed struggle.

For years the United States and Maoist China had no kind word for each other. While they hurled polemical insults at each other on many planes, they also were negotiating secretly in remote Warsaw, Poland, in efforts to discover real areas of congruity in their peoples' interests.

The crisis in South Africa has reached the point where the Africans on the frontline negotiate where it is possible, just as they laid down their lives when need for this arose. Peoples who have been fighting each other for more than three hundred years cannot and will not suddenly forget the cruelties and humiliations inflicted on them by history. The developing crack in the mind of the Afrikaner monolith on the need to consult with the African could be transformed into a factor of political significance in the crisis. People who do not as yet have guns could do worse than deepen the crack. Merely to say, "We shall not collaborate!" when non-collaboration gave Matanzima the green light to accept vassalage does not solve our problem at the level of fundamentals. The logic of our bicipitous mind and the Evolving Revolt demands that we should always be ready with political and military choices; that we should work as much for an *evolving transfer of power* to the majority as we should be ready to take up arms when these become available. In the context provided by the prospect that South Africa might be one of the main battlefields of World War III, Buthelezi's and Botha's priorities are not altogether irreconcilable. This calls for a serious and informed confrontation of minds between the African and the Afrikaner for the purposes of: a) creating a Black-White consensus on a unifying national identity, b) signing a Black-White treaty to solve the Afrikaner's *survival problem,* c) realising that majority rule means one thing in a unitary state, another in a race dictatorship like the one we have in South Africa and a third in a federal union, and d) ensuring that Black-White unity prevents South Africa from becoming a battlefield in a war over Africa's resources.

In blunt language again, history tells us that a united front of like-minded Africans, Coloureds, Asians, Afrikaners, English, etc., is the only guarantee that South Africa shall not be reduced to ashes.

Buthelezi and Botha have a responsibility here to see to it that South Africa does not become one of the battlefields of World War III, to lead South Africa along safer routes to a better future. A face-to-face meeting between Buthelezi and Botha might be a turning-point in the drift to disaster.

Buthelezi is in a position to obtain a Black mandate for offering the Afrikaner an alternative guarantee of survival. Buthelezi wants this alternative negotiated; that is why he calls for a constitutional conference.

Above all, Buthelezi has the mandate to use the military potential of the Zulu people to contribute if conditions change, to the defence of South Africa as a whole. Afrikanerdom needs this potential, just as all South Africa needs it. On the other hand the Afrikaner has the ability to procure arms. Buthelezi needs this ability, just as all South Africa needs it. Redefining the "race" problem could produce a synthesis of needs or a consensus on the defence of South Africa which could eliminate the need for an armed struggle and move Black and White to a political solution, to the realisation that no prescribed destiny will ever work in South Africa because it will at all times act against the will of the African people.

The African people's will, as their history in the last hundred years shows, is an evolving attitude; it is a mode of adapting to the demands of a changing situation; it is a habit of thinking and a lifestyle designed to create new and relevant cultural and political anchors in the conditions created by conquest. No disarmed and deprived nation ever made these adaptations overnight.

The last armed protest the Zulu section of our people made was in 1905-06 when Bhambada ka Mancinza refused to pay taxes to a government in which he was not represented. In the seventy years which followed, our various language-groups unified themselves into a new nation on the basis of a clearly stated philosophy, and set themselves equally clearly stated goals. They developed a readily recognisable strategy for moving to these goals.

Largely as a result, they can be said today to be the only community which has developed a realistic and viable plan for normalising relations between Black and White—for creating a political order which all races can accept with honour. The secret of Inkatha's growth and Buthelezi's influence lies in the fact that they adhere to this plan and move Black and White to their goals in spite of unparalleled difficulties inside South Africa and abroad.

The Collective Will brings us to the last word on the armed struggle. While this Will is aggressive where the African people are strong, it conciliates where they are weak. One day, large-scale flows of arms from across the borders of Mozambique, Zimbabwe, Botswana and Namibia to South Africa will place the Africans in a situation of obvious strength. This strength will be able to destroy South Africa from within.

The Afrikaner has made himself the most hated White group in the Republic. Afrikaner farmers are placed in isolated corners of the country. The White army and police are altogether inadequate for the purpose of protecting every farm, manning the borders, keeping order in the urban areas and ensuring that South Africa is safe for the White man. That between three and four thousand Whites per year are fleeing the country while they can, shows that some Whites, who include Afrikaners, have reached the point where they realise that the relativity of White power is now a fact of South African life.

Botha, his government and the leadership stratum in the Afrikaner monolith do not realise that they live in a changed world; they think they can shoot their way to security and see no need for changes to accommodate the aspirations of Africans, Coloureds and Asians as long as Israeli and German technology promises them the nuclear bomb.

But the nuclear bomb will be as effective in protecting the status quo as the Maginot Line was in preventing the German conquest of France in World War II. The Africans do not need to have guns to crush apartheid; they have the option to paralyse the economy in general and the mines in particular with a stay-at-home strike.

From 1912 to the present, they have been patiently and consistently building the potential to bring the South African economy to a halt. In the final analysis, White South Africa does not have the potential to stop the African majority if and when it decides to paralyse the economy. Buthelezi has been told by his people on several occasions to warn the Whites that if they do not abandon their racial policies, the Africans will withdraw their labour. Buthelezi's response to this has been that his people's options are his options.

This warning must be seen against developments in Rhodesia. Joshua Nkomo started his political career as what most Whites would describe as a moderate. White intransigence drove him from this position to acceptance of the armed revolt as the only answer to race oppression in his country. This acceptance was the final option open to his people and Nkomo was obliged to make it his option.

South Africa is fortunate in one respect: the time has not yet come for Africans to commit themselves to armed struggle. The existence of viable options is one factor responsible for this. The options open to the Afrikaner monolith are another deterrent. But the day is coming when the African will choose the military argument.

The interval between now and the day of decision gives the African and the Afrikaner, who are South Africa's key communities, a little more time to run as fast as they can toward a negotiated solution. But running is precisely what Botha and his government are incapable of doing, as the failure of the Mondale-Vorster discussions shows. This calls for an overhaul of Free African, Frontline, OAU, Third World and Western attitudes to the crisis; for a re-evaluation of power dispositions in the Afrikaner community and for a strategy which will hit apartheid where it is weakest.

The structure of the Afrikaner monolith is the Afrikaner's point of greatest strength and maximum vulnerability. Its stratification into the apartheid regime, the leadership stratum and the rank-and-file combines with its political potential to give it a number of options. Only two will be mentioned here.

If Pretoria seriously wanted to split and crush the South African Black Alliance, for example, it would offer the whole of Natal to the Zulus and *at the same time* urge the Coloureds and the Asians to identify themselves with the Whites. In spite of everything that has been written in this discussion, there still are Coloureds and Asians who would jump for the opportunity to be identified with the Whites. So-called progressive Indian organisations in Natal continue to sit on the fence when it comes to joining the SABA in the hope that Pretoria might offer them better terms than the three-tiered government and second-class citizenship.

Declaring Natal an autonomous Zulu state would have a number of advantages for the Afrikaner monolith. Natal is not Afrikaner country; for apartheid's purposes, it is Zulu-English-Asian territory. By restoring Natal to the Zulus, Pretoria would get rid of South Africa's most "troublesome" communities: the Zulus, English and Asians.

Natal's English are more or less traditional secessionists while Pretoria regards the Asians as a potential fifth-column on the Indian Ocean, precisely in the way that the United States viewed the Japanese-Americans on the West coast as probable allies of Japan during the second World War.

Pretoria regards the Zulus as the only African community which has consistently never accepted defeat and which is not likely to. To get these communities out of "White" South Africa would leave the Afrikaner free to create the order he desires.

In the climate of hostility to Buthelezi which exists in sections of Free Africa, the OAU, the United Nations and among groups of Western liberals and Moscow surrogates, the Zulus might be forced into the position where they would join the English secessionists, accept provincial autonomy and eventually secede from South Africa to form the nucleus of the Federal Union of the Autonomous States of Southern Africa. The nucleus would include Natal, Lesotho, Swaziland and Transkei (including Ciskei) and would form a strategically placed nation in Southeast Africa controlling the ports of Durban and Richards Bay and with the potential to develop St. Lucia Bay into a major naval base. The establishment of the nucleus would confront Free Africa, the OAU, the Frontline States, the United Nations and Western liberals with awkward choices. In addition, the nucleus would have enough resources to build a powerful army to protect its freedom.

The second option concerns Matanzima and Mangope. If the Afrikaner monolith felt really cornered, it would not hesitate to offer Matanzima and Mangope terms of alliance which would place these two men in better positions to secure their power. They would accept arms from Botha to protect their "independence."

An important aspect of this option is that if Botha's knees quaked at the prospect of an accommodation with the Africans, the Afrikaner monolith is not incapable of rejecting him and choosing a leader with the courage to strike a deal with the Africans. The Afrikaner's allergy to race equality it was said in an earlier chapter, is a variable which responds to the demands of survival. If the Afrikaner's *survival problem* demands the rejection of Botha, the Afrikaner monolith will throw him out, just as it rejected Hertzog and Smuts.

For there is only one situation in which the Afrikaner monolith can have no options: when it comes face to face with what it regards as threats to its survival. The Arnold-Bergstraesser initiative, if combined with a controlled economic crisis which would be supported at least by American, British, Canadian, French and West German investors, would be one such threat.

The inner logic of developments in the Afrikaner monolith suggests that armed struggle would for a long time to come play into the hands of the apartheid regime; at the same time it makes it clear that Afrikanerdom is most vulnerable on the political and diplomatic planes. If this conclusion does anything, it argues the case for the co-ordination of internal and external campaigns against apartheid for the purpose of moving events visibly and effectively toward a political solution; toward a disciplined social order in South Africa which will be based on the primacy of the person, the simultaneous legitimacy of different cultural self-definitions and political federalism. In the final analysis, this order is the only basis for a national identity which will enable the African and the Afrikaner in the first instance, and elsewhere, the Africans, Coloureds, Asians and Whites, to prevent the reduction of South Africa to ashes if war finally comes to that country.

The question this raises is: Where can the start be made to move all races toward the national identity under discussion? The "race" problem has to be redefined. Stress has to be laid, not on "petty apartheid," which is one way of perpetuating the status quo, but on the development of a Black-White policy for preventing the reduction of South Africa to ashes; on the creation of a Black-White consensus on a joint policy for coping with external threats.

Such a consensus is possible only with acknowledgement of the fact that the attitudes which inspire Sudic and Graeco-Romano-Hebraic civilisations are polarities which have brought into being the African perspective and the Caucasian perspective. Where the African perspective attaches maximum importance to the fundamentals of conflict, the White perspective sets the greatest store by the operational aspects of race conflict.

In these conditions, the first precondition for a consensus on the prevention of South Africa's reduction to ashes is a formula for co-existence which all races can accept with honour. The second is open and effective support for this formula by the Frontline States, the OAU and the rest of the international community. External groups cannot define destiny for Black and White in South Africa. In the final analysis, they would have to accept what Black and White agreed upon. Their support is necessary only to the extent that the vacuum in Western thinking on the crisis subjects all new ideas from South Africa to approval by Free Africa, the OAU and the Frontline States, which have not done all their homework on power dispositions inside South Africa.

Now for the formula for co-existence.

A UNIFYING NATIONAL IDENTITY

The answer to the crisis in South Africa is a process which will redefine the "race" problem, produce a formula for co-existence which will be acceptable to all races and peoples and create a consensus of the like-minded for the purpose of stabilising economic and political conditions in Southern Africa as a whole. This process will move coterminously on two planes: inside South Africa and in the rest of Southern Africa.

The Programme of Principles for moving people and events toward the resolution of conflict in the sub-continent includes:

i.   *The redefinition of the "race" problem.*
     The crisis in South Africa needs to be recognised as a war of minds that can be settled by a serious and informed confrontation in order to move events visibly and effectively to a political solution. Free Africa has shown that she is more effective on the political plane than in armed struggles.

ii. *The creation of a state based on the primacy of the person.*
     Southern Africa is inhabited by peoples with different racial and cultural backgrounds. Most of these define fulfillment in their terms and want to do this for as long as they need these self-definitions. Others want to prescribe destiny for their neighbours. Emphasis on the primacy of the person will create a synarchy, which is an open, non-racial state based on the primacy of the person, the simultaneous legitimacy of cultural self-definitions, political federalism, economic mutualism and cultural autonomy.

iii. *The development of a unifying Formula for Co-Existence for Southern Africa.*

The racial, economic and other problemns which afflict all the races, peoples and nations of Southern Africa are related and inseparable aspects of a larger Southern African problem which calls for a larger Southern African solution, hammered out by all the races, peoples and nations which have made Southern Africa their home. Such a larger solution or Formula for Co-Existence is the transformation of all the races, nations and peoples of the sub-continent into a co-operating economic and political community.

iv. *Phased movement toward the unification of all the nations, peoples and races of Southern Africa into the Federal Union of the Autonomous States of Southern Africa.*

The federal union would be large, wealthy and powerful enough to ensure that Southern Africa does not become the football of international politics. At the same time, it would reconcile the conflicts created by apartheid's fragmentation of the African community.

v. *The convention by the Security Council of the Southern African Treaty Conference at which all the races, nations and peoples of the sub-continent will start working together on the Formula for Co-Existence.*

No power or combination of powers would start war in Southern Africa if all the peoples of the region were seen effectively negotiating a formula for co-existence in their part of the world. The Security Council is the only body with enough authority to call for such a gathering.

vi. *The establishment of a Stabilisation Fund to revitalise and normalise all the economies of Southern Africa which have been affected adversely or paralysed by race conflict.*

The economies of Southern Africa cannot be treated in isolation from each other; they dovetail and interlock at so many points that they can be stabilised only if they are treated as a unity.

vii. *The formation of a Southern African Development Authority to guide development in an open, person-centred society.*

While conflict features prominently in African-Afrikaner relations, there also are important areas of congruity in the experiences of the two communities. One of these is the mixed economy developed mainly by the Afrikaner monolith. This eliminates the need for extensive radical nationalisation and creates the conditions which would facilitate the systematic redistribution of wealth. To produce the desired results, the redistribution should be related to conditions in other parts of the sub-continent.

viii. *Proportional Partition as the basis for the establishment of the Federal Union of the Autonomous States of South Africa.*
To resolve the war of minds and establish a democracy of cultures, each self-defining community must have enough power—that is, enough land and other forms of wealth—to ensure that its wishes are respected and to establish a Collective Sovereignty which will unify by constantly reinforcing the disparate sovereignties of the autonomous states of the Federal Union.

ix. *Relevant guarantees of security for all sections of the population which have a survival problem.*
Proposals for the resolution of conflict which ignore the Afrikaner's *survival problem* are most likely to fail. The Afrikaner's definition of the "race" quarrel needs to be confronted with a clearly stated alternative to apartheid as a guarantee of survival. But the Afrikaners are not the only community which feels threatened. The Asians have reason to fear being crushed between any two monoliths; they have the right to demand guarantees of security, even when these might be dissimilar to those which would satisfy the Afrikaner.

x. *The radical redistribution of land and other forms of wealth on the basis of mutualism.*
The abolition of race discrimination, without social and economic justice to those whom the White man's racial policies deprived for more than a century, would be a mockery of freedom. Those who benefited from the exploitation and humiliation of the African either have to pay reparations or integrate the African in the economy on the principle of co-ownership.

xi. *The principle of a mixed economy to be preserved in South Africa.*
An important area of congruity in the African and Afrikaner experiences is the nationalisation by different Afrikaner governments, of a number of primary resources. This laid foundations for mutualism and would facilitate the redistribution of wealth.

xii. *The re-unification of Kwa Zulu and "White" Natal into an autonomous nonracial state which could unite with Swaziland, Lesotho, Transkei and Ciskei to form, if need arises, the nucleus of the Federal Union of the Autonomous States of Southern Africa.*

Such a course would have obvious advantages and disadvantages. Let us start with the latter, because they can be readily disposed of. Some of Buthelezi's critics would charge that by moving farther away from the unitary state he would be extending the area of "collaboration" with the apartheid regime.

But, as he himself has often pointed out, the Africans had nothing to do with the formation of the unitary state. It was imposed on them, as on the Afrikaners, by the British. Sections of Cape African opinion which followed the Jabavu tradition of collaboration have rejected working with the Whites.

If the quarrel between Black and White is a war of minds, there is no possibility that the majority will ever accept the destiny prescribed for it by the minority. In like manner, it is not likely that the latter will give up their attitude to the person. If current indications are any guide, the minds in collision are moving Black and White to a war whose final outcome will be the ruin of South Africa and the expulsion of the Whites.

After the overthrow of White rule, the peoples of Southern Africa would still have to come together in a federal union because of intertwining economic and defence needs.

The advantages of a federal union for the sub-continent are overwhelming. To begin with, by re-unifying Natal and seceding in order to form the nucleus state, the NCLM would transform the nucleus into a majority-ruled federation. The transformation could keep the nucleus out of the war to which the apartheid regime is driving South Africa.

The complete encirclement of "White" South Africa by Black states would reinforce the Black minority which would remain in the White state, and extend the area of race equality.

The commitment to proportional partition and secession would give focus to the thinking of the masses of the African people. The divided mind on the strike during the Soweto Rebellion arose partly from the circumstance that the leaders have not as yet confronted the advocates of White supremacy with a clearly stated geopolitical alternative to the status quo. There is a vacuum in African thinking on the geopolitical goal toward which the Black people are being led.

Movement toward the Federal Union of the Autonomous States of Southern Africa would be in three stages. There would first be the creation of the consensus on final goals which would be followed by the convention of a constitutional conference of all races to give legal form to the formula for co-existence produced by the consensus. The second stage would be the establishment of the Federal Union of the Autonomous States of South Africa. This would lead eventually to the formation of the Federal Union of the Autonomous States of Southern Africa.

The involvement of the Coloured community on the side of the Africans during the Soweto Rebellion, the formation of the South

African Black Alliance, the shift in Big Business thinking on race discrimination and the Viljoen-de Klerk initiative have all prepared ground for movement toward the consensus.

This movement calls for the assertion of statesmanlike leadership initiatives to lead Black, Coloured, Asian and White opinion toward agreement on final goals. As things stand at the moment only Buthelezi and the National Cultural Liberation Movement can give this type of leadership. As the Freiberg Report and other researches show, Buthelezi has enough organised power to be a representative of the majority of the South African people at the ·moment.

These advantages give Buthelezi the freedom to call out his followers in a national stay-at-home strike to paralyse the economy and to back this with a crisis of dual-authority conflict, or to secede from the Republic to form the nucleus of the Federal Union of the Autonomous States of Southern Africa.

This union might be formed in one of two ways: either with or without the co-operation of the Whites. The crisis in South Africa has reached the point where the conquering minority has lost the power to impose its will but still has enough authority to delay the march to majority rule. The increase in the numbers of Whites who flee the country shows that cracks have developed in the foundations of White power. These cracks give Buthelezi his chance.

He could unify Kwa Zulu and "White" Natal and secede from the Republic specifically to form, with the Ciskei, Transkei, Lesotho, Swaziland and Mozambique, which have contiguous borders with Natal, the nucleus of the Federal Union of the Autonomous States of Southern Africa.

The psychological effects of such a nucleus need no emphasis. The goal of a Black-ruled federation which every Black man in South Africa could regard as his own would introduce a new dimension in the relations between Black and White. And this dimension would, in turn, prepare ground for a Black-White defence policy which would make it impossible for any combination of powers to plunge Southern Africa into war.

The nucleus can be seen from another angle. The international community has rightly taken the position that it will not recognise the vassal states which have accepted the "independence" offered by the apartheid regime. But this negative reaction cannot be the policy of the international community forever. At some time in the future, the world must realise that the treatment of Transkei and Bophuthatswana as international pariahs creates problems for mankind.

While there is need for reinforcing rejections of the vassalage which apartheid offers as independence, the Free World should develop a policy for recognising the Federal Union of the Autonomous States of Southern Africa as the geopolitical structure that would re-unite the peoples apartheid divides.

The nucleus of the Federal Union would make it possible for some Africans to secede from apartheid's satellite system and regroup to form a nucleus of their own design.

In India Mahatma Gandhi and Mohamed Ali Jinnah reached the point where the differences dividing their communities forced them to accept partition. As already shown, there are Africans who do not want to belong to the same state as the Whites. Some of these are prepared to accept "independence" itself if it takes them out of the racial dictatorship imposed by the Afrikaner monolith.

There are many ways of moving toward the Federal Union; establishing the nucleus, which would evolve into a larger regrouping of Southern African peoples, is one of them.

The PAC popularised the slogan: *Izwe lethu*! (It is our country!) Before it, the ANC had demanded: *Mayibuye i Afrika* (Let Africa be restored to her glory). In the view of the man or woman whom White rule crushes every day, these slogans have little or no meaning; they do not define goals which have vital meaning in his or her life. In the conditions created by apartheid, goals with a specific geopolitical focus are likely to evoke a positive mass response.

One of the weaknesses on the side fighting White rule has always been the absence of a clearly stated alternative to the national identity prescribed by apartheid. Black and White have never been confronted with a real choice of worlds—with an alternative to the racial dictatorship which would have relevance in the lives of ordinary people.

The Bloemfontein Unity Conference gave us an Ideal of Nationhood while the Umtata Conference of 1973 gave geopolitical content to the Ideal. Since then, nobody has stated in precise terms what shape the geopolitical form should take.

The ordinary person who is crushed by race humiliation and oppression does not have the time or equipment to familiarise himself with abstract principles; he is concerned with concrete situations because these affect his life visibly.

The nucleus would give Lesotho and Swaziland direct access to the sea.

The re-unification of Natal and the formation of the nucleus would attract investments and would lay the foundations for the transformation of the Federal Union into the industrial heart of Africa. The establishment of the nucleus would go beyond opening the markets of the continent to goods from the nucleus; it would create an altogether new type of relationship between Free Africa and the peoples of the nucleus.

Above all, the nucleus would have a greater potential for developing a more prosperous economy than the "White" state. Apart from crushing the satellite system which Pretoria dreams of it would have two major ports facing the Indian Ocean and St. Lucia Bay, which is almost surrounded by national game parks, and has the potential to be one of the finest holiday resorts on the Indian Ocean. The nucleus would have coal, iron, wood pulp, sugar, maize, livestock and other resources which would make it the industrial gateway into Africa.

The nucleus, in which the majority of Africans live, could be extended to include the homelands of the North if and when they are ready to confront the Afrikaner monolith with the inevitable implication of Ethnic Grouping.

xiii. *A common defence policy for all the peoples of South Africa initially and all the communities of Southern Africa later.*

The most important developments on the homefront in the clash between Black and White during the first, nine months of 1978 were, first, the decision, by Dr. Gerrit Viljoen, chairman of Die Broederbond, Dr. Willem de Klerk, editor of *Die Transvaler* and other leaders of the Afrikaner monolith, to exchange ideas with African leaders and, second, Premier Vorster's resignation from the leadership of the apartheid regime.

The resignation took place in curious circumstances. Chief Buthelezi, in common with some Coloured, Asian and White leaders, had for years called upon Vorster to convene a constitutional conference to hammer out a formula for co-existence which would be acceptable to all races. Vorster had opposed this. Then, early in the second half of 1978, the chairman of Die Broederbond and *Die Transvaler's* editor and other Afrikaner leaders met Drs. Nthato Motlana and Maurice Nyembezi, leaders respectively of Soweto's Committee of Ten and Inkatha branch.

Some of the points made by Afrikaner leaders were: that the Afrikaner monolith would have to change its commitment to excessive Afrikaner protectiveness; that it would have to adopt riskier positions to maintain its culture; that all "unnecessary" colour bars would have to be rejected; that Africans should move away from their commitment to the unitary state and the Westminster concept of "winner take all" if victorious in general elections; that the government was becoming aware that South Africa had entered a new political era in which "the essential factor is maximum consensus"; that if Black nationalism and the Afrikaner had to make sacrifices to secure their common future, in the new thinking of the Afrikaner, provision had to be made for "the political fulfillment of the urban black"; that the Afrikaner was thinking of some sort of confederal structure for South Africa and believed this could reconcile conflict.

xiv. *The return to their original homes or ancestral lands of all African communities and others removed from these homes and lands by the White man's laws and the payment, to all people thus deprived, of reparations and such other forms of compensation as the majority government will authorise.*

We should under no circumstances believe that just because some Afrikaner leaders now talk of policies based on "maximum consensus" they have changed their basic attitudes to us. We should develop our own yardsticks for determining basic changes in their thinking. One of these is the return to our people of all lands which belonged to us before conquest. These are African lands; they have always been African lands and will forever be African lands.

Jordan K. Ngubane

The Afrikaners, if the points they made are any guide, came to set in motion a political process; their name for it was *maximum consensus*. They met the Africans in the effort to sound African reactions to Afrikaner alternatives to the status quo. These alternatives had two fundamental weaknesses: they were conceived within the concept of separate freedom on one hand and, on the other, they were based on demonstrable Afrikaner ignorance of developments in the African's Evolving Revolt in the last sixty-six years.

The doctrine of separate development is unacceptable because it is based on what the Afrikaners regard as the White man's right to prescribe destiny for the African. The prescription might be seen in Afrikanerdom's hostility to the Bloemfontein Ideal of Nationhood and the dishonest offer of vassalage in unviable mini-states.

The ignorance of African history emerged in Afrikaner insistence on the abandonment of the commitment to a unitary state. The Africans rejected the concept on January 8, 1912, when they formed themselves into a new nation whose destiny was not to be integrated in a unitary state, nor in a racial dictatorship of the type established by apartheid, but to establish "a new and unique civilization."

The African rejected the Westminster concept of nationhood when he chose this destiny.

The Africans had said, over a hundred years ago, that the philosophy by which they gave meaning to freedom defined the person in terms which emphasised his primacy regardless of who his parents were and recognised the simultaneous legitimacy of different cultural self-definitions.

The facts which gave significance to the exchanges were, first, that the chairman of Die Broederbond and the editor of *Die Transvaler* had virtually gone over the head of the Vorster government to meet the leaders of the African people in an exchange of views which, though not formal, had some of the makings of a first step toward negotiating a political settlement.

The second fact was that at about the time the Africans met the Afrikaners, rumours started circulating to the effect that Vorster was planning to resign, which he did.

His resignation drew into sharper outlines the conflict between the advocates of the narrower ideal of nationhood based on the principle that *die wit man moet baas bly* and that section of Afrikaners who are moving toward a larger concept of nationhood which would include the Africans, the Coloureds, the Asians and the Whites on the basis of "separate freedoms."

The two developments throw into bolder relief the vacuum which has developed in Afrikaner thinking on the future of South Africa. The void demands that the Africans, particularly in Free Africa, should be ready to fill it with a political alternative; that is, with a clearly stated final goal while readying themselves for armed struggle should the apartheid regime play them dirty tricks.

The people on the homefront have already indicated their determination to negotiate with the Afrikaner if he wants a real alternative to apartheid. Realism demands that Free Africa should adapt to the demands of this situation on the homefront instead of shouting ineffective slogans about armed struggle.

The alternative is simple: The Africans on the homefront will proceed to settle their quarrel with the Whites in their own way, regardless of what the advocates of the armed struggle say or do.

In the meantime it does not do the African harm to move the argument with the Afrikaner away from separate lavatories for Black and White to a Black-White defence policy for South Africa. This would be an assertion of leadership initiatives in a situation of challenge.

This is not written to threaten Free Africa. On the contrary it is a plea to those Black countries which have made colossal sacrifices in support of our cause—sacrifices which we honestly and deeply appreciate—to take note of the changing dispositions of power on the homefront and develop strategies for adapting to these changes.

One consequence of not adapting before armed conflict is the unnecessary bloodshed we saw in Rhodesia. The other was the humiliating position where the Free Africans who clamoured for armed struggle did nothing effective to stop the massacre of our children during the Soweto Rebellion, other than to saturate the air with angry verbiage. They did the same when Smith killed Mozambicans on their own territory.

Other points from the above Programme of Principles call for comment. These will be discussed in their order of importance rather than as listed in the Programme.

Proportional partition is the most important of these. To begin with, proportional partition is not a new development in African history. As we have shown, Seme, Jabavu and Selope-Thema gave thought to the idea; so did H. Selby Msimang and Paul Mosaka.

It has been argued throughout this discussion that Black and White attitudes to the person produce mutually exclusive ideals of nationhood. The resulting conflicts make a poor foundation for a unitary state of the type imposed by the English in 1910. And, in any case, we Africans were not a party to the formation of the unitary state. In 1912, however, we united ourselves into a single nation. This nation needs to consolidate its territory first. This means that it must start by forming the nucleus of a federal union of the states which face the Indian Ocean, which would grow gradually to include all the states of the sub-continent in the end.

While opposing White domination in all its forms in every possible way, we Africans should also take note of the specifically geopolitical problems apartheid creates for us and should develop our Federal Union idea in such a way that it eventually solves these problems.

Proportional partition on the bases of simultaneous legitimacy and validity, proportional redistribution of the land, resources and other forms of wealth and eventual unification into a federal community of Black and White states of Southern Africa seems the type of state structure which conditions in the subcontinent call for.

Instead of wasting time, energy and money exchanging polemical insults with Pretoria, the international community generally and Free Africa in particular need to move away from concentrating on the functional aspects of apartheid, toward confronting the Whites in South Africa with a geopolitical alternative to the status quo.

The above might be stated in different terms. If the evolution, forms and functioning of racism and race discrimination in South Africa, the United States and in the relations between the Black and White nations together constitute a process which translates into action a given attitude to the person, the answer to the crisis in South Africa is a counter-process which would move the Africans and the Whites to a face-to-face confrontation on a clearly stated geopolitical alternative to the status quo; it is the launching of a political initiative which would set the counter-process in motion and lead Black and White to a Southern African Treaty Conference in which all the racial, language and other groups which have made Southern Africa their home would together hammer out a formula for co-existence that would transform the subcontinent into a cooperating economic and political community which would develop by stages into a federal union of the autonomous states of Southern Africa.

South Africa would be partitioned into two states, one Black and the other White as shown in the accompanying map. The Black state would have to control enough land and resources to withdraw Black communities in the White state if necessary.

Like the Black state, the White state would have the right to accede to the Federal Union. If it wanted to, it could remain out of it and throw in its lot with the West. The expectation is that self-interest would enable it to join the Federal Union.

Two main points need to be noted about the above formula for co-existence. The formula proposes a treaty between Black and White to settle the race quarrel for all time. This is the only way to build for peace, mutuality, co-operation and stability where two races, controlling given reserves of power, are committed to two different attitudes to the person.

The three elements of the formula for co-existence proposed above are: the dismantling of the unitary state-structure as a first precondition for the demonolithisation of South African society; adequate guarantees of political independence, economic security and survival not for the Whites only, but for all the peoples of Southern Africa, and the unification of all these peoples into a co-operating economic and political community.

On one hand these elements provide moulds in which diametrically opposed evaluations of the person could co-exist in an environment which recognised the simultaneous legitimacy, validity and importance of different cultural self-definitions. On the other, they would create a collective sovereignty whose first task would be to protect the national-group sovereignties and preserve a satisfactory relationship between the whole and its constituent parts; that is, between the collective sovereignty and the national-group sovereignties.

The collective and constituent sovereignties would be bound together by a consensus on final goals; that is, by the recognition of all the nations of the subcontinent as a community with a common economic and political destiny. For this consensus to produce the desired effects, it has to be developed now, before armed conflict breaks out in South Africa. Urgency is given to its establishment by the circumstance that it is an important insurance against civil wars in the African community.

The apartheid regime is incapable of giving leadership in the directions outlined by the formula for co-existence; only the Security Council can do this. The government in Pretoria is deliberately creating the conditions which make war inevitable. The Soviet Union, acting through the Cubans, would not be human if it ignored Pretoria's role as its best ally in Africa. Partly as a result, the Soviets and Cuba are pouring large amounts of military materiel into Africa, first, to impress on the Africans the fact that the Soviet Union is an effective ally because it supplies arms when they are needed and, second, to be within striking range of Pretoria when war comes to South Africa.

The second point to be noted about the treaty conference is that it is designed to ensure that no foreign power or group of powers imposes solutions to Southern Africa's race problem. The peoples of the subcontinent themselves must produce a solution and they would do this, not in an appointment on the battlefield, but by sitting together in a treaty conference to agree on how they propose to live together.

In order to move events in this direction, machinery needs to be established for the co-ordination of the internal (South African) and external campaigns against apartheid. Such machinery would ensure that if and when the African majority came out in a general strike to paralyse the apartheid economy, the international community would be ready to act decisively to bring race oppression crashing to the ground.

The co-ordination would confront the Afrikaner with equitable partition as a guarantee of security for, and a possible solution to, his *survival problem*. The global fight against racism in South Africa continues to be handicapped by the fact that nobody in the international community has seriously confronted the Afrikaner with such an alternative.

When the Afrikaners have a state of their own, in which to nurture their culture, preserve their identity and segregate themselves to their hearts' desire, they would no longer have a *survival problem*; they would cease to make a nuisance of themselves in the subcontinent; they would stop making a mess of the lives of Africans, people of mixed blood,

312

English and Asians inside South Africa. Instead of living in uncertainty about the future, all races would be guaranteed security in the African sun.

No foreign power can give the peoples of the subcontinent this guarantee. Only they can give it to themselves in a treaty conference. The international community can help move events in this direction by exerting pressure on the Security Council to do the work it was established to do: to build for peace by calling the Southern African Treaty Conference with a minimum of delay.

Map of the proposed Federal Union of the Autonomous States of Southern Africa, showing South Africa partitioned into the Black state, the Republic of Sudia, and the White Homeland.

The fashion in South Africa, as in the outside world, is to define the quarrel between Black and White only in racial terms. This simplistic approach ignores the facts that the Afrikaners and the English, though White, have problems between themselves which are as intractable as some of those which characterise Black-White relations; that their histories, cultures and positions in the state give them conflicting attitudes to many of the country's problems.

The Afrikaner has a *survival problem* which the English do not have. Where the Afrikaner sees the retribalisation and fragmentation of the African majority as one of his guarantees of survival, the English, when they ruled South Africa, did not regard African unity as the threat to the Whites which the Afrikaners think it is.

In the schools and churches they established for the Africans, the English welcomed Black people from all language-groups. They are not averse to the African community's ambition to transform Southern Africa into the Ruhr of Africa.

Thus, to define the Black-White quarrel only in racial terms has the effect of adding to the complexity of an already complicated problem; it forces all concerned to speak in terms of absolutes and unnegotiable positions.

What the crisis in South Africa calls for is the realisation that while race features prominently in the quarrel between Black and White, it is only a vehicle used in a conflict which involves fundamentals like different attitudes to the person, the mutually exclusive ideals of nationhood to which these attitudes have given rise, and the irreconcilable strategies adopted for marching to final goals.

Defined in these terms, the problem will cease to be racial only; it will be seen to have aspects which call for a political solution; it will even project majority rule arrived at as a result of negotiation involving all the peoples of Southern Africa as the Afrikaner's only real guarantee of survival. Defining the race problem in terms of monolithal power dispositions will emphasise the need to create a Black-White consensus on final goals; the need to develop a formula for co-existence which will demonolithise South African society and provide new guarantees of survival for those who need them; and the need to accelerate movement to the transformation of Southern Africa into a co-operating economic and political community.

The treaty conference would produce the formula for co-existence on which to develop a consensus on final goals. Proportional partition, which would be the second stage, would give each group adequate guarantees of security. For those Afrikaners and English who detest race equality and majority rule, a separate state would be provided. In this state, they would practice apartheid to their hearts' desire and would not have a single Black person to annoy them.

Up to now, the race problem has been treated as though all White people were against the Black race. This is not the case. While it is true that the majority is for White supremacy—during the November 1977 elections the liberal Progressive Reform Party bought large amounts of newspaper advertising space to let the White electorate know that it opposed universal adult suffrage—there also are Whites who would feel comfortable in a Black state or in one ruled by a Black majority.

It is important that the Whites should be encouraged to choose freely between living in an all-White apartheid state and living in one based on race equality and majority rule. The separatists would be a free and sovereign independent community in their own homeland if they wanted things that way.

The treaty conference, the Consensus on Final Goals and Proportional Partition would be no more and no less than related stages in the march toward the final goal: the establishment of the Federal Union of the Autonomous States of Southern Africa.

Proportional Partition would enable the White segregationists to be separated from those they do not want as neighbours and would leave the anti-racists free to co-operate with the Black majority in transforming Southern Africa into the Ruhr of Africa. We Africans need to reject those who reject us and embrace those who embrace us; we want to stand shoulder to shoulder with the latter in our march to the Federal Union.

The Coloureds, Asians and Whites who would remain in the Black Republic of Sudia would be denied no right that the Africans want for themselves; they would become Africa's children by identifying themselves with Africa's first-borns and would choose to do the thing which the Africans do in Africa: to reject the idea of punishing the person for being the child of his particular parents.

Movement to the treaty conference, Proportional Partition and the transformation of Southern Africa into a co-operating economic and political community would of necessity be a process which would involve all Africans, Coloureds, Asians and Whites who regard all the communities of Southern Africa as peoples with a common economic and political destiny.

One of the weakest points in internal and external campaigns against apartheid is that they lack positive focus. Up to the end of the era of the wars, between 1870 and 1880, African opposition to White domination defended the Black peoples' right to call their lands their own. Conquest, defeat, deculturation and proletariatisation created dangerous problems for our people. All sorts of Caucasian theological and ideological groups came in to divide us and create confusion in our ranks.

Partly as a result, we began to define ourselves in the incongruous terms prescribed by the conquerors. That held out the prospect that we might one day take up arms against each other in the defence of the borrowed self-definitions.

We sent our children to White-oriented schools in South Africa and the West where they were taught the techniques of self-definition, not in their own terms, but in Graeco-Romano-Hebraic terms which avoided the fundamentals of conflict and focused on the operational aspects of apartheid—on segregated residential areas, the pass laws, the differential wage, influx control, etc.

At every conference on South Africa I attended in the ten years I was in America, African scholars read "learned" papers in which they played around with statistics collected by the White power-structure to show where tactical retreats and adjustments could be made to ensure that White domination functioned with the minimum of friction.

Our scholars did not, as a rule, address themselves fully to the need to think in terms of solutions; to the need to confront White domination with well-reasoned and clearly stated alternatives to the status quo in South Africa.

If this helped to surrender the initiative to influence events to Pretoria, it did not give our people the clearest possible view of their alternative to apartheid.

It was not enough merely to say: "Abolish Apartheid! Establish Majority Rule!" The mass of the African people ask: "How do you abolish apartheid? What is Majority Rule? How do you go about establishing it?" Our scholars, particularly those in exile and who are, for this reason, freer to think and write independently, are shy of addressing themselves to this aspect of our struggle.

But our scholars are not the only people who allow the advocates of apartheid to do most of the thinking on the type of South Africa for which so many have sacrificed so much in the years since 1910.

While the NCLM and the Black Consciousness Movement have done magnificent work in politicising our people, they continue not to give positive focus to the struggle they lead. They demand Majority Rule and, in the next breath, do not tell their readers precisely what Majority Rule means and the steps to take to move toward it.

It is true that there are all sorts of legal obstacles to the free discussion of moves to establish Majority Rule. But it is difficult to see why legal institutions like homelands assemblies, which are to a certain extent privileged platforms, are not used fully as platforms from which to educate the masses of our people on what Majority Rule is and on how the Africans can reach it via a political solution.

The proposal for proportional partition is one way of moving toward Majority Rule. Other people might think of other measures. All these need to be aired as freely and as extensively as possible. The Whites are doing this on every conceivable plane. We, who stand to lose or gain most, do not make the best possible use of the channels we have to give positive focus to our struggle or to confront the Whites with clear alternatives.

Proportional partition sets aside the largest portion of South Africa for the Black people because, first, they are in the majority and, second, because those Whites, Coloureds and Asians who would elect to live in Sudia would have to be provided for.

The boundaries of the White state would stretch in a straight line from Knysna to Prieska, through Calvinia to Koekenaap on the South Atlantic. This part of the country has the areas where the Whites first settled.

Those Whites who hate the idea of being ruled by Africans would be free to live in the White homeland and would be free not to join the Federal Union. In like manner, the Union would be free to refuse to accept the White state as a member if the latter pursued policies which would not be acceptable to Africans.

The proportional reapportionment of the land, its resources and other forms of wealth is unnegotiable. No African in his senses accepts the position that Whites own 87 per cent of the land and the Blacks the remainder. The resources of South Africa must be distributed according to population needs on both sides of the colour line.

Speaking for myself, I might add that it would not harm the majority if the van Plettenberg formula, which laid down the Kei River as the eastern boundary of White territory, were modified in such a way as to create what can be called the Prieska Polygon. Prieska's position, near the Orange River, would place the waters of this river at the disposal of the White state. For this reason, Prieska is a pivotal point in the geographic and economic forms of the Polygon.

The rest of South Africa would belong to the Africans. People of mixed blood and Asians would be free to live where they chose.

It is possible that mine might be a minority view. Apartheid's excesses against the majority are driving increasing numbers of Africans to the view that the expulsion of the Whites from all South Africa is the Black man's only guarantee of a satisfying life in his land.

I am a serious exponent of the Sudic evaluation of the person and would regard the right of the White man to live in Africa, if he faced the challenge of belonging to Africa, as an unnegotiable absolute.

Negotiable matters, like population transfers and the distribution of water, would be issues in which Black and White interests could be reconciled.

Areas of congruity would include those issues where there are fundamental affinities in Black and White interests. I would regard the right of the Whites to a place in the African sun as an area of congruity, just as I would the nationalisation by successive Afrikaner governments of basic resources like water, etc.

One of the criticisms levelled against the Geopolitical Alternative is that it leaves the bulk of South Africa's industries in what would be Black territory. This point deserves attention.

The Whites were able to develop industry and commerce with the enforced co-operation of the African. Forced African labour (Isibhalo) was used in the construction of sections of the Durban-Johannesburg railway line. The Differential Wage paid to the African, the exploitation on White farms, and the humiliations of segregation made it possible for the Whites to be one of the most affluent groups in the world.

The African's share of his land's wealth and what he was paid for his labour were a scandal when compared with the way the Whites rewarded themselves. These injustices clamour for redress; they require that the Whites should pay reparations for their crimes against African humanity.

These reparations can be paid by giving the industrialised section of South Africa to the dispossessed majority.

While saying this, note should be taken of the fact that many resources of the section proposed as Black territory have to a large extent been exploited by the Whites. Take the gold mines of the Transvaal for example. Many of them are not very far from depletion-point while the mineral resources of the Cape Western district, which would be on White territory, have barely been touched.

The logic of a political solution demands that the right of the Whites to a place in the African sun should be recognised. The African has the right to claim South Africa as the Black man's land; he can argue that he is entitled to every inch of it; he can even lay down his life for it, as he has done so often in South Africa. If he did that, history would be on his side; but that approach will never lead to a political solution to the race problem to which I, for one, am committed.

What I propose in the Geopolitical Alternative is not a magic formula which will transform South Africa into a paradise for everybody in a day; what I offer is a formula, first, for a Black-White consensus of final goals and, second, for co-ordinated, phase-by-phase movement to these goals; a formula for giving the Africans and the Whites feelings of certainty about their future, whereas apartheid moves all concerned to a future that is "too ghastly to contemplate," as Vorster once said.

The Soweto Rebellion on the homefront, the virtually complete isolation of the apartheid regime on the international plane and the acceptance of Majority Rule by the world combine to mark the end of one phase in our struggle and to signal the beginning of another. In the new era, as in the old, our first guarantee of victory against policies based on pessimistic attitudes to the person is the ability to give effective leadership; to be ready with alternatives to fill the vacua which Sudic initiatives create in White thinking on a satisfying relationship between Black and White.

The creation of a world consensus on proportional partition would enable like-minded Blacks and Whites to start planning for a new society, in Sudia, in which the person would be equipped, enabled and seen to make the best possible use of his or her life regardless of race, colour, sex,ethnicity or creed; they would establish machinery for creating an altogether different set of relations with Free Africa and the rest of the international community; they could set out to transform Southern Africa into the Ruhr of Africa and ask the industrial nations to be involved in a mutually satisfying manner in the transformation of the peoples of the subcontinent into a co-operating economic and political community.

The advocates of apartheid are incapable of leading us or the Whites to the above goals; their attitude forces them to lead all concerned, including the Afrikaner monolith, to ultimate destruction. The political initiative proposed in this discussion will stop this crusade of insanity.

MAJORITY RULE

Majority Rule is controversial in so far as the White communities are concerned. Space does not allow a full discussion of this all-important goal but enough will be said to give at least a working idea of how some Africans understand it.

Majority Rule means the use of political and economic power by the many to raise the living standards of all citizens in a balanced, person-centered society.

Translated into action in South Africa, Majority Rule means:

i. The redrawing of borders for the purpose of creating autonomous states in Sudia in which different communities would have enough living-space to guarantee their survival in ways best suited to their genius;

ii. The language and culture of each majority group in an autonomous state would be the dominant factor in that state;

iii. People whose attachment to their language and culture makes them feel uncomfortable when they have to live with other communities would be free to confine themselves to their state;

iv. Policy would aim at the free movement of populations, the mutualisation and broadening of contacts and the exchange of cultural contributions; the Afrikaner, to give one example, would be encouraged to place at the disposal of the Zulus, for example, those contributions which would help enlarge the Zulu personality and vice versa;

v. Municipalities like Verulam or Stanger in Natal, where racial minority groups constitute the majority would automatically belong to the autonomous state;

vi. Larger urban areas, in particular the industrial areas, would become open, non-racial non-ethnic states in which no cultural pattern would dominate;

vii. Each state would control all its internal affairs with the exception of Defence, Finance, Foreign Affairs and Economic Development;

viii. In its own interest and in the interest of the larger whole, each state would surrender some of its sovereignty to create a head of state who would be a rotating, executive president;

ix. The president, who would hold office for four years, would be elected by the Federal Parliament from a list submitted by a different state every four years; the rotating right to nominate candidates within each state would moderate excessive preoccupation with narrowly ethnic and other concerns;

x. When the turn of the next state came to propose candidates, it would nominate its own citizens;

xi. Each citizen in an autonomous state would have the vote on reaching the age of eighteen (18) regardless of race, colour or creed;

xii. The executive president's cabinet would have at least one member from each autonomous state plus as many members as the federal union might decide to have; the president would choose his cabinet on the basis of merit, regardless of whether or not they were members of the legislature;

xiii. The minorities would have the right to veto legislation which affected adversely their cultural rights pending an appeal to a Human Rights Court which would be a branch of the Appellate Division established to ensure that no cultural group was denied the right to make the best possible use of its life as long as such life did not limit similar rights of other communities.

Many of the points listed above call for comment or explanation. The principle of autonomy requires that the distinction should be drawn between the proposals I made for a federal union about fifteen years ago and what Pretoria is offering. When I referred to the Swiss system and its cantons, I had in mind an arrangement which would be hammered out by all the communities of South Africa and not the frauds foisted on my country as "independence" for the Africans or "participation" in the government offered the people of mixed blood and the Asians.

There are fundamental differences between the type of autonomy I proposed and what the government offers today. Agreement on final goals was the first precondition for movement to the Federal Union of Autonomous States. Each of the main language-groups would submit its proposals for the redelimitation of borders for the autonomous states. Natal, with its Zulu majority, would be an open nonracial state in which Zulu and English would be the official languages.

In so far as the other Black communities are concerned there would have to be extensive restorations to them of the lands taken away from them by the White conquerors. Each such deprived community would present its claims in writing and these would be discussed in open debate by all the groups represented in the official body considering boundaries. Lesotho, for example, cannot survive without the lost lands on the Orange River. The Swazi have extensive claims to land in the Piet-Retief-Barberton-Nelspruit sections of the Transvaal; so do the Pedi, Tswana, Shangane and Venda people in the North. There is need for boundary adjustments in the neighbourhood of the Transkei and the Ciskei.

Unlike the English, the people of mixed blood—why can't we call them the Sudians? I find it humiliating constantly to be calling them Coloureds or people of mixed blood; humiliating to me because these labels insult them; they define them as people who do not belong anywhere when they are the children of Africa—and the Asians, the Afrikaners have a *survival problem* which works for the creation and continuous extension of areas of conflict in Southern Africa. I am committed to the Sudic evaluation of the person and this commitment binds me to recognise the Afrikaner's right to a place in the African sun if he is prepared to face the challenge of belonging to Africa.

I would want to see an autonomous state set aside for the Afrikaner in which he would take care of his *survival problem,* develop the habits of living which make a people the children of Africa, and contribute constructively to the enrichment of the freedom experiment which the Africans launched at the Bloemfontein Unity Conference. The Afrikaner is a human being; he has the potential to do better things than make himself a nuisance to his neighbours. I would want to do all I could to see the potential translated into reality.

In each state, the language of the majority would be the official language, in common with one European language or another. There would also be the option of a third language—say, Portuguese—to facilitate communication among the peoples of the Federal Union.

There would be two types of states in Sudia: those based on cultural autonomy and those in which the language-groups were so mixed that people had no identity problems. In Sudia the Witwatersrand area, for example, would be an open state in which no language-group would be dominant.

Each open state would make adequate provisions for all the cultural groups within it. These provisions, like guarantees of individual rights, would be spelt out in the Constitution of the Federal Republic of Sudia.

The basic point always to bear in mind is that in South Africa, as in other parts of the continent, we are dealing with conflicting processes—with power dispositions which create these conflicts. The only way to evolve effective solutions is to realign the power groupings and set in motion an altogether different process which will move men and events to goals agreed upon by all races. Apartheid's proposals for change are doomed to fail because they are designed to serve the ends of predation and are not based on any consensus.

A united front of militants and moderates was established to fill the vacuum created by the mass resignations from the government-sponsored Urban Bantu Council. The new unity cut across language and territorial barriers. To demonstrate the growing solidarity of the African community the predominantly urban supporters of the united front met in conference in Hammanskraal, near Pretoria, where the delegates resolved to wage a co-ordinated fight against vassalage in unviable mini-states which the government peddles as independence.

Whether or not by design, South Africa's then predominantly rural National Cultural and Liberation Movement (Inkatha) met in annual conference in Natal almost at the same time that the Hammanskraal assembly was in session.

These events prepared ground for a larger type of unity; for the co-ordination of urban and rural opposition to apartheid. A united front of the urban and rural Africans could call for a general strike which would paralyse the economy. Those OAU countries which export labour to South Africa could use it to paralyse the mines, in support of the general strike. The co-ordination of internal and external pressures against apartheid would force the economy to grind to a halt.

The radical redistribution of wealth enters the picture at this point. A united African community could either paralyse the economy or wreck it by using arson as a political weapon. The intransigence which would try to wreck the unity would create a political vacuum which would march South Africa straight to armed conflict and arson.

What this calls for is not the nationalisation of industry; it calls for a bold sharing of political and economic power on the basis respectively of majority rule and mutualization. The acceptance of the principle of effective co-ownership could be part of the evidence those Whites who claim to work for a political solution would have to give to establish their seriousness.

In *An African Explains Apartheid,* I made the following comments and proposals on federation:

The Afrikaner's fear of being swamped by the Africans in a non-racial society constitutes a challenge that any statesman-like approach to South Africa's race crisis must take into account.

The federal constitution . . . would ensure that the Afrikaans minority had areas in the country it could regard as its "homelands." Within these, it would be free to develop its culture and language and, at the same time, make its distinctive contribution to the progress and prosperity of the whole.

In each ethnic province, the language and culture of the dominant group would become the main influences, and non-racial areas would, of course, be free to adopt cultural patterns of their choice. This arrangement gives each culture not only the soil, as it were, in which to nurture itself, but the room for adapting itself to changing circumstances, and it places a premium on collaboration, more or less in the way the different Swiss cultural groups have one loyalty but different homelands.

What I had in mind was an evolving ideal of nationhood; a concept all communities could grow into because all would have contributed to its formulation. Working together could teach all of us the habits of co-operating to create the open society in which we could all feel wanted. The Afrikaner had no right to saturate the air with his screams about his threatened survival when he thrived on the ruin of other peoples. If he wanted to belong to South Africa, he had to face South African realities and adapt to the fact that we were a very mixed nation. If he could not do that, it would be wise of him to clear out of South Africa and leave us to solve our problems with those Whites who would want to work with us in building the Federal Union of the Autonomous States of Southern Africa. We would attract as many of them as we would need. They would come from Western Europe, the Americas and other parts of the world. In spite of the Mau Mau Revolt, Kenya was beginning to have more Whites after independence than she had under British rule.

The specifics of my proposals for a federal state based on cultural autonomy included:

The real friends of South Africa should insure that the legal and political structure of the nonracial society to replace apartheid is a federal constitution, which makes provision for four types of federating provinces—those in which Afrikaner initiatives are the dominant influence, those in which the African has the biggest say, those in which the British are the key factor, and the nonracial provinces.

The division of the country into a number of culturally autonomous provinces.

The union of these provinces into a federal republic.

Voluntary union with the Protectorates of Basutoland, Bechuanaland, and Swaziland, and the mandated territory of Southwest Africa.

Universal adult suffrage for all on a common voters' roll.

Entrenched guarantees of personal liberty and individual rights.

The restoration of the Commonwealth connection.

Friendly alliances with the states of Africa.

Provision for territories and peoples who would like later to join the federal republic.

The immediate and unconditional release of all political prisoners, the lifting of the bans, and the return of all political exiles to their homes.

The procurement of active United Nations assistance in establishing the federal republic as an additional protection to the minorities and a precaution against the dislocation of the country's economy. . . .

Some Afrikaner nationalists might argue in all sincerity that the homelands in a federal republic would be no guarantee of survival for Afrikanerdom. The homelands idea, of course, is borrowed from their side; but if they think it is good for the African, surely it must be good for them too. If, however, what they mean is that their domination of the African is the only guarantee of survival they will accept, then we might as well face the fact frankly that salvation for the African would lie in preparing for war as the only solution to the race problem.

If they want to have the lion's share of the land of Africa and shunt the African majority to the eroded and crowded reserves, the Black man will not have much of a choice other than to teach himself and his children to know no rest until they drive the last Afrikaner out of South Africa, back to Europe. These realities must be faced because people are thinking and talking about them. If the Afrikaner is determined to keep by force of arms what he holds, he should realize that the African will one day seize by force that which was taken away from him. The emergence of African states will have been in vain if it does not enable them to supply arms to the Africans in the republic to redress a historical injustice. Force provokes force. It might not be to-day; it must come sooner or later.

I wrote these words in 1962, before going into exile. The government's answer was to impose a five-year ban on me. One of the laws under which I was banned was the Suppression of Communism Act! Neither the bans nor the long years I have been in exile have changed the views expressed above—except that where, in 1962, I was prepared to demarcate a part of Natal as English territory, the Soweto Rebellion and the apartheid regime's determination to force the African majority out of South Africa made it clear to me that the majority of the Whites did not want a negotiated solution. If they pushed us to war, I told myself, all the African communities should insist on reversion to their ancestral boundaries. This would be one of our war aims.

In 1974 Buthelezi went to Cape Town to deliver that year's Hoernle Memorial Lecture organised by the South African Institute of Race Relations. He went to great pains to explain how the federation of autonomous states we had in mind would be formed, and laid great stress on parallels with the cantonal system of the Swiss.

I could not believe my eyes, two years later, when *Newsweek* published the gist of an interview which Mr. de Borchgrave, one of the weekly's senior correspondents, had with General van den Bergh, South Africa's security police chief and head of the Bureau of State Security (BOSS). De Borchgrave reported, among other things, that at the headquarters of BOSS in Pretoria he had been made to understand that BOSS chiefs favoured the establishment of a Swiss type of federation! BOSS promptly denied that it had given the information Mr. de Borchgrave passed on to *Newsweek*.

Subsequently, the cabinet appointed a committee, chaired by Defence Minister P.W. Botha (now the Prime Minister) to examine the constitution of South Africa with a view to effecting changes in it which were acceptable to the government.

The international edition of the Johannesburg *Star* (May 28, 1977), reported Chairman Botha as having made the following statements before a student audience in Pretoria University:

I have said before that a possible road to the future is a canton system for our extraordinay situation. It will guarantee the maintenance of identities for each group and consultation between them. Unique arrangements need to be made for our situation.

Two days before the Botha statement, another cabinet minister, Dr. Koornhof, had flown another kite to test reactions to a Swiss-type of cultural confederation. Premier Vorster neither associated himself with the kite-flying nor rejected it. His neutrality created the type of confusion which, some commentators argued, could give him the image of a unifying influence in the ranks of Afrikanerdom.

Significance was given to this view by the fact that early in 1977 the government announced its plans for granting "full autonomy" to those homelands which did not accept "independence." Buthelezi's Kwa Zulu was uncompromising in its rejection of the vassalage which Pretoria offered as independence. The change in policy suggested that Pretoria had reached the point where its "independence" policy could not work. Kwa Zulu was a mass of islands which could not be consolidated into a single state without hurting White interests. Apartheid set out to protect White interests. In addition, the English in Natal made it clear that they were not averse to the idea of forming an alliance with Buthelezi's Zulus. Pretoria promptly dropped its offer of "independence" in order to prevent the formation of a united front of the Zulu and English monoliths which could demand independence and secede from the Republic.

The appointment of the Botha committee was a government admission that the South African constitution was due for change.

OPEN SOCIETY

The evolving programme outlined above would be designed to achieve two objectives: to enable all the groups to learn the habits of living, working and planning together for their corporate good, and to ready themselves in the process, for movement to citizenship in a larger state where race and ethnicity will be of no political significance; where merit alone will determine the position of the person in the life of the Federal Republic of South Africa.

In an open, person-centred society, each community would have enough land and resources to maintain its viability; it would, in other words, have enough living-space to define itself freely. The entrenchment of this fundamental freedom would be the first pillar on which the Federal Republic would be established.

The executive president would be the second source of strength. His office would be vested with a great deal of power to ensure that each community which felt deprived or unjustly treated would redress the wrongs against it when the time came for it to nominate its candidate for the federal presidency. No community would have the right to nominate a candidate before everyone had exercised their right to nominate. At this level, collective sovereignty would be a moderating influence in a society where citizens' personalities would have been moulded and honed by different evaluations of the human being.

After, say, thirty years, the constitution would come up for review. The points of strength and weakness noted in the life of a whole generation would provide insights into necessary changes and adjustments.

The definition of Majority Rule given here gives those Africans and Whites who want a negotiated solution the opportunity to assert informed leadership initiatives toward the convention of the Southern African Treaty Conference to pre-empt war.

The Stabilisation Fund and the Southern African Development Authority call for a few remarks. In the situations created by White domination in Southern Africa, Majority Rule or the granting of political "freedom" without social justice would be a fraud, an invitation to disaster, and a perpetuation of tyranny in a new guise. Those sections of the nation which White domination placed in positions of economic and cultural advantage would dominate the new society and continue to give to freedom a meaning that would humiliate the African and force him to use the political power he would have to crush the economic power of the advantaged groups. That would move us full circle back to where the Soweto Rebellion found us.

A community of have-nots owes no loyalty to those institutions it regards as the means for exploiting or oppressing it. Its responses sooner or later become influenced by what we might call the temper of the dispossessed—the mood which seeks to destroy that which cannot be changed, if it is unjust.

But White domination has encouraged the development of the temper of the dispossessed over such a wide area in Southern Africa that it would be folly to separate the economic problems of Southern Africa from the political or to deal with each country in isolation. What is needed is a sub-continental programme for the development of a sound, integrated economy within an integrated political structure. The Stabilisation Fund and the Development Authority would complement political freedom with social and economic justice.

Finally, reference has been made to the Africans and the Afrikaners as key communities. While the relations between the two are characterised mainly by conflict, fundamental congruities exist which the Africans and the outside world have not up to now given the attention they deserve. Both have always lacked enthusiasm for the unitary state because it facilitated the imposition of the will of one group on the others. Granting "independence" to the Transkei is the Afrikaner's way of dismantling the unitary structure. Matanzima's acceptance of "independence" might, in a sense, be said to be a rejection of the unitary state.

The Africans and the Afrikaners are deprived majorities on different planes. While the Afrikaners control the government, their share of the actual wealth of the country is not worth writing home about. Their position in the government projects them as the main exploiters of the African when the English-speaking sections collect the bulk of the profits from the oppression of the African. On this plane, the Afrikaner gets all the knocks and the blows from the outside world for defending a racial policy which gives him relatively marginal profits when it comes to the possession of actual wealth.

The Black majority is kicked and knocked in different ways—to protect those who benefit most from their exploitation. Left-wing albificationists have suddenly discovered that there is no uglier political and moral evil than Black racism. Taking their cue from these, a number of Western liberals and intellectuals have started beating drums against Black racism. If an African defines himself and his people's struggle in non-Caucasian terms, he is branded a racist. The intention is to make it difficult for African Nationalism to free the African on his terms; to tie him to leadership by the albificationists so that when freedom comes, he will not be in the position to use the political power he will then have to dispossess the White supremacists.

Congruities exist, also, when it comes to African and Afrikaner attitudes to state ownership of resources like water, electricity, shipping, harbours, railways, airways, etc. The nationalisation of these resources is part of what some Africans call the redistribution of wealth. By vesting control of important sources of wealth in the state the Afrikaners laid foundations on which the Africans would build to raise the living standards of all the peoples of their country.

These congruities call for an informed dialogue on alternatives over the heads of the apartheid regime if necessary, between the Africans and Afrikaners who genuinely seek to resolve conflict and are ready to make the adjustments called for. These Afrikaners realise that provoking the African beyond a certain point will commit him irrevocably to armed conflict. They take note of the fact that when South Africa entered the Angolan war, the West regarded that as a kiss of death for UNITA, and preferred to see Angola taken over by the Marxists than appear to be anywhere near South Africa. That Western world which would not give aid to the side supported by South Africa in Angola wasted little time in finding ways to send some form of help to Zaire to suppress the Katangese revolt. The writing on the wall was clear. The West would rather see South Africa taken over by Black Marxists than come to the assistance of the advocates of White supremacy.

In order for us Africans to conduct a meaningful dialogue with the Afrikaner we need to say more clearly what we mean when we talk of the redistribution of wealth. No Black political party inside the country has stated its goals on this plane in the clearest terms possible. The open debate on economic alternatives to apartheid still goes on.

Without the redistribution of wealth and social justice, political autonomy for the African people would be one more trick designed to perpetuate White domination in a new guise. There would be no point in us accepting a political federation in which the wealth of our land continued to be controlled by the minority groups. We oppose apartheid because we want to control the wealth of our country; we want political power because it will enable us to develop this wealth and use it in ways which will give to freedom a meaning that will be seen to be valid in the lives of all the peoples of South Africa. If we cannot have this meaning, our alternative would be to expel the Whites from our country. Speaking for myself, this would do more harm to all concerned than the apartheid evil we oppose.

The principles on which the redistribution of wealth is based have their origins in the mutualism of the Sudic Ideal. These principles include:

- stress on the primacy of the person regardless of race, colour, sex or creed;

- the right of the person to make the best possible use of his life in the light of his abilities and choices;

- the function of society is to create the conditions in which the person will make the best possible use of his life; it is to ensure that the person is equipped, enabled and seen to realise the promise and the glory of being human regardless of who his particular parents were;

- state ownership of primary resources like land, water, roads, harbours, airways, minerals, etc.;

- the radical redistribution of wealth with the minimum of unavoidable dislocations of the economy;

- the development of an evolving synthesis of economic experiences which will keep control of primary resources in the hands of the federal government and mutualise the ownership and control of the means of production and distribution;

- minimise the interest of the dispossessed in the use of arson and sabotage as political weapons and make them feel and see that they are effective co-owners of all the wealth of their country;

- the recognition of labour unions for all races in order, among other things, to create a well-educated, disciplined and thrifty labour force which would establish responsible labour-management relations and provide an expanding internal market for goods of South African manufacture;

- the introduction of radical land reforms to open the ownership of land to all South Africans;

- the maximum utilisation of all human resources in the modernisation of equipment, increasing production and the generation of capital from savings;

- increasing the personal savings ratio to reduce the dependence on foreign investments;

- the modernisation of industrial structures to obtain maximum advantage from resources by eliminating the weakness of exporting raw materials instead of converting them into manufactured goods inside South Africa;

- relating modernisation and technology to the needs of large, medium and small concerns so that progress in one field might stimulate progress in other sectors of industry;

- giving constructive purpose to the tensions and conflicts produced by the deracialisation of the economy;

- the co-ordination of policies by the government, industry and labour for solving the problems created by deracialisation;

- the recognition of an expanding economy as a precondition for peace, stability and growth in South Africa;

- the removal of all impediments to growth in education, land utilisation, labour mobility, energy production, raw materials procurement and the expansion of markets;

- the establishment of machinery to study the problems political decentralisation might produce in the economy and propose solutions to these.

The type of mutualisation described in these principles would seek to create internal cohesion and stability and extend the area of co-operation with the outside world. Movement toward these goals would be in three stages. There first would have to be agreement on the need radically to redistribute wealth. The first reaction of most people in Africa and the West is that redistribution means nationalisation of the type seen in Marxist states. This method is not suitable to South Africa, with its legacy of race discrimination. It would transfer power from one racial group to another and give the Africans a vested interest in using their numbers and the political power in their hands to dispossess the Whites who oppressed and humiliated them. The Whites would retaliate in different ways. The end result would be violent revolts which would not do anybody any good.

A CHANGED ROLE FOR NIGERIA

The redefinition of the "race" problem made in the present discussion, the stress on the primacy of the person, and the Ideal of Nationhood developed by the Black South Africans combine with the Evolving Revolt, the Bicipitous Mind, the Collective Will and the policy for isolating the advocates of apartheid to set the spotlight on the role Africa could play in the turn the crisis has taken in South Africa.

If Free Africa, in particular, did all her homework on power dispositions in the Black and White communities, she would realise that she, like the OAU and the Black people in South Africa, are strongest, not on the military plane, but at political and diplomatic levels, and would develop a strategy for asserting informed leadership initiatives also in these areas.

These initiatives would include the re-evaluation of the strategies against White domination which Free Africa has been using in the last ten years. Free Africa would be badly equipped for the liberation of South Africa if she did not re-examine her attitudes for the specific purpose of fighting where she is strongest and hitting apartheid where it is most vulnerable.

An error which clamours for correction by the OAU is the exclusion of Lesotho and Swaziland on one hand and, on the other, Nigeria, from the Frontline States. The first two are important windows on what is going on inside South Africa and would give the Frontline States valuable insights on Pretoria's thinking on race conflict; they should have seats in the Frontline States.

Nigeria has a special role to play in the crisis in South Africa. The apartheid problem has been before the United Nations almost from the foundation of this body. In spite of this, the international community continues to be unable to build an effective consensus on how best to fight apartheid. One of the reasons for this is that the world organisation defines the crisis mainly from Caucasian perspectives. After the collapse of White rule in Rhodesia, the international community is likely to stand face to face with the White supremacists in Pretoria in a life-and-death-struggle that has the gravest implications for the future of the world.

This calls not only for clarity on the forces involved in the crisis into which apartheid has thrown the Republic; it calls, in particular, for the correction of some of the blunders which today continue to surrender to the apartheid regime the initiative to influence events.

The first of these errors is the failure to appreciate Nigeria's potential for becoming the decisive factor in the struggle for the liberation of Southern Africa. This failure is all the more amazing because of Nigeria's known commitment to liberation in the South. Not only have her leaders spoken in clear and unmistakable terms in support of liberation, Nigeria has backed her words with deeds befitting her size, commitment and position of leadership in Africa.

In spite of all this, Nigeria is not a member of the Frontline States; this means that if she continues to be excluded, she would not be a negotiator before collapse. For Free Africa to allow this state of affairs to continue is not only to give apartheid a new lease on life; it is unwittingly to sacrifice our children, who are showing that we are prepared to pay the supreme sacrifice rather than be slaves to apartheid.

As one of the larger producers of oil, Nigeria occupies a strategic position among the oil-producing nations whose importance in the fight against apartheid should never be underestimated. Nigeria is in the position to put persuasive pressures on the African members of OPEC to enable them to make a decision on whether or not to use African oil as a weapon against those who make it a crime for the children of Africa to exist in their own continent.

Africa's oil-producers are members of the OAU; they can be persuaded to use oil as a political weapon if the OAU addressed itself to the actualities of power disposition inside South Africa today. Nigeria, with her tremendous sense of responsibility is in the position to lead an African stand in the world oil producers organisation in favour of the use of oil as a weapon against apartheid. I was in Nigeria in 1958 and saw their performance in the Accra Conference of that year; I returned to my country with a tremendous amount of respect for their wisdom, ability to lead, and grasp of the complexities of the Black struggle.

OPEC, in turn, has the potential to approach some of South Africa's main suppliers, which sell oil to the Republic—with the request to suspend their exports as long as apartheid remains official policy in South Africa.

Nigeria, acting alone or in concert with Africa's producers, is in the position to approach the United States and ask it, first to stop exporting oil to South Africa and, second, to approach others with the request for co-operation in suspending oil supplies to South Africa to prevent a war that could set Africa and the Indian Ocean on fire. They could be told that by selling oil to South Africa they subsidize movement to a war that could some of their own enemies.

Lastly in the list of fundamental weaknesses is the power the homelands administrations now have to create a dual-authority crisis if they want to. The homelands administrations provide a privileged platform from which apartheid can be attacked. All the homelands have a land problem which the pegging of African land at 13 percent complicates every year. The reserves or homelands are not able to carry their present populations. This has created a problem in the rural areas which is moving toward being explosive.

Sooner or later, the homelands administrations will have to stand together and join the militants in calling all their people out in a general strike in demand for majority rule. The homelands administrations are better-placed to lead on this plane and confront White authority with legal Black authority to bring apartheid face to face with the absurdity of its assumptions.

Let us conclude this discussion with brief references to the main issues raised in what has been written up to now.

Attempts by Western and Socialist countries (China excluded) to create a class of ideological menials who will function either as the political managers of an economic estate owned by the West or as the Black surrogates of Moscow after victory will land South Africa in the disasters we see in South Vietnam, Iran and Taiwan on one hand and, on another, in quarrels which produced the Sino-Soviet split, Tito's revolt and the suppressions of popular uprisings in Hungary and Czechoslovakia. The emergence of Eurocomunism shows that Socialism is no cure for the ills which afflict mankind, just as capitalism is not. If it was, the Soviet Union would not be buying American wheat to feed the Soviet people.

It is an invitation to disaster for us Africans to throw in our lot with the West or with the Soviet Bloc. What our situation calls for is a re-alignment of internal forces for the purpose of moving Black and White toward the transformation of all the peoples of Southern Africa into a co-operating economic and political community.

The first step in this direction is a meaningful dialogue between the Africans and the Afrikaners for the purpose of building a Black-White consensus on the above goal. The second would be proportional partition. Mutualism, which would recognise the compatibility of private ownership of property on given planes, community ownership on others and state ownership elsewhere, would be the third. The fourth would be the unification of the autonomous, proportionally partitioned states into the Federal Union of South Africa which would negotiate with Angola, Botswana, Bophuthatswana, Lesotho, Mozambique, Namibia, Swaziland, Transkei, Zambia and Zimbabwe for the creation of the Federal Union of the Autonomous States of Southern Africa.

Where the Whites in South Africa continue to waste time talking about separate lavatories when the issue before them is whether or not the Africans, Coloureds, Asians, Afrikaners and English shall have the sense speedily to develop and agree on a formula which will enable them to stand together to prevent their country from being reduced to ashes by internal insurrection or external intervention or both; where the Whites are proving that they are incapable of leading a racially mixed country, it becomes the duty of the Africans to assert vigorous leadership initiatives to give their country the character they want for it.

The obvious priority here is a policy *yokubophana amanxeba* (of binding each other's wounds) which will create a consensus of the like-minded on the homefront and abroad to extend the area for the co-ordination of internal and external campaigns against White domination. Such a policy would seek to re-unite those whom White domination divided.

It would enable the people on the homefront and the exiles to speak with one voice against Western talk of capitalistic "interests" and guarantees for minority rights when these "rights" are the issue on which Black and White are quarrelling. The West might be making itself irrelevant when it places its "interests" and so-called "minority rights" before the people of Southern Africa.

What it should be thinking about is the creation of a controlled credits crisis to accelerate movement to the establishment of majority rule with the minimum of violence in South Africa.

But as experience in Iran and Taiwan shows, the West will shout itself hoarse about the need to secure its "interests." When the time comes for it to protect these, it will do nothing effective. That shows an important dimension of the vacuum in Western thinking on the crisis in relations between the West and the Third World.

The Soviet Bloc is moving toward a parallel position of irrelevance. It supports the clamour for armed struggle in the hope that this will prepare ground for another European ideology, after the failure of Christianity, Colonialism, Slavery and Capitalism. Soviet imperialism is committed to the Graeco-Romano-Hebraic attitude to the person which Africa rejects.

What conditions demand of the Soviet Union in Africa is not to prescribe destiny for the Black people as many other Whites tried to do in the past, but to launch an informed and constructive conversation with Black Africa on the basic materialism of the Buntu or Sudic Ideal.

The Soviet Union needs to conduct an informed conversation of minds with African Nationalism on this brand of materialism instead of calling African Nationalists names.

This takes us back to the proposal, by some Afrikaners, that Black and White should exchange ideas on alternatives to the status quo on the basis of what they called "maximum consensus." If, by this, they mean a consensus based on "separate freedoms" or any other apartheid-oriented philosophy, they are wasting their time, as Sharpeville and Soweto should have warned them by now.

If, as some hope, they plan to establish a satellite system which they hope to operate indefinitely with the co-operation of "difficult" African leaders like Buthelezi, they must be told in clear terms that they are also wasting their time.

No African in his senses will rush to see in the words "maximum consensus" a statement of surrender terms. At the same time it would be an error to disregard the fact that the Afrikaner is under intense pressure on all sides to get out of the laager and belong to the twentieth century. In a situation where he presides over a power-structure where labour and technology are controlled respectively by the Africans and the English, he does not have much of a choice; he has to start moving into the twentieth century. We, Africans, need to develop a quality of diplomacy which will deal with this change in his thinking—if only to determine if it is a real change. Armed struggle will not determine this; it will mend the cracks in the united front of White monoliths and create new problems for us.

Our business is to create helpful polarisations on the side of all racists and not to unify them.

NOTES ON CHAPTER V

1. Eds: Mohamed A. El-Khawas and Barry Cohen, Lawrence Hill & Co., Westport, Connecticut, 1976, Pp 105-06.

HONEST MONEY NOW!

DONT TREAD ON ME

**SELECTED ESSAYS By
HOWARD S. KATZ**

*Arise then ye freemen, use liberty's hand
And drive this vile paper from liberty's land,
And let the gold dollar be coin for the poor
And circulate freely to every man's door,
Awake up to freedom and not be controlled,
Submit not to bankers to pocket your gold.*

100 years ago it was common knowledge that gold money was in the interest of the average citizen and that paper money served the interests of bankers and charlatans. History shows that the struggle between paper money and hard money had been the dominant political issue in the United States until World War I.

Today, the fight between hard money and paper money is again becoming the primary political issue of our time.

Honest Money Now! is the first shot fired in the action-phase of this struggle. In **The Paper Aristocracy**, Howard Katz explained why the gold standard was essential to our nation. In **The Warmongers**, he showed how the paper money interests were moving our nation toward war. In **Honest Money Now!**, he explains how the Gold standard can be acheived now, and what you ought to be doing about it!

To order send $3.95(plus 80ᶜ p.&h.) to Books In Focus. 30 day return privilege.

• •

RUDEBARBS

*By
RANDY HYLKEMA*

RUDEBARBS are cartoons with a message! Some of the funniest economic, political, and social lampoons ever created; thanks to the genius of Randy Hylkema. Guaranteed to have you in stitches or your money refunded.

To order, Send **$5.95** (+80ᶜ P. & H.) to: BOOKS IN FOCUS. 30 Day Return Priveleges.

Conflict of Minds
Changing Power Dispositions in South Africa

by Jordan K. Ngubane

Conflict of Minds is a brilliant redefinition of the South African Crisis in terms of two conflicting philosophies of life, rather than a racial struggle.

Ngubane shows how the Sudic philosophy of Africa, and attitude toward the person evolved from ancient Egyptian theology, being passed on from generation to generation through the oral tradition; and he traces it to present day Zulu philosophy.

Conflict of Minds is the first written presentation of this philosophy ever, and therefore represents a major cultural achievement. It is a clear demonstration that there is a unifying world view throughout Africa, and that contrary to popular belief this view is in respects actually in advance of the Judeo-Christian structure. This has implications for that structure which cannot be ignored.

ABOUT THE AUTHOR:

Conflict of Minds represents a labor of 10 years for Mr. Jordan K. Ngubane. During this period he has been in exile from his home and people in the Zulu areas of South Africa. Living in Washington, D.C. and lecturing at Howard University, Jordan has maintained an objective attitude and has remained very much in touch with Black leadership within South Africa.

This is Jordan Ngubane's fifth book. He was the editor of a South African Black newspaper for eight years and was the correspondent for Mahatma Ghandi's newspaper. He has written 10 articles for the McGraw-Hill New Encyclopedia of World Biographies.
To order send $10.95(plus 80¢ p.&h.) to Books In Focus. 30 day return privilege.

- -

"It is by far the best and most comprehensive statement for liberty I have come across."
Leon Louw
Founder and Executive Director
Free Market Foundation

In Search of Liberty

FRED MACASKILL

IN SEARCH OF LIBERTY advances the concept that the more liberty a society enjoys, the stronger it will be, with greater material and moral benefits available to its individual members.

THE PRINCIPLES AND CONCLUSIONS of *In Search of Liberty* are based on the solid bedrock of individual rights. Taking nothing for granted, the author proceeds from the most basic right - the right to live. Then, considering more complex derivative rights, *In Search of Liberty* examines the most pressing issue of our time - the proper role of government in the life of man. Statism is shown to be destructive to individual rights; the free market is demonstrated to be an approach consistent with man's nature. These free market conclusions are underscored by the fact that author Macaskill lives in the highly authoritarian South African society. The concluding chapter appropriately shows how the individual rights approach (without regard to color or nationality) is the best and possibly the only hope in the South African situation.

"It's no exaggeration to say that the future of Western Civilization depends on ideas set forth in this book."
James U. Blanchard
Chairman, National Committee
for Monetary Reform

To order, Send $8.95 (+80¢ P. & H.) to: BOOKS IN FOCUS 30 Day Return Privelege

Immortal Light of Genius

Flight

In this volume
you will find the immortal light
of genius at its moments of greatest
inspiration discovering truth, creating
beauty, moving Humanity to fulfill its
dream of Glory... freedom, achievement
and joy.

Touch this blue fire of genius, this
immortal light, this glory, with your
mind and with your heart and it will
set fire to your spirit.

The immortal light of genius
is the energy for life.

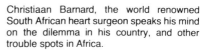

Christiaan Barnard, the world renowned South African heart surgeon speaks his mind on the dilemma in his country, and other trouble spots in Africa.

"In an unquestionably heartfelt expression of his views as a white Afrikaner proud of his heritage and land, he asserts his reasoned opinion that apartheid should be ended immediately — for practical as well as moral reasons."—PUBLISHERS WEEKLY (review)

Here is a view of South Africa for the reader who wants to form his own judgment, a view based on practical knowledge of the situation as analyzed by an intelligent mind. As the situation there threatens to explode and intrude more and more into our lives, concerned persons will want to understand this viewpoint.

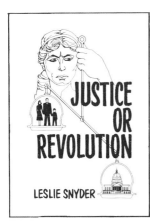

AMERICAN JUSTICE IS IN TROUBLE

*THOUSANDS OF NEW LAWS ARE
BEING ENACTED EACH YEAR, YET
JUSTICE IS DISAPPEARING FROM
THE AMERICAN SCENE. WHY?*

JUSTICE OR REVOLUTION examines justice in America—not in terms of legalistic structure—but from the viewpoint of our inalienable individual rights, and comes to some surprising conclusions:

- That the greater part of the American system of justice as achieved by the American Revolution, has been obstructed.

- That complex laws are MORE OFTEN THAN NOT, enacted to serve one special interest group or another, and are actually one of the greatest barriers to justice in our society.

- That a revolt is building, because Americans are fed up and are taking matters into their own hands, as with California's Proposition 13.

- That unless this action is based on the sound principles of individual rights, it will lead to an even greater loss of justice, to a condition of dictatorship.

JUSTICE OR REVOLUTION traces the concept of justice as understood by the great minds of the past, particularly those thinkers who developed the philosophy of rights on which America was based. JUSTICE OR REVOLUTION points out the injustices of the present system, and presents the way to re-establish political and economic rights, in a principled and peaceful way. *The alternative is revolution!*

To order send $9.95 (plus 80ᶜ p.&h.) to Books In Focus. 30 day return privilege.

....

Adventures with *Liqueurs*

Lucienne M.L. De Wulf
and
Marie-Françoise Fourestier

For centuries liqueurs have provided a special flavor to sophisticated living and have been valued as elixirs, potions, curatives, digestifs, and even as aphrodisiacs.

ADVENTURES WITH LIQUEURS introduces you to the world of liqueurs. It gives their fascinating history, telling the story of how they were discovered and are made, and best of all **ADVENTURES WITH LIQUEURS** describes in detail how you can use liqueurs to add to your enjoyment of food and beverages, and enhance your lifestyle. Hundreds of elegant food and beverage recipes using liqueurs are presented, from simple mixtures to gourmet productions!

ADVENTURES WITH LIQUEURS has been written by two French Ladies to help you bring the sensuous intriguing and sophisticated tastes and experiences afforded by fine liqueurs into your life. Join Francoise and Lucienne in this adventure with liqueurs, as they share their knowledge and experience on this exquisite topic.

To order send $11.95 (plus 80ᶜ p.&h.) to Books In Focus. 30 day return privilege.

SPECIAL DISCOUNTS TO READERS

The following quantity discounts are available to readers who want to help spread the message of this book. (The same discount applies to all books available through Books In Focus).

10 copies	20%
25 copies	30%
50 copies	40%
100 or more	45%

Add 25¢ per book for postage and handling. New York residents add sales tax also. Mail your order and check to: BOOKS IN FOCUS, P.O. Box 3481, Grand Central Station, New York, N.Y. 10017.

- -

To Order Books

Send The Following Information:
(You can send this sheet or photocopy it)

Book Title(s)	Quantity	Cost

Name:_____   Total quantity: _____

Address:_____   Total Cost: _____

City:_____ State: _____   Minus % Discount: _____

ZIP: _____   Plus Postage: _____

Total Due: ════════
(check included)

Send your personal check or money order payable to:

BOOKS IN FOCUS, INC.
P.O. BOX 3481
GRAND CENTRAL STATION, New York 10017

If you have a question, phone (212) 490-0334